COERCION AND SOCIAL WELFARE IN PUBLIC FINANCE

Economic and Political Perspectives

Although coercion is a fundamental and unavoidable part of our social lives, economists have not offered an integrated analysis of its role in the public economy. The essays in this book focus on coercion arising from the operation of the fiscal system, a major part of the public sector. Collective choices on fiscal matters emerge from and have all the essential characteristics of social interaction, including the necessity to force unwanted actions on some citizens. This was recognized in an older tradition in public finance, which can still serve as a starting point for modern work. The contributors to the volume recognize this tradition but add to it by using contemporary frameworks to study a set of related issues concerning fiscal coercion and economic welfare. These issues range from the compatibility of an open access society with the original Wicksellian vision to the productivity of coercion in experimental games.

Jorge Martinez-Vazquez is Regents Professor of Economics and Director of the International Studies Program in the Andrew Young School of Policy Studies at Georgia State University in Atlanta. He has published more than twenty books and numerous articles in academic journals, such as *Econometrica*, the *Journal of Political Economy*, the *Journal of Public Economics*, the *Southern Economic Journal*, and the *Review of Economics and Statistics*. He has directed multiple fiscal reform projects, having worked in more than seventy countries including China, Indonesia, Mexico, Russia, and South Africa. He is the current coeditor of *Hacienda Pública Española/Review of Public Economics*. Professor Martinez-Vazquez holds M.A. and Ph.D. degrees in Economics from Washington University in St. Louis.

Stanley L. Winer is the Canada Research Chair Professor in Public Policy in the School of Public Policy and Administration and the Department of Economics at Carleton University in Ottawa. He is the author, with Walter Hettich, of *Democratic Choice and Taxation: A Theoretical and Empirical Analysis* (Cambridge University Press, 1999). His recent book with Kathleen Day, *Interregional Migration and Public Policy in Canada* (2013), was awarded the Purvis Prize from the Canadian Economics Association. He has also published widely in leading academic journals on the political economy of fiscal systems and other topics. Professor Winer is the chair of the editorial board of the Carleton Library Series. He holds M.A. and Ph.D. degrees in Economics from the Johns Hopkins University.

Jorge Martinez-Vazquez:
To Isaac, Jonah, Lily, Amelia, Oliver, Eleanor, and Emma

Stanley L. Winer:
To Navah and Zev

Coercion and Social Welfare in Public Finance

Economic and Political Perspectives

Edited by

JORGE MARTINEZ-VAZQUEZ
Georgia State University

STANLEY L. WINER
Carleton University

CAMBRIDGE
UNIVERSITY PRESS

CAMBRIDGE
UNIVERSITY PRESS

32 Avenue of the Americas, New York, NY 10013-2473, USA

Cambridge University Press is part of the University of Cambridge.

It furthers the University's mission by disseminating knowledge in the pursuit of
education, learning, and research at the highest international levels of excellence.

www.cambridge.org
Information on this title: www.cambridge.org/9781107052789

© Cambridge University Press 2014

First published 2014

A catalog record for this publication is available from the British Library.

Library of Congress Cataloging in Publication Data
Martinez-Vazquez, Jorge.
Coercion and social welfare in public finance : economic and political perspectives / Jorge
Martinez-Vazquez, Georgia State University, USA, Stanley L. Winer, Carleton University,
Canada.
pages cm
Includes bibliographical references and index.
ISBN 978-1-107-05278-9 (hardback)
1. Finance, Public.   2. Public welfare.   3. State, The.   4. Social policy.   I. Winer, Stanley L.,
1947–   II. Title.
HJ141.M37   2014
336.001–dc23   2013040676

ISBN 978-1-107-05278-9 Hardback

Contents

Figures

Tables

Contributors

Lucy F. Ackert, Kennesaw State University, United States

Robin Boadway, Queen's University, Canada

Giorgio Brosio, University of Turin, Italy

Elena Cettolin, Maastricht University, The Netherlands

Roger D. Congleton, West Virginia University, United States

Léonard Dudley, Université de Montréal, Canada

Ann B. Gillette, Kennesaw State University, United States

Bernard Grofman, University of California, Irvine, United States

Walter Hettich, California State University, United States

Edgar Kiser, University of Washington, United States

John O. Ledyard, California Institute of Technology, United States

Jorge Martinez-Vazquez, Georgia State University, United States

Michael McKee, Appalachian State University, United States

Michael C. Munger, Duke University, United States

Mark Rider, Georgia State University, United States

Arno Riedl, Maastricht University, The Netherlands

Saloua Sehili, African Development Bank, Tunisia

Stergios Skaperdas, University of California, Irvine, United States

George Tridimas, University of Ulster, United Kingdom

John Joseph Wallis, University of Maryland, United States

Stanley L. Winer, Carleton University, Canada

George R. Zodrow, Rice University, United States

Editors' Preface and Acknowledgments

The papers and formal discussions presented in this volume emerged from the workshop on "Coercion and Social Welfare in Contemporary Public Finance," held at Stone Mountain, Atlanta, in October 2010. This conference was designed and organized by us with the intention of creating the book on the meaning and role of coercion in public finance that is before you. The idea for working on public finance in the Wicksellian tradition emerged in the course of our own individual research activities, and we are fortunate to have been able to collaborate in bringing together a distinguished group of scholars to explore this line of thought more fully than we could do on our own.

We are indebted to the authors and discussants for their participation at the workshop and for their work in helping turn a stimulating workshop into a cohesive book. We thank Roger D. Congleton, Walter Hettich, Michael C. Munger, George Tridimas, and John Joseph Wallis for reviewing early drafts of our Introduction to the volume, as well as two anonymous reviewers of the manuscript for their helpful suggestions. We also want to thank Luc Noiset, Tom Rutherford, and David Wildasin for their participation at the seminar.

Financing for the workshop was provided by the International Center for Public Policy of the Andrew Young School of Policy Studies at Georgia State University. This generous support was essential for the project, and we are grateful for it. Winer's participation was partly supported by the Canada Research Chair Program. Finally, we thank our editors at Cambridge University Press, Scott Parris and Kristin Purdy, for their assistance.

1

Coercion, Welfare, and the Study
of Public Finance

Jorge Martinez-Vazquez and Stanley L. Winer

1. The Purpose and Outline of This Book

Social interaction necessarily requires limits on the freedom of individual choice. As soon as we are part of a group, different voices must be heard and compromises must be made. Major questions will inevitably arise about whether some people have more to say than others do when acceptable limits to individual actions are specified, how such limits or rights are to be defined and circumscribed, and how they will be enforced once agreement on their nature is achieved.

Coercion is an essential part of this process. Although voluntary agreement may underlie some of the compromises achieved, coercion is a part of all widely used collective decision mechanisms. Coercion will also be involved in the enforcement of group decisions after they are made, to deal with free rider problems and other types of strategic behavior by individuals or groups who attempt to take advantage of their fellow citizens.

Coercion is therefore a fundamental and unavoidable part of our social lives. For this reason, it is not surprising that philosophers and legal experts have examined its nature at length. Economists, however, have not yet offered a fully integrated analysis of its role in either the private or the public economy. Contemporary economic analysis of the public sector usually does not deal with coercion in a direct or formal manner, although a concern with it often lies below the surface, especially when contentious issues such as taxation are involved. The essays in this book are different. Because collective choices on fiscal matters emerge from and have all the essential characteristics of social interaction, including the necessity of coercion, and because there is an older tradition of work on coercion in public finance (introduced later) that we can build on, the essays presented here focus directly on the study of coercion arising through the operation of the fiscal system.

The initial questions that were put to the contributors to this volume on coercion in public finance are challenging: How does the coercive power of the state evolve, and what are the implications of this history for the structure of public finances? How can we understand the meaning and role of coercion in contemporary societies? Can we measure it? What is its role in modern public-sector economics, which is, after all, concerned with figuring out how governments should interfere with our private and social lives? How does a concern with coercion in public finance conflict with, or mesh with, welfarist objectives? And what are the important issues and problems that may guide contemporary research?

Detailed answers, and more questions, are found in the individual contributions by the group of thoughtful authors and discussants we have brought together here. In this introductory chapter we hope to convince the reader that a deeper understanding of coercion in fiscal affairs is important for the study of the public economy and of public policy generally. We shall also explain the structure of the book and briefly outline what the reader can expect from each contribution.

Our enterprise is both old and new. A concern with coercion was central to an older tradition in public finance that was initiated by Knut Wicksell (1896) and Eric Lindahl (1919), and which is an important part of the equally celebrated work of James Buchanan and Gordon Tullock (1962). We shall have more to say about this tradition shortly. For the moment, however, we shall point out that with the exception of one special type of work that originates with Lindahl, and which is well represented in this book, *explicit* concern with, and analysis of, coercion is not reflected in the mainstream of contemporary research on the public economy. Contemporary public economics is a field that is primarily guided by a social planning approach to welfare analysis, in which a benevolent planner is allowed to coerce anyone to any extent, for example, by taking from the rich to give to the poor, as long as aggregate social well-being is increased.

Two specific and basic sources of coercion in public finance are at play in the essays in this volume. Coercion in public finance arises (1) as a result of external control by the state over one's life and that of the country exercised through threats of violence or sanctions; and (2) as a by-product of the compromises that all citizens must agree to in a democratic society as part of the process by which collective decisions are made. These two situations, while conceptually different, are related, and the issues of how a society progresses from the first to the second, as well as their coexistence, also arise.

The first source of coercion – external control by the state – is closely connected to what has become one of the most influential theories of the state. In Max Weber's (1919, p. 78) view, "a state is a human community that (successfully) claims the monopoly of the legitimate use of physical force within a given territory." How such a state evolves from anarchy to one in which state sanctions are severely constrained under an impersonal rule of law, and the nature of the public finances that arise at different stages of this development, are key issues in the first part of the book.

In market economies, coercion is pervasive in *private* contracts and can be productive. As Thomas Hobbes put it some time ago in *Leviathan* (1651, part II, chapter XVII): "Covenants, without the Sword, are but Words, and of no strength to secure a man at all." Oliver Williamson (1975) draws on this idea by observing that it is possible to think of most human interactions as undergoing a "fundamental transformation." Before a private contract is signed, there is no coercion in the negotiating process. Each party can exit without harm. After the contract is signed, however, exit from the agreement may be expensive, and failure to meet its terms may trigger punishment. So it is likely that the contract would never have been signed unless there was an *ex ante* expectation that *ex post* sanctions would be imposed. That is, both parties are inviting coercion voluntarily, as a means of making a credible commitment, and without this the contract would not be effective.

Coercion also arises naturally in the *public* life of liberal democracies. This brings us to the second source of coercion in public finance identified earlier – coercion that arises through the operation of a collective choice process. To fix ideas, consider a group of people who have come together in a room for a common purpose and who must collectively set the temperature on a thermostat and then pay for the resulting use of energy. Inevitably, some will be too hot and some too cold, and even those for whom the temperature is just right may be unhappy with the resulting balance between what they pay and what they get. Individual citizens can escape the situation if they move to another room or out of the building that represents the collectivity in this example. If they stay, however, they must cope with the coercion implied by their assent to the collective decision.

Coercion in this situation – that is, not getting what you *think you deserve* at the tax price you have to pay – cannot be avoided whatever collective choice procedure is employed in deciding on the public budget, as we implied earlier. Nor does anyone want to do so if on balance we value the goods and services made possible by collective action, provided (and here we mimic the logic of private contracts) that we can be sure that others will also be forced, if necessary, to carry through with *their* tax obligations.[1] On the other hand, it is our understanding that if coercion of the individual by the state or by special interests acting through the state becomes too great, unrest, emigration, and eventually failure of the state may occur.

The two sources of coercion introduced in the preceding discussion are just that – situations that lead to coercion, not measures of the degree of coercion itself. In the second part of the book, we shall see that it is not easy to come up with a practical definition or measure that incorporates the counterfactual, the state of relative freedom from coercion that any careful definition unavoidably must encompass. (What is the precise meaning of what we *think we deserve* in the definition of coercion suggested in the previous paragraph?) Still, we must do so if we want to proceed further, and this leads, as we find out here as well, to reappraisal of aspects of the foundations of welfare analysis.

In the third and longest part of the book, the task of actually doing public economics when coercion is an explicit part of the framework of analysis is tackled, first from the theoretical perspectives of mechanism design and optimal taxation, and then in the somewhat more applied contexts of the study of fiscal incidence and fiscal federalism. Finally in the fourth part of the book, experimental methods are used to investigate the collective action problem citizens face in organizing resistance to coercion, and to explore the productive role of coercion in organizing public life.

In addition, the reader will find short formal discussions of the essays at strategic points in the volume. These discussions are presented to help the reader gain a critical perspective on what has been said, while at the same time provoking a contest of ideas.

Before we introduce the individual contributions in greater detail, it will be both helpful and interesting to go further into the history of thought concerning the role of coercion in public finance.

2. Reflections on Coercion in the History of Public Finance

It is fair to say that the role of coercion in public finance was drawn to our attention by Wicksell in his book *Finanztheoretische Untersuchungen* (1896), part of which was published as the chapter titled "A New Principle of Just Taxation" in the Musgrave-Peacock (1958) collected readings of *Classics in the Theory of Public Finance.*

---

[1] One should note that such reciprocal coercion is also part of the foundation for one important view of what is, and why people obey the law. See, for example, Hart (1961).

As we have noted, contemporary public economics remains a field largely guided by utilitarianism and social planning. The state in this approach stands outside the polity and the economy. The tradition initiated by Wicksell, in contrast, views public finance as the study of how people act collectively to achieve their various ends. In this view, as Richard Wagner reminds us, the state does not stand above the economy and its participants, and the fiscal system that emerges through the collective choice process may be, depending on the nature of governance in place, beneficial for a large majority or only for an elite (Wagner 1988, 1997).

Wicksell was especially concerned with the possibility that the fiscal system could be used to coercively redistribute from one group of citizens to another. Indeed, since spending and taxing decisions in the modern legislature are usually not coincident and the decision-making rule departs substantially from unanimity, this is more than a possibility: it is obviously politically tempting to deliver publicly financed benefits to favored groups at the expense of other taxpayers. It is a testimony to the importance of the issue to be able to say that it is one of the key problems addressed by contemporary political economy, which is focused to a considerable extent on the study of why such coercive redistribution happens and on the precise form it takes in various political systems.[2]

Wicksell recognized that the design and operation of fiscal systems is intimately bound up with the way in which they are determined, because fiscal policies are *always* the outcome of a collective choice process in a democratic society. He advocated the adoption of an approximate unanimity rule voting process to consider packages that combined public expenditures with the taxes required to finance them as a way of making decisions about the public finances that he thought would achieve both economic efficiency *and* the absence of coercion. Wicksell's purpose, as James Buchanan (1967, 1986) emphasizes, was to insure that as far as possible, government actions embodied a quid pro quo process of exchange among citizens that was mutually beneficial.[3]

---

[2] This sort of redistribution is often referred to as rent seeking. See Congleton, Hillman and Konrad (2008) for a comprehensive collection of work on this topic.

[3] We are reminded of this important aspect of the Wicksellian perspective and of Buchanan's discussion of it by Mueller (2003, 5). Readers interested in further reading about the role of coercion on public finance, in addition to what is provided in this Introduction and in the volume as a whole, may wish to look at the work of Buchanan and Tullock cited earlier, as well as later work by Johansen (1963), Buchanan (1968, 1975), Head (1974), and Breton (1996). For textbook discussions, see Mueller (2003, chapters 1 and 4) and Besley (2006, Chapter 2)

Avoiding coercion while pursuing efficiency by seeking a broad consensus about both spending and the taxes required to support that spending before action is taken was, for Wicksell, a valued end in itself. In later work, for example by Lindahl (1919) and Buchanan (1959), this was also seen as a way of uncovering what people actually want in public-goods situations where market prices that guide an invisible-hand process toward an efficient allocation do not exist.

No doubt on purpose, Wicksell swept many of the difficult issues raised by using coercion as a criterion with which to judge fiscal systems. In particular, he knowingly left aside the problem of injustice in the initial distribution of income, dealing with which may require coercive redistribution from rich to poor, and the problem of how we control a (Weberian) state that has a monopoly on violence while still ensuring that the state has sufficient power to tax.[4]

He must have been aware of the many issues involved in dealing with coercion more deeply, as it has long been an important subject in philosophy. To take one famous example, Jean-Jacques Rousseau, perhaps the most important theorist of the social contract, offered an analysis of coercion more than 130 years before Wicksell's work. In his *Social Contract* (Book IV, 1762) he states in a passage worth quoting at some length:

When the state is instituted, residence constitutes consent; to dwell within its territory is to submit to the Sovereign. Apart from this primitive contract, the vote of the majority always binds all the rest. This follows from the contract itself. But it is asked how a man can be both free and forced to conform to wills that are not his own. How are the opponents at once free and subject to laws they have not agreed to? I report that the question is wrongly put. The citizen gives his consent to all the laws, including those which are passed in spite of his opposition, and even those which punish him when he dares to break any of them.

Similar reasoning has found its way into thinking about the public sector, though not generally in the public finance literature. For a recent example, we can read William Baumol (2006, 613), who echoes Rousseau in stating

---

[4] As to the first issue, Wicksell notes (Musgrave and Peacock 1958, 108) that "it is clear that justice in taxation tacitly presupposes justice in the existing distribution of property and income." As Besley (2006, 53) points out, he then goes on to say that society may revise the existing property structure if it is in contradiction to modern concepts of law and equity, although how this was to be done was not then discussed. We are not aware of how he thought about the second issue of controlling the state. For a recent discussion of why the twin issues of controlling state power while still ensuring sufficient power to tax are important, see, for example, Levi's Presidential Address to the American Political Science Association, "Why We Need a New Theory of Government" (2006, 5–19).

that "the essential feature that defines a democratic government is voluntary agreement by the members of the public to subject themselves to its coercion."

About twenty-five years after Wicksell's seminal contribution, his student Eric Lindahl (1919) presented a dissertation in which he attempted to find a positive solution, or mechanism, to implement the Wicksellian ideal.[5] Lindahl's contribution appeared during the same year in which Weber introduced a monopoly on violence as *the* defining characteristic of the modern state, in his famous Munich lecture titled "Politics as a Vocation." However, we are not aware of any direct connection between Lindahl and the Weberian conception of the state, a view that still is of substantial importance in political science.

The problem of constraining the state aside, Lindahl's attempt to find a mechanism to implement a non-coercive and efficient allocation of public goods set off a quest that has occupied mechanism design theorists for many years. This still-active area of theoretical research, well represented in this volume, is the only one in public-sector economics in which coercion explicitly plays an important role. Coercion – or more precisely, its complete absence – is imposed on the abstract economies explored in this work by requiring that all agents in the economy have the option of withdrawing without cost to some outside alternative, thus ensuring that no one is coerced in any solution of the model.

While a concern with non-coercive implementation in economies with public goods has become an established part of the contemporary mechanism design literature, Wicksell's approach to the study of the public sector more or less disappeared from the mainstream of public finance after being introduced to the English-speaking audience by Richard Musgrave in an early paper (1939) and especially in his *Theory of Public Finance* (1959). This was so despite the rise of the public choice school led by Buchanan and Tullock, who generalized Wicksell's framework in their *Calculus of Consent* (1962) to determine the socially optimal degree of consensus for collective choice.[6] Social planning as an expression of utilitarianism, following the work of Francis Edgeworth (1897), Arthur Pigou (1932), and

---

[5] This work is also provided in the Musgrave-Peacock volume in a chapter titled "Just Taxation – A Positive Solution."

[6] See Chapter 6 and especially Figure 6.3 where the optimal degree of consensus for a collective choice process is determined. Buchanan's book on the *Demand and Supply of Public Goods* (1967) is also an important contribution, standing between the Wicksellian tradition and post–World War II developments.

especially Paul Samuelson (1947, 1954), emerged after World War II as the predominant approach in public economics and economic policy research.

In terms of the stylized collective choice scenario introduced earlier, modern social planning leads to the study of how to set the temperature on the thermostat to optimize an objective that combines and allows for trade-offs between aggregate social welfare and equity among heterogeneous citizens. It is implicit in this approach that one accepts, or should accept, the solutions favored by the planner as a matter of social solidarity. Also implicit in this approach are the assumptions that the community is well organized to take advantage of collective action by the state on behalf of its citizens under the rule of law, and without the exercise of violence. In this volume, none of these conditions are taken for granted.

3. A Tour through the Individual Contributions

We turn now to the individual chapters. The emphasis in our introduction to these essays will be on their general thrust and on how they fit together.

3.1. Violence, Structured Anarchy, and the State

We begin in Part I, and appropriately so for a book on coercion in public finance, with two essays that deal with the connection between violence and the public finances in societies in which democracy under the rule of law is not already well entrenched.

Chapter 2 by John Wallis sweeps across the history of human organization. In this work he extends to the study of public finance, his recent book with Douglass North and Barry Weingast on *Violence and Social Orders* (2009). It will not come as a surprise to the reader of this Introduction that Wallis begins with the Weberian conception of the state. He asks how a society capable of limiting a government that has a monopoly on violence must be structured to constrain the government's use of violence, and how an answer to that difficult question bears on the use of unanimity in taxing and spending that was Wicksell's solution to the problem of limiting coercion. Wallis then shows at some length – in part using arguments developed in his book and extended here – how an understanding of the evolution of impersonality in the application of the rule of law bears on the study of public finance. He concludes on the basis of this analysis that Wicksell's idea is too simple; that it is not consistent with a solution to the problem of constraining the state because it leads to too much detail or attention to individual preferences in public finance, which is at odds with the requirements of an open access society with limited government under the impersonal application of the rule of law.

In rejecting Wicksell's approach, Wallis is in accord with the *Calculus of Consent*. But the argument here takes a different route, bypassing the problem of how to structure the collective choice mechanism itself. In this respect, his conclusions – though not his precise reasoning – are similar to those of Henry Simons (1938) and of Buchanan and Roger Congleton (1998), all of whom advocated broad tax bases that, to paraphrase Simons, prevent government from dipping deeply into great incomes with a sieve. The idea here, cast in the original language of Wallis's analysis, is that to prevent the breakdown of impersonality in the application of (tax) law, and the higher level of coercion and even violence this leads to as groups then sort themselves out for reasons of self-protection, the state should not be able to use tax discrimination to effectively play favorites.[7]

These nondiscriminatory tax systems are the antithesis of an Optimal Tax system, which is a generally more complex structure proposed by a benevolent planner to maximize social welfare in a world of heterogeneous taxpayers. (For examples, see, among others, Ramsey 1927; and Diamond and Mirrlees 1971a, 1971b.) While reading this chapter, one wonders how far one can go in a democratic, open access society where interest groups must compete openly and vigorously and hence on unfavorable terms for government favors, toward such an Optimal or economically efficient fiscal system without regressing back into the world governed by bargaining among interest groups. That is one of the unpalatable alternatives to a society based on the impersonality Wallis favors, where membership in a group is what matters, and the waste of resources in protecting one's common interest with other members of the clan, tribe, or party, as in much of the world today, reduces social welfare substantially.

In Chapter 3, Stergios Skaperdas investigates at length a world of structured anarchy that is certainly unpleasant by modern democratic standards. The societies Skaperdas describes are the ones where elites compete to provide security for the larger society, and where each rent-maximizing elite uses the fiscal system to exploit the citizens under their control. There is no Weberian state, a type that looks benign by contrast. The proprietary

---

[7] This idea works reasonably well whatever the tax base chosen, such as with a broad-base consumption tax, as Buchanan and Congleton realize. But it seems that advocates of the broad-base income tax in particular (in the tax expenditure literature) have not generally understood the basic idea, and would not, it seems, be opposed to such deviations from nondiscriminatory treatment if it were instead delivered by explicit discrimination in the provision of public expenditure.

state – one in which the state is "owned" by a ruler who maximizes revenues net of the cost of governing and which are common in the history of the world (Finer 1997) – emerges here out of anarchy given the state of military technology, but faces difficulties surviving because of the problem of providing effective security. This is a more or less stable world in which the center of power establishes itself at great expense in terms of enforcement and security.

Skaperdas's model includes, as an exceptional case, Mancur Olson's (1993) roving bandits, who arise and survive only when military-scale economies are absent so that there is no surplus that can be captured by an "entrepreneur" who offers to rid the peasants of these bandits in exchange for tax payments that leave them with a subsistence existence.

In his formal discussion of the Wallis and Skaperdas essays, Leonard Dudley characterizes Wallis's chapter as one that deals with bargaining between elites and the associated commitment problems that these elites must cope with as they try to maintain their rents. He thinks of the essay by Skaperdas as an analysis of the role of scale economies in military technology in the outcome of elite competition. Dudley then argues that these two chapters are parts of a bigger picture and that they may be unified by thinking about the first paper as an essay on the demand for governance, and about the second as providing a theory of its supply. Rents play a key role in this unified framework because they provide the incentive for and currency via which elites can make stable agreements. He goes on to argue that coercion in public finance – in the sense of tax prices in excess of willingness to pay – will be a key feature of regimes in the (possibly substantial) period of time following important shocks to the economy or society, especially when the private sector becomes more efficient (after a technological shock), and will be less important in long periods of stability. We leave the "proof" of this assertion, along with the many interesting details of the arguments in the main essays, for the readers to discover.

Before continuing to introduce the other contributions in the book, it is important to note that in the essays in Part I, more than in the following chapters, the emphasis is on the kind of governance in which rulers and elites use fiscal instruments to satisfy private interests without direct concern with the public interest, and in which competition between elites often generates unequal and even destructive outcomes. In the following parts of the book, some constraints such as exist in a democracy on the powers of the government and the bureaucracy are regarded as a normal, albeit still problematic, aspect of society.

3.2. Voluntary and Coercive Governance in Welfare Analysis

We pointed out earlier that definitions of coercion often are phrased in terms of its source, and that we need to go further in order to construct measures of coercion. The two essays in Part II move in that direction. In Chapter 4, Roger Congleton attempts to clarify the meaning of coercion by developing a representation of voluntary and coercive proposals first suggested by Alan Wertheimer (1990). The new development in this chapter is Congleton's demonstration that coercion cannot be defined without the use of a baseline proposal or counterfactual, which is the situation that would have occurred had the proposal of interest not been made.[8]

We must imagine what the counterfactual could have been in any particular situation. Congleton argues that often this baseline can be considered the exit option or, more precisely, the alternative realized when an offer is rejected. This reasoning obviously could form a rationale for the use of participation constraints in the mechanism design approach, though not necessarily the costless migration form of the constraint usually used in that literature. Coercive proposals, in his view, do two things: they attempt to eliminate this baseline as an option, and they involve the person making the offer also determining the payoff that the person receiving the offer obtains by acceptance or rejection of it.

To move toward measurement, Congleton uses as a baseline the outcomes in an ideal society where rent extraction through the public sector is completely absent. This corresponds to a world of costless exit from the community in question, which is one among many possible scenarios. He argues that estimates of rent extracted per non-privileged member of society can form the basis of a simple measure of the *aggregate* amount of coercion, thus linking the large literature on rent seeking to the present discussion. He also speculates about the implications of using rent (that is, coercion) minimization as a criterion for social action compared to one of maximizing GDP per capita.

---

[8] For another interesting, recent paper on the definition of coercion, which is illustrative of the importance and endurance of the issue in political science, see Valenti (2011). See also, for example, Greif (2005) and the various essays in Reidy and Riker (2008), Brautigam, Fjeldstad, and Moore (2008), and Marciano and Josselin (2007). We note that in contrast to the present book, these works do not focus directly on coercion in the discipline of public economics. The Brautigam, Fjeldstad, and Moore volume deals with coercion in taxation in a contemporary developing country context and is, like the other works cited here, a useful companion to the present volume.

Chapter 5 also identifies the subjectivity of coercion as a central issue, but in quite a different manner. In this essay, Michael Munger explores the implications of not knowing exactly what people regard as coercive for the foundations of welfare analysis. He does so by comparing the Kaldor-Hicks-Scitovsky (KHS) criterion to Coasian bargaining (Coase 1960). The essence of the application of the KHS "Compensation Principle" is the summing of gains to gainers and comparing the result to the sum of losses to the losers. The choice among feasible allocations that results produces a greater social surplus than any other, assuming (as did Wicksell) that justice and equity questions are somehow handled separately by the political process. Munger notes that Coasian bargaining is precisely isomorphic in the sense that it discovers the maximal social welfare. On the other hand, in his view the two approaches differ importantly in the degree of their potential for coercion by the central authority and by their capacity to elicit accurate information about costs and benefits. Coasian bargaining between individuals by its nature involves no direct coercion by the state and necessarily brings out individual valuations of the contracting parties.

By describing them in this manner, Munger is attempting to unify two approaches to welfare analysis that until now have been considered to be separate, placing them on a continuum according to which one might choose one or the other as a mechanism for revealing preferences, reducing coercion, and achieving efficient solutions to public good problems.

Munger's chapter also explains how you can get out of the need for a standard of reference to define coercion in public finance if you live in a (non-Coasian) world of cheap bargaining. Of course, bargaining, like migration, is not costless, and we can conclude that the measurement of coercion in the public sector is not easy, depending as it will on an operational definition of some sort of counterfactual or standard of reference. The essays in the following section on public economic theory and application struggle with this issue, one to which we will return.

In his review of the two essays in the second part of the book, Edgar Kiser reminds us that the nature of coercion in these discussions is fundamentally subjective. He notes that Congleton considers both the subjective nature of coercive proposals and the use of an ideal counterfactual with which to 'objectively' define coercion, while Munger discusses the problem of subjectivity in assessments of adequate compensation, without which proposed reallocations will be coercive. Kiser then points out that while both authors acknowledge the subjective nature of coercion in their analyses, neither of them asks what he sees as the obvious next question: If ideas about coercion are fundamentally subjective, what factors determine the degree of coercion that individuals deem appropriate? He then introduces us to the long tradition of research by sociologists who have worked at understanding how individual preferences are molded and shaped, suggesting an important place for such work in the contemporary study of coercion.

3.3. Coercion in Public-Sector Economics: Theory and Application

We move from the nature of public finance in structured anarchy and under impersonality, and from discussion of the philosophical foundations of coercion, to deal with the role of coercion in mainstream models used in public-sector economics. To present ideas sharply and to cover as much ground as possible, the first two chapters in Part III purposively lie at opposite ends of the continuum concerning the voluntariness of participation in the social situations in which coercion might arise. These are theoretical analyses. The second two essays are more applied in nature, dealing with two standard topics in public finance – namely, fiscal incidence and federalism.

In Chapter 6, John Ledyard presents a survey and extension of research on participation constraints in mechanism design in the presence of public goods, work that emerged out of Lindahl's contribution in 1919. A "mechanism" in this literature is a process through which individuals communicate and arrive at a social allocation of resources. Bargaining over tax shares as Lindahl described it in 1919, a collective choice process like majority rule and a competitive decentralized market are examples of such mechanisms. As in Congleton's analysis in Part II, the participation constraints allow individuals to exit the community, and in this case to do so without cost.

Ledyard first asks if a mechanism of some sort exists that exhibits both efficiency in the equilibrium supply of public goods along with strictly voluntary participation – that is, one that achieves the Wicksell-Lindahl ideal – despite Samuelson's (1954) guess that coercive taxation will always be required to deal with free riders. The answer is a qualified yes, and so Samuelson was too pessimistic. It is possible to achieve a solution in which everyone contributes voluntarily and the public good is supplied in just the efficient amount, and this will precisely be the one proposed by Lindahl, in which individualized tax prices are equal to everyone's marginal evaluation of the public good (Hurwicz 1979).

We learn next that such a nice outcome depends importantly on who knows what. The classic Lindahl result applies when there is complete information about individual preferences. If, however, individual agents are assumed to know only their own "types" – that is, what they alone want from the public sector – the answer is a gloomy one. In this kind of economy we will likely not have any public goods, at least not without coercion. (Here is another reason why some coercion may be a good thing.) It then turns out that putting us all behind John Rawls's (1971) veil of ignorance, or considering the matter *ex ante* before people know their own preferences, makes things easier. However, it is not obvious as to how comforting this last result is if we need governments to engage in contemporary policy reform.

The results described so far are based on frameworks in which it is assumed that everyone knows that everyone else is behaving rationally – that there is a "common knowledge of rationality." If we do away with that assumption, and allow for full knowledge in all *other* respects, we again find that the Wicksell-Lindahl ideal is unobtainable with any mechanism that is non-coercive.

Ledyard speculates about some very recent work that may change the last conclusion. Apparently by using MRI imaging to observe a neuro-signal that is correlated with the individual's demand for public goods, it may be possible to figure out a tax price that will induce truthful revelation of an individual's demand for the public service, despite the incentives for free riding. Would this MRI be voluntary or compulsory, one might ask (half) jokingly? More seriously, this discussion provides another example of the fact that constraints on mechanism design and policy making generally are not determined by nature alone. They depend on such matters as attitudes toward privacy and on the extent to which we will allow the state to fix our outside options.

He concludes with a discussion of the classic problem of ensuring the proper behavior of the state, the issue Leonid Hurwicz took up in his Nobel lecture in 2007. In the mechanism design literature, this issue plays out in a different manner than in the chapters by Wallis and Skaperdas. If we dispense with the usual assumption that the state (somehow) enforces property rights, and allow for the possibility that endowments can simply be seized, the imposition of participation constraints obviously does not imply that coercion is entirely absent. And knowing this, agents will behave differently than has been assumed in the theory introduced earlier. How the results reported in this chapter are then altered is left for future research.

In contrast to Ledyard's approach, the next chapter by Stanley Winer, George Tridimas, and Walter Hettich (hereafter WTH) begins with a completely different perspective on the nature of participation in a community. In Chapter 7, it is assumed that exit, as opposed to voice in domestic politics, to use Albert Hirschman's (1970) categorization of alternatives, is not possible at all because it is too costly to leave "home." The authors go on to explore the grammar of optimal fiscal structure when constraints on the social planner are (somehow) imposed so that coercion does not exceed an arbitrarily chosen level, either for the community or, alternatively, for each individual. The difference between these two types of exogenously imposed coercion constraints corresponds to the difference between the Kaldor-Hicks-Scitovsky criterion analyzed by Munger in Part II and the strict Pareto criterion which requires that no individual actually lose out in any reallocation that moves society toward the efficiency frontier.

The approach taken by WTH requires the use of an operational measure of coercion. As suggested by Buchanan (1968) and Albert Breton (1996), WTH take the tax share or tax price as socially determined, as in private markets where the price is given by the market and consumers' quantity adjust, and define coercion as the difference in welfare between the situation in which individuals could hypothetically adjust the quantity of public services and the actual social situation they are presented with. They refer to this as the individual-in-society definition of coercion. Defining the counterfactual here thus depends on knowing individual demands for public services.

They then vary the allowed degree of coercion and ask how the economically efficient fiscal system changes as a result, comparing standard optimal tax and coercion-constrained tax formulas. Because coercion depends on what the constrained planner does, and the planner must take constraints on coercion into account in making policy choices, the degree of coercion actually experienced is endogenously determined in this analysis.

For a simple (Cobb-Douglas and linear tax) economy, there arises a concave trade-off between aggregate social welfare and the aggregate degree of coercion. The standard optimal tax solution, in which the social planner has coerced the rich and transferred to the poor just the right amount to maximize aggregate social welfare, is at the peak of the curve, and it is possible to actually calculate the amount of coercion imposed here by the unconstrained social planner and to study its determinants. Intuitively, coercion in the socially optimal plan rises with the magnitude of demands for the public good because the welfare losses resulting from departures from preferred counterfactuals are larger then, and it also rises with the heterogeneity of tastes for the public good, because it is harder to satisfy a more heterogeneous community with the same restricted set of fiscal policy instruments. (Giorgio Brosio follows up in a later chapter on the possibility suggested here that decentralization may reduce coercion at little cost in terms of social welfare; the idea turns out to be less promising than it appears at first glance.)

WTH also compare the degree of coercion in the traditional socially optimal plan with what would happen under majority rule. Coercion in this political system *exceeds* that imposed by the social planner, *and* social welfare is lower. The reason is that majority rule, or any choice process short of unanimity, introduces discrimination according to political influence in addition to that adopted by a social planner.

In his discussion of the WTH essay, Robin Boadway raises several issues that point the way toward further work on coercion in public finance. We summarize three of these matters here. First, there is the question of whether coercion should in some way enter the individual's utility function, or at least the social welfare function. (One answer is probably that one should proceed in various ways and that to include coercion as constraints on a planner as WTH do, does not mean that their paper is "non-welfarist" in a broad sense). Second, following some recent research he introduces, Boadway suggests that it would be reasonable to define coercion with respect to what people think is an appropriate *social* outcome, instead of using the approach of WTH, and of Congleton and Munger earlier, in which what matters is the *individual's* preferred outcome. A further issue for future work concerns the fact that in the comparison with majority rule, neither voters nor political parties take coercion directly into account. With respect to Ledyard's chapter, Boadway's comments center on whether or not it is appropriate to use a completely binding participation constraint and on the reasonableness of alternative assumptions about what agents know about each other.

3.3.1. Fiscal Incidence and Fiscal Federalism

In the context of this book it makes a lot of sense to ask if ideas about coercion can inform the analysis of standard topics in public finance. The contributions in the second half of Part III deal with the role of coercion in the study of two well-traveled issues: fiscal incidence and fiscal federalism.

Saloua Sehili and Jorge Martinez-Vazquez analyze fiscal incidence using the Lindahl solution as a standard of reference. In Chapter 8, they present an incidence study in which the Lindahl solution – one that everyone would vote for unanimously at given tax prices (equal for each individual to their marginal evaluations of the public good being supplied) – is used as a standard of reference to distribute net gains (relative to this solution) from fiscal policy across individuals or groups. In this study, the calculation of the difference between the tax people pay and what they would pay in a hypothetical Lindahl solution for the given quantity of the public good is essentially a measure of coercion because of the operation of the fiscal system.

Note here the use of a counterfactual tax payment to define coercion, rather than a counterfactual level of benefits received as in the WTH approach. Whether the conclusions reached from using counterfactual tax payments or, alternatively, counterfactual quantities as a metric for defining coercion differ in some important manner remains to be investigated.

Another issue that arises at this point concerns the distinct difference between the *act of coercing* and the *amount of coercion* in a fiscal equilibrium. Sehili and Martinez-Vazquez would like to label as coerced only those citizens who pay more than they would like to pay in the Lindahl solution. One could also say that people who pay less than they should, or who receive more in benefits, are coercing others through the fiscal system. In contrast, WTH do not say who is coercing whom but do include in their aggregate measure all differences across individuals, whether positive or negative, between the values of public benefits received and what people think they ought to receive. (These values do not cancel out because individual preferences are heterogeneous).

In the Sehili-Martinez-Vazquez approach, the level of public goods may or may not be set at the Pareto-efficient level, in contrast to the full Wicksell-Lindahl equilibrium, although in every case, tax prices are adjusted until they "match up" with individual marginal willingness to pay for the level of the public good being provided in the counterfactual. Note that it is assumed here that everyone pays their taxes whether they are coerced a lot or a little.

Their empirical application uses a numerical general equilibrium framework to model the Lindahl incidence in the state of Georgia, where, despite the logic of Lindahl taxation at the national level, some taxes levied by Georgia are allowed to be exported to nonresidents in the rest of the United States. They find that the distribution of Lindahl net fiscal benefits across income groups at the regional level is regressive, meaning that poorer residents are coerced relative to richer ones. They show that this conclusion is robust to alternative assumptions about efficiency in the supply of public services. Moreover, their calculations show that tax exporting – that is, coercing nonresidents in other states – makes residents of Georgia on balance better off despite any deadweight losses coming from public sector expansion that this exporting may create. This last situation obviously leads on to thinking about the organization of public finance in federal systems.

In his discussion of the Sehili-Martinez-Vazquez paper, George Zodrow points to a limiting assumption in their model, to the effect that the public good entering the individual utility functions is a single pure public good, especially in relation to local services. The standard assumption in the local public finance literature is that local public services are "publicly provided private goods." A second related limitation is the assumption that all residents consume the same level of public services. In Zodrow's view, relaxing those assumptions brings into play the Tiebout (1956) model of local public finance.

Charles Tiebout's model shows that, under certain conditions, competing jurisdictions coupled with perfect or costless individual mobility results in efficient local public goods equilibria, as individuals sort themselves into homogeneous jurisdictions with no conflict regarding the optimal level of service provision. In this sense the Tiebout mechanism effectively results in a Lindahl-type equilibrium, in which no coercion exits *in each local jurisdiction*, because at home everyone gets what they pay for. However, in the Sehili-Martinez-Vazquez approach, net incidence would still vary across communities because of restrictions on the sorts of fiscal instruments used by governments. The implications of this point, of course, depend on the relevance of the Tiebout model in general and, in particular, for local jurisdictions in Georgia, which is the case studied in this chapter.

Even though the Tiebout model necessarily describes reality imperfectly, Zodrow argues that many observers believe that the model provides important insights into the operation of the local public sector, meaning that fiscal federalism at the local level, coupled with household mobility across jurisdictions, can act to limit coercion of the kind discussed by WTH and by Sehili and Martinez-Vazquez. So it is entirely appropriate that in Chapter 9, Giorgio Brosio considers the possibility – one suggested much earlier by Roland Pennock (1959) in a different context as well as by Tiebout – that formal decentralization will reduce the aggregate amount of coercion inherent in a fiscal system.[9]

Students of public economics will be reminded here of the decentralization theorem of Wallace Oates (1972). In the Oates framework, demands for public services are heterogeneous, and a uniform centralized supply at the national level is replaced with, say, two "provinces" supplying the same kind of public service, each doing so at the provincially efficient level where the sum of marginal evaluations of the public good of citizens in each province equals its marginal cost. Because heterogeneity of demands in any province can be no greater than in the country as a whole, and generally

---

[9] Pennock actually considers the number of people who would be in a majority on a given issue (such as the size of public expenditure) in the country as a whole versus in the equivalent decentralized state. His logic may or may not carry over to coercion in fiscal affairs.

will be less, the social planner in each province can match its chosen level of public goods supply more exactly (even if not perfectly) to the demands of its provincial citizens than can a planner in a centralized state constrained to supply a uniform level of public services everywhere. In this way we can see that with benevolent government, decentralization will always lead to an increase in the aggregate, national level of social welfare.

The question Brosio tackles is different, because he is dealing with the possibility that decentralization reduces coercion in the political equilibrium of a newly decentralized state, whether or not public goods are efficiently supplied. His answer is that formal decentralization can reduce coercion *if* it is accompanied by lower dispersion of preferences in the subcentral units, or if it produces better governance. However – and this is his major claim – such a result is context specific and does not provide a general a priori argument in favor of decentralization. Although the Oates theorem still applies, provinces where the local dispersion of preferences is substantial may experience an increase in coercion as defined by WTH, depending on how the level of the public good is determined (e.g., to satisfy a median voter). He argues that in such cases, voluntary *centralization*, also known as asymmetric centralization, may do better than decentralization, especially when one realizes that centralization does not necessarily imply uniformity in public provision at the local level.

This chapter also includes a discussion of the interesting and difficult case of Macedonia after the breakup of Yugoslavia, where Brosio worked for the World Bank following the civil war that was ended by NATO's intervention. This is a highly divided society of Macedonians (the majority) and ethnic Albanians where concern with coercion of one group by another is still at the core of public life and where there was significant decentralization despite the fact that there are only about two million people in this small country.

In his discussion of the Brosio paper, Bernard Grofman raises several issues that broaden the landscape of the discussion of coercion in public finance to include the nature of alternative collective choice institutions. Grofman notes that two key approaches to address the problem of preference heterogeneity are super-majoritarianism (including unanimity and veto rules) and segmentation of control over outcomes. One form of the latter approach deals with the partition of voters into more preference-homogenous voters. It is here where Oates' decentralization theorem fits according to Grofman. Even though the decentralization theorem simply assumes that localized decision making does go along with or creates more preference homogeneity, Grofman points out that such an assumption seems empirically well substantiated.

The question remains, however, whether homogeneity is necessarily better when collective choice rules are considered. It would not be the case, Grofman argues, if, for example, national level (centralized) decisions are done through some proportional allocation rule based on population shares, while local level (decentralized) decisions are monopolized by the majority group.

Concerning the Macedonian case, ethnic concentration led to the redrawing of municipal boundaries to increase the Albanian population's representation, and that group was also given a sort of minority veto. Grofman identifies these kinds of provisions, along with elections based on proportional representation, as *consociational* arrangements (Lijphart, 1977). Both Grofman and Brosio worry that such arrangements may lead to the hardening of ethnic differentiation, with increased self-segregation of the minority group and state support for arrangements that minimize contacts across ethnic lines.

3.4. Coercion in the Laboratory

The fourth and last part of the book brings experimental methods to bear on the nature of coercion: "Coercion in the lab!" as discussant Michael McKee calls it. There is little work that investigates in an experimental setting how cooperation is affected by the presence of players who are "obliged" to contribute to the collective enterprise. The first study focuses on the determinates of resistance to coercion in a public goods game. The second experimental chapter is motivated by the educated guess, expressed at various earlier points, that some coercion may be socially productive.

The nature and extent of coercion, whether in structured anarchy, natural states, or advanced democracies, will depend in large measure on how people cooperate to resist it. Lucy Ackert, Ann Gillette, and Mark Rider (AGR) address the fact that cooperating to deal with coercion is essentially a public good of the usual kind for those resisting. In Chapter 10, they follow up on this observation using a laboratory experiment with students.

The AGR team adapts a threshold public goods game to investigate whether people are able to cooperate to resist coercion despite individual incentives to free ride. The experimental game they set up works like this: A randomly chosen decision maker, who remains anonymous, is given the opportunity to expropriate all or part of the endowments of four experimental subjects – the "others." Others can resist the decision maker's demands by making voluntary contributions to a resistance fund, and if the balance in the fund reaches a commonly known threshold, the Others do not have to pay what is demanded by the decision maker. Whether or not resistance is successful, contributions to the fund are lost.

Behavior in this resistance game turns out to be similar to that observed in multi-period public goods games. They observe "out-of-equilibrium" outcomes not predicted by the standard theory in which everyone free rides and a decrease in successful resistance in later periods of a session compared to earlier ones. Nevertheless, cooperation remains relatively high even in the later periods. In addition, the AGR team does find that increasing the resistance threshold has a substantial negative effect on the probability of successful resistance. We can only speculate at this point on how the coercion we observe in democratic or developing societies, including the state of Georgia and the country of Macedonia, depends on the costs of organizing resistance to it, the role of institutionalized constraints of various kinds as a substitute for the need to organize resistance, and the incentives that remain for rent seeking.

The second experimental chapter is by Elena Cettolin and Arno Riedl. In Chapter 11, they investigate whether partial coercion can increase contributions to a public good. What they mean is described by the structure of their experimental game. Three subjects are randomly matched, and each receives fifty tokens as an endowment. One of the three is randomly chosen and forced to contribute thirteen (low coercion) or thirty-eight (high coercion) of his fifty tokens. They then have to decide individually how much to contribute to provision of a public good. In a final treatment, members are allowed to voluntarily commit to a minimal contribution of zero, thirteen, or thirty-eight.

They are especially interested in the behavior of the *non-coerced* populations in these situations. This is sensible – it is clear from our earlier discussion that cooperation depends on people knowing that others will be required to take part even if they find it advantageous to shirk on their responsibilities as citizens.

The main finding is that partial coercion is not a strong enough force to increase overall contribution levels. Although there is a pure coercion effect (contributions by the coerced member are higher), and non-coerced subjects appear to adjust their beliefs about the contribution behavior of coerced subjects, they do not increase their own contributions to the public good accordingly. Voluntary commitment seems to yield the same results. They suggest that these results cast some doubt on the actual strength of conditional cooperation as a mechanism to overcome social dilemma problems.

Michael McKee in his discussion considers the two essays in this section of the book in the context of the main body of experimental work on public goods economies and also links them to contemporary research on tax compliance issues. He suggests that coercion can be identified with compulsory tax withholding, which occurs along with more voluntary participation by other citizens. The question of whether coercion aids cooperation in the laboratory experiments is set against studies which show that tax compliance is higher than one should expect from looking at penalties from a tax audit. Apparently even simply informing people (untruthfully) that they are going to be audited is enough to increase self-reporting, suggesting that coercion may be more powerful than is suggested by the experiments.

McKee speculates about the possibility that players' views about what is fair are also involved in the outcome of the experiments in both essays along with the role of coercion, to some unknown extent. This suggests that further investigation will be required to separate the role of coercion from the effect of views about redistribution.

McKee also asks whether the use of coercive methods – in Congleton's sense of altering baseline options or fixing the payoffs from them – in tax collection can lead to social norms that encourage or discourage cooperation over time, a key issue raised by John Wallis in Chapter 2 and also by Robin Boadway. The extent to which tax evasion is a response to social actions that are regarded as coercive by taxpayers is not known, although as he points out, some experiments in which taxpayers vote on the budget indicate that evasion declines as meaningful participation by taxpayers increases. To go further into this issue, McKee argues that we will need to bring the issue of commitment of government to the proper use of funds into the experimental setting, which he thinks must be involved in people's assessment of what is and what is not coercive taxation. A useful line of future experimental inquiry, he then suggests, would be to decouple the link between tax compliance (or coercion) and the use of public funds in the experiments and to study the willingness to be coerced and its effectiveness in the absence of any direct link between revenues and expenditures. In other words, more coercion in the lab is warranted.

4. Concluding Remarks

We return to where we started by pointing out that social interaction necessarily requires limits on individual choice and that coercion is an essential part of whatever process is adopted to provide for the common good. The book before you stems from the view that, despite the conceptual and practical difficulties, it is important to analyze the meaning, nature, and role of coercion that is *always* part of the practical organization of any democracy, and especially in the formation, structure, and operation of its public finances.

Our intention in initiating the workshop from which this book emerged was to contribute to the approach to public finance initiated by Wicksell and Lindahl, an approach that combines a concern with efficiency in public goods supply with a related concern with coercion in the financing of government. The result is something of an adventure. The essays and discussions in this volume address a variety of important, challenging, and interconnected issues concerning the evolution, measurement, and implications of coercion in public finance. These include the emergence and persistence of coercion in the financing of structured anarchies; its role in the transition from natural states to the open access society; the measurement of coercion and its connection to the foundations of welfare analysis and to the sociology of preference formation; coercion in mechanism design problems with public goods; as constraints on optimal policy design and under alternative collective choice rules; and the question of whether federalism is a less coercive solution to problems of highly divided societies. The implications for contemporary tax policy of the Wicksell-Lindahl solution, for the calculation of the incidence of the fiscal system, and for experiments with coercion in laboratory settings as a potentially productive force are also explored.

All of this work is prompted by asking about the role of coercion in public finance, a basic issue that, we think it fair to say, has been neglected in contemporary work on the public economy. We hope that the reader will find the essays and formal discussions of coercion and its role in public finance interesting and that at least some of them will provoke further inquiry.

References

Baumol, William J. (2006). "Welfare Economics and the Theory of the State." In C. Rowley and F. Schneider (eds.), *The Encyclopedia of Public Choice*, Vol. II. Dordrecht: Kluwer Academic Publishers, 610–613.

Besley, Timothy (2006). *Principled Agents: The Political Economy of Good Government*. Oxford: Oxford University Press.

Brautigam, Deborah, Odd-Helge Fjeldstad, and Mick Moore (2008). *Taxation and State-Building in Developing Countries*. Cambridge: Cambridge University Press.

Breton, Albert (1996). *Competitive Governments: An Economic Theory of Politics and Public Finance*. Cambridge: Cambridge University Press.

Buchanan, James M. (1959). "Positive Economics, Welfare Economics and Political Economy." *Journal of Law and Economics* 2: 124–138.

Buchanan, James M. (1967). *Public Finance in Democratic Process*. Chapel Hill: University of North Carolina Press.

Buchanan, James M. (1968). *The Demand and Supply of Public Goods*. London: Rand McNally.

Buchanan, James M. (1975). *The Limits of Liberty: Between Anarchy and Leviathan*. Chicago: University of Chicago Press.

Buchanan, James M. (1986). *Liberty, Market and the State*. New York: New York University Press.

Buchanan, James M. and Roger D. Congleton (1998). *Politics by Principle, Not Interest: Towards Nondiscriminatory Democracy*. Cambridge: Cambridge University Press.

Buchanan, James M. and Gordon Tullock (1962). *The Calculus of Consent: Logical Foundations of Constitutional Democracy*. Ann Arbor: University of Michigan Press.

Coase, Ronald H. (1960). "The Problem of Social Cost." *Journal of Law and Economics* 3: 1–44.

Congleton, Roger D., Arye L. Hillman, and Kai A. Konrad (eds.) (2008). *40 Years of Research on Rent Seeking. Vols. I and II*. New York: Springer.

Diamond, Peter A. and James A. Mirrlees (1971a). "Optimal Taxation and Public Production I: Production Efficiency." *American Economic Review* 61(1): 8–27.

Diamond, Peter A. and James A. Mirrlees (1971b). "Optimal Taxation and Public Production II: Tax Rules." *American Economic Review* 61(3): 261–278.

Edgeworth, Francis Y. (1897). "The Pure Theory of Taxation: Parts I, II and III." *Economic Journal*. VII, 25(46–70), 26 (226–238), 28 (550–571).

Finer, Samuel (1997). *The History of Government from the Earliest Times: The Intermediate Ages*. Oxford: Oxford University Press.

Greif, Avner (2005). "Commitment, Coercion, and Markets: The Nature and Dynamics of Institutions Supporting Exchange." In C. Ménard and M. Shirley (eds.), *Handbook of New Institutional Economics*. Amsterdam: Springer, 727–786.

Hart, H. L. A. (1961). *The Concept of Law*. Oxford: Oxford University Press.

Head, John G. (1974). *Public Goods and Public Welfare*. Durham, NC: Duke University Press.

Hirschman, Albert O. (1970). *Exit, Voice, and Loyalty: Responses to Decline in Firms, Organizations, and States*. Cambridge, MA: Harvard University Press.

Hobbes, Thomas. (1651). *Leviathan*. Edwin Curley (ed.), Indianapolis/Cambridge: Hackett Publishing Company, 1994.

Holcombe, Randall G. (2002). *From Liberty to Democracy: The Transformation of American Government*. Ann Arbor: University of Michigan Press.

Hurwicz, Leonid (1979). "Outcome Functions Yielding Walrasian and Lindahl Allocations at Nash Equilibrium Points." *Review of Economic Studies* 46(2): 217–224.

Hurwicz, Leonid (2007). "But Who Will Guard the Guardians?" Nobel Prize Lecture, http://nobelprize.org/nobel_prizes/economics/laureates/2007/hurwicz-lecture.html

Johansen, Leif. (1963). "Some Notes on the Lindahl Theory of Public Expenditures". *International Economic Review* 4: 346–358.

Levi, Margaret (2006). "Why We Need a New Theory of Government." *Perspectives on Politics* 4(1): 5–19.

Lijphart, Arend (1977). *Democracy in Plural Societies: A Comparative Exploration.* New Haven, CT: Yale University Press.

Lindahl, Eric (1919). "Just Taxation: A Positive Solution." In R. A. Musgrave and A. T. Peacock (eds.), *Classics in the Theory of Public Finance.* London: Macmillan, 168–176.

Marciano, Alain and Jean-Michel Josselin (eds.) (2007). *Democracy, Freedom and Coercion.* Cheltenham: Edward Elgar.

Mueller, Denis (2003). *Public Choice III.* Cambridge: Cambridge University Press.

Musgrave, Richard A. (1939). "The Voluntary Exchange Theory of Public Economy." *Quarterly Journal of Economics* 53: 213–237.

Musgrave, Richard A. (1959). *The Theory of Public Finance: A Study in Public Economy.* New York: McGraw-Hill.

Musgrave, Richard A. and Alan T. Peacock (1958). *Classics in the Theory of Public Finance.* London: MacMillan.

North, Douglass, John J. Wallis, and Barry R. Weingast (2009). *Violence and Social Orders: A Conceptual Framework for Interpreting Recorded Human History.* Cambridge: Cambridge University Press.

Oates, Wallace E. 1972. Fiscal Federalism. NY: Harcourt Brace Jovanovich.

Olson, Mancur (1993). "Dictatorship, Democracy and Development." *American Political Science Review* 87: 567–576.

Ostrom, V. (1984). "Why Governments Fail: An Inquiry into the Use of Instruments of Evil to do Good." In J. M. Buchanan and R. D. Tollison (eds.), *Theory of Public Choice II.* Ann Arbor: University of Michigan Press, 422–435.

Pennock, Roland. (1959). "Federal and Unitary Government – Disharmony and Frustration." *Behavioral Science* 4(2): 147–157.

Pigou, Arthur. (1932). *The Economics of Welfare,* 4th edition. London: Macmillan and Co. Ltd.

Ramsey, Frank (1927). "A Contribution to the Theory of Taxation." *Economic Journal* 37(145): 47–61.

Rawls, John (1971). *A Theory of Justice.* Cambridge, MA: Harvard University Press.

Reidy, David A. and Walter J. Riker (eds.) (2008). *Coercion and the State.* New York: Springer Science.

Rousseau, Jean-Jacques. (1762). *The Social Contract.* Penguin Classics. Maurice Cranston, transl. 1968.

Samuelson, Paul A. (1947). *Foundations of Economic Analysis.* Cambridge, MA: Harvard University Press.

Samuelson, Paul A. (1954). "The Pure Theory of Public Expenditure." *Review of Economics and Statistics* 36(4): 387–389.

Samuelson, Paul A. (1955). "Diagrammatic Exposition of a Theory of Public Expenditure." *Review of Economics and Statistics* 37: 350–356.

Samuelson, Paul A. (1958). "Aspects of Public Expenditure Theories." *Review of Economics and Statistics* 40: 332–338.

Simons, Henry (1938). *Personal Income Taxation: The Definition of Income as a Problem of Fiscal Policy.* Chicago: University of Chicago Press.

Tiebout, Charles M. (1956). "A Pure Theory of Local Expenditures." *Journal of Political Economy* 64(5): 416–424.

Valenti, Laura (2011). "Coercion and (Global) Justice." *American Political Science Review* 105(1): 205–220.

Wagner, R. E. (1997). "Choice, Exchange, and Public Finance." *American Economic Review*, Proceedings, 87(May): 160–163.

Wagner, Richard E. (1988). "The Calculus of Consent: A Wicksellian Perspective." *Public Choice* 56: 153–166.

Weber, Max. (1919). "Politics as a Vocation." In H. Gerth and C. Mills (eds.), *From Max Weber*. Essays in Sociology. New York: Oxford University Press, 77–128.

Webber, Carolyn and Aaron B. Wildavsky (1987). *A History of Taxation and Expenditure in the Western World*. New York: Simon and Schuster.

Wertheimer, Alan. (1990). *Coercion*. Princeton, NJ: Princeton University Press.

Wicksell, Knut. (1896). "A New Principle of Just Taxation." In R. A. Musgrave and A. T. Peacock (eds.), *Classics in the Theory of Public Finance*. London: Macmillan. An excerpt from Knut Wicksell, *Finanztheoretische Untersuchungen* (Jena: Fischer, 1896), 73–118.

Williamson, Oliver E. (1975). *Markets and Hierarchies: Analysis and Antitrust Implications*. New York: Free Press.

PART I

VIOLENCE, STRUCTURED ANARCHY,
AND THE STATE

2

The Constitution of Coercion

Wicksell, Violence, and the Ordering of Society

John Joseph Wallis

1. Introduction

In the essay in which Max Weber defines the modern state as the organization with a "monopoly on the legitimate use of violence," he prefaces his definition with a discussion of the relationship of states and violence:

> But what is a "political association" from the sociological point of view? What is a state? Sociologically the state cannot be defined in terms of its ends. There is scarcely any task that some political association has not taken in hand, and there is no task that one could say has always been exclusive and peculiar to those associations which are designated as political ones: today the state, or historically, those associations which have been the predecessors of the modern state. Ultimately, one can define the modern state sociologically only in terms of the specific means peculiar to it, as to every political association, namely, the use of physical force.
>
> "Every state is founded on force," said Trotsky at Brest-Litovsk. That is indeed right. If no social institution existed which knew the use of violence, then the concept of "state" would be eliminated, and a condition would emerge that could be designated as "anarchy," in the specific sense of this word. Of course, force is certainly not the normal or the only means of the state – nobody says that – but force is a means specific to the state. Today the relationship between the state and violence is an especially intimate one. In the past, the most varied institutions – beginning with the sib – have known the use of physical force as quite normal. Today, however, we have to say that a state is a human community that (successfully) claims the monopoly of the legitimate use of physical force within a given territory. Note that "territory" is one of the characteristics of the state. Specifically, at the present time, the right to use physical force is ascribed to other institutions or to individuals only to the extent that the state permits it. The state is considered the sole source of the "right" to use violence. Hence, politics for us means striving to share power or striving to influence the distribution of power, either among states or among groups within a state. (Weber 1948, 77–78)

If we define coercion as the threat of violence as Weber would have, then a major tool for ordering societies is the use of coercion. The threat of violence by the government – through police actions, seizure of property, imprisonment, and corporeal or capital punishment – lies behind many of the incentives governments create to shape individual and group choices. The arrangements under which governments use coercion and violence are loosely what I call the "constitution of coercion." The constitution can be formal or informal, written or understood, and has a direct connection to what Weber would call the legitimate use of physical force.

Knut Wicksell (1958) laid out a framework for making decisions about taxation in a representative (parliamentary) democracy designed to ensure that fiscal decisions promoted social welfare. He proposed that tax legislation be paired with expenditure legislation, so that every legislator knew what the costs and benefits of the legislation would be, and then only legislation that passed with unanimous consent (or close to unanimity) would be enacted. Wicksell's unanimity criteria guaranteed that no legislator was coerced, in the sense of accepting a tax burden that was less than the benefits of the associated expenditures. Wicksellian coercion "arises whenever citizens experience a mismatch between what they receive from the public sector in the way of goods, services or transfers and what they pay in taxes" (Winer, Tridimas, and Hettich, Chapter 7). Wicksell's coercion is a mild form of the threat of violence, but to the extent that the government does enforce the payment of taxes by threatening financial or physical penalties, we can think of this as a species of coercion reflecting the threat of violence.[1]

Many have noted that the genius of Wicksell's essay is not the unanimity approval for tax legislation but his recognition that the efficiency and equity properties of a tax system can only be evaluated when taking the associated system of expenditures into account. The unanimity rule works only because unanimity simultaneously applies to taxes and expenditures. This is true both at the level of the individual considered as an individual, and the individual considered as part of a larger society. An individual cannot know whether she should consent to a particular tax or not without knowing what the associated benefit from the tax is. Similarly, an individual may not be able to ascertain the burdens of a tax or benefits of an expenditure without knowing the distribution of taxes and expenditures among the entire population of taxpayers and beneficiaries.

---

[1] Note that governments coerce all taxpayers, because the punishments for not paying taxes apply to all persons regardless of the benefits they receive from the expenditures funded by the taxes. Winer, Tridimas, and Hettich (Chapter 7 in this volume) formally "define coercion for an individual as the difference between this person's utility under what he or she regards as *appropriate* treatment by the public sector, and the utility that he or she actually enjoys as a result of social planning."

Wicksell made no explicit assumptions about coercion, but I suspect he would do so were he writing today. The reason is the slippery distinction between coercion and voluntarism implicit in Wicksell's notion of consent. Imagine two individuals who are willing to consent today to legislation that proposes to levy taxes and finance expenditures in the future but who can both see that neither party will have an incentive to pay his tax share in the future unless he is "coerced." In this case, both parties may be willing to agree to the legislation only if they credibly believe that they both will be "coerced."[2] Is their consent voluntary or coerced? Both Roger Congleton and Mike Munger raise this question in slightly different forms in their essays in this volume.

My concern is different. Credible beliefs about government actions are critical to the preceding example. The political economy question is whether or not the government can play the role of third-party enforcer to its own agreements, that is, to levy taxes, make expenditures, and enforce agreements through coercion. This question usually falls beyond the reach of public finance, but it cannot be left unexamined if we wish to talk intelligently about coercion in Wicksellian terms. In particular, we cannot dismiss out of hand the incentives that the government has to provide third-party enforcement in a biased or unbiased way. We cannot assume that the government always fulfills its promises. The constitution of coercion – the norms and institutions by and through which the government exercises violence and thus coercion – will be central to the expectations of the parties and, therefore, central to whether an agreement to be coerced in the future should be considered coercive or voluntary in the present.

Is Wicksell's unanimity idea consistent with the social dynamics necessary to limit the government's use of coercion? The central question of this essay is how a society capable of limiting a government with monopoly on violence must be structured to constrain the government's use of violence. It then asks whether the economic and political forces necessary to limit the government is consistent with the spirit of Wicksell's unanimity ideal. I think the answer is no, but it is neither a simple question nor a simple answer. Implicit in Wicksell's argument is the assumption that the government uses violence "impersonally," meaning the same rules for the legitimate use of violence against individuals and organizations apply in the same way to all organizations and citizens. We might call this a rule-of-law application of the constitution of coercion. To sustain the impersonal use of violence,

---

[2] Wicksell dodged all of these problems in his paper by noting that taxes levied to repay debts should not come under the universality rule.

taxes and expenditures must also be levied in an impersonal manner. This means that the distribution of taxes and expenditures across individuals and organizations within the society is based on some impersonal criteria such as income or geography. The need for governments to adopt impersonal taxes and expenditures constrains, indeed may prevent altogether, the ability of governments to implement unanimity rules. Some historical examples are given in the last section to show that over the course of the nineteenth century Britain, the United States, and France moved toward impersonal, rather than unanimous, rules.

In a recent book, *Violence and Social Orders*, Doug North, Barry Weingast, and I (hereafter NWW) proposed a way of thinking about how societies manage to control violence (not solve the problem of violence because no society has ever done that). Our answer is that a political coalition of powerful individuals and groups manipulates the economic system; the manipulations create rents for powerful organizations that are at risk if violence breaks out; and the rents serve as a means for a "dominant network" of powerful organizations to credibly commit to deal with one another in ways that do not include violence (although they always include the possibility of violence). This is the question that Skaperdas asks in his essay in this volume on proprietary public finance, anarchy, and the provision of security: Is it possible for a group of elites to provide security for the larger society? We asked and answered the question in a different way. NWW lay out two fundamental types of social orders that differ in how the larger society creates organizations that limit the use of violence by structuring the incentives facing powerful individuals and groups: limited access orders and open access orders.[3]

The key to the two social orders is the way the dominant network structures organizations. Weber's formulation of the state as an organization that uses coercion as the *means* to attain its goals misses an essential element of how states actually work. The violence or threat of violence (coercion) that governments use is always "organized." It is not violence wreaked on others by a single individual (e.g., a king) but is always violence wielded by an organized group. In the simplest terms possible, Weber's formulation assumes the problem of organizing violence away.[4] Once we acknowledge that violence has to be organized within the state or the government before

---

[3] The third type of social ordering – foraging societies – made up of small hunter-gatherer bands is not of interest here.

[4] Weber is not alone in doing this. Single actor theories of the state are prominent in North's "revenue maximizing monarch," Olson's "stationary bandit," as well as Bates (1989, 2001, 2008), Bates, Greif, and Singh (2002), Barzel (2001), Bueno de Mesquita, et al. (2003),

the government can hope to use the threat of violence to influence taxpayers and beneficiaries of government policies, it becomes obvious that the way violence is organized constrains the kinds of coercion that government can use on the public.

I begin by considering the problem of voluntary consent and coercion, then move to a consideration of how societies limit violence. This leads into a discussion of organizations and the nature of personal, identity, and impersonal relationships. The key distinction is between societies that sustain social order through incentives embedded in organizations and societies that sustain social order through incentives embedded in impersonal rules. With those concepts in hand, I turn to emergence of impersonality in modern societies and the implications it has for Wicksell's unanimity ideas.

2. Coercion and Voluntary Choice

By definition, free choices are not coerced. In Wicksell's framework, a person who realizes $75 in benefits from the public provision of education, but is required to pay $100 in taxes to finance the education, will not freely and voluntarily choose to support that public policy. If that person is, nonetheless, required to pay $100 in taxes, she has been coerced. A rational individual will, nonetheless, choose to pay the taxes if the threatened costs imposed on her by the government for failing to pay her taxes are greater than $25.[5] Thus a person who rationally opposes a government policy may also rationally find it in their interest to submit to the policy. The problem usually has a temporal dimension: one votes first and pays taxes later. However, it can also be represented at the same instant of time in the contradictory answers to two similar questions: Will you vote to support this government policy? Will you support the policy if it is passed by the legislature? In the example, the answer to the first question is no and the second question is yes.

To be clear, Table 2.1 provides general schedules of expenditures, taxes, and coercion for all the individuals (or legislators) in the society who influence the choice of policy. Expenditures, taxes, and coercion vary across

---

Levi (1988), North (1981, 1990), Olson (1982, 1983,), and Tilly (1993), just to name a few prominent scholars.

[5] Because coercion is the threat of violence, the costs imposed by coercion are always expectations about possible future consequences, weighted by the individual's subjective assessment of the probabilities associated with the outcomes. This is particularly important in the case of violence, because it is difficult to apply violence in measured doses. Circumstances can quickly change and consequences can escalate unpredictably.

Table 2.1. *Expenditure, tax, and coercion schedules, and their utility equivalents*

Levels of				Utility of		
Individual (1)	Expenditures (2)	Taxes (3)	Coercion (4)	Expenditures (5)	Taxes (6)	Coercion (7)
1	E_1	T_1	C_1	UE_1	UT_1	UC_1
2	E_2	T_2	C_2	UE_2	UT_2	UC_2
n	E_n	T_n	C_n	UE_n	UT_n	UC_n
Society	Sum of E_i	Sum of T_i	??	Sum of UE_i	Sum of UT_i	Sum of UC_i

Note: Expenditures and taxes are dollar values, and coercion is of the form "if you do not pay your taxes, go to jail for one year." Therefore, coercion measures do not add up. Utility of expenditures, taxes, and coercion may depend on the expenditures, taxes, and coercion an individual faces, as well as the expenditures, taxes, and coercion facing other individuals. In Wicksell's terms, individuals support legislation *ex ante* if UE_i > UT_i. However, *ex post*, individuals pay taxes if UT_i < UC_i. Remember that the UT and UC are "disutilities."

individuals. The schedules are in dollar terms for expenditures and taxes, but coercion is measured in penalties (like jail sentences for tax evasion) and thus is in units that do not add up. The utility of expenditures and disutility of taxes and coercion are in comparable units and provide the basis for the Wicksell criteria (columns (5) – (7)). Note that the utility and disutility of expenditures and taxes to individual (i) depend on his own taxes and expenditures, as well as the expenditures and taxes of others. According to Wicksell unanimity criteria, individuals only support a tax and expenditure schedule if (5) > (6), the utility of expenditures exceeds the disutility of taxes.

An individual may freely choose to engage in behavior that requires that they subject themselves to coercion. Suppose we have a two-person legislature with a Wicksellian unanimity rule. Person A builds schools, person B teaches school, and both people have children. The collective benefits of educating their children in the second period are sufficient to both pay for the construction of the school in the first period and pay the teacher in the second period. The school costs more to build than it does to operate, and rising marginal costs of taxation make it more efficient to raise the same amount of tax revenue in period 1 and period 2 and to borrow to cover some of the cost of construction. Because A is paid in the first period and B in the second period, it may be the case that A's benefit from sending his children to school in the second period is less than the tax burden he bears in the second period. There may be many possible schemes that alter the pattern of taxation over time to solve the credible commitment problem, but by assumption those solutions come at some cost because they involve shifting the tax burden temporally. Nonetheless, the coordination problem may be easy to solve if A and B agree that anyone who does not pay their taxes is put in jail for one year (assuming that the government can jail a person at low enough marginal cost). By agreeing to be coerced in the future, A and B can credibly commit to an arrangement in the present.[6]

The example demonstrates how Wicksell's problem must be extended beyond the consideration of taxes and expenditures to include the structure of coercion that the government will employ. Once we admit that coercion can be an efficient way for governments to solve coordination problems between citizens and that it can be in all citizens' interests to allow coercion, then we face a difficult problem when we try to apply the unanimity rule in the absence of coercion.

These intertemporal problems of commitment are very important. Willingness to submit to coercion may be a very low-cost way to commit, particularly if both individuals can see that it will be in their own interests and the interests of the other to avoid violence/coercion by paying their taxes (honoring their commitment). A government that can effectively threaten to use violence may be able to induce compliance among its citizens to agreements without ever having to use violence. I return to this problem in the next section, because it involves the very tricky problem of establishing credible third parties. In this case, the government apparently serves as a third party to its own arrangements, because the enforcement of public agreements about expenditures and taxation involves both the government and an explicit agreement between private individuals.

The coordination problem need not be intertemporal, however. Suppose that legislator A is only willing to pay $75 in school taxes for an education bill costing him $100, but he is willing to pay $150 in road taxes for a highway bill that will cost him only $100. Legislator B is willing to pay $125 for the education bill costing $100 but only $80 for the road bill costing $100. There are obviously gains from packaging the two bills together. However, such a compromise depends on the willingness of both legislators (and their constituents) to pay taxes for one public service that exceeds the value they place on the service. The ability of the government to coerce may be integral to making these kinds of arrangements.

An alert reader may have already reached the next conclusion. Even if a bill passes the legislature under conditions of Wicksellian unanimity,

---

[6] The example is very simple. Cettolin and Riedl (Chapter 11 in this volume) have a much more sophisticated discussion of cooperation and coercion in the provision of public goods.

individuals may still have an incentive not to pay their taxes. Voluntary tax payment, without coercion, will only occur under conditions in which tax payment and service delivery are credibly connected. If individuals enjoy the benefits of expenditures whether they pay their taxes or not, then what induces them to pay taxes is the threat of the disutility of coercion. This brings us back to the venerable free-riding problem of Mancur Olson (which he presumed the government could solve through coercion) and the work of Buchanan and others on the nature of constitutions. Wicksell's unanimity solution depends on unstated assumptions about the nature of the violence and threats of violence that the government can deploy.

A straightforward way to extend Wicksell is to require that all expenditure and tax legislation also explicitly include the coercive measures necessary to enforce the payment of taxes. Individuals then make a decision about the net benefits of the legislation, the utility of expenditures minus the disutility of taxes and coercion. That is all perfectly fine theoretically, as long as we take into consideration the effect of government coercion on the way the rest of society actually works. The remainder of this essay focuses on that problem: How does the interaction of individuals, organizations, and incentives affect the use of violence and coercion and vice versa? It turns out that only some ways of structuring coercion are politically sustainable. In terms of Table 2.1, there are only a limited number of ways to distribute coercion over the population in column (4).

There are two final caveats to keep in mind as we move on to consider the nature of coercion more closely. The first is to avoid the assumption that voluntary coordination without coercion (like Olson's voluntary association) precedes coordination with coercion. Rather than beginning with a theoretical perspective in which coercion is absent and then adding coercion into the mix to see how it changes things (like Wicksell added expenditures to taxes), we should start with the possibility of violence and see what role coercion plays in limiting and shaping the possibilities of violence. In a world where violence is not deterred by the presence of a third-party enforcer that punishes anyone who uses violence, any relationship between two individuals contains the possibility that one or both of the parties will become violent – that is, that coercion, the threat of violence, is always a part of relationships between people.[7]

The second is that the structure of coercion is highly problematic. We can think of the penalties imposed for not paying taxes, as in the examples

---

[7] I first became aware of this in the work of Stergios Skaperdas (see Chapter 2 in this volume and the references therein).

given earlier. Modern legal codes contain extensive lists of such coercive penalties, as well as the conditions under which the government and its agents can use force and the degree of force allowed. The nature of the threat of violence to be used by the government is essential to the concepts of the rule of law and of limited government. Note, however, that the idea of a rule of law coercion schedule that applies impersonally to all citizens is a very specific form of coercion, one in which the same coercive action applies to all individuals. The notion that the same coercive force will be applied to everyone does not follow from the nature of the threat of violence in relationships between individuals. In the absence of credible impersonal third-party enforcement of rules against using violence, when I consider a possible relationship with an individual, I do not want to know what the general rules about the use of violence are, I want to know what the costs and benefits facing that individual are. I want personal knowledge, not impersonal rules. This is the starting point for NWW's analysis of how societies come to limit violence: the highly personal relationships between powerful individuals and groups which create incentives that limit violence and, in the process, create organizations capable of using violence in systematic ways. The logic of the natural state they develop depends, however, on the fact that individuals are treated uniquely, rather than being treated the same. As a result, there is no violence schedule that applies impersonally to all citizens.

If we want to think about legislators A and B (and C, D, etc.) making arrangements within a framework that utilizes Wicksell's unanimity concept, but is extended to include taxes, expenditures, and coercion, do we need to have an impersonal violence schedule? Does there need to be a constitution of coercion that delineates when the government can use violence against citizens as well as the extent of the violence? We cannot answer that question intelligently without understanding more basic features of violence and the organization of society, to which we turn now.

3. Violence and the Logic of the Natural State

Until ten thousand years ago, archeological evidence suggests that the typical human society was small, organized in bands of roughly thirty people who occasionally came together in larger groupings. There were no Weberian "states," no large organizations with a monopoly on the legitimate use of violence, indeed no large organizations at all. Over the last ten millennia, societies have evolved that are both larger and more intricately organized. Few of these societies approached the Weberian ideal either. Whether there was a formal government was often problematic. Even when a formal government existed, powerful groups within society but outside of the formal government often retained not only their arms and military training; social norms also did not confer a legitimacy on government violence that was denied to other groups (for example, England as late as the seventeenth century). It is difficult to understand how coercion is used in these societies if our starting point is a modern society where the government does possess a monopoly on legitimate violence and is, therefore, the only source of legitimate coercion.

In *Violence and Social Orders*, NWW (2009) lay out a conceptual framework for understanding how societies can control the problem of violence. They also provide an understanding of the process by which societies become better organized. They begin their analysis with a world in which individuals base trust on personal interaction and ask how some individuals can deal with dangerous and potentially violent individuals with some degree of confidence. Think of two specialists in violence, each of who is associated with a group of clients. The specialists mistrust one another and will not lay down their arms and coexist because each believes such behavior will lead the other specialist to destroy or enslave him. Armed conflict is the equilibrium outcome. The NWW solution, in simple terms, is for the violence specialists to agree to divide the land, labor, and capital in their world between themselves and agree to enforce each other's privileged access to their resources. The rents they receive from privileged access depend on their continued cooperation. If the value of the rents they earn from their privileges are larger under conditions of peace rather than violence, then the rents from peace can enable each specialist to credibly believe that the other will not fight. The specialists remain armed and dangerous and can credibly threaten the people around them.

The arrangement is represented graphically in Figure 2.1, where A and B are the two violence specialists, and the horizontal ellipse represents the arrangement between the specialists that create their organization/institution. The vertical ellipses represent the arrangements the specialists have with the labor, land, capital, and resources they control: their "clients," the a's and b's. The horizontal arrangement between the specialists is made credible by the vertical arrangements. The rents the specialists receive from controlling their client organizations enable them to credibly commit to one another, since those rents are reduced if cooperation fails and the specialists fight. There is a reciprocal effect. The existence of the agreement between the specialists enables each of them to better structure

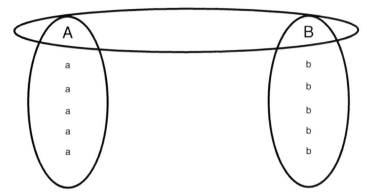

Figure 2.1. Violence specialists, clients, and related (adherent and contractual) organizations.

their client organizations, because they can call on each other for external support.

A and B are the violence specialists, the a's and b's are their clients, respectively. The horizontal ellipse represents the violence specialists organization, the "dominant network." The dominant network is an adherent organization. The specialists limit the ability to form organizations to themselves. Their client organizations, the vertical ellipses, are contractual organizations, which can utilize the dominant coalition as a third-party enforcer.

Organizations are groups of people with shared interests and goals. An *adherent organization* is one in which all of the members have an interest in cooperating with each other (on the relevant dimensions of the organized activity) at all points in time. In an adherent organization interests are structured in such a way that all individuals have an interest in belonging to the organization, even if their interests result from being coerced. Adherent organizations are self-enforcing.

In contrast, a *contractual organization* is one in which relationships between the group members are not inherently self-sustaining, and the group maintains itself only through the presence (or potential presence) of an external third party. The third party may enforce relationships within the organization or between the organization and other external parties. In Figure 2.1, the horizontal relationship between the violence specialists creates an adherent organization. The vertical relationships between the violence specialists and their clients are contractual organizations because they rely on the external presence of the other violence specialists. The vertical client organizations might be organized as kin groups, ethnic groups, or patron-client networks. The combination of multiple organizations – the "organization of organizations" – mitigates the problem of violence between the really dangerous people – the violence specialists – creates credible commitments between the specialists by structuring their interests, and creates a modicum of belief that the specialists and their clients share a common interests because the specialists have a claim on the output of their clients.

The nature of the rents that hold the network and the organizations together must exhibit certain properties. First, for A and B to believe that they will continue to cooperate, some of the rents that A and B enjoy must depend directly on their cooperation. Likewise, their credible belief that the other will not fight depends on the existence of rents from peace for A and B. That is, the rents that A and B derive from their organizations must be sufficiently lower in the presence of violence to sustain beliefs that A and B will not fight.[8] The agreement between A and B enables B to serve as a credible third party for A's organization, and A to serve as a credible third party for B's organization. By enabling A and B to form larger and (potentially) more productive organizations, rents are created that depend on the cooperation of A and B. The relationship between A and B is made credible by the existence of rents that depend on their continued cooperation, and it does not matter whether those rents raise or lower social output; it only matters that the cooperation creates rents for A and B. The rents from peace and cooperation arise because only A and B can form contractual organizations that the coalition will support – that is the "limit" in limited access order that matters.

There is no inherent dynamic that would lead A or B to structure organizations that raise productivity, but equally there is no inherent dynamic that leads A or B to structure organizations that reduce productivity. This is the central problem in North's (1981) neoclassical theory of the state. North models the decision-making process confronting a monarch constrained by political competition and transaction costs and who, therefore, often chooses to pursue policies that reduce total output rather than raise total output: taking a bigger share of a smaller pie, rather than a smaller share of a bigger pie. North, however, assumes the monarch is a unitary actor. In contrast, NWW view the dominant network as facing an internal problem of organizing the network and an external problem of dealing with society.

---

[8] As with all of these statements, terms such as *must* and *sufficiently* should not be interpreted to mean that these conditions will always hold but that if they do not hold, the social arrangements will fall apart.

How the network solves the internal problem depends on the solution to the external problem, and vice versa.

Figure 2.1 is a very simple representation. In a functioning society, members of the dominant network include economic, political, religious, and educational specialists (elites) and organizations whose privileged positions create rents that ensure their cooperation with the dominant coalition and create the organizations through which the goods and services produced by the population can be mobilized and redistributed. Limited access orders are hierarchical, with interlocking groups of elites whose interests are tied by networks of economic privilege. Their political systems tend to be clientelistic, with patron-client networks playing a prominent role in many. Societies ordered by the logic of the natural state live in the shadow of violence: either the threat of imminent violence that requires ongoing changes in institutions to balance the interests of potentially violent groups, or the fact that key institutions were established in the wake of past violence to establish incentives for controlling it in the future.

Recall the two caveats from the preceding section. We cannot understand the structure of human organizations by beginning with non-coerced voluntary cooperation and then adding in violence and coercion. The dominant network in a natural state is an adherent organization whose members are held together only by interests and forces created by the interaction of themselves, but coercion plays an integral role in holding the organization together. The threat of violence is an inherent part of the incentives that make arrangements between members of the coalition credible. In Figure 2.1, A must be able to threaten B, and vice versa. In turn, the existence of the network makes it possible for each of the network members to have stronger organizations that can utilize the third-party services of the coalition. The member organizations are contractual, because they can access the third-party coercion of the coalition.

The second caveat is that the structure of rents in this society is the result of "privileges" that are often unique to specific individuals, rather than "rights" that apply widely to classes of people such as citizens. As a result, the structure of coercion is idiosyncratic as well. Whether you are threatened by violence, and by how much violence, depends on your position in the society. More powerful individuals typically are threatened by more coercion than the less powerful but accordingly have more resources to defend themselves. There is no organization that possesses a monopoly on violence, much less a monopoly on the legitimate use of violence. As a result, there is no uniform schedule of coercion, but there may be specific, even formal, threats of violence that are supported by the network.

4. Organizations, Identity, and Impersonality

The logic underlying Figure 2.1 can produce a set of interests in and out of the government that will result in schedules of expenditures, taxes, and coercion that look like Table 2.1, but it is a table in which taxes, expenditure, and coercion vary widely from individual to individual. In most limited access societies, laws do not apply equally to everyone; taxes are not paid in equal portion by everyone; tax and expenditure policies usually favor one group and disadvantage others; and, in general, relationships between powerful individuals tend to be personal and fluid. Coercion is not applied in an impersonal way by the government. In many developing societies, the government is not even in a position to coerce powerful nongovernment organizations. The pattern of coercion cannot be represented simply as a vector of punishments, because these are not Weberian modern societies with a state monopoly on the use of legitimate violence.

Fascinating as the question is, this essay will not go into the transition from societies where rules and laws cannot be credibly enforced for everyone all the time to societies were they can be.[9] Instead, the contrast between the role of coercion in limited access societies illuminates several features of the role of coercion in the open access societies that Wicksell considered. A key difference is between weak governments and limited governments. We can define "weak governments" as governments that cannot coerce all the organizations within its society and "limited governments" as public organizations that operate within constraints acknowledged by the government and recognized as such by the "citizens."[10] Paradoxically, modern societies with strong governments that possess a monopoly on the use of violence and whose governments are more powerful organizations than the world has ever seen are, nonetheless, characterized as societies with limited government. Societies with weak governments that cannot discipline significant parts of their societies, nonetheless regularly terrorize their populations through the use of torture, coercion, and even genocide. Weak governments exercise unlimited powers; limited governments do not.

---

[9] Wallis (2011) considers this question in greater detail. The transition from limited to open access societies is the subject of chapters 5 and 6 in NWW.

[10] "Political scientists have long emphasized the problems created in many less developed nations by 'weak states,' which lack the power to tax and regulate the economy and to withstand the political and social challenges from non-state actors" (Acemoglu, 2005, abstract). A weak state exists when some private organizations are beyond the control of the government.

Weak governments are constrained in their use of violence not only by the presence of other powerful groups with the ability to be violent but also by the interlocking set of rents that governments and other organizations create. The essential logic of the natural state is that rent creation (and the threat of losing rents) ultimately constrains powerful actors, not institutional rules enforced by the government. When weak governments decide to use violence, they are only constrained by the costs imposed by other powerful groups and the loss of rents. As a result, their use of violence is sometimes unlimited.

The constraints that limit violence by governments are not embedded in credible threats by other groups to use violence against the government but by the way that organizations are formed and structured by the society.[11] Weber's definition of the modern state is very helpful in illuminating the point for open access societies: a government with a monopoly on the use of violence cannot be constrained from abusing that monopoly by the threat of violence against the government from elsewhere in society, because by definition, the government has a monopoly on violence.[12] The constraints on the government have to come from the interests that political, economic, and other social organizations can mobilize to discipline the government. This is equally true in a limited access society.

Looking at the problem this way highlights the critical role organizations play in the logic of the natural state and in the logic of open access societies. It seems obvious, in retrospect, that if violence must be organized to be effective, then the way in which violence is organized will have marked influence on the way it is used. In a limited access society, the political and economic dynamics determine the use of violence and coercion within the dominant network and within the member's organizations. What is "limited" is not the ability to use violence; what is limited is the ability to form an organization that the dominant network will support. Support can include coercion and, if necessary, violence. The limits create rents and the rents shape incentives in a way that encourages both limits on violence and extended coordination and cooperation. In contrast, what is "open" in

---

[11] Wallis and North (2011) develop a set of implications that build on the idea that the power of the state is grounded in its ability to structure (or remove) organizations, rather than its capacity for violence.

[12] We can quibble about the extent of legitimate vs. illegitimate violence capacity, but the fact is that in modern developed societies the government possesses such a preponderance of violence capacity that, if it chooses to use its capacity, it can overwhelm any organized interest within the society. The exceptions occur only when the military and police forces of the government themselves divide, as occurred in the U.S. Civil War in the 1860s.

an open access society is the ability to form organizations that the larger society, through the agency of the government, will support. As a result, the structure of violence and coercion has to be different in an open access society.

In limited access societies, the capacity for violence is possessed by many organizations. In contrast, in open access societies the capacity for violence is consolidated in a limited number of military and police organizations. Those organizations are under the direct control of the political system. The political system is subject to competition and entry. Political organizations are disciplined by economic competition. Open entry in the economic system produces a constantly changing constellation of economic interests that the political system can control only at the margins. As long as the society maintains open entry to economic organizations (and implicitly to markets), then political competition ensures that the government will maintain open economic access.[13] When the government uses violence against organizations and citizens, it must do so in prescribed ways and adhere to certain limits. Governments must obey the constitutional rules about the use of coercion. Governments that attempt to go beyond those limits may be successful in doing so but only if they are able to prevail against the economic and political forces that organize to resist it. If the government is able to exceed the constitutional limits on coercion, it will unravel the internal dynamics of open access (so far in history this has not happened in an open access society).

To this point the discussion has focused on the level of organizations and societies, but individuals must also find it in their interests to adhere to the rules inherent in constitutional arrangement. An even stronger requirement is that individuals find it in their interests to support social rules even when it may appear that it is in their immediate interest not to. The collective action problem is most often cast as a conflict between the interests of individuals versus the interests of groups. However, a more revealing way to conceptualize the problem is the interest individuals have in supporting the organizations they belong to versus supporting the social rules, even when those rules may harm the organization and individual.[14] An example is the easiest way to illustrate the framing.

[13] The structure of the sentence is circular, because political and economic access are critical elements in an equilibrium. NWW call this the "double balance," meaning that you cannot have open access politics and limited access economics, or vice versa. Both systems must be open, or both must be limited.

[14] The remainder of this section is based on Wallis (2011).

In the American presidential election of 2000, George Bush and Al Gore ran an extremely close race that turned, in the end, on the results of voting in the state of Florida. The governor of Florida was George Bush's brother, Jeb, and the attorney general of Florida ruled that Bush had won the Florida balloting when many felt that more investigation was warranted. The Florida ruling was immediately taken up through the court system. When the legal rules had played out and the Supreme Court ruled in favor of Bush, Gore and the Democrats accepted it at considerable cost to Gore as an individual and the Democrats as a political organization.[15] In contrast, in December 2007, when the presidential election in Kenya produced a close result and the incumbent, Mwai Kibaki, was declared the winner, Raila Odinga, the candidate of the losing Orange Democratic Movement protested the results. Over the next two months, violence repeatedly broke out in Kenya and hundreds of people were killed. At the end of February, a negotiated agreement, the National Accord and Reconciliation Act, created the framework for the competing factions to restructure the Kenyan constitution, including the creation of a new office of prime minister, filled by Odinga and substantially increasing the number of cabinet posts to accommodate the organizations of Kibaki and Odinga. In the United States in 2000, Democrats acted to support the rules and acted against the interest of their organization. In Kenya in 2008, Kenyans acted to support their organizations against the rules and ended their organized conflict only after the formal rules had been fundamentally altered in a very personal way. When do individuals find it in their interest to support their organizations and when do they find it in their interests to support impersonal social rules, when the two are in conflict? Wicksell assumes that people will pay their taxes if the legislature asks them to. However, why would individuals pay taxes if they bear no costs for not paying them? Why should they simply obey a rule?

Institutional economics has made considerable progress in thinking about these kinds of problems over the last three decades, but there has been confusion about the nature of "impersonality." Impersonal relationships occur when two individuals interact in a way that does not depend on their personal identity. Impersonal relationships only occur in societies that

---

[15] In his concession speech Gore said, "Over the library of one of our great law schools is inscribed the motto, 'Not under man but under God and law.' That's the ruling principle of American freedom, the source of our democratic liberties. I've tried to make it my guide throughout this contest as it has guided America's deliberations of all the complex issues of the past five weeks. Now the US supreme court has spoken. Let there be no doubt, while I strongly disagree with the court's decision, I accept it." As quoted in the *Manchester Guardian*, December 14, 2000.

are capable of creating and sustaining an impersonal identity of "citizen" or "resident" that applies equally to a large number of people.[16] The essence of impersonality is treating everyone the same. Impersonality pervades open access societies in law, markets, education, religion, politics, and the delivery of public services.

While there is nothing controversial in this definition of impersonal relationships, it is not always the one most often used in the social science of institutions. Instead, the problem of impersonal relationships or impersonal exchange is often motivated by considering how two individuals who do not know each other personally and have no expectation of a continuing relationship in the future can come to agree on a social relationship. Defining impersonal relationships as dealings between individuals who do not know each other personally, however, differs from impersonality defined as treating everyone the same. To separate the two types of relationships, define *identity relationships*, or *identity exchange*, as situations in which people who do not personally know each other interact on some dimension, although the parties know the social identity of the other in the relationship. The social identity of the group, organization, tribe, city, and so forth that an individual is identified with is a key element of identity relationships. In contrast, *impersonal relationships* are situations in which people are treated according to the same rules, whether they are personally known to each other or not. Social identity is not a part of impersonal relationships because, in the limit, all people are treated identically.

Both Wicksell and Lindahl set up their essays as problems of identity relationships, the interaction of two groups, rather than a problem of impersonal relationships, a set of tax rates that applied impersonally to all individuals. Lindahl begins his essay on just taxation with the statement that "[w]e may begin by assuming that there are only two categories of taxpayers; one, A, relatively well-to-do, and the other, B, relatively poor" (1958, 168). Taxes and expenditures are different for the two groups. Wicksell and Lindahl were both concerned about wealthy and poor individuals as groups because of their recent social experience, rather than just for theoretical convenience. However, their formulation followed naturally in a society where individuals looked to the organizations they belonged to protect and define their interests, rather than an impersonal set of rules.

The tendency to assume that organizations already exist or are inherently self-organizing is a strong assumption in economics and other fields.

---

[16] Impersonal rules do not have to apply to everyone universally. Whether a rule is impersonal or not always depends, in part, on the identity of the people it applies to.

For example, Hirshleifer's (1995) well-known paper on anarchy includes the statement that "I will generally treat *groups* as unitary actors that have somehow managed to solve the internal collective action problem."[17] How violence is organized internally within organizations will influence how those organizations behave in external interactions with other organizations. It is simply wrong to assume that the solution to the internal collective action problem does not matter to the behavior of the organizations. What I want to focus on here, however, is the implications of identity relationships for the role of organizations. Organizations can only secure relationships between individuals in different organizations if the organizations have unique identities. That is, I have to know which organization you belong to and something about that organization for your identity as a member of that organization to convey information that allows me to trust you in an anonymous way.[18]

If we were to restructure Table 2.1 to allow for anonymous relationships, then individuals in the table would have to be identified by the organization(s) they belong to. As noted, Wicksell and Lindahl did this implicitly by discussing rich and poor groups (see the graphical treatment in Escarraz 1967). In the Kenya example, it would be followers of Kibaki or Odinga. In Shakespeare it would be Capulets and Montagues; in *West Side Story* it would be Jets and Sharks. These organizational identities are not the same as Democrats and Republicans in the United States, or Labour and Conservatives in the United Kingdom, because these organizations possess the capacity to be violent.

Social stability and order can be sustained in a limited access society, through identity relationships in which individuals are identified with organizations. The dynamics of those societies, however, cannot support impersonal relationships in which all individuals or citizens are treated the same.

5. Getting Impersonal

The changes that have to occur in society to support impersonal relationships involve organizations and explicit rules about the use of violence. The

---

[17] Hirshleifer is not alone in making this kind of assumption nor is the assumption confined to economics. For a discussion of considering groups (or the government) as a unitary actor, see Tilly (1993, 34). Olson's "stationary bandit" (1993) or North's "revenue maximizing monarch" (1981) are also unitary actor models. Also see Bates (2008) and Barzel (2001).

[18] Greif's work community responsibility system and other institutional arrangements (2006) are clear examples of how anonymous relationships can structure societies.

dynamic relationships necessary to sustain impersonal relationships (and open access) also create the necessity of an impersonal constitution of coercion. We cannot reach this conclusion if we consider a world populated only by individuals; we must explicitly consider organizations.

An earlier paper (Wallis 2011) lays out the logic by which impersonality can be created and sustained. The logic has two parts. First, powerful organizations must find it in their interest to support a set of rules for the formation of organizations that allows any citizen to create an organization and that treats all organizations in the same manner. Why powerful organizations might be willing to concede special privileges in return for equal ability to organize is discussed at length in NWW. The United States, the United Kingdom, and France all moved in the mid-nineteenth century to allow equal access to forms of organizations in economics, politics, religion, and education. An inherent part of allowing anyone to form an organization is formally denying nongovernment organizations the ability to use violence, and thus coercion, as a tool for structuring internal or external relationships. I return to this important point in a moment.

The second part of the logic is that individuals – not just elite individuals – must find it in their interest to support impersonal rules rather than the interests of the organizations they belong to. The logic is straightforward. For example, an individual with a specific bundle of human capital (an occupation, for instance, an accountant) chooses to work for firm A. The rents that individual receives from firm A depend on the value of his human capital in his next best employment, for instance, at firm B. Call these "organization specific" rents, because these are the rents that arise from the decision to work at firm A. In contrast, the rents that the individual receives from choosing to be an accountant depend on the relative returns in his next best choice of occupation. Call these "individual specific" rents. Suppose that the number of firms who hire accountants increase and competition for accountants increases as well. The rents the accountant gets from working for a specific firm (the difference between his return in firm A and in firm B) are likely to decrease, as competition drives earnings for accountants at competitive firms toward equality, whereas the rents the accountant receives from being an accountant are likely to increase as the number of alternative employments for his human capital rises.

If the rules for forming organizations become open and more firms are created, individual specific rents increase relative to organization specific rents. At some point, the individual may find that his interests in supporting the organization he belongs to are outweighed by the interests he has in maintaining rules that increase the number of outside options he can exercise.[19]

Individual level incentives alone, of course, will be too idiosyncratic to result in individuals always preferring the abstract rules over the interests of their specific organizations. However, if powerful organizations also find it in their interest to support abstract rules that allow entry (that is, that treat all organizations and citizens the same), then a set of interlocking interests can emerge. It is here that violence comes back into the picture. As long as organizations can potentially use violence or coercion to protect (or project) their interests, there are strong incentives to constrain organizations through rent creation by special privileges. An individual organization must either possess the ability to project violence or be allied with another organization that can do so. The potential use of violence by organizations creates the need for special privileges to create interests that limit the use of violence.

If all organizations are to be treated the same, however, organizations must be prohibited from using violence against each other. Specifically, if the rule is to be that all citizens have the right to form legally sanctioned organizations, then no organization must be able to use violence or coercion to prevent another organization from forming. Prohibiting the use of violence by organizations is accomplished by locating control over violence in a small number of public, government controlled organizations. In *Coercion, Capital, and European States*, Charles Tilly (1993) calls this process "disarming the population."

Powerful organizations will be willing to concede the option of using violence *only if* all other organizations make the same concession. There is a serious coordination problem here. The use of violence will not disappear just because organizations concede their right to use it. The government must formally undertake to enforce rules against the use of violence by organizations (weak governments cannot do this) which requires that the rules about the use of violence be applied equally to all organizations – that is, impersonally. The other side of the agreement is that all individuals who wish to form organizations be allowed to do so. A powerful group that loses

---

[19] Kobe Bryant is a concrete example. Bryant is a star basketball player who makes about $21 million from his team, the LA Lakers. Bryant would be willing to play basketball for $1 million, so his rents from being a basketball player are $20 million. However, there are many NBA teams willing to pay him $20 million to play for them, so his rents from playing for the Lakers are $1 million. Would Bryant cheat to enable the Lakers to win? If his cheating harms the NBA, perhaps not, because he risks the $20 million in basketball rents to increase the $1 million in rents from the Lakers.

out today can reorganize and return in the future. Conceding control of violence to the government is matched with the ability of all interests to form organizations. If organizations cannot freely form, an interest that is forced out of power or influence today may not be able to reorganize and reenter the fray. All organizations, as a result, have an incentive to support free entry.[20]

Conceding power over coercion to the government, then, is an inherent part of making credible and impersonal social arrangements. As the discussion has stressed, impersonal social rules must appear at the level of organizations for those rules to be credible at the level of individuals. Organized violence is the truly dangerous type of violence. Conceding coercive power to the government organizations necessarily requires that private organizations no longer use organized violence. The complementary arrangement is allowing any citizen to form an organization that the government will recognize. Government violence is "legitimate" in the narrow sense that the citizens agree that the government has the ability to use violence. Government violence also becomes legitimate in the broader sense, as there must be a "constitution of coercion" that lays out conditions under which it is appropriate for the government to use violence and, thus, the structure of coercion.[21] It is not just that the society agrees that the government can use coercion, but only in agreed on circumstances is it appropriate for the government to use violence. Private organizations are willing to concede this power to government because they feel that, through the operations of a competitive political system, sustained by a competitive economy, they can discipline any use of government violence outside the agreed on limits.

What are the implications for Wicksell?

6. Wicksell, Unanimity, and Impersonality

Wicksell began his paper on just taxation by accepting the charge that he was engaged in armchair speculation: "I accept the charge happily, since it was my purpose above all to construct a complete, comprehensive, and internally consistent system." (1958, 73) In the spirit of Wicksell, I have tried to make our considerations more complete and comprehensive by explicitly thinking about coercion. Drawing on the conceptual framework

---

[20] For any specific organization, the benefit from open entry must be balanced against the specific rents that an organization might receive from limiting entry. This kind of rent seeking is common in open access societies.

[21] Weingast uses the notion of "bright lines" to denote the conditions under which the government can and cannot use coercion.

Table 2.2. *Impersonal expenditure, tax, and coercion schedules and their utility equivalents*

| Individual (1) | Levels of | | | Utility of | | |
	Expenditures (2)	Taxes (3)	Coercion (4)	Expenditures (5)	Taxes (6)	Coercion (7)
1	$E(x_1)$	$T(y_1)$	C	$U_1 E(x_1)$	$U_1 T(y_1)$	$U_1 C$
2	$E(x_2)$	$T(y_2)$	C	$U_2 E(x_2)$	$U_2 T(y_2)$	$U_2 C$
n	$E(x_n)$	$T(y_n)$	C	$U_n E(x_n)$	$U_n T(y_n)$	$U_n C$
Society	Sum of $E(x_i)$	Sum of $T(y_i)$	??	Sum of $U_i E(x_i)$	Sum of $U_i T(y_i)$	Sum of $U_i C$

Note: Where x and y are impersonally defined measures that vary across individuals, so that expenditures and taxes are a function not of individual identity, but of an impersonally defined characteristic.

of NWW, we can see that the structure of coercion is fundamentally different in limited access and open access societies. Limited access societies require some dispersion of violence capacity between powerful organizations to maintain credible relationships between elites. They also require coercion that varies across individuals, particularly in relationships between powerful individuals. In contrast, open access not only requires consolidation of control over violence in public government organization. It also requires that the government enforce the rules that prevent individuals and organizations from using violence and those rule apply equally to all individuals and organizations. The government's use of violence must be impersonal for the consolidation of violence capacity to be credible and sustainable.

Impersonality pervades many aspects of open access societies. Any citizen must be able to form an organization that the government recognizes and supports, as long as that organization does not use violence. Rules are often written impersonally and applied in an unbiased manner (rule of law).[22] What the Western world considered personal rights are often manifestations of impersonality. Rights are distinguished from privileges by the range of people that possess the privilege. Rights are possessed by all citizens. Rent creation through special privileges does not stop in an open access society; people are still rent maximizers after all. However, rents in an open access society tend to be competed away by open entry and by the development of institutions that implement impersonality in government policies.

Tax and expenditure policies can be personal or impersonal. Table 2.2 presents an impersonal analog to the schedules in Table 2.1. Impersonal

---

[22] The existence of rules in and of itself does not imply impersonality. Rules themselves can be personal, applying differently to different individuals or different groups of people, and rules can also be enforced in a biased way.

expenditures and taxation does not imply that everyone pay or receive the same amount. Allocating taxes and expenditures impersonally requires that some impersonal criteria (such as income) are used to allocate taxes, and other impersonal criteria (such as geography) are used to allocate expenditures.[23] Impersonal enforcement requires that the same punishments apply to all individuals, which Table 2.2 represents as a fixed punishment C.

When open access societies find themselves confronted with a trade-off between more unanimity (perhaps more consensus is a more intuitive way of saying it) and more impersonality, they tend to choose more impersonality. This is my own reading of the history of the modern world.[24] Societies that have been successful at moving toward open access have also moved toward impersonal rules and policies. Societies that have remained limited access societies have, particularly in crises, been unable to introduce or maintain impersonal rules and policies. Thinking about the trade-offs between unanimity and impersonality bring up very deep questions in the structure of modern societies, questions that those societies are still in the process of answering.

New democracies often place considerable importance on the normative goal of consensus and the idea that some Wicksellian minimum core of public policies will obtain the approval of all of the people. This is probably no less true of independence movements in late twentieth-century Africa than it was in early nineteenth-century United States. The will of the people becomes an important concept, even if no one knows how to define it. Threats to popular sovereignty are almost uniformly identified as the result of special organized political or economic interests.[25] As late as the 1840s in the United States, Americans were still arguing that in a true democracy there would only be one party that truly represented the people. This was after several decades in which the inevitability of multiparty politics was

---

[23] For example, the current formula for allocating highway funds between the states is one-third population, one-third land area, and one-third miles of rural post roads (Johnson and Libecap 2003).

[24] My intuition is drawn primarily from the economic and political history of the United States over the last two centuries as well as from European history and the experience of new democracies in the nineteenth and twentieth centuries.

[25] For example, read George Washington's farewell address, which identifies the major threat to American democracy as political parties and organized economic interests, or the first revolutionary French Constitution in 1791, which bans corporations several times in the preamble. This argument and some evidence is presented in NWW, Chapter 6. The importance of the idea of consensus in the early history of the United States is stressed in Hofstadter (1969).

apparent to most political observers.[26] Early nineteenth-century Americans thought that a democratic republic should be based on a wide degree of consensus, but their political system did not evolve in that direction.

Unanimity does not serve as the basis for building workable open access political and economic systems for a number of reasons. Most of the reasons have to do with the dynamic features of societies over time, rather than static mechanisms for making political and economic decisions. One central reason is static, however: the features of a government monopoly on violence that we have already talked about.

Recall the discussion of strong and weak governments and the contrast with limited and unlimited governments. When powerful organizations concede the possibility of using violence to the government, the government becomes stronger in a very real sense. As stressed earlier, powerful organizations will concede control over violence only under three conditions. First, the government must enforce a prohibition on the use of violence by any nongovernment organization. Second, the government must adopt a clear set of guidelines for when the government will use violence to discipline organizations. Third, the government must allow any organization to form that does not use violence or engage in prescribed activities.

These conditions require a "strong" state, with the capacity to discipline organizations within society according to impersonal criteria. Although these requirements are static, they are necessary to sustain a political and economic dynamic that both maintains open access and disciplines both the political and military parts of the government. The selection of political leaders to decide government policy, the political part of the government, must be open and competitive. Universal suffrage and democratic institutions are not the only way to achieve political competition, but so far in history something like an electorally competitive democracy is what societies have moved toward. The political side of the government must be strong enough to discipline the military part of the government. The political side cannot coerce the military, so it must be able to mobilize political, economic, and social forces to discipline the military if necessary. Political competition for leadership must be sustained by economic competition. A political faction must not be allowed to manipulate economic privileges to consolidate political support. Economic entry must remain open, which brings us back to the necessity for allowing organizations to form at will.

---

[26] The best treatment of the realization that political parties were an inevitable part of American politics is Richard Hofstadter (1969).

What happens to theses political dynamics if we require unanimity? Political consensus requires compromise. Obtaining a compromise between individuals or groups whose interests are not identical usually involves mutual accommodation. One group gets more of what it wants in return for conceding a competing group more of what it wants. This amounts to tax and expenditure schedules, T_i and E_i, that vary systematically across individuals (or groups) as in Table 2.1, not in Table 2.2. This is precisely the solution that Wicksell and Lindahl propose. This is not impersonal taxation. It is also possible, perhaps likely, that the government might choose to implement a coercion schedule that treats different groups differently.

Think of the Alien and Sedition Acts in the United States in 1798 that allowed President Adams to shut down opposition newspapers and put their editors in jail. The acts explicitly allowed the government to treat and coerce organizations in a way that was not impersonal. In the case of the Alien and Sedition Acts, political competition pushed back, and in the Jefferson administration the government foreswore the necessity of treating different organizations differently and repealed the acts.[27]

The most frequent problems in the United States, however, did not involve coercion through violence but rather coercion through structure of taxes and expenditures. Under a unanimity rule, individuals who receive higher benefits from expenditures should receive them if they are willing to pay higher taxes. Farmers in the old Northwest (Ohio, Indiana, and Illinois) wanted to build better transportation infrastructure. They understood the logic of unanimity and obtained a political compromise to build canals using debt finance by switching their property taxes from per acre taxes to *ad valorem* taxes. The explicit argument was made that those who benefited most from the canal should pay higher taxes, and because property values capitalized the value of lower transportation costs and *ad valorem* tax system, New York, Ohio, Indiana, and Illinois were able to obtain political consensus that enabled their enormous investments (for their time) in transportation infrastructure (Wallis 2003, 2005).

These investment looked good *ex ante*, but *ex post* they turned out to be real problems. After the economic downturn in 1839, states stopped construction on their canals, property values fell (particularly along proposed canal routes), and tax payers throughout the state ended up bearing an unexpected tax burden. Wicksell understood that the unanimity rule should not apply to taxation to repay debts. However, tax payers were

---

[27] Hitler and the National Socialists after 1933 show a similar pattern, but one in which political competition is too weak to discipline the politicians.

now forced to endure higher taxes to repay debts that were supposed to be serviced out of promised canal revenues. Voters and tax payers could foresee this happening again and again. As a result, in the 1840s many American states began changing their constitutions. An important change was a movement to general taxation, which required that all property be assessed on the same basis and taxed at the same rate. States began requiring that legislatures pass general incorporation laws allowing anyone to form a corporation and began prohibiting legislatures from creating special corporations with unique privileges. To round out the package, states began requiring statewide bond referendums to approve higher taxes before any new debt could be issued.

The motivating idea for these changes was not unanimity, but impersonality. State governments learned that a general political consensus could more easily be crafted by legislatures if they were allowed to treat different individuals differently (different in either their geographical or economic location). *Ex ante* these compromises looked good politically, but *ex post*, if the compromise did not work out as anticipated, some groups were inevitably left holding a bigger bag than they anticipated.

The solution was to move to restrictions on legislature that required them to treat everyone the same. In the United States these are called "general laws." State constitutions began mandating legislatures to pass general laws for property taxation and business corporations in the 1840s, for municipal governments in the 1850s, for a wide range of legislative functions (such as granting divorces) in the 1850s, and for forming political parties in the 1880s.

These changes did not have to occur at the constitutional level, however. Britain and France also moved to general incorporation and open political parties between 1840 and 1880. In France, open access for political parties was ensured when the Republican government elected in 1879 refused to use the "assembly" laws that had allowed the party in power to suppress and disrupt competing political parties by denying competing parties the power of assembly.

The point is not that democratic political institutions have an inherent tendency to move toward impersonal institutions. It is rather to emphasize the opposite. Go back to the idea of the dominant network in a limited access society. The dominant network is an adherent organization whose members coordinate only because it is in their interest to do so. There is no external coercion involved in the network. There is internal coercion: members of the network remain armed and threaten (coerce) each other. Coercion is part of the threats that maintain credible commitments within the network. The network has voluntary unanimity with coercion, because all members find it in their interest to belong to the network. However, the price of unanimity within the network is that each member of the coalition must be treated differently – that is, personally.

Democratic political systems face the same set of problems whether they are in limited access or open access societies: how to coordinate powerful individuals and groups and limit their use of violence. The natural way to do this is by creating special, individualized privileges for powerful groups. If the value of the privileges is reduced if violence breaks out or if coordination within the coalition breaks down, the systematic creation of privileges can sustain a social order. An unequal distribution of violence capacity and use of coercion is an inherent part of the special privileges. Democratic elections will not, in and of themselves, eliminate special treatment. There is nothing in the recent history of new democracies around the world to suggest that democracies move toward impersonality.

Wicksell wrote at a time when many European nations were in the process of making the transition from limited access to open access societies (not all of them would make it). Governments in those societies were becoming stronger. Political scientists and economists, both theoretical and empirical, were wrestling with the problem of how best to limit the powers of these stronger governments. Wicksell's unanimity rule was one such proposal. It remains a proposal with very attractive theoretical properties.

Enforcing unanimity or strong consensus between dominant groups, however, does not guarantee open access. The unanimity rule limits "coercion" in the Wicksellian sense only in the context of a preexisting set of conditions in which the government has obtained a monopoly on violence. Wicksell assumed that everyone would pay their taxes. I have argued that this requires a government with a monopoly on violence that can create incentives through the threat of violence to ensure tax compliance. How does a government arise that is strong enough to be capable of enforcing the rules with regard to taxation, without government simply engaging in predation?

The social arrangements that make limited government possible involve the explicit constitutional agreement (whether the constitution is a written document or not) that organizations will be allowed to form at will; that organizations will not be allowed to use violence; that the government will use violence only within prescribed limits; and that the use of government coercion will be applied impersonally. In the dynamic behavior of societies as they develop politically and economically, constraining government policies to be impersonal appears to be a much stronger survival characteristic for open access. The kind of individualized treatment of people and organizations by the government necessary to implement Wicksell's unanimity rules is inconsistent with impersonal rules and, therefore, is inconsistent with social dynamics necessary to allow a government to possess a monopoly of violence without creating tyranny and dictatorship.

7. Wrapping Up

The powerful insight in Wicksell is that taxes and expenditures must be considered simultaneously if we are to reach intelligent conclusions about what government policies should be. My attempt to extend Wicksell's logic to include decisions about coercion simultaneously with decisions about taxes and expenditures ran into a serious problem: in most developed societies, coercion is applied impersonally. There are fixed punishments for specific crimes, such as not paying your taxes, and those punishments do not vary with the social identity of the individual. Unanimous consent will only arise if every individual is treated differently, and each individual finds that the legislation provides him with expenditure benefits that exceed his tax costs. It is difficult to see how such an outcome will regularly occur under impersonal tax, expenditure, and coercion policies.

We cannot assume that a government capable of impersonal enforcement already exists and go from there. Because organized violence is necessary for coercion, how violence is organized effects how it can be used. Until the last two centuries, governments that could credibly administer impersonal justice, enforcement, and coercion were very rare (perhaps nonexistent).

Following the logic of the natural state developed in NWW, in most societies the administration of coercion is identity based, not impersonal. Rules apply differently to people in different organizations and different places in the social hierarchy. Powerful organizations maintain the ability to use violence. Powerful organizations and individuals will only be willing to concede their ability to use violence to the government if they are convinced that violence will not subsequently be used against them. This requires that (a) the use of violence by all organizations is prohibited by rules; (b) the government organization charged with control of violence enforces the rules by punishing any individual or organization that uses violence; (c) the government organization adheres to a constitution of coercion that stipulates the level of violence appropriate for different circumstances; and (d) all citizens have the ability to form organizations that the government will recognize and support. The impersonal use of violence and the impersonal application of rules for the formation of organizations are necessary parts of these arrangements.

Open access societies involve more than impersonality. They involve institutional arrangements that provide for political and economic entry. Entry fuels the competitive process, and the dynamics of economic and political competition are what makes it possible for a strong government with a monopoly on the legitimate use of violence to credibly accept limits on the use of violence. Impersonal government policies are the hallmark of open access societies.

Wicksell's unanimity rule can be accomplished by tailoring taxes, expenditures, and coercion to individuals and groups in such a way that everyone is in favor of the policy. However, the assumption that the government can credibly enforce rules when the rules are different for everyone is a Herculean assumption. Perhaps we should be satisfied with a modicum of consensus under rules that are truly impersonal.

References

Acemoglu, Daron (2005). "Politics and Economics in Weak and Strong States." *Journal of Monetary Economics* 52(7): 1199–1226.

Acemoglu, Daron (2010). "Institutions, Factor Prices, and Taxation: Virtues of Strong States?" NBER Working Paper 15693, January.

Bates, Robert H. (2008). *When Things Fell Apart: State Failure in Late Century Africa*. New York: Cambridge University Press.

Bates Robert H. (2001). *Prosperity and Violence: The Political Economy of Development*. New York: W. W. Norton.

Bates, Robert H. (1989). *Beyond the Miracle of the Market*. Cambridge: Cambridge University Press.

Bates, Robert H., Avner Greif, and Smita Singh (2002). "Organizing Violence." *Journal of Conflict Resolution* 46(5): 599–628.

Barzel, Yoram (2001). *A Theory of the State*. New York: Cambridge University Press.

Escarraz, Donald Ray (1967). "Wicksell and Lindahl: Theories of Public Expenditure and Tax Justice Reconsidered." *National Tax Journal* 20(2): 137–148.

Fearon, James D. and Laitin, David D. (2003). "Ethnicity, Insurgency, and Civil War." *American Political Science Review* 97(1): 75–90.

Greif, Avner (2006). *Institutions and the Path to the Modern Economy*. New York: Cambridge University Press.

Hirshleifer, Jack (1995). "Anarchy and Its Breakdown." *Journal of Political Economy* 103(1): 26–52.

Hofstadter, Richard (1969). *The Idea of a Party System*. Berkeley: University of California Press.

Johnson, Ronald N. and Libecap, Gary D. (2003). "Transaction Costs and Coalition Stability Under Majority Rule." *Economic Inquiry* 41(2): 193–207.

Lindahl, Eric (1958). "Just Taxation – A Positive Solution." In R. A. Musgrave and A. T. Peacock (eds.), *Classics in the Theory of Public Finance*. New York: MacMillan Company.

North, Douglass C. (1981). *Structure and Change in Economic History*. New York: Norton.

North, Douglass C. (1990). *Institutions, Institutional Change, and Economic Performance*. New York: Cambridge University Press.

North, Douglass C. and Barry R. Weingast (1989). "Constitutions and Commitment: The Evolution of Institutions Governing Public Choice in 17th Century England." *Journal of Economic History* 49: 803–832.

North, Douglass C., John Joseph Wallis, and Barry R. Weingast (2009). *Violence and Social Orders: A Conceptual Framework for Interpreting Recorded Human History*. New York: Cambridge University Press.

Olson, Mancur (1965). *Logic of Collective Action*. Cambridge, MA: Harvard University Press.

Olson, Mancur (1982). *The Rise and Decline of Nations*. New Haven: Yale University Press.

Olson, Mancur (1993). "Democracy, Dictatorship, and Development." *American Political Science Review* 87(3): 567–575.

Tilly, Charles (1993). *Coercion, Capital, and European States: 990–1992*. London: Blackwell Publishing.

Wallis, John Joseph (2003). "The Property Tax as a Coordination Device: Financing Indiana's Mammoth System of Internal Improvements." *Explorations in Economic History* 40(3): 223–250.

Wallis, John Joseph (2005). "Constitutions, Corporations, and Corruption: American States and Constitutional Change, 1842 to 1852." *Journal of Economic History* 65(1): 211–256.

Wallis, John Joseph (2006). "The Concept of Systematic Corruption in American Political and Economic History." In Claudia Goldin and Ed Glaeser (eds.), *Corruption and Reform*. Chicago: University of Chicago Press, pp. 23–62.

Wallis, John Joseph (2011). "Institutions, Organizations, Institutions, Organizations, Impersonality, and Interests: The Dynamics of Institutions." *Journal of Economic Behavior and Organizations* 79(1–2): 35–48.

Wallis, John Joseph and Douglass C. North. (2013). *Leviathan Denied: Governments, Rules, and Social Dynamics*, manuscript.

Weber, Max (1948, 1919). *From Max Weber: Essays in Sociology*. Translated and edited by H. H. Gerth and C. Wright Mills. London: Routledge and Kegan Paul, Ltd.

Wicksell, Knut (1958, 1896). "A New Principle of Just Taxation." In R. A. Musgrave and A. T. Peacock (eds.) *Classics in the Theory of Public Finance*. New York: MacMillan Company, pp. 72–118.

3

Proprietary Public Finance

On Its Emergence and Evolution Out of Anarchy

Stergios Skaperdas

1. Introduction

Proprietary public finance is a term that, to my knowledge, was first introduced by Grossman and Noh (1994). It refers to the ideal type of a state owned by a single entity – the emperor, the king, the ruler – who maximizes the difference between tax receipts and the costs of running the state. These costs may well include expenditures on public goods because such goods typically enhance production and thus increase tax receipts up to a point. This is a very different type of public finance than the traditional ideal type, whereby taxes and expenditure policies are considered to be welfare maximizing. It is also different from the more pragmatic approaches in which public finance is determined by mixtures of lobbying and parliamentary politics.[1]

Given that the vast majority of states that have existed up to modern times have been autocracies and, at least for many of them, there was no essential distinction between the finances of the state and the finances of its ruler, proprietary public finance has received comparatively little attention. Brennan and Buchanan (1985), while recognizing the historical importance of "Leviathan," concentrate on normative issues on how to constrain "Leviathan." To my knowledge, Engineer (1989) was the first to model the basic choices of a proprietary ruler and contrast them to the case of welfare-maximizing public finance. Findlay (1990) also developed a basic model of a proprietary ruler with reference to the political economy of development, whereas Findlay (1996) presented a spatial model of the extent of empire, of which public finance was a concern. Grossman and Noh (1994)

---

[1] See Winer and Hettich (2006) for an overview and the exchange in Buchanan and Musgrave (1999). Wintrobe (1998) goes beyond public finance to provide a more comprehensive analysis of autocratic rule (which is not synonymous with proprietary rule).

emphasized the endogeneity of the horizon of a ruler's rule on the ruler's own policies – that is, how a ruler, by overtaxing and underspending on public goods, would likely have a shorter rule because of a higher probability of successful revolt. Therefore, a ruler who is more likely to survive in the long run should be someone who does not tax and spend like there is no tomorrow. Such an insight is probably behind McGuire and Olson's (1996) and Olson's (1993) more celebrated argument that a *stationary bandit* is superior to a *roving bandit*, even though there was no formal argument made in the static model of McGuire and Olson (1996). Moselle and Polak (2001) have explored difficulties in proprietary rule achieving anything close to efficiency, as has Robinson (1997). A distinct rationale for the relative superiority of the stationary bandit to that of Grossman and Noh is found in Myerson (2008), who shows how rulers could do better when there are restraints on their rule, interpreted as constitutional checks on a ruler's power, and how these can emerge as equilibria in dynamic contests for power.

Apart from the analysis of the proprietary state when it is taken as given, there is also the question of why such states have been so common in history and why in many places in the world today autocracies and kleptocracies (which can be approximated by the proprietary ideal type of state) are still rather common. In this paper I argue that proprietary states are likely to emerge out of anarchy as the dominant form of state organization because violence or the threat of violence is the primary means of enforcement in such settings. Unlike the case of a modern state where anyone can buy security services from a firm such as Brinks Security without fearing its personnel for extortion (because Brinks can be sued, and one ultimately relies on the courts and enforcement agencies of a modern state), under anarchy security and protection cannot be bought and sold like other goods and services because the service itself is about the means of enforcement. There is nothing holding back the provider of security in demanding even more than those who originally threatened the purchaser of protection and induced the need for that purchase. If Brinks and its employees did not face the threat of being sued and jailed, there would be nothing other than social norms in holding them back from extorting their clients. Sometimes police officers with low supervision, especially in weak states, as well as Mafiosi do play the dual role or protector and extortionist. There is a reason that the defining characteristic of the state in its common Weberian definitions centers around the near-monopoly in the use of force because without that near-monopoly, contracts on everything else become difficult or impossible to enforce.

I explore the provision of protection systematically, starting from the proverbial state of nature or anarchy and analyzing the industrial organization of protection using a simple model. In doing so I rely on Skaperdas (1992), Konrad and Skaperdas (1998), Skaperdas (2008), and especially Konrad and Skaperdas (2012). Following the logic previously described, in this analysis no contract can be enforced in any other way than the relative ability of adversaries to use force.

Section 2 introduces a very simple model of atomized anarchy and describes how collective protection could improve outcomes over that condition. Collective protection can be employed either by self-governing groups or by for-profit, proprietary rulers. Section 3 analyzes the case of a monopolistic proprietary ruler who provides collective protection to producers in exchange for tribute, the size of which is determined by the relative ability of producer and ruler to use force. Although total output can be higher than output under atomized anarchy, all the extra output is appropriated by the single ruler so that producers could even be worse off than under anarchy. Section 4 examines how different proprietary rulers compete to essentially capture producers within a given territory and behave in other ways just as a single monopolistic ruler does. In the long run, the number or rulers is endogenous, and all the benefits of collective protection are shown to be dissipated in the competition among rulers. It is also argued that self-governing political entities that could provide collective protection in a democratic fashion have difficulties surviving in the presence of proprietary rulers, primarily because of the small size that is needed to control free-rider problems. Thus, competitive proprietary rule (or organized anarchy) appears to be the type of market structure that is the more stable among those examined.

Section 5 explores avenues through which competitive proprietary rule could evolve to become more consolidated and efficient, although still remaining proprietary and perhaps more hierarchical. After discussing the problems with folk-theorem type of arguments, I briefly discuss ways in which the rulers themselves could make investments in elementary forms of commitment devices so as to increase efficiency.

2. Atomized Anarchy and Collective Protection

Consider first a hypothetical simple setting in which individuals are truly atomized so that they have no connection to any other individual and no collective organizations of any kind exist. There are two possible occupations: those of *producer* and *bandit*. Producers have one unit of time that they can devote to two activities: self-protection against bandits (x) and production $(1 - x)$. Bandits engage full-time in their occupation, which is trying to locate producers and extract from them as much as possible. For simplicity,[2] we suppose that a producer can keep a share x of his output away from bandits, so that his payoff is the following:[3]

$$\pi_p = x(1 - x). \tag{1}$$

The remainder of the production of each producer, $(1 - x)(1 - x) = (1 - x)^2$, is appropriated by bandits. Moreover, the more producers there are relative to bandits, the higher is the payoff of a bandit. Letting P denote the number of producers and B the number of bandits, the payoff of a particular bandit is as follows:

$$\pi_b = (1 - x)^2 \frac{P}{B}. \tag{2}$$

Given the producer's payoff in (1), the optimal choice of self-protection is $1/2$, leaving the remainder $1/2$ for production. Thus, the payoff of a producer is $\pi_p^* = (1/2)(1/2) = 1/4$.

If the payoff of bandits were higher than the payoff of producers, then there would be a tendency of producers becoming bandits. Similarly, if the payoffs of bandits were lower than that of producers, bandits would want to become producers. Therefore, a long-run equilibrium condition for an atomized anarchic economy is that the payoffs of producers and peasants are equalized, or that $\pi_p^* = \pi_b^*$ (which, in this example, equals $1/4$). Given the payoff for bandits in (2), $\pi_p^* = 1/4 = (1/2)^2 \frac{P}{B}$ and the equilibrium condition in our example imply that the number of producers equals the number of bandits ($P^* = B^*$). Letting N denote the total population, the constraint $P^* + B^* = N$ implies $P^* = B^* = N/2$. That is, in long-run equilibrium under atomized autarky we have the following outcomes:

- Payoffs of producers and bandits: $\pi_p^* = \pi_b^* = 1/4$
- Populations of producers and bandits: $P^* = B^* = \frac{1}{2}N$
- Total output: $\frac{1}{4}N$

---

[2] For more general formulations of this and other parts of the model, see Skaperdas (2008) and Konrad and Skaperdas (2012).

[3] Technologies of protection, violence, and fighting, of course, can get a lot more complicated than that. Hirshleifer (1989) first compared different functional forms, and a sizable literature has emerged on the properties of such functions (see, e.g., Jia 2008; Rai and Sarin 2009; Corchón and Dahm 2010).

Changes in such technologies over the course of history have been critical in creating new types of states and in the "industrial organization of protection." Dudley (1991) has examined the role of such changes in the technologies of fighting in history.

Note that total potential output, under which the whole population would become full-time producers, is N. The long-run equilibrium output, $\frac{1}{4}N$, is lower than that because bandits do not contribute anything to production and producers have to divert some of the resources to defending against bandits. The nature of the technology of self-protection is critical in how many resources are wasted on banditry and self-protection. A more effective technology of self-protection would induce both fewer resources devoted to self-protection and less banditry.

2.1. Collective Protection and Self-Governance

Typically, however, we can expect measures that do not just protect an individual producer but have positive (external or other) effects on other producers to be collectively more effective. Such measures could include warning systems about the presence of bandits in the area, the formation of a militia that becomes active when there is a threat, the building of rudimentary fortifications to protect crops or other property, the employment of full-time guards and police officers, or even the building of villages with an eye toward security.

Consider a group of m producers and suppose that y resources per producer were to be devoted to such a type of *collective* protection. If such protection were to be more effective than individual self-protection, then each individual producer should be able to keep more of his production away from bandits by using this collective protection and committing y to it than by devoting the same resources to self-protection. That is, denoting by $h(\frac{\Sigma y}{m}) = h(y)$ the share of a producer's output that is kept away from bandits when all the members of a group of size m contribute y to collective protection, we expect $h(y) > y$. For simplicity, from now on we suppose that $h(y) = \sqrt{y}$, and for arbitrary contributions of members of the group y_i, we have $h(\frac{\sum_{i=1}^{m} y_i}{m}) = \sqrt{\frac{\sum_{i=1}^{m} y_i}{m}}$.

This collective protection technology could be employed not just by groups of producers contributing their own time and effort but also by entrepreneurs who could hire "guards" to protect peasants from bandits. The two possible methods of employing the collective protection technology – a self-governing group of producers and a specialized entrepreneur who hires guards – might seem equivalent. It could be argued, for example, that, instead of the producers contributing their own time and effort, they could pay the corresponding amount to a group of guards or a security agency that would hire guards to protect the producers against bandits. This, however, assumes that there is already a third party that would be able to enforce a contract between the producers and the security agency, something that clearly assumes an answer already exists to the protection and security problem that we have sought to examine in the first place. In the absence of third-party enforcement, instead of protecting the producers, a group of guards or a leader who has managed to put together a group of guards under his aegis could conceivably extract even more out of the producers than simple bandits could.

Unless the security agency consists of the rough but moral do-gooders who appear in movies such as *The Seven Samurai* or *The Magnificent Seven*, relying on such organized enforcers to protect a group of producers against bandits does not appear to be a realistic alternative to the producers just banding together and using the collective protection technology themselves. Analyzing how groups of producers who do use the collective protection technology in a self-governing fashion is straightforward (for a detailed analysis, see Konrad and Skaperdas, 2012). Under Nash equilibrium behavior in the contribution of producers to collective protection, there is predictably under-contribution relative to the efficient outcome, and the contribution is lower the larger the group size is. However, the payoff of producers is always higher than the payoff under atomistic anarchy because the more efficient collective protection technology allows the producers both to decrease the resources they devote to protection – thus increasing useful output – and to increase the share they keep away from bandits. With the total population dividing itself into groups of producers and individual bandits, the bandits would also be better off (otherwise, they would not want to become bandits), but there would be fewer of them. That is, the collective protection technology allows an increase in total output for two reasons: both the output of individual producers and the number of producers increases.

Such a state of affairs supposes the absence of large predators, organized bandits, or entrepreneurs who can use the collective protection technology for their own benefit. I will briefly come back to a discussion of the long-run viability of self-governing groups only after analyzing the industrial organization of collective protection in the presence of for-profit, proprietary rule.

3. Monopolistic Proprietary Rule

We consider first a single entrepreneur, a ruler or "Leviathan," who has a monopoly in the provision of collective protection. The ruler hires guards to protect producers from bandits and receives taxes (or tribute) from the producers. His objective is to maximize the difference between taxes and costs.

Even for proprietary rulers, tax rates are typically assumed to be passively set by the ruler (that includes all the related literature cited in the

Introduction, including Grossman and Noh 1994 and McGuire and Olson 1996). The producers react to such rates by optimally setting their productive effort, something that results in deadweight costs of reduced production compared to the cases without taxation and with optimal, welfare-maximizing taxation. Nevertheless, a proprietary ruler who has significant enforcement power in dealing with bandits would also be tempted to use that power against the producers and perhaps exceed the taxation levels that could have been promised. The producers themselves are also less likely to just believe any promised tax rate unless it is close to what the ruler could extract given his potential for violence and will therefore take defensive measures against the ruler in a similar way that they take defensive measures against bandits. The costs that could come from such posturing and the resource misallocation that they bring about would be in addition to those that come just from having a suboptimal tax rate.

Let G denote the number of guards hired by the ruler and continue denoting by P the total number of producers. Then, each producer would receive collective protection against bandits of $h(\frac{G}{P}) = \sqrt{\frac{G}{P}}$. The wage received by guards is the going rate in this economy, which would be the payoff received in the other available occupations of producer and bandit. For given numbers of guards and producers, and self-protection level x by a producer, the maximum share of output that could theoretically be retained by the producer is $x + \sqrt{\frac{G}{P}}(\leq 1)$. Given, however, the ruler's coercive machinery of guards at his disposal, producers could retain only whatever they can keep from being snatched away from them. One possibility is that producers can keep away from the ruler what they keep away from bandits, which is x in the example we have been following. It is possible, however, that the ruler could extract more than simple bandits can – an issue that we will revisit shortly at the end of this section. For now, we suppose that producers can keep away x share of their output away from the ruler.

That is, each producer obtains a payoff of $x(1 - x)$, and the ruler obtains from each producer what is kept away from bandits $(x + \sqrt{\frac{G}{P}})(1 - x)$ minus what the producers can retain $x(1 - x)$ for a net amount of $\sqrt{\frac{G}{P}}(1 - x)$ (and a tax rate of $x + \sqrt{\frac{G}{P}} - x = \sqrt{\frac{G}{P}}$). Bandits, if any were to exist, take away $(1 - x - \sqrt{\frac{G}{P}})(1 - x)$ from each producer. The net payoff of the ruler is then

$$\sqrt{\frac{G}{P}}(1 - x)P - x(1 - x)G, \qquad (3)$$

where the first term represents the revenues obtained from the producers, and the second term is the cost of hiring the guards. In maximizing this payoff, the ruler needs to take into account several constraints. First, any choice of guards he makes subtracts from the population that is available to become producers and bandits. That is, he needs to take into consideration the following population constraint:

$$N = P + B + G. \tag{4}$$

Second, the choice of guards affects the payoff of bandits, which is the following:

$$\pi_b = \left(1 - x - \sqrt{\frac{G}{P}}\right)(1 - x)\frac{P}{B} \quad \text{if } 1 > x + \sqrt{\frac{G}{P}}$$
$$= 0 \quad \text{otherwise} \tag{5}$$

Bandits can receive positive payoff only if there is imperfect security (i.e., $x + \sqrt{\frac{G}{P}} < 1$). If there is perfect security ($x + \sqrt{\frac{G}{P}} = 1$), by definition no bandits exist.

The third constraint that the ruler needs to take into account is that, if any bandits were to exist, they would need to have the same payoff as producers. Given that the payoff of a producer is $x(1 - x)$, the optimal choice of x is the same as under atomized anarchy of $1/2$, leading to payoffs for producers, bandits (if any), and guards of $1/4$.

The ruler then maximizes (3) subject to (4), (5), and the conditions that the payoffs of all occupations are equalized. It turns out that the maximizing choice of guards is the one that yields perfect security, so that $x + \sqrt{\frac{G^r}{P^r}} = 1/2 + \sqrt{\frac{G^r}{P^r}} = 1$. That choice along with the other characteristics imply the following outcomes under monopolistic proprietary rule:[4]

- There are no bandits in equilibrium ($B^r = 0$) with $G^r = \frac{1}{5}N$ and $P^r = \frac{4}{5}N$.
- Total output is $\frac{2}{5}N$.
- The ruler obtains a maximal payoff of $\frac{3}{20}N$.
- Producers and guards receive a payoff of $\frac{1}{4}$.

---

[4] It can be checked that the derivative of the ruler's payoff function evaluated at G^r, the point at which security becomes perfect, is positive, and therefore no level of guards lower than G^r is optimal. Perfect security with no bandits would not necessarily be true under other functional forms for the collective and self-protection technologies. The qualitative features of the equilibrium, however, in terms of comparisons with atomized anarchy are general (see proposition 2 in Konrad and Skaperdas, 2012).

Compared to atomized anarchy, there are a lot more producers under the single ruler, and output is higher. Using the collective protection technology is responsible for all this increase in the number of producers and total output. Nevertheless, all the extra output compared to atomized anarchy ($(\frac{2}{5} - \frac{1}{4})N = \frac{3}{20}N$) is appropriated by the ruler with what was received under anarchy by producers and bandits now going to producers and guards.

3.1. When the Ruler Is Better at Extraction than Bandits

In this analysis of the monopolistic ruler, we have assumed that producers can resist the ruler just as easily as they can resist bandits or, equivalently, that bandits are as good at extraction as the ruler is. What if the ruler were to be better than bandits at extracting ("taxing") the producers' output? Again, for simplicity, we consider an example. In particular, suppose that for any choice of x, producers can keep away from the rulers only $x^2 (< x)$ share of their output. In that case the payoff of producers would be $x^2(1 - x)$. The optimal choice of x would be $x^e = \frac{2}{3}$, the share that could be kept away from the ruler would be $x^{e^2} = \frac{4}{9}$, the output of the producer would be $1 - x^e = \frac{1}{3}$, all resulting in equilibrium payoff of a producer of only $\frac{4}{27}$ (compared to $\frac{1}{4}$ under atomized anarchy or under a ruler who has the same extractive capacity as bandits). Despite the greater effort devoted to self-protection (against the ruler), producers receive a lower share of their output and produce less output.

Whereas the ruler can enjoy a higher tax rate (for any given choice of guards), the output to be taxed is lower. Additionally, however, the hiring of guards is also cheaper because the "going" wage – the equilibrium payoff of producers – is lower. It can be shown that the optimal choice of guards for the ruler in this case is $G^e = \frac{1}{10}N$, which results in perfect security and a number of producers, $P^e = \frac{9}{10}N$. Thus, the ruler hires fewer guards now than when extraction is not as easy and guards are more expensive to hire and there are more producers, and, given that each producer produces less, total output turns out to be lower ($\frac{3}{10}N$ versus $\frac{4}{10}N$, although total output is still higher than under atomized anarchy).

The tax rate is higher ($\frac{5}{9}$), total output is lower, and the total cost of hiring guards can be shown to be lower ($x^{e^2}(1 - x^e)G^e = \frac{4}{270}$). Overall, however, it can be shown that the payoff of the ruler is still marginally higher than when his extractive power is lower. That is, if the ruler could commit to the lower tax rate than he can impose, he would not want to do so.

4. Competitive Proprietary Rule (or Organized Anarchy)

The profits received by the monopolistic ruler can be expected to attract competitors. The type of competition usually examined by economists is one in which different firms (or, adapted for this case, polities) would attempt to attract mobile producers with lower prices (i.e., tax rates) and better provision of the public goods and services they offer. However, the central question that emerges in such an anarchic setting is how the contract between the firms and the producers will be enforced. A ruler could still extract more from producers than promised and provide less collective protection, and there would be no legal recourse on the part of a producer in enforcing a previously agreed on contract. Moreover, the presence of potentially violent competitors who contest a given ruler's territory implies that the ruler might not be even around to honor a contract even if he wanted to do so. That is, the ubiquitous presence of coercion implies a very different type of competition than that of competing security agencies in a modern rule-of-law state.

Suppose there are R rulers. Each ruler controls territory and his relationship to producers within that territory is the same as that of the monopolistic ruler: the collective protection technology is the same, and he hires guards to protect the producers against bandits but also to extract tribute from them. Again, for simplicity, producers are supposed to be able to keep away from rulers the same amount that they alone could keep away from bandits (i.e., the share of output kept by a producer is x).

The major difference from both monopolistic rule and the ordinary modeling of competition, however, is that rulers compete for territory and the producers within them by fighting with one another or by threatening to fight. To do so, they need to develop a military capacity by hiring warriors, where W_i denotes the number of warriors hired by ruler $i = 1, 2, \ldots, R$, with each warrior having the same payoff as producers and guards. In particular, for a given total number of producers, P, the number of producers within ruler i's territory is (assuming $\sum_{j=1}^{R} W_j > 0$)

$$P_i = \frac{W_i^k}{\sum_{j=1}^{R} W_j^k} P \quad \text{for each } i = 1, 2, \ldots, R; \, 0 < k \leq 1. \quad (6)$$

The parameter k represents the effectiveness of conflict, the relative ease with which a ruler can grab more territory at the expense of other rulers.

Letting G_i denote the number of guards hired by i, the payoff of ruler i (provided $\sqrt{\frac{G_i}{P_i}} \leq \frac{1}{2}$) then becomes

$$\sqrt{\frac{G_i}{P_i}}(1 - x)P_i - x(1 - x)(G_i + W_i),$$

which, given (6) and that producers choose $x = \frac{1}{2}$, becomes

$$\frac{1}{2}\sqrt{\frac{G_i}{\frac{W_i^k}{\sum_{j=1}^{R} W_j^k}P}}\frac{W_i^k}{\sum_{j=1}^{R} W_j^k}P - \frac{1}{4}(G_i + W_i), \quad \text{provided} \quad \sqrt{\frac{G_i}{\frac{W_i^k}{\sum_{j=1}^{R} W_j^k}P}} \leq \frac{1}{2}. \quad (7)$$

Each ruler chooses the number of guards and warriors he hires strategically, so that these choices form a Nash equilibrium. For convenience, and in an analogy with perfect competition in the theory of the firm, each ruler takes the total number of producers as given. The population sorts itself among producers, bandits, guards, and warriors, with individual identity not being essential because all occupations receive the same payoff. All occupational choices and the rulers' strategic choices are made simultaneously and have to be consistent so that they add up to the total population. The equilibrium concept defined next is similar in spirit to notions in general equilibrium in which some players can have some strategic influence on a variable.

Let a *short-run equilibrium* be numbers of peasants ($\hat{P}$), bandits ($\hat{B}$), and for each ruler ($i = 1, 2, \ldots, R,$) guards ($\hat{G}_i$) and warriors ($\hat{W}_i$) such that

1. each ruler with a payoff function described in (7) takes $\hat{P}$ as given and chooses $\hat{G}_i$ and $\hat{W}_i$ simultaneously with other lords so that these choices form a Nash equilibrium;
2. the payoff of each occupation other than producer should be the same or higher than that of a producer;
3. the number of bandits, $\hat{B}$, equals the sum of the bandits in all of the rulers' territories; and
4. $N = \hat{P} + \hat{B} + \sum_{j=1}^{R} \hat{W}_j + \sum_{j=1}^{R} \hat{G}_j.$

It is theoretically possible for different rulers to choose different numbers of guards and warriors resulting in different security levels (in terms of the total fraction of output that is protected from bandits) across different territories. In our example, however, the equilibrium can be shown to be unique and symmetric and involves – just as in the case of monopolistic rule – perfect security, so that $\hat{B} = 0$.[5] Moreover, there are analytical solutions to the equilibrium numbers of the other occupations. It is instructive to first see how equilibrium guards and warriors vary with the number of producers as well as the number of rulers themselves (this is obtained by solving for the Nash equilibrium in equilibrium condition 1):

$$\hat{G}_i = \frac{\hat{P}}{4R}$$

$$\hat{W}_i = \frac{k(R-1)\hat{P}}{R^2}. \tag{8}$$

On the one hand, both guards and warriors are increasing in the number of producers: the former are increasing because more guards are needed to guard (and tax) the producers as the number of producers increases, whereas the warriors are increasing in the number of producers because, as there are more producers, there are more rents to be fought over, and the marginal benefit of an extra warrior increases. On the other hand, both guards and warriors are decreasing in the number of rulers. However, the total number of individuals hired as warriors ($R\hat{W}_i = \frac{k(R-1)\hat{P}}{R}$) is increasing in the number of rulers, something that shows that the intensity of this violent competition increases with the number of rulers. Finally, we should mention the role the effectiveness-of-conflict parameter k plays, as warriors are increasing in proportion to the value of that parameter.

By substituting the values at (8) into equilibrium condition 4, we obtain the equilibrium number of producers:

$$\hat{P} = \frac{4R}{M}N,$$

where $M = (5 + 4k)R - 4k$. The number of producers (and, consequently, total output) can be shown to be decreasing in the number of rulers. By substituting for $\hat{P}$ into (8) and multiplying by R, we obtain the total number of guards and warriors:

$$R\hat{G}_i = \frac{R}{M}N$$

$$R\hat{W}_i = \frac{4k(R-1)}{M}N. \tag{9}$$

Whereas the number of guards is decreasing in R (to maintain perfect security guards decrease proportionately to producers), the number of warriors

---

[5] For general existence and uniqueness results for such an equilibrium, see proposition 3 in Konrad and Skaperdas (2012).

increases as the number of rulers increases, as rulers compete with one another more intensely over a smaller number of producers. (This reduction in producers and increase in warriors as the number of rulers increases is not just a feature of this example but also a characteristic of more general models – see proposition 3 in Konrad and Skaperdas, 2012.)

By substituting all the equilibrium values into the payoff function of a ruler in (7), we obtain the equilibrium payoff:

$$\pi_i(R, k) = \frac{(3 - 4k)R + 4k}{4RM} N. \tag{10}$$

As can be expected, the more rulers are around, the lower the equilibrium payoff of each ruler (i.e., $\frac{\partial \pi_i(R,k)}{\partial R} < 0$) – that is, competition drives down profits. Moreover, it can be shown that profits are decreasing in the effectiveness of the technology of conflict (i.e., $\frac{\partial \pi_i(R,k)}{\partial k} < 0$). The reason for this result is that a higher effectiveness of conflict increases the number of warriors that each ruler hires and thus reduces profits.

Thus far, we have assumed the number of rulers as given. Given that the profit of each ruler is decreasing in the number of rulers, there are obviously numbers of rulers for which profits would be too low or even, possibly, negative. In the long run, in an analogous fashion to the theory of the firm, with free entry and exit we can expect the number of rulers to be endogenous, given a fixed cost of entry into the protection business $F \geq 0$. In particular, we define a *long-run equilibrium* to be a short-run equilibrium (that is, numbers of producers, bandits, guards, and warriors) and a number of rulers, $\hat{R} \geq 2$, such that:[6]

$$\pi_i(\hat{R}, k) \geq F \quad \text{and} \quad \pi_i(\hat{R} + 1, k) < F. \tag{11}$$

Given the properties of $\pi_i(R, k)$, the equilibrium number of rulers is decreasing in the effectiveness of conflict, k. That is, for higher levels of k, when rulers have to hire more warriors for given values of the other parameters, the resultant lower profits imply that fewer rulers can be supported in the long run.

There is a general tendency in a long-run equilibrium for the number of producers to approximate from above the number of producers (and output) under atomized autarky, with a higher entry cost F inducing more production than a lower entry cost. In the limiting case of $F = 0$ and for high enough values of k, the number of producers equals exactly the

---

[6] If $\pi_i(2, k) < 2$, then the long-run equilibrium involves just one, monopolistic ruler: the case we have examined in the previous section.

number of producers under atomized anarchy ($\frac{1}{2}N$), whereas the number of guards equals $\frac{1}{8}N$ and the number of warriors equals $\frac{3}{8}N$. (When $k = 1$, the number of rulers $\hat{R} = 4$ and for $k = \frac{7}{8}$, we have $\hat{R} = 7$.) That is, all the extra output that could be saved by using the collective protection technology is dissipated in the conflictual competition among rulers. What is appropriated by bandits in atomized anarchy is now used in the employment of guards and warriors, with some bandits possibly surviving on the edges (not in our example, but this can occur more generally).[7] Atomized anarchy is replaced by a different form of anarchy, that of organized, hierarchical entities clustered around multiple, feuding rulers.

The model of this section can be interpreted as either a simple model of interacting sovereign, proprietary states or as a model of profit-seeking warlordism (within a formerly unitary state). Whereas the latter interpretation is the one usually associated with the word *anarchy*, the former is also literally true. After a short excursus on the viability of democratic rule, the last section will explore how rule could become consolidated in the case of warlordism.

4.1. On the Viability of Democratic Rule

In Section 2, I briefly alluded to what would occur if groups of producers were to use the collective protection technology in a self-governing fashion, something we can identify as "democratic" rule. Although there is a free-rider problem that becomes greater with an increasing size of the group, individual welfare is higher than under atomized anarchy, monopolistic rule, or organized anarchy. Therefore, instead of producers acquiescing to proprietary rule, why would such groups not form?

The challenge that such groups would face is that proprietary rulers would attempt to conquer them, just as they do so against one another. The members of the group would need to provide resources not just for internal protection against bandits but also for external defense against proprietary rulers. Even if they were to provide the needed resources for external defense at the group-optimal level, the relatively small size that is needed for the more effective provision of internal protection would not leave much for production. In fact, in examples along those lines (found in section V of Konrad and Skaperdas, 2012) the needed resources for

---

[7] If rulers could extract taxes from producers more easily than bandits, by the example analyzed under monopolistic proprietary rule, we can expect competitive proprietary rule to be strictly worse than atomized anarchy.

external defense leave very little for production and internal protection, so that internally there are too many bandits relative to both proprietary rule and atomized autarky. No examples have been found in which individual welfare under that type of democratic rule was as high as that under atomized autarky.

That absence of examples in which democratic rule is viable mirrors the historical rarity of that rule. It is, of course, of interest to find examples and characterize the conditions under which democratic rule is viable. Among the conditions that could be explored are the following:

- By introducing different productivities, producers with higher productivities could form their own groups. This feature would allow them sufficient resources for adequate internal and external security, despite their small size. This characteristic would fit the later medieval Italian city-states: they were usually more productive than other polities (primarily as a result of their trading and specialized manufacturing) and also smaller than their more autocratic competitors.
- Less effective technologies of conflict would reduce the cost of external defense enough to allow democratic rule. The early city-states of Sumeria and perhaps (depending on the interpretation) the city-states of classical Greece would fit this feature. (The Greek city-states would also fit the higher productivity case, especially in the initial stages when the combination of olive, vine, and fruit cultivation as well as trade provided an advantage.) The introduction of the Macedonian phalanx and later of the Roman legion can be interpreted as increasing the effectiveness of conflict, thus increasing both the size of proprietary states as well as making democratic rule less viable.

5. Paths to Consolidation

Competitive proprietary rule or organized anarchy involves at least as much waste of resources as atomized anarchy. Instead of just individual bandits forming the main nonproductive block, under organized anarchy, guards, warriors, some bandits, and rulers take their place without offering anything that improves economic efficiency. Societies cannot withstand such conditions for long periods, as life is "nasty, brutish, and short." Empires, kingdoms, even feudalism (for which competitive proprietary rule can be considered a reasonable model) involve less waste and disorder. Mechanisms develop so as to reduce the worst inefficiencies and further consolidate rule, although the benchmarks established by the coercive arrangements examined thus far have lasting influence on what follows, especially as far as distribution is concerned.

There are two areas in which resources could be saved. First, there is the deep adversarial relationship between ruler and producer, whereby producers reduce production to take defensive measures against the agents of the ruler. Second, rulers could reduce the amount of resources expended on contesting one another's territory and the producers within them. Both types of inefficiencies could be reduced if the *commitment* ability of rulers, with respect to both producers and one another, were to increase.

5.1. The Folk Theorem to the Rescue?

In economics and rational-choice political science, one mechanism of implicit commitment that has been emphasized is long-term relationships, with folk-theorem type of arguments providing game-theoretic underpinnings. Under indefinite repetition of the static interactions I have examined in previous sections, the different agents could initially, in an implicit or explicit agreement, adopt more efficient strategies: the peasants could devote fewer resources to protection and more to production, the rulers might demand less in tribute than they could extract and, simultaneously, hire fewer warriors but keep dividing territory and peasants among themselves as prescribed by the static equilibrium. If one side of a dyadic interaction were to choose to renege on the agreement, then the other side would revert to a punishment strategy that would involve the static inefficient equilibrium for at least a number of periods and possibly indefinitely. Under a sufficiently high discount factor (a "long shadow of the future"), such strategy combinations, and thus more efficient outcomes, can form an equilibrium.

There are, however, a number of issues in considering a folk-theorem argument as a plausible mechanism for alleviating the problems of organized anarchy. First, there is a great multiplicity of equilibria, in terms of levels of efficiency and punishment, and the static, inefficient equilibrium is still an equilibrium in the repeated game. How do the many different sides coordinate on the particular strategy they will follow? Well, simplicity is one criterion, and the simplest, and focal, strategy is the static equilibrium. Moreover, the punishment strategies are typically "non-renegotiation proof" – that is, once someone cheats, he or she could say, "Sorry, I made a mistake and I will not do it again. Could we just go back to the good strategies?" That is, the static, inefficient equilibrium appears to be the most plausible one to follow by all sides.

Second, in our case, both the number of players involved is large and, even more important, there are interactions at multiple levels. How would the producers coordinate among themselves and with the ruler about the amount of resources they will devote to production and protection and the level of tribute their ruler will ask in return? Moreover, if different rulers agree on different levels of tribute and resources with their own producers, then there might be incentives for some rulers to increase the number of warriors they hire so as to take additional territory with more producers and possibly reneging on the agreement the previous ruler of the newly acquired producers. Additionally, with such serious loose ends in the background, the rulers themselves need to coordinate on a lower level of warriors. Therefore, in the case of our model, folk-theorem arguments not only face the problem of coordination among a large number of players but more seriously also involve significant interdependencies across essentially different games in ways that would make even the definition of appropriate punishment strategies difficult and coordination across them even more so.

Third, folk-theorem arguments are made on the basis that the same game will be played period after period. In the conflictual conditions we have examined, however, an equivalence that may exist between conflictual and settling under the threat of conflict in one-period interactions can no longer be assumed in multi-period interactions.[8] In particular, if two rulers were to fight instead of settling on a division of territory, the winner would gain an advantage (more territory) not just in the current period but also, by virtue of his increased fiscal capacity, well into the future. The loser might even be eliminated altogether. This type of non-stationarity makes punishment strategies less likely to exist, and in limiting cases they might not exist at all. Furthermore, higher discount factors in such settings, instead of facilitating cooperation, induce more intense conflict because the winner has more to gain and the loser more to lose (for such models, see Garfinkel and Skaperdas 2000 and McBride and Skaperdas 2010).

Finally, the fourth problem with relying on folk-theorem arguments to explain the emergence of more cooperative types of state rule is that such arguments do not require any institutions, laws, courts, police, and other state infrastructure that is observed in actual states. Solely relying on the folk theorem would seem to imply no need for any organizations whatsoever.

---

[8] In the previous sections we have actually assumed that the rulers never fight it out and they just settle with the shares of producers they receive determined by their relative number of warriors. However, these payoffs would be equal to the expected payoff under overt conflict. In multi-period interactions, this equivalence of payoffs is no longer valid. (See Garfinkel and Skaperdas 2000 or McBride and Skaperdas 2010.)

5.2. Investing in Commitment (or Building a State)

In late medieval Genoa, after decades of internecine warfare the main competing clans made an agreement to bring an external limited enforcer, the *podesta* (Greif, 1998). A new podesta was hired from outside Genoa every year and he performed basic administrative and police duties, but his power was limited so that he could not effectively ally himself with one of the clans against the others. All the clans contributed to the cost of maintaining the podesta, and in return they received some assurance that inter-clan warfare would not take place, and this appears to have worked well for a number of decades. That is, we can think of the clans, through their contributions to hire a podesta, as making investments in (limited) commitment.

Those investments can take other forms as well, from meeting for social and diplomatic purposes with other rulers, to creating a more formal "assembly of rulers," to creating laws, courts, and enforcement agencies. Such measures can contribute to increasing the rulers' abilities to commit to one another that they will not fight or cheat in their dealings with one another, although imperfectly so.[9]

We can model the "degree of commitment" that can be achieved by modifying the sharing function in (6) as follows:[10]

$$
P_i = \left[\sigma \frac{1}{R} + (1 - \sigma) \frac{W_i^k}{\sum\limits_{j=1}^{R} W_j^k} \right] P \quad \text{where } \sigma \in [0, 1]. \tag{12}
$$

The parameter σ represents the degree of commitment (or security). Equation (6) is the special case of (12) for $\sigma = 0$. The polar opposite of that is the case of $\sigma = 1$, whereby commitment is perfect, and the sharing of the producers among the rulers is fixed at $\frac{1}{R}$. The greater σ is, the higher the degree of commitment that the rulers can achieve. The closer 1 is to σ, the closer to the "rule of law for elites" (North, Wallis, and Weingast 2009) or to the state having the monopoly in the means of coercion (Wallis, this volume) we can consider the outcome to be.

[9] Ostrom (2010) brings attention to a large number of empirical case studies and experiments in which face-to-face communication as well as other agreements on monitoring and sanctions for cheaters reduce inefficiencies in common-pool settings. Although our setting is somewhat different from those that Ostrom has studied, the lessons are likely transferable.

[10] The approach follows McBride et. al. (2011). A probabilistic approach to the same problem is found in Genicot and Skaperdas (2002). Both of those papers employ multi-period models in contrast to the static model we use in this paper.

By modifying the payoff function in (7), we can derive a new Nash equilibrium among rulers that eventually leads to the following modified version of equilibrium in number of producers, guards, and warriors:

$$\hat{P}(\sigma) = \frac{4R}{M(\sigma)} N$$

$$R\hat{G}_i(\sigma) = \frac{R}{M(\sigma)} N, \tag{13}$$

$$R\hat{W}_i(\sigma) = \frac{4k(1 - \sigma)(R - 1)}{M(\sigma)} N, \tag{14}$$

where $M(\sigma) = (5 + 4k(1 - \sigma))R - 4k(1 - \sigma)$. An increase in σ (i.e., higher commitment or higher security) plays the same role as a decrease in the effectiveness of conflict (lower k). Higher commitment capability increases the total number of producers and increases the number of guards hired but, given that rulers trust one another more, decreases the number of warriors.

Naturally, given that there are more producers within each ruler's territory and fewer warriors need to be hired, a ruler's equilibrium profits increase as well:

$$\pi_i(R, k, \sigma) = \frac{(3 - 4k(\sigma))R + 4k(1 - \sigma)}{4RM(\sigma)} N. \tag{15}$$

Because σ can be thought of as a collective good for the rulers and there might be actions they could take to modify it (by, for example, hiring a podesta or simply starting to meet with one another for diplomatic reasons), we can think of commitment as a function of investments made by the rulers themselves. That is, let $\sigma = \sigma(\sum_{j=1}^{R} I_j)$, assumed to be strictly increasing in its argument, where I_i denotes the cost of the investment by ruler $i = 1, 2, \ldots, R$. Then, by first making investments before making the other choices, the ruler's payoff function is modified as follows:

$$\pi_i\left(R, k, \sigma, \sum_{j=1}^{R} I_j\right)$$

$$= \frac{\left(3 - 4k\left(\sigma\left(\sum_{j=1}^{R} I_j\right)\right)\right)R + 4k\left(1 - \sigma\left(\sum_{j=1}^{R} I_j\right)\right)}{4RM\left(\sigma\left(\sum_{j=1}^{R} I_j\right)\right)} N - I_i. \tag{16}$$

We can analyze the Nash equilibrium in investments in commitment, with straightforward results, with investments being higher the larger the population N and the smaller the number of rulers R (see McBride et. al. 2011, for details in a more general, dynamic model but with similar characteristics). There are, however, some other important considerations that merit discussion:

- The equilibrium and payoffs we have described here are for a given number of rulers. Because there might still be entry of new potential rulers, another consideration in the collective interest of existing rulers is to take measures that will make new entrants less likely.
- The investments that maximize the sum of profits in (16) are clearly higher than those obtained in Nash equilibrium. Therefore, a complementary consideration to increasing commitment and trust might be in engaging in more cooperative behavior by making investments that are higher than those in Nash equilibrium. Therefore, there are multiple areas in which existing rulers could cooperate and increase individual and collective profits: investing in commitment; increasing investment in commitment to their collectively maximal levels; and engaging in entry-deterring measures against potential challengers.
- All the rulers have been assumed to be identical up to this point. Breaking that symmetry can not only change some key results but also bring new insights. For example, a simple way to break the symmetry would be to modify (12) in the following way:

$$P_i = \left[\sigma\alpha_i + (1 - \sigma)\frac{W_i^k}{\sum\limits_{j=1}^{R} W_j^k}\right]P \quad \text{where} \quad \Sigma_{j=1}^R \alpha_j = 1; \; \alpha_i \in (0, 1),$$

where the share received by each ruler is replaced in the case of perfect commitment by an arbitrary share α_i instead of the equal share $\frac{1}{R}$. This change might reflect some initial advantage that some rulers might have over others. When calculated, the equilibrium results with this change and end with a modified equilibrium payoff function of (16) (which would be different for different rulers); therefore, we can show that only the ruler with the highest α_i would have an incentive to invest in commitment. We could conceive of that ruler as providing leadership, being first among equals, and providing a way of thinking about how a king could emerge out of an originally undifferentiated mass of rulers.

- One important caveat to the preceding discussion of asymmetry is that a king, once he gains greater power than other rulers, might no longer want to invest in commitment measures that benefit all rulers but would want to enhance his power by creating a "king's court" or a "Star Chamber." Rule of law for elites is no simple matter to achieve.

- Also, the collective and individual interest of rulers is to decrease the costs of extraction from producers. That could also be achieved through investments in changing norms, through the acceptance and dissemination of ideologies and religions that enhance their profits. For example, having producers believe that there is a single God whose sole representative on earth is their current ruler is helpful in reducing resistance and acceptance of the taxes they pay to that ruler.

Such considerations indicate the rich set of possibilities that exist in evolving beyond organized anarchy into the hierarchical proprietary states that have existed in most of history (Finer 1997 provides a great overview as well as detail of states in history). Their organization is more complex and involves not just extracting tribute and providing collective goods but also developing and maintaining intra-elite cooperation and propagating unifying and profit- (and efficiency-) enhancing ideologies among its subjects.

References

Brennan, Geoffrey and M. James Buchanan (1985). *The Reason of Rules*. New York: Cambridge University Press.

Buchanan, James M. and Richard A. Musgrave (1999). *Public Finance and Public Choice: Two Contrasting Views of the State*. Cambridge, MA: MIT Press.

Corchón, Luis and Matthias Dahm (2010). "Foundations for Contest Success Functions." *Economic Theory* 43(1): 81–98.

Dudley, Leonard M (1991). *The Word and the Sword: How Techniques of Information and Violence Have Shaped our World*. Cambridge, MA: Blackwell Publishers.

Engineer, Merwan (1989). "Taxes, Public Good, and the Ruling Class: An Exploration of the Territory Between Brennan and Buchanan's Leviathan and Conventional Public Finance." *Public Finance/Finances Publique* 44: 19–30.

Findlay, Ronald (1990). "The New Political Economy: Its Explanatory Power for the LDC's" *Economics and Politics* 2(July): 193–221.

Findlay, Ronald (1996). "Towards a Model of Territorial Expansion and the Limits of Empire." In M. R. Garfinkel and S. Skaperdas (eds.), *The Political Economy of Conflict and Appropriation*. New York: Cambridge University Press, pp. 41–56.

Finer, Samuel (1997). *The History of Government*. Vols 1–3. New York: Oxford University Press.

Garfinkel, Michelle R. and Stergios Skaperdas (2000). "Conflict without Misperceptions or Incomplete Information: How the Future Matters." *Conflict of Journal Resolution* 44(6): 793–807.

Genicot, Garance and Stergios Skaperdas (2002). "Investing in Conflict Management." *Journal of Conflict Resolution* 46(1): 154–170.

Greif, Avner (1998). "Self-enforcing Political Systems and Economic Growth: Late Medieval Genoa." In R. Bates, A. Greif, M. Levi, and J.-L. Rosenthal. *Analytic Narratives*. Princeton: Princeton University Press, pp. 23–56.

Grossman, Herschel and Suk Jae Noh (1994). "Proprietary Public Finance and Economic Welfare." *Journal of Public Economics* 53: 187–204.

Hirshleifer, Jack (1989). "Conflict and Rent-Seeking Success Functions: Ratio vs. Difference Models of Relative Success." *Public Choice* 63: 101–112.

Jia, Hao (2008). "A Stochastic Derivation of the Ratio Form of Contest Success Functions." *Public Choice* 135(3–4): 125–130.

Konrad, Kai A. and Stergios Skaperdas (1998). "Extortion." *Economica* 65: 461–477.

Konrad, Kai A. and Stergios Skaperdas (2012). "The Market for Protection and the Origin of the State." *Economic Theory* 50(2): 417–443.

McBride, Michael and Stergios Skaperdas (2010). "Conflict, Settlement, and the Shadow of the Future." Working paper.

McBride, Michael, Gary Milante, and Stergios Skaperdas (2011). "Peace and War with Endogenous State Capacity." *Journal of Conflict Resolution* 55(3): 446–468.

McGuire, Martin C. and Mancur Olson (1996). "The Economics of Autocracy and Majority Rule: The Invisible Hand and the Use of Force." *Journal of Economic Literature* 34: 72–96.

Moselle, Boaz and Ben Polak (2001). "A Model of a Predatory State." *Journal of Law, Economics, and Organization* 17(1): 1–33.

Myerson, Roger B. (2008). "The Autocrat's Credibility Problem and Foundations of the Constitutional State." *American Political Science Review* 102(1): 125–139.

North, Douglass C., John Joseph Wallis, and Barry R. Weingast (2009). *Violence and Social Orders: A Conceptual Framework for Interpreting Recorded Human History*. New York: Cambridge University Press.

Olson, Mancur (1993). "Dictatorship, Democracy, and Development." *American Political Science Review* 87(3): 567–76.

Ostrom, Elinor (2010). "Beyond Markets and States: Polycentric Governance of Complex Economic Systems." *American Economic Review* 100(3): 641–672.

Rai, Birendra K. and Rajiv Sarin (2009). "Generalized Contest Success Functions." *Economic Theory* 40: 139–149.

Robinson, James A. (1997). "When Is a State Predatory?" Department of Economics, University of Southern California.

Skaperdas, Stergios (1992). "Cooperation, Conflict, and Power in the Absence of Property Rights." *American Economic Review* 82(4): 720–739.

Skaperdas, Stergios (2008). "An Economic Approach to Analyzing Civil Wars." *Economics of Governance* 9(1): 25–44.

Winer, Stanley L. and Walter Hettich (2006). "Structure and Coherence in the Political Economy of Public Finance." In B. Weingast and D. Wittman (eds.), *The Oxford Handbook of Political Economy*. New York: Oxford University Press, pp. 441–463.

Wintrobe, Ronald (1998). *The Political Economy of Dictatorship*. New York: Cambridge University Press.

Discussion

A Spatial Model of State Coercion

Léonard Dudley

Although the essays by John Wallis on "The Constitution of Coercion" and Stergios Skaperdas on "Proprietary Public Finance" both deal with the use of force to compel citizens to pay taxes, the two chapters are quite different. Wallis uses a non-formal approach, focusing on the division of power between groups of violence specialists *within* states. In contrast, Skaperdas employs formal modeling to examine the degree of competition *between* states. I will nevertheless show that the two approaches are highly complementary. Borrowing from two German theorists, Walter Christaller (1966) and August Lösch (1954), I will make explicit an element that is implied in each chapter, namely, the spatial dimension.

THE DEMAND FOR PUBLIC SERVICES

Wallis's approach to public finance follows Knut Wicksell (1958) in comparing the valuations that difference people place on the public services they receive under exogenously set tax rates. In other words, the emphasis is on the demand side. Assume that individuals in the general population are ranked in decreasing order of their willingness to pay taxes, WTP in Figure D.2.1. Here the horizontal axis measures the population of a state and the vertical axis its tax rate (assumed identical for all taxpayers). Add the corresponding marginal willingness to pay schedule, MWP. Finally, assume that the average cost of supplying collective goods, AC, is constant.

Throughout history, Wallis argues, the typical political unit has been the "natural state" in which groups of violence specialists use their power to exploit nonviolent subjects. He assumes that military power is held by distinct groups, for example, a king with his followers, X, and a group of nobles, Y. Neither group has a monopoly on violence. Together, they constitute an *adherent* organization – that is, a coalition that always has an interest in

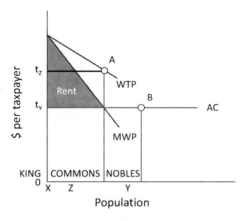

Figure D.2.1. The natural state.

cooperating because of the threat of violence in case of disagreement. These individuals in turn exploit members of the general population who do not have access to military technology, the commons, Z. The latter have *contractual* relationships – that is, relationships that require enforcement by a third party – with both X and Y. Here X enforces Y's contracts and Y in turn enforces X's contracts. However, neither X nor Y has a monopoly on the legitimate use of violence. The resulting arrangement is *anonymous* but *not impersonal*, because the group to which each individual belongs is common knowledge.

The society Wallis describes is logically consistent, but can it help us understand the history of the West over the last millennium? I would say yes, with one qualification: namely, that there have been long periods in most states when one small group of violence specialists had a monopoly on the legitimate use of military power. Consider, for example, the case of France. Between roughly 1450 and 1870, it was the king or emperor who dominated the nobility, because of the former's command of the tremendous scale economies of gunpowder technology (McNeill 1982). In England, the story was similar except that the Glorious Revolution of 1688 led to a transfer of legitimate power from the monarch to a coalition of landholders – an arrangement that lasted until the Reform Bill of 1832.

Figure D.2.1 illustrates the type of equilibrium just described. The king, who controls the army, is a discriminating monopolist, setting tax rates, t_Y and t_Z, for the nobles and commons, respectively. The nobility have a privileged position in that they pay only the average cost of the collective good, usually in the form of military service. Their situation, explained by the nobility's mobility or its mastery of violence, might be called Tiebout coercion ($t_y = AC$), analogous to a golfer's membership in a club. However, the unarmed and immobile commoners pay a higher rate, one that maximizes the king's rent. Their situation might be called Cournot coercion, because they pay a tax that is higher than the average cost of public services but below their willingness to pay ($WTP > t_Z > AC$).

Wallis also cites Wicksell to describe what might be defined as Wicksell coercion, in which the tax rate is greater than the willingness to pay ($t > WTP$). However, if the king attempts to set such a tax (greater than t_Z), he risks destroying his tax base, because the willingness of the marginal taxpayer at A to pay is presumably her production less the subsistence wage. In equilibrium, then, we will not observe Wicksell coercion.

The alternative to this vertical structure is what Wallis defines as the "open access society." In the preceding model, groups X and Y may be persuaded to give up their privileges if the government allows any organization to form provided that it does not engage in violence or other prescribed activities. The result is a society in which the relation between the state and the individual is *impersonal*. Taxation must now be based on some impersonal criterion such as the taxpayer's income rather than on the group to which she belongs.

What Wallis does not explain is the transition from the natural state to the open access society. Why should group X or Y give up its violence monopoly and allow competing organizations to be formed? To answer this question, it is useful to turn from coercion to consent, making explicit the society's information technology. One of the fundamental transformations in Western societies between 1500 and 1914 was the spread of literacy. Arguably, it was the arrival of near-universal literacy that made it possible for group Z creditably to challenge the political power of X and Z, insisting on the dismantling of the restrictions that limited access to political decision making.

THE SUPPLY OF PUBLIC SERVICES

At first glance, Skaperdas's model of *proprietary rule* would seem to be similar to Wallis's *natural state*. In each case, a rent-maximizing elite uses the fiscal system to exploit the majority of the population. However, whereas Wallis emphasizes the *cooperative* contractual relations within the elite group, Skaperdas studies the *competition* between military entrepreneurs, each with his own territorial base. By making explicit the military technology, he is able to model a continuum of state types between absolutism and

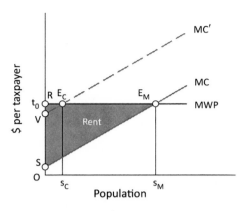

Figure D.2.2. The proprietary state.

anarchy. Abstracting from demand considerations, assume that the marginal willingness to pay taxes, *MWP* in Figure D.2.2, is constant.

Imagine, for example, a uniformly fertile plain that stretches far in any direction. A proprietary ruler of a given territory is then able to extract all production greater than the subsistence wage in the form of taxes.

At one extreme is the *monopolistic proprietary* equilibrium, E_M. When military scale economies are high, the marginal cost of holding territory is low, as shown by the curve *MC*. In this case, there is a single ruler who expands his territory to s_M. Note, however, he will not be interested in expanding beyond this point. Applying the tax rate $t_0 = MWP$, he collects rent equal to the shaded triangle $RE_M S$.

At the other extreme is the *competitive proprietary* equilibrium, E_C. Here, because of a fall in military scale economies, the marginal cost curve has shifted upward to position *MC'*. There are now many small states of size s_C. The rental share is much smaller: together, the multiple triangles of size $RE_C V$ are smaller than $RE_M S$.

Both of these cases are examples of Olson's (1993) *stationary* bandit, although the scale of the rational tax collecting, of course, differs. Skaperdas also provides an elegant model of the latter's *roaming* bandit. Imagine a case in which military scale economies are nonexistent and the marginal cost curve cuts the horizontal axis at *R*. In this case there are no rents. In equilibrium, each bandit pillages wherever and as much as he chooses, not caring about whether the peasants have enough food to survive until the next season. However, as long as military scale economies are positive, such a situation will not occur in equilibrium. It will always be profitable for an entrepreneur to offer to get rid of the bandits in return for a tax level

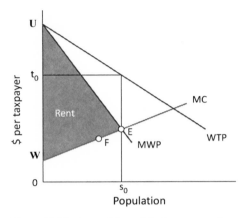

Figure D.2.3. A spatial model of state coercion.

that leaves the peasants a subsistence wage plus. For example, in eleventh-century Normandy, young duke William ended a state of near anarchy by persuading a group of like-minded young nobles to follow his leadership (Bates 2004, 77–82).

A MORE GENERAL MODEL

By combining Wallis's demand-side approach to the public sector with Skaperdas's supply-side approach, we obtain a more general spatial model of state coercion. In Figure D.2.3, assume that individuals are ordered by their willingness to pay taxes, *WTP*, and that the marginal cost curve, *MC*, has a positive slope. Furthermore, let the rankings of the population by each of these measures be identical. Then in equilibrium, the typical state will have population s_0 and tax rate t_0. In addition, there will be a triangle of rent, *UEW*, to be distributed among the state's interest groups.

This spatial model includes the "natural state" and the "proprietary state" as special cases. However, there are many more possibilities, depending on the homogeneity of population, military and communications technology, and transport costs. For example, if the private sector suddenly becomes more efficient than the public sector at providing public services such as protection, garbage collection, and education, the *WTP* and *MWP* curves will shift downward. During the transition to the new equilibrium at *F*, a considerable portion of the population will experience Wicksell coercion, the tax rate being greater than their willingness to pay – a "Tea Party" situation. At the same time, there will be pressure on the state's borders – "imperial overextension," to use Kennedy's (1987) term.

In conclusion, the theories of state coercion proposed by Wallis and Skaperdas suggest three considerations that must be taken into account when we study the welfare impact of coercion in fiscal systems:

1. As the synthesis in Figure D.2.3 makes clear, both the absolute size of the state and the relative size of its public sector are endogenous. For a given geography and degree of cultural heterogeneity, Skaperdas's military-technology variable will play a key role in determining both the frontiers of the state and the public share.
2. This approach shows that except in the degenerate case of Olson's roaming bandits, there will always be rents to be distributed. Therefore, Wallis's emphasis on the relationships within and between the dominant groups in a society is an essential part of fiscal welfare analysis.
3. For any given level of willingness to pay, there are various levels of coercion to be considered. To the extent that voters are immobile, the efficient ideal of Tiebout coercion, in which the tax rate is equal to the average cost of public services, will be rare at the level of the sovereign state. However, the other extreme of Wicksell coercion, with tax rates greater than people's willingness to pay, is likely to be an exceptional situation while a society adjusts to a shock. In general, the dominant coalition will tend to set tax rates at the intermediate Cournot level that maximizes its rents.

Ultimately, there is the question of who is supreme, the sovereign or the state. At age sixteen, the impetuous sun king, Louis XIV, uttered his famous pronouncement, "L'État c'est moi." However, sixty years later, on his deathbed, the king was considerably wiser. "Je m'en vais," he wheezed, "mais l'État demeurera toujours."[1] Roughly translated, his last testament becomes, "I'm out of here, but the rest of you guys and your descendants will be paying taxes to the French state forever."

References

Bates, David (2004). *William the Conqueror.* Stroud, UK: Tempus.
Christaller, Walter (1966). *Central Places in Southern Germany.* Englewood Cliffs, NJ: Prentice-Hall.

---

[1] Marquis de Dangeau, *Mémoire sur la mort de Louis XIV.* Paris: Firmin Didot, 1858, p. 24.

Graff, Harvey J. (1991). *The Legacies of Literacy: Continuities and Contradictions in Western Culture and Society*. Bloomington, IN: Indiana University Press.

Kennedy, Paul (1987). *The Rise and Fall of the Great Powers*. New York: Random House.

Lösch, August (1954). *The Economics of Location*. New Haven: Yale University Press.

McNeill, William H (1982). *The Pursuit of Power*. Chicago: University of Chicago Press.

Olson, Mancur (1993). "Dictatorship, Democracy and Development." *American Political Science Review* 87: 567–576.

Wicksell, Knut (1958). "A New Principle of Just Taxation." In Richard A. Musgrave and Alan T. Peacock (eds.), *Classics in the Theory of Public Finance*. London: Macmillan, 72–118.

PART II

VOLUNTARY AND COERCIVE TRANSACTIONS
IN WELFARE ANALYSIS

4

Coercion, Taxation, and Voluntary Association

Roger D. Congleton

Since that which is done under compulsion or by reason of ignorance is involuntary, the voluntary would seem to be that of which the moving principle is in the agent himself, he being aware of the particular circumstances of the action.
Aristotle, *Nicomachean Ethics* (book III)

1. Introduction: Baselines and the Nature of Voluntary and Coercive Transactions

Voluntary and coercive relationships among persons play important roles in ethics, political theory, and Western law. For the most part, voluntary relationships are considered to be morally neutral or good as long as the voluntary relationships do not harm others. Coercion on the other hand tends to be considered to be a "bad," because coercion by definition tends to make at least one person worse off – namely the person(s) coerced. Consequently, contractarian, Paretian, and other natural rights-based normative theories tend to denigrate coercive relationships, as do utilitarian theories and Western law. It is partly the consensus on the repulsive nature of coercion that leads to the ever wider rhetorical use of the term coercion in public policy debates, although often with subtle shifts of meaning.

Most of the essays in this volume assume that the nature of coercion is obvious and proceed without giving the concept careful attention; however, systematically identifying the nature of coercive relationships is more difficult than one might first imagine. For example, if a club, firm, or government can impose penalties on its members, can club membership, employment, or citizenship ever be truly voluntary? If so, what then does coercion mean?

This chapter attempts to clarify the meanings of voluntary association and coercion using matrix representations of the consequences of various proposals. The matrices are extended versions of those developed in

Wertheimer (1990), who uses matrices to clarify several properties of coercive relationships. His matrices, however, lack an explicit representation of the "baseline," which is not a minor neglect, because voluntariness is largely determined relative to a baseline of some kind. Wertheimer's neglect of the baseline is remedied in this chapter by adding a third row to his matrices.

For most of this chapter, the relevant baseline is the situation (future time series) that would have occurred had the proposal of interest not been made. In many cases, such a baseline can be considered the exit option: the alternative realized when an offer is rejected, although as will be noted, the exit option is not always the *status quo ante*. Such baselines have long played (implicit) roles in normative assessments. For example, Paretian norms are relative to an initial point, often interpreted as the *status quo ante*. This chapter suggests that *ex ante* baselines also provide a systematic way to distinguish coercive proposals such as "your money or your life" from non-coercive proposals to join groups or engage in voluntary exchange.

Two settings are focused on in this chapter: The first is one in which an individual (or organization) makes proposals that another individual (or organization) can accept or reject. The second is one in which governments make explicit or implicit proposals that an individual or organization can only indirectly accept or reject by emigrating to another polity. Baselines turn out to be important aspects of relationships among persons and for those between governments and "their" citizenry, although the relevant baseline is often more difficult to identify in the governmental cases. In the case of governmental relationships (and those between individuals and other organizations with the ability to impose rules on their members), the relevant baseline often differs according to whether exit is easy, difficult, or infeasible.

The next section of this essay shows how baselines can be used to classify private transactions into entirely coercive, entirely voluntary, and partly coercive subsets. In the following section, parallels are constructed between these transactions and those between governments and individuals. The analysis is necessarily abstract and incomplete but sheds light on a question of interest to economists, political scientists, and legal scholars. The last section explores rationales and uses of hypothetical and normative baselines other than the *status quo ante*. For example, rights-based arguments usually use (implicitly) an ideal baseline in which particular rights are well protected to judge both offers and outcomes. It suggests that the ideal baseline of a zero-rent-extracting government can be used to judge the degree of coercion under a given government. The rent-extraction concept has previously been used in the Skaperdas essay on proprietary government, but its value as an index of coercion was not fully worked out in that chapter.

For the most part, this essay assumes that the Wallis problem of violence has been solved, although the analysis of coercion and voluntariness developed can also be applied to those circumstances, as well as the Hobbesian and Lockian ones. Ledyard's essay on decentralized, non-coercive solutions to public goods problems is similar in spirit to the following analysis but focuses less attention on the nature of coercion and is less concerned with external constraints on the range of policies and degree of coercion that may be adopted by governments in the short and long run. Ledyard analyzes a broader range of institutional alternatives than analyzed in this essay, albeit somewhat abstractly. The institutional settings explored in this essay are modest refinements of ones often used by public finance and public choice scholars.

2. A Matrix Representation of Voluntary Relationships

Completely voluntary interactions among individuals and organizations can be represented with the following matrix. Consider a setting in which A approaches B with a proposal of some kind that B is free to accept or reject (see Table 4.1). Row 1 characterizes the result if B agrees to A's proposal. Row 2 characterizes the result if B rejects the offer. Row 3 characterizes the state that would have existed had no proposal been made by A. This is the *status quo ante* representation of the baseline.

The payoffs associated with the baseline have been normalized to zero, so all payoffs greater than zero are improvements over the baseline, and all payoffs less than zero are reductions in welfare relative to the baseline. The case depicted is one in which B accepts A's proposal because B's welfare is increased by A's proposal relative the baseline (3 > 0).

Two characteristics are associated with a completely voluntary transaction: (a) both A and B prefer the proposal to their baselines and (b) in the

Table 4.1. *Case 1: Completely voluntary relationships*

	A	B
B accepts A's proposal	4	3
B rejects A's proposal	0	0
Baseline	0	0

case in which B rejects A's offer, the consequence is a return to the *status quo ante*, that is, the *ex ante* baseline remains feasible. Such proposals cannot make B worse off. A very wide range of proposals approximately meet this criteria, including the exchange transactions economists focus on, as well as voluntary contributions to charities, voting in (most) popular elections, and unanimous group decisions to form common enterprises. Philosophers often refer to proposals that frame or initiate voluntary transactions as "offers." (See Nozick 1974, Frankfurt 1973, or Wertheimer 1990.)

2.1. Transactions Costs and Voluntariness

There are also cases in which B may accept A's proposal, but the transaction is not completely voluntary, because the proposal *incidentally eliminates the baseline as a possibility*. Listening to a proposal and evaluating it nearly always consumes valuable time and attention. In such cases, rejection of the proposal yields an outcome that is not the same as the baseline, but somewhat below it, because evaluating the offer has consumed time and attention that could have been more beneficially employed along the baseline. A telephone call may interrupt a conversation or meal. Even if the offer thus delivered is accepted, the baseline has been affected by the call: a conversational thread was lost or a tasty hot meal became cold.

The payoffs to such cases are illustrated in Table 4.2. In Case 2A, the proposal is accepted, and the final result is better for both players than the baseline – that which would have happened without the proposal (3 > 0). In Case 2B (with the bracketed payoffs), the proposal is rejected and each person is worse off than they would have been in the absence of the proposal (0 > −1).

If A can make costly proposals to B without B's consent, it is clear that A has the ability to make B worse off by doing so. Beggars in public streets often have such an ability, as do salespeople of various kinds, whether in stories, on the phone, or through Internet ads and other interruptions.

Table 4.2. *Case 2: Less than completely voluntary relationships*

	A	B
B accepts A's proposal	4 [4]	3 [−3]
B reject A's proposal	−1	−1
Baseline	0	0

In general, B will allow A to make proposals – will listen to and evaluate them – only if B anticipates that A's solicitations are more likely to produce gains than losses, on average. In such cases, B "wins" on some occasions and "loses" on others, as in Case 2A and Case 2B. Listening to such proposals may be said to be voluntary insofar as B could have rejected such proposals out of hand (by, for example, disconnecting or turning off the telephone during supper, although this too has a cost).

However, this is not true of all solicitations. Here we may consider proposals by telephone salespeople made to persons eating dinner, between beggars and passersby, or lonely men and pretty women. Offers that are always refused often make the person receiving the proposal worse off.[1] If B cannot costlessly limit A's ability to make a proposal, then the resulting negotiations can be said to be voluntary or not based on *the average net return* from listening to and evaluating such proposals. If the average outcome of a series of offers makes the person solicited better off, then the series may be regarded to be voluntary; if not, then the solicitations are not entirely voluntary and may, in some cases, be coercive.

Matrices similar to Cases 2A and 2B can also be used to characterize the overall net benefits of relatively complex proposals, which may take considerable time and attention to evaluate. For example, A might offer B a job or membership in an organization that requires accepting a variety of rules, rewards, and punishments. If B accepts, she (he or they) must abide by the organization's rules or face punishments of various kinds. B may carefully weigh the benefits and costs of accepting the proposal, including both the opportunity cost of doing so and the likelihood that he or she will be wrongfully punished by the organization's management or government. In such cases, a whole series of future decisions are contrasted with those that would have occurred in the absence of the offer.

B will voluntarily take a job, join a club, or enter into a society, when the anticipated time stream of (risk-adjusted) net benefits are greater than that associated with the baseline. Note that if B's membership in such organizations is voluntary, so is her subsequent rule-bound and punishment-encouraged behavior within the organization, unless she is unpleasantly surprised by the operation of the organization. The mere use of punishments, fines, fees, or taxes does not imply that membership in a club or society is not voluntary.

---

[1] There are also cases in which simply receiving an offer makes one feel better off even if one rejects the offer, as when fine dancer A asks lonely B for a dance at a local dance club.

It bears noting that most organizations have systems of conditional punishments and transfer resources among members. This is, after all, largely what makes them organizations. If joining a club correctly anticipates the day-to-day benefits and costs associated with membership, and the baseline is not affected by the offer of club membership, those joining the club have relative payoffs similar to those of Case 1. Voluntary membership resembles Case 2A, if evaluating the offer takes time.

The same logic applies to insurance policies under which "transfers" are made to those harmed by chance events from those that are not. The mere existence of "transfers" does not necessarily imply that the relationship is coercive.

It also bears noting that most settings in which offers are made and evaluated can be factored into a series of sub-transactions. However, it is the net result of the overall series that is relevant when a choice commits oneself to a complex contract (or to a particular game tree).

Complex cases analogous to 2B also exist in which complex proposals may be regarded as coercive or partly coercive. Opportunities to purchase poorly made products, join expensive or unattractive clubs, or accept poorly paying jobs or enlist in demanding religions are almost routinely rejected, but the process of listening to such offers and rejecting them absorbs time and attention that could be better used elsewhere. Listening to such offers is not always a voluntary activity, because the "offers" predictably worsen the baseline. Fraudulent transactions are not voluntary undertaken insofar as losses are realized by B instead of the benefits implied by B's offer.

2.2. Coercive Proposals

Coercive proposals are analogous to those of Case 2B, in that a coercive proposal eliminates the baseline as an alternative and would otherwise be rejected. Coercive proposals, however, differ from Case 2B in that the person making the offer *intentionally* manipulates (or at least substantially determines) both the payoffs that B obtains by accepting the proposal and those associated with rejecting the proposal. Controlling the baseline allows A to induce B to accept offers that he or she would otherwise have rejected. Faced with "your money or your life," most rational persons will hand over their wallet or purse, yet it is clear that this is not voluntary action, nor a voluntary relationship.

When a thief says "your money or your life," he or she is determining both the payoff associated with accepting the proposal (your money) and

Table 4.3. *Case 3: Coercive proposals*

	A	B
B accepts A's proposal	4	−3
B rejects A's proposal	1	−P
Baseline	0	0

with rejecting it (your life). A return to the *ex ante* baseline is ruled out by the conditional punishment (assuming that the threat is credible). The recipient of a coercive proposal cannot simply walk away after answering "neither."

Table 4.3, Case 3, illustrates the essential properties of coercive proposals for the case in which a punishment, P, is associated with rejecting the offer.

Coercive proposals have three characteristics: (a) the person making the proposal (A) controls (or influences) the payoffs associated with accepting and rejecting the proposal; (b) rejection of the proposal leads to a penalty imposed by A that is worse than the baseline; and (c) acceptance of A's proposal also generates a result that is worse than the baseline, although normally greater than that associated with rejection. Returning to the *ex ante* baseline, exit, is not an option, because a (credible) threat of punishment rules out the *status quo ante*.

A coercive proposal succeeds when the punishment for rejecting the offer is sufficiently large. Such offers are "accepted" even though doing so makes the person worse off than under the baseline. For example, if P equals −4, B will accept A's proposal, because B is better off accepting it than rejecting it. However, given a choice between a coercive proposal and the baseline, the recipient will always prefer the baseline $(0 > −3 > −4)$. He or she would be better off if such proposals were never made. Note that the person making the coercive offer may actually gain more from B's acceptance than the B loses, although this is not always, or very often, the case. The offer is coercive because the punishment for rejecting the proposal, P, has been manipulated by A to increase the likelihood that B accepts an offer that would otherwise make B worse off.

"Your money or your life," clearly differs from "your money or continue your pleasant walk." The new exit option is worse than the original one.

Threats (promised punishments) are always associated with coercive proposals, although as noted, the use of punishments may also be associated with a subset of voluntary transactions such as joining an organization with demanding rules that are well enforced.

2.3. Subjective Nature of Coercive Proposals

The payoffs associated with voluntary and coercive proposals are subjective, so it is not always possible for an observer to know whether a transaction falls into Cases 1, 2, or 3. However, net benefits are often correlated with observable (substantive) phenomena, which allow many coercive proposals to be distinguished from non-coercive ones by outsiders observing them. C sees A show B a gun, at which point B hands over her purse to A, and A takes both the purse and the gun away with him. The gun implies a threat, and the fact that A did not exchange the gun for B's purse is consistent with that interpretation. Voluntary transactions do not require the threat of bodily harm associated with the gun. This allows C to infer that a coercive transaction has taken place between A and B.

There is, however, often some chance of error, because one can imagine scenarios under which the gun was involved, but the transaction was completely voluntary. Perhaps A knew that B enjoyed role playing, and B gave A her purse because it belonged to D who A would see later that day. The subjectivity of the payoffs implies that misinterpreting the nature of a transaction is nearly always possible, although some cases are very clear, as when A shoots B and takes B's purse. (It is unlikely that this transaction was B's preferred method of suicide.)

2.4. Natural Baselines: Hard Choices Can Be Voluntary Transactions

It is important to keep in mind that baselines are not always attractive, and so many voluntary transactions yield outcomes that are unattractive. For example, nature generates low baselines during natural disasters, essentially by definition. Aristotle discusses a case in which a storm at sea induces a captain to propose throwing valuable merchandise overboard to avoid even worse results.

Something of the sort happens also with regard to the throwing of goods overboard in a storm; for in the abstract no one throws goods away voluntarily, but on condition of its securing the safety of himself and his crew any sensible man does so. Such actions, then, are mixed, but are more like voluntary actions; for they are worthy of choice at the time when they are done, and the end of an action is relative to the occasion.

Both the terms, then, "voluntary" and "involuntary," must be used with reference to the moment [*baseline*] of action (Aristotle, *Nicomachean Ethics*, book III, 1908: sec 1).

Throwing valuable merchandise overboard during a storm is voluntary in the sense used in this essay. Those adopting this strategy – accepting this proposal by the captain or fellow shipmates – benefit relative to the baseline produced by nature (drowning at sea).

Many centuries later, similar arguments were used to characterize legitimate forms of governments, given violent, unattractive, baselines that might be produced by human nature. The best known of these arguments is the one developed by Thomas Hobbes in the seventeenth century, a time of civil warfare in England and colonization in North America. Hobbes (1651) postulated a gruesome baseline – a war of every man against every other.

Whatsoever therefore is consequent to a time of War, where every man is Enemy to every man; the same is consequent to the time, wherein men live without other security, than what their own strength, and their own invention shall furnish them withal. In such condition, there is no place for Industry, because the fruit thereof is uncertain, and consequently no culture of the earth; no navigation, nor use of the commodities that may be imported by Sea, no commodious building, no Instruments of moving, and removing such things as require much force, no knowledge of the face of the Earth, no account of Time, no Arts, no Letters, no Society; and which is worst of all, continual fear, and danger of violent death. And the life of man [is] solitary, poor, nasty, brutish, and short.

To this war of every man against every man, this also is consequent; that nothing can be unjust; the notions of right and wrong, justice and injustice have there no place. Where there is no common Power, there is no Law: where no Law, no Injustice. Force, and Fraud, are in war the two Cardinal virtues. (I have updated the spellings to their modern form. Hobbes [1651/ 2011]: 71.)

Hobbes argued that the only possible escape is the acceptance of a largely unconstrained government that would have sufficient power to assure peace. He concludes that the order that emerges from an irrevocable transfer of rights to the sovereignty is always better than nature's anarchy, although he acknowledges that the result is not always the best that can be imagined.

[T]hey that have already instituted a commonwealth, being thereby bound by covenant, to own [obey] the actions, and judgments of one [the sovereign], cannot lawfully make a new covenant, amongst themselves, to be obedient to any other, in anything whatsoever, without his permission. And therefore, they that are subjects to a Monarch, cannot without his leave cast off Monarchy, and return to the confusion of a disunited multitude; nor transfer their person from him that beareth it, to another man, or other assembly of men: for **they are bound**, every man to every man, **to** own, and be reputed author of all, that **he that already is their Sovereign, shall do, and judge fit to be done.** (Hobbes 1651/ 2011: 95–96)

A few decades later, Locke (1689), perhaps inspired by the Dutch and American experiences, challenged Hobbes' conclusions with respect to sovereignty by arguing that the baseline (the natural state) is not as bad as Hobbes' war of every man against every other. Given a better baseline, some authorities would never be transferred to a sovereign. The members of a commonwealth might prefer the natural state to rule by an unconstrained tyrannical sovereign. Moreover, Locke suggests that sovereignty may be revoked when the bounds of proper authority are overstepped. Given a better baseline, only more limited social contracts would be accepted by freemen.

A few decades later, Montesquieu (1748) and Madison, Hamilton, and Jay (1788) suggested several institutional solutions that freemen might prefer to Leviathan. Constitutions that include checks and balances, representative chambers of government, and decentralized authority might be adopted, even if one accepted Hobbes' characterization of the baseline for human society. If the interests of Leviathan can be better aligned with those governed through institutional design, those institutions may be voluntarily adopted.

3. Voluntary and Coercive Governance

At this point, we shift the analysis from the formation and limits of voluntary agreements and organizations to cases in which anarchy has been left behind and several polities, each with their own government and rules, exist. Because all governed societies have a broad range of rules and punishments – essentially by definition – it is important to distinguish between rules and punishments that are voluntarily accepted and those that are not. Rules and punishments may be voluntarily accepted when they increase net benefits for the person (or group) of interest, as emphasized by contractarians from Hobbes (1651) to Buchanan (1975). Membership is coerced when an organization's rules produce net benefits that are below the relevant baseline.

Individuals will voluntarily join organizations and societies that use punishments to solve social dilemmas whenever the value added by solving coordination, shirking, and public goods problems exceeds the expected cost (including costs associated with being punished). Being a member of such organizations produces payoffs that are larger than the baseline. Indeed, Hobbes argued that civilization is a consequence of solutions to such problems. In voluntary associations, the benefits of continued association must be greater than the costs, including costs associated with efficiency-enhancing punishments (duress, wrongful conviction, etc.).

Again, it is important to distinguish between unattractive settings and coercive proposals. A club or government that rescues someone from very unattractive settings may charge high fees or taxes without engaging in coercion. However, few baselines are as bad as posited by Hobbes, so there are clearly cases in which laws and taxes are coercive.

In civilized societies, the *status quo ante* is not usually anarchy or some similar setting but rather the set of rules, fees, procedures, and punishments already in place. Shifts between societies are possible, and both continued residence and exit can be said to be results of implicit proposals made by the governments that an individual or family is free to choose among. When shifting between polities is costless, continued membership is always voluntary in the sense of Case 1 and implies that residents find their particular communities to be at least as good as all others.

When shifting among communities is easy, but not costless, the choices resemble those of Cases 2a and 2b. In cases in which the persons occupying offices of authority in government – "the state" – drive up the cost of exit to induce its residents to accept otherwise unattractive "proposals," the relationships may be coercive in the sense of Case 3. The iron curtain of the old Soviet Union is only one of many clear instances in which exit costs were manipulated by governments to induce acceptance of "offers" that reduced citizen welfare below their previous baselines.

3.1. On the Appeal of Liberal Societies and Limits to Coercion

To make the preceding analysis somewhat less abstract, consider locational choices among several preexisting polities. First, consider transactions that are analogous to those of Cases 1 and 2. Suppose that a person or family is free to exit from a somewhat disorganized baseline society, S, and enter one of two more organized societies. One of the alternatives is a rent-extracting society, country R, in which privileged families (the elite) use lump-sum taxes to transfer resources (extract rents) from the non-privileged families (the non-elite) to the privileged families. The other is a liberal society, country U, which has adopted rules and procedures that maximize a Benthamite social-welfare function, subject to various constraints, which may include bounds on threats and punishments, and civil law. By assumption, no rent extraction takes place in the liberal society, so there are no "elite" families that receive unearned privileges (rents).

To simplify analysis, countries R and U are both assumed to use punishments efficiently to solve their internal coordination and social dilemma problems. This is a somewhat strong assumption for a rent-extracting society, but it allows us to compare outcomes more easily in countries R and U and to draw conclusions about policies that may be coercive in the sense of Case 3. The assumption that only efficient methods of taxation are used does not affect many of the conclusions drawn from the analysis, but it does simplify it.[2]

To further simplify the analysis, notation, and discussion, all payoffs are expressed in dollar value or additive utility terms, and a single social dilemma is assumed to be solved with Pigouvian fines, F, that are imposed on "social shirking." The fines are used to encourage team production or free riding, whereas the revenues are used to fund the associated monitoring and enforcement institutions. Shirking would otherwise produce a payoff of $P + L$ (income and leisure) that is individually greater than that of not shirking, M. The fine reduces this to $P + L - F < M$, with M greater than the payoff realized when everyone shirks, as in the disorganized society. Average collections are assumed to be just sufficient to solve the problems of interest and to pay for the monitoring and enforcement systems required.[3]

In the rent-extraction country, additional revenues are generated through lump-sum tax, T, which is imposed on non-elites. Political elites in rent-extraction societies extract some or all of the benefits that non-elites gain from solutions to social dilemmas in their society. The elite profits from the "extraction taxes" are assumed to be exempt from the shirking fines, which implies that members of the political elite may choose to simply live off their share of the extraction tax receipts without working (non-shirking), with $P + L + T > M + T$, although this is not critical for the present analysis.

Society S plays the role of the "state of nature" or natural baseline in the present analysis. In the relatively disorganized community, it is assumed that few social dilemmas are addressed ($F = 0$), but rates of rent extraction are low ($T = 0$). In that society, property rights and other public goods that increase marginal productivity are underprovided, which implies that the marginal product of working and shirking is individually and collectively

---

[2] For the purposes of this essay, the possibility that the residual claimant status of the elite may induce a less than completely encompassing interest is ignored. A less than fully encompassing interest in maximizing national income is quite likely when the rent-extracting individual or group cannot use lump-sum taxes (Olson 1993; Congleton and Lee 2009). Such problems are neglected here to focus on essential features on coercive and voluntary uses of conditional punishments and the importance of baselines.

[3] Fines can be used to solve essentially all social dilemmas; however, the analysis could have been conducted using Lindahl fees instead. These could be collected and used to subsidize the desired behavior, rather than to punish the undesirable (shirking) behavior as in the Pigouvian fine case. The analysis can be generalized by considering F to be a vector of fines that address a variety of dilemmas.

Table 4.4. *Case 4: Choosing among societies*

	Rent-extracting society			Utilitarian society	
	Payoffs by social status			Payoffs by social status	
	Non-elite	Political elite		Non-elite	Political elite
Work	$M - T$	$M + T$	Work	M	M
Shirk	$P + L - T - F$	$P + L + T$	Shirk	$P + L - F$	$P + L - F$
Baseline	S	S	Baseline	S	S

The cell entries are utilities, the rank order of subjective payoffs for the members of the society. It is assumed that $M > S > P - F$.

less than that in the rent-extraction and liberal states $M > M'$ and $P > P'$. Moreover, because problems of social shirking are not addressed, the normal behavior in society S is shirking, with a payoff of $S = P' + L < P + L < M'$.

The efficiency-enhancing fines of countries U and R are assumed to reduce the payoffs associated with social shirking to levels less than that associated with the baseline, $S > P + L - F$. This allows persons to avoid the Pigouvian fines by working in or by emigrating to society S. However, solving social dilemmas allows resources to be used more efficiently, and thus the payoff from both working and shirking in U or R are higher than they are in the disorganized society, S. These payoffs vary among individuals, although identifying subscripts are not used, because the focus is, for the most part, on a "typical" person's choice.

The matrices of Table 4.4 characterize payoffs for typical elite and non-elite persons who are free to choose among the three communities. The matrix can be used to analyze a person's choice of society and, by providing alternative notions of baselines, to shed light on the extent to which government policies in the three states are coercive or not.

Note that elites and non-elites tend to rank the three societies differently. A non-elite person who places relatively little value on leisure and believes that fines are accurately applied in the liberal society, prefers the liberal society to the baseline of the disorganized society and also to the rent-extracting society $M > M - T$ and $M > S$). Non-elite persons living in either society R or society S would, thus, tend to emigrate to country U. For non-elites, the extraction of rents, even via non-distorting lump-sum taxes, is analogous to the "your money or your life" proposal of the robbery case and is a proposal to be avoided rather than embraced. Members of the elite, however, prefer the rent-extraction society to the liberal and disorganized societies as long as significant rents are harvested and shared.

Note that relative to the baseline of the liberal state, rent extraction is a coercive enterprise. No non-elite person will voluntarily join a rent-extracting society when a liberal society is available. In contrast, members of the privileged families of country R will prefer society R to both S and U, because $M + T > M$. Members of the elite would regard a forced move to country U to be coercive, because it reduces their welfare by eliminating their rents.[4]

Persons who greatly value leisure (with relatively high L) would tend to rank the societies differently. Such persons may find that $S = P' + L > M$ and choose to stay in or emigrate to country S. Although they would rank the liberal (utilitarian) society over the rent-extracting one, people work "too hard" in the liberal society. For such persons, a forced move from S to U would be coercive. Even efficiency-enhancing fines may be coercive, although this depends on the person and the extent to which their productivity is increased by such fines and the value placed on leisure.[5]

In the long run, emigration pressures imply that rent-extracting societies are not viable, if liberal states exist and exit costs are low. Freedom of exit and entry implies that all non-elites emigrate from R to U, whereupon privileged families would find themselves with no one to extract rents from. Only productive forms of punishment are viable in settings in which persons are free to choose among societies that include liberal ones, although not everyone emigrates to U or prefers the liberal society to rent-extracting or disorganized societies.[6]

3.2. Settings in Which Ideal Alternatives Do Not Exist: Competition among Rent-Extraction Societies without Exit Costs

Extraction Societies without Exit Costs
A similar logic, perhaps surprisingly, applies to cases in which liberal utilitarian societies initially do not exist. In such cases, migration will also favor

---

[4] Note that even lump-sum taxes cannot be entirely neutral if emigration is possible, because they influence a variety of locational decisions at the margin.
[5] Many academics may be said to make similar choices in their decision to teach in universities rather than work in the private sector or in a governmental bureaucracy, although of course not all academics are shirkers.
[6] This argument is not exactly the same as that developed by Tiebout (1956), although it is very similar. A rent-extracting regime may be completely efficient, but the rent extraction necessarily reduces net benefits for its non-elite residents relative to other communities without rent extraction. See Congleton (2000) for models of how mobility limits rent seeking and rent extraction in settings in which less efficient methods of transfer are used. See Epstein, Hillman, and Ursprung (1999) for an analysis of how privileges may be assigned given exit possibilities.

relatively liberal societies (those with more nearly optimal levels of F and relatively low rates of rent extraction).

The relevant baseline for determining whether rent extraction is coercive is less obvious in this setting than in the case in which country U exists. A move from S to a rent-extraction society makes the migrant better off, as long as $M - T > P' + L$. Thus, relative to society S, membership in the rent-extracting society for many non-elite individuals is voluntary, and the rent extraction is unpleasant, but not coercive.

In such cases, residence in a rent-extracting state is analogous to purchasing goods from a monopoly supplier that charges more than the competitive price for a desirable product. Many persons will voluntarily pay a monopoly price rather than do without. Both Apple and Microsoft currently profit from such choices by consumers. Similarly, many persons will voluntarily pay a monopoly price for governmental solutions to social dilemmas. Indeed, the use of a disorganized state as the baseline may yield conclusions that are similar to those of the pessimistic contractarians, such as Hobbes, who use an unpleasant "state of nature" as their baseline.

Within rent-extracting societies, changes in rates of rent extraction can also be evaluated using their own *status quo ante* as the baseline. Given that baseline, it is clear that an increase in the rate of rent extraction is coercive for non-elites. Non-elites are "forced" to pay higher taxes (to "give" more money to privileged families) or to pay penalties for tax evasion, without any compensating improvement in their collective productivity. The effects of an increase in rent-extraction are thus similar to Case 3 for non-elites. However, only if extraction taxes are increased to the point at which all the surplus generated from solutions to social dilemma is extracted would hardworking non-elites emigrate to the disorganized society.

However, community S is not the only alternative or constraint in the setting being analyzed. Non-elites may also emigrate to other rent-extracting states. This may induce competition among elites in different states for non-elites to extract rents from. Such competition tends to generate reductions in rent-extracting taxes – "a race to the bottom." A polity that reduces its rate of rent extraction implicitly or explicitly makes an offer analogous to Cases 1 or 2 for non-elites in other countries who decide to emigrate. When exit costs are zero or low relative to differences in rates of rent extraction, non-elite members of society will tend to move to the efficient state with the lowest rate rent extraction. In such cases, a small decrease in rent-extraction lump-sum tax T may induce a sufficiently large increase in the number of non-elites, N, that it increases the rents of the polity's elite.

Thus, in cases in which migration is easy, competition for non-elite persons tends to induce a race to the bottom in which rent extraction, T, is gradually reduced in each country until the limit of zero is reached. In the long run, competition causes liberal states to emerge.

Reductions in rent-extraction possibilities for elites in other polities induced by tax competition are analogous to Case 2b, rather than Case 3. The reduction in elite rents in other countries is not accomplished by an intentional manipulation of penalties to induce changes in their behavior. Indeed, a government that reduces its own extraction rates would prefer that no other government changes its rate of extraction. Extractive tax competition is thus not coercive, although it is inconvenient for elites.

3.3. Competition among Rent-Extracting States with Exit Costs

The previous Tiebout-like analysis suggests that only punishments and taxes that enhance efficiency are sustainable in the long run if the persons taxed or punished are completely mobile. Truly coercive governments can persist in the long run only if there are significant exit costs. Unfortunately, exit costs are significantly greater than zero in most real world settings.

We now turn to the case in which significant exit costs exist. When exit costs are significant, members of the non-elite move from one polity to another only in response to relatively large differences in rates of rent extraction. In our illustration, an individual will move from community 1 to community 2 only if $T_1 - T_2 > E$, where E is the individual's exit cost.[7] Consequently, community 2 may have rent extraction rates, T_2, less than T_1, yet attract few emigrants from community 1. To attract additional persons from whom to extract rents will require a significant reduction in extraction rates.

In this case, there is no necessary race to the bottom in rent extraction. Whether it pays to reduce rates of rent extraction varies with the distribution of exit costs in other communities, as well as the levels of rent extraction and public services in the communities of interest.

Consider the case in which a continuum of exit costs among residents exists in all relevant communities, with some persons (or other sources of rent payments) having high exit costs, others low, and others in between. Suppose there are two efficient rent-extracting states and elites cannot engage in "price discrimination" because exit costs cannot be directly observed. It is clear that competition for non-elite immigrants may take place. If there are different rates of rent extraction in the two rent-extracting

---

[7] By exit costs, I mean both the total cost of moving from country 1 and settling in country 2. In this it could be said that E includes both exit and entry costs. Both costs tend to vary among countries and persons within countries.

communities, with $T_1 > T_2$, all persons with exit costs less than $E = T_1 - T_2$ will leave community 1 and take up residence in community 2. Moreover, all the emigration from the disorganized society S now goes entirely to the organized society with the lowest rate of rent extraction. Emigration from S will take place for all residents with $M - E > S$. Others will stay at home.

Let function f characterize the fraction of all persons who live in community 1, given the distribution of exit costs that exists in the three communities and their initial populations, N_1^0, N_2^0, and N_S^0, respectively. That fraction falls when $T_1 - T_2 > 0$ and increases when $T_1 - T_2 < 0$. If the distribution of exit costs is continuous and differentiable for the communities of interest, function f will also be continuous and differentiable and will be monotone decreasing in $T_1 - T_2$. The number of non-elites in community 1 can be represented as

$$N_1 = f(T_1 - T_2)\left(N_1^0 + N_2^0 + N_S^0\right) \tag{1}$$

and per capita elite rents as

$$R_1 = \left[f(T_1 - T_2)\left(N_1 + N_2 + N_S^0\right)\right] T_1/H_1. \tag{2}$$

The rent-maximizing member of the elite in community 1 will prefer the tax that satisfies

$$R_1 = [f'(T_1 - T_2)]T_1/M_1 + [f(T_1 - T_2)]T_1/H, \tag{3}$$

which is satisfied when

$$f' + f(T_1 - T_2) = 0. \tag{4}$$

Together equation (4) and the implicit function theorem imply that elite 1's ideal rent-extraction rate can be written as

$$T_1^* = g(T_2). \tag{5a}$$

A similar best reply function can be derived for community 2:

$$T_2^* = h(T_1). \tag{5b}$$

The Nash equilibrium occurs when both communities are simultaneously on their best reply functions:[8]

$$T_1^{**} = g(T_2^{**}) \tag{6a}$$

$$T_2^{**} = h(T_1^{**}). \tag{6b}$$

---

[8] Recall that function f is continuous and bounded at 0 and 1. This implies that a fixed point exists.

Competition among rent-extracting states for mobile non-elites tends to produce convergence in the levels of rent extraction, whenever the relevant societies are similar. Whether this entails high or low rates of rent extraction varies with the distribution of exit costs and the extent to which solving social dilemmas increases marginal products.

If communities 1 and 2 have no other distinguishing characteristics, the Nash equilibrium will tend to be a symmetric one, with $T_1^{**} = T_2^{**}$, and each of the rent-extracting communities will have

$$N_1^* = f(0) \left(N_1^0 + N_2^0 + N_S^0\right) \ residents, \tag{7a}$$

and members of their elites will each receive rents equal to

$$R_1^* = N_1^* T^{**}/H_1. \tag{7b}$$

The extent to which competition limits rent extraction varies with the implied population flows among communities. (There may be multiple equilibria.)

If rent extraction was reduced on the way to the Nash equilibrium, persons may emigrate from community S to one of the rent-extracting states. In that case, the marginal resident of community S is indifferent between staying and leaving for one of the rent-extracting states, $M - T - E = S$, at the Nash equilibrium. That is to say, community S's most mobile resident is indifferent between the disorganized society and the least extractive alternative, given his or her exit costs and productivity gains in the rent-extraction societies.

If, however, rent extraction has increased on the way to the Nash equilibrium, there may be migration from the Rs to S. In that case, the marginal member of the rent-extraction societies is indifferent between staying and leaving for $S : M - T = S - E$.

Exit costs, perhaps surprisingly, imply that rent extraction may exceed the social surplus from solving social dilemmas for some or all non-elites. Exit costs imply that migration occurs only if, $S - E > M - T$, only if net of exit cost benefits exceed the net of extraction benefits of the rent-extracting society. If $S > M - T$, it can be said that all non-elite members of the rent-extracting societies would have emigrated to the disorganized society, but for their exit costs.

Although beyond the scope of this essay, it bears noting that exit (and entry) costs may also be adjusted by rent-extracting states in much the same manner that a thief may adjust the baseline with greater threats. An increase in exit costs in combination with an increase in T tends to be coercive in exactly the same manner as Case 3. Such policies are clearly coercive, because they combine offers that make persons worse off with changes in their baselines designed to induce acceptance of the offer.

Overall, the preceding analysis suggests that the term coercion can be applied to governments whenever we use a baseline that is more attractive than the one suggested by Hobbes. It also suggests that governments can be regarded as more or less coercive according to the degree of rent extraction present, which in turn varies with exit costs and the extent of tax competition among states for residents.

4. Baselines and Distinctions among Volition, Voluntariness, and Coercion

It should be kept in mind that coercive proposals do not literally force a result, as when the police physically carry a person to a jail cell and lock the door. Instead coercion normally involves the creation of strong incentives that induce particular choices, as when threats induce a person to walk "voluntarily" into a jail cell and close the door or induce a person to "tip" his or her executioner. The characterization of coercive offers developed in Section I allows us to distinguish among settings in which behavior is volitional, but is coerced rather than voluntary. The matrices also allow us to distinguish between settings in which conditional punishments are used to solve social dilemmas and those in which threats are used to extract rents. There are no efficiency-coercion tradeoffs once this distinction is recognized.

Generalizations of the matrices imply that the existence of conditional punishments does not necessarily imply that a proposal is coercive. Individuals freely join clubs, firms, and societies in which conditional punishments are used, because they value the results achieved by the behavior induced by those systems more than their *status quo ante*. For example, a firm's conditional punishment system solves a wide variety of team production, coordination, and public goods problems that allow it to pay higher wages than available in atomistic market alternatives. Similarly, a government that effectively solves social dilemmas increases productivity and the incomes of its resident-citizens by, among other things, reducing losses from externalities, theft, and fraud. (That efficiency is increased in the preceding illustrations: $M > M'$, is the reason that Pigouvian fines, F, are preferred by the residents of U to their absence in society S.) In contrast, individuals never voluntarily subject themselves to entirely extractive organizations or governments, because such practices reduce individual net benefits relative to their baseline.

In the real world, all governments use conditional punishment systems, but not all such punishments are coercive in the sense developed here. The use of violence or threats of violence may simply be a means to advance ends that benefit a broad cross section of a country's residents. Residents may be attracted rather than repulsed by such policies.

Coercive governments use similar tools, but in a different manner. They are extractive even if they are also productive organizations. Citizens who exit after a new policy is announced demonstrate the coercive nature of that new fiscal or regulatory package. Others who do not exit may also be worse off but fail to leave because their exit costs are relatively high. It is the propensity to exit, not the existence of threatened punishments, that provides the best evidence of whether a new policy or reform is coercive or not.

4.1. Using Ideal Baselines to Measure Coercion

When real baselines are used, coercion is context dependent. In a nasty circumstance, an offer might be accepted that would be rejected in less nasty circumstances. Thus, whether a given change in policy is coercive or not varies with the baseline of every individual in the society of interest. Do new policies alter incentives (payoffs for accepting and rejecting offers) in a manner that makes a given citizen-resident worse off or better off than the previous policy?

For the purposes of assessing policies without having to examine the context in detail, it is often useful to use an ideal or hypothetical baseline and measure coercion relative to that imaginary baseline, rather than to the actual baseline. For example, the use of an ideal baseline of zero rent extraction or zero exit costs allows a relatively simple index of coerciveness to be constructed by measuring the (total) rents extracted per non-privileged member of society. This measure is bounded at zero and has an upper bound at $M - S$, whether S ensures only subsistence levels of consumption (as might be true in a Hobbesian jungle) or S is well above subsistence (in a Lockeian or Nozickian natural state).

Rent extraction, as demonstrated, is nearly always coercive, and one government can be considered more coercive than another – other things being equal – if it engages in more rent extraction. Of course, it is not always easy to measure rents extracted, but rent extraction can often be estimated. In contemporary dictatorships this can be approximated by the personal budgets and secret bank accounts of the ruling elite. In medieval Europe it can be approximated by the size and décor of royal palaces. Within democracies, the rents of the political elite are less obvious than in medieval systems where formal titles separated nobles from commoners, but implicit and explicit transfers to relatively wealthy rent seekers might serve as a first approximation.[9]

To the extent that rent extraction is accomplished by designing rent-seeking contests, rent-seeking expenditures can also be used to estimate the extent of rent extraction and coercion (Tullock 1967, Hillman and Katz 1984, Congleton, Hillman, and Konrad 2008). Laband and Sophocleus (1992) attempted to measure all rent-seeking expenditures in the United States and estimated that up to 25 percent of gross domestic product (GDP) is devoted to rent-seeking activities. However, not all rent extraction is undertaken by governments, so such broad estimates tend to be greater than appropriate for an indicator of government coercion. If all governments had the same interest and ability to maximize their rents, exit costs could also serve as an indicator of the extent of the rents extracted.

4.2. A Digression on other Ideal Baselines, "Unacceptable" Baselines, and Voluntariness

Universal baselines have two quite different applications. The first, as noted earlier, is pragmatic. An ideal baseline can be used to simplify analysis in a manner that allows governments to be more readily compared and critiqued. This essay suggests that rent-extraction can be used as such an index; other essays in this volume use other ideal baselines. For example, the Winer, Hettich, and Tridimas essays use Lindahl taxes as their idealized baseline, in part because it facilitates analysis of fiscal systems.

The second use is a related, but different, one. A universal normative baseline can also be used to assess the normative properties of choice settings themselves. It may be argued, for example, that some voluntary proposals "should not be made" and when made "should be" refused, because they are unfair or exploitative. Such idealistic baselines can be derived from a

---

[9] Transfers to the poor may also be examples of rent extraction, insofar as the poor are able to organize effective political parties. However, many transfers to the disadvantaged appear to be instances of social insurance, rather than rent extraction. As noted earlier, individuals voluntarily purchase insurance policies in the private sector (Congleton 2007).

Table 4.5. *Case 5: Unreasonable proposals*

	A	B
B accepts A's proposal	4	1
B rejects A's proposal	−1	0
Actual baseline	0	0
Proper or ideal baseline	2	2

variety of normative frameworks, including religious norms for behavior, natural rights theories, and modern welfare economics.

Such normative baselines, like coercion itself, play a role in ethics and Western law. For example, B may have to make a choice under duress or in a setting that is reprehensible in some sense (B might be starving, a slave, or in prison). Contracts made under duress are normally deemed invalid under civil law. Such baselines do not attempt to assess coercion by individuals or governments but rather the existing baseline relative to what it should be.

As a consequence, a subtle shift in the meaning of the term *voluntary* occurs when idealistic baselines are used. Idealistic baselines are often used to argue that a particular transaction is not "truly" voluntary behavior – even though an offer is not coercive in the sense used in this essay – because in an "ideal world," B would never make or even confront such choices. A's proposal may make B better off, relative to his or her baseline but only because the baseline is so low, indeed "improperly" so.

Case 5 illustrates the essential logic of this use of baselines (Table 4.5). The first three lines are the same as those of Case 1, but the fourth line is the ideal baseline. Note that under the "normatively acceptable" baseline, the offer should be rejected if made, and because this would be known, such offers would unlikely to be made in the first place.

Under this norm, the status quo (baseline) should be sufficiently attractive that many potentially voluntary transactions (selling oneself into slavery or indentured service for many years) cease being voluntary. Such baseline analyses do not characterize coercion per se but rather whether the society or situation is in some sense "morally unacceptable," "unfair," or "unreasonable." (It was this type of reasoning that Aristotle's storm example was meant to challenge.)

A slightly different but similar line of reasoning occurs in settings in which B does not understand the full implications of the offer or the baseline, because he or she is ignorant of relevant details or is misled about them. In such cases, B may accept an offer that turns out to be worse than the baseline.

Such proposals may be fraudulent, but they are not coercive, because B is free to reject them and return to the status quo before the proposal was made, but they are not entirely voluntary either. B would have been better off if such fraudulent proposals were never made. There are also innocent mistakes in which B accepts a "well-intentioned" offer from A that nonetheless makes B worse off, because B misunderstands the offer. In a world with irreducible uncertainty or ignorance, some bargains will always turn out to be less attractive than they appeared. There will be mistakes. (See the Ledyard essay for more on informational problems and voluntariness.)

The use of idealized "knowledge baselines" is found in Western law and ethics. Contract law presumes a common understanding of the agreement (a meeting of the minds). Fooling a person into accepting offers that actually make him or her worse off implies that a meeting of the minds has not taken place. Moreover, fraud is subject to criminal sanctions. Many products cannot be sold, because it is believed that most persons buying such products make mistakes in their purchases, as with highly addictive drugs. Such considerations are also often evident in bills of rights and civil liberty sections of constitutional documents, which attempt to outlaw some kinds of government policies as mistakes to be avoided.

5. Minimizing Coercion as an Alternative to Maximizing Per Capita GDP and Other General Conclusions

Relative to many idealistic theories, the use of *status quo ante* baselines and rent extraction as foundations for measuring coercion may seem a bit crude. However, this approach provides a more practical and universally acceptable index of governmental quality than other idealistic baseline approaches, which tend to rest on particular norms and are often idiosyncratic in their application. The use of coercion, as defined in this essay, does not require committing to a specific normative framework, because coercion is "bad" from the perspective of a broad cross section of normative theories. The analysis also suggests that coercion can be operationalized at the level of society by focusing on rent extraction and/or exit costs, which provide evidence of and constraints on governmental coercion, rather than measure coercion itself.

Per capita GDP is often argued to provide an analogous estimate of utilitarian social welfare. However, GDP does not distinguish rent seeking from productive activities, values government services at cost, and neglects nonpecuniary transactions and environmental degradation. It also fails to take account of diminishing marginal utility of income (especially among privileged families), which plays a role in both utilitarian and contractarian normative theories of distributive justice.[10] An efficient rent-extracting society may maximize gross national product (GNP) and elite rents without producing an attractive society for non-elites.

Such societies might have been rejected from behind the veil of ignorance, because the risk of being a "loser" (target of rent extraction) was too great. Non-privileged families would all emigrate to other polities with lower rates of rent extraction, even if per capita GNP was lower, were it not for high exit costs. (Such an emigration, for example, took place from Sweden during the late nineteenth century.) For all of these reasons, per capita GNP tends to overstate Benthamite social welfare and is at best only a very rough first approximation of average welfare. Migration patterns provide more direct information about the distribution of welfare within a given society but tends to understate coercion (and governmental inefficiency), because exit costs are often very high.

If minimizing coercion is accepted as a policy or constitutional norm, the analysis of this essay has several general implications. First, policies and institutions that reduce exit costs tend to improve governance directly and/or indirectly by increasing the mobility of non-elites and thereby increasing rent-extraction competition and reducing coercion. Second, institutions that curtail rent extraction, of which there are many, tend to produce more attractive societies. For example, civil law and takings clauses by defining and protecting property rights tend to reduce the scope for governmental and private rent extraction. Third, institutions such as federalism that promote tax and service competition tend to reduce coercion by reducing exit costs. Federalism also tends to encourage governmental efficiency (in the Pigouvian and Lindahl senses of inducing more nearly ideal fees, F in the preceding models), which tends to produce more attractive societies for both elites and non-elites.

Other baselines have other implications for the degree and optimal manner of curtailing coercion, as evidenced in several of the other essays in this volume. The zero rent-extraction baseline, however, may be more broadly applicable and useful insofar as it potentially provides measureable indices of government coercion and institutional quality that

---

[10] Diminishing marginal utility plays an important role in contractarian theories that rely on the veil of ignorance or uncertainty to analyze social compacts, because diminishing marginal utility implies risk aversion and that persons choosing societies are not indifferent about the distribution of income and/or other rewards.

are relevant for a broad range of non-utilitarian and utilitarian normative analysis.

References

Aristotle (1908). *Nicomachean Ethics.* Translated by W. D. Ross. Available on line at: http://classics.mit.edu/Aristotle/nicomachaen.1.i.html.

Arnold, D. G. (2001). "Coercion and Moral Responsibility." *American Philosophical Quarterly* 38: 53–67.

Brennan, G. and J. M. Buchanan (1980). *The Power to Tax: Analytical Foundations of a Fiscal Constitution.* Cambridge: Cambridge University Press.

Buchanan, J. M. (1975). *The Limits of Liberty: Between Anarchy and Leviathan.* Chicago: University of Chicago Press.

Cohen, G. A. (1988). *History, Labor, and Freedom, Themes from Marx.* Oxford: Clarendon Press.

Congleton, R. D. (2000). "A Political Efficiency Case for Federalism in Multinational States: Controlling Ethnic Rent-Seeking." In G. Galeotti, P. Salmon, and R. Wintrobe (eds.), *Competition and Structure: The Political Economy of Collective Decisions: Essays in Honor of Albert Breton.* New York: Cambridge University Press, 365–397.

Congleton, R. D. (2001). *Perfecting Parliament: Liberalism, Constitutional Reform, and the Emergence of Western Democracy.* Cambridge: Cambridge University Press.

Congleton, R. D. (2007). "On the Feasibility of a Liberal Welfare State: Agency and Exit Costs in Income Security Clubs." *Constitutional Political Economy* 18: 145–159.

Congleton, R. D., A. L. Hillman, and K. A. Konrad (eds.) (2008). *40 Years of Research on Rent Seeking.* Heidelberg: Springer.

Congleton, R. D. and S. Lee (2009). "Efficient Mercantilism? Revenue-Maximizing Monopolization Policies as Ramsey Taxation." *European Journal of Political Economy* 25: 102–114.

Epstein, G. S., A. L. Hillman, and H. W. Ursprung (1999). "The King Never Emigrates." *Review of Development Economics* 3: 107–121.

Frankfurt, H. (1973). "Coercion and Moral Responsibility." In T. Hoderich (ed.), *Essays on Freedom of Action.* London: Routledge.

Hettich, W. and S. L. Winer (1999). *Democratic Choice and Taxation: A Theoretical and Empirical Analysis.* Cambridge: Cambridge University Press.

Hillman, A. L. and E. Katz (1984). "Risk-Averse Rent Seekers and the Social Cost of Monopoly Power." *Economic Journal* 94: 104–110.

Hobbes, T. (1651/2011). *Leviathan.* Boston: Digireads.com Publishing.

Laband, D. N. and J. P. Sophocleus (1992). "An Estimate of Resource Expenditure on Transfer Activity in the United States." *Quarterly Journal of Economics* 107: 959–983.

Locke, J. (1689/1988). *Two Treatises of Government.* Cambridge: Cambridge University.

Madison, J., A Hamilton, and J. Jay (1788). *The Federalist.* New York: J and A. McLean.

Montesquieu, C. (1748/1914). *The Spirit of the Laws.* London: G. Bell and Sons.

Nozick, R. (1969). "Coercion." In S. Morgenbesser et al. (eds.), *Philosophy, Science and Method.* New York: St Martin's Press.

Nozick, R. (1974). *Anarchy, State, and Utopia.* New York: Basic Books.

Olson, M. (1993). "Dictatorship, Democracy, and Development." *American Political Science Review* 87: 567–576.

Tiebout, C. (1956). "A Pure Theory of Local Expenditures." *Journal of Political Economy* 64: 416–424.

Tullock, G. (1967). "The Welfare Costs of Tariffs, Monopolies, and Theft." *Western Economic Journal* 5: 224–232.

Wertheimer, A. (1990). *Coercion.* Princeton: Princeton University Press.

5

Kaldor-Hicks-Scitovsky Coercion, Coasian Bargaining, and the State

Michael C. Munger

Make a change when total income increases; don't worry about how it is distributed.
Stokey and Zeckhauser on cost-benefit analysis (1978, 279)

1. Introduction

The core questions and subsidiary questions relevant to the study of coercion include the following:

- *Core:* What are necessary and sufficient conditions for justifying the existence of the state?
- *Subsidiary:* Accepting that the state legitimately exists, what justifies state coercion of citizens?
- *Core:* What is the basis for making moral statements?
- *Subsidiary:* Accepting this basis, do individuals have an obligation to act morally outside of the threat of coercion by the state?

With respect to these questions, my goal in this essay is to distinguish the *ex post* enforcement of an agreement voluntarily entered into *ex ante* from the initiation of coercion based on utilitarian precepts. Coercion as *enforcement* of an agreement freely entered into can be justified, even in a purist libertarian minimal state setting. The justification is simple, but powerful: the threat of *ex post* enforcement is what binds *ex ante* agreements. Unenforceable agreements prevent people from achieving mutually beneficial gains from trade or cooperation.

With most sincere thanks to Jonny Anomaly, Geoffrey Brennan, Roger Congleton, Bernard Grofman, Libby Jenke, William Keech, John Ledyard, Stergios Skaperdas, and Stan Winer for useful comments. The remaining problems are largely the result of my inability to solve fully the problems highlighted by their objections.

However, the argument for *utilitarian* justifications for *initiation* of coercion violates any possible conception of consensual contractarianism. Utilitarians use an organic conception of society in which individual consent, although perhaps desirable for other reasons, is essentially irrelevant to the problem of group choice.[1] The problem to be solved is simply to add up the total gains to the winners and compare this sum to the total losses to the losers. Clearly, the utilitarian must somehow solve two problems: utility must be interpersonally comparable in a cardinal sense, with common units, and government officials must solve the Hayekian problem of generating sufficient, accurate information to identify a determinate outcome.

None of these arguments are novel, and so I will move through them quite quickly. The core of what is novel about this essay is the comparison between two approaches to extending the Pareto criterion: the Kaldor-Hicks-Scitovsky approach and the Coasian approach. I will make the comparison in five steps. First, the Kaldor-Hicks-Scitovsky (KHS) "compensation principle" is fundamentally coercive, because it justifies takings without consent or compensation.[2] Second, the Coasian Bargaining (CB) principle is at least potentially *euvoluntary*,[3] under certain assumptions about the distributions of rights and powers prior to the initiation of bargaining. Third, the outcomes of Kaldor-Hicks-Scitovsky processes and Coasian processes are not just similar, but mathematically isomorphic, under the conditions of full information and negligible transactions costs. Fourth, if these assumptions are breached, the performances of the two processes are context dependent. In the presence of very high transactions costs of a collective action variety, Kaldor-Hicks-Scitovsky might perform better. However, in the presence of high transactions costs of the informational variety, the market signals generated by Coasian bargaining are very valuable. Finally, Coasian bargaining has an additional advantage: it is voluntary and requires that compensation is agreed to and then actually paid. Kaldor-Hicks-Scitovsky is "potential Pareto," but Coasian bargaining is a means of achieving unanimous consent – or something like it – for a policy.

---

[1] For a comprehensive review of utilitarian and efficiency arguments, see Gaus (2008). For specific consideration of the ethics of cost-benefit analysis, see Schmidtz (2001).

[2] It would be more accurate to say that the KHSC principle *allows* taking without compensation, because the question of compensation is relegated to an "equity" problem irrelevant to efficiency.

[3] *Euvoluntary* means "truly voluntary," in the sense of Munger (2011) or Guzman and Munger (2013).

2. Coercion

The essential utilitarian claim that justifies coercion by government is clear: systems that allow government coercion are (potentially) better for everyone in the society than systems that allow no coercion. This Hobbesian justification for coercion is clear, but it cannot distinguish among competing social systems. For Hobbes, nearly *any* coercive social system in which citizens are not murdered by the state is better than "nature," which is characterized by the *absence* of state coercion but which leaves too much liberty in the hands of individuals. Hobbes argues:

> [T]hat a man be willing, when others are so too, as far forth as for peace and defence of himself he shall think it necessary, to lay down this right to all things; and be contented with so much liberty against other men as he would allow other men against himself. For as long as every man holdeth this right, of doing anything he liketh; so long are all men in the condition of war. But if other men will not lay down their right, as well as he, then there is no reason for anyone to divest himself of his. (Hobbes 1651/1996, 92)

The question – for most analysts at least – is not whether state coercion can be justified as an abstract principle. The question is how to select *among* specific justifications, because the account we choose has important implications for the way the state is conceived. There are (at least) three different justifications one might offer for endowing the state with coercive powers: securing Lockean natural rights, ensuring contractarian consent of the governed, and utilitarianism, or "guaranteeing the greatest good for the greatest number."[4] To foreshadow the central claim of this essay, the differences among these three will turn to be exactly the same as the differences between KHS and CB.

A Lockean natural rights theorist would claim that the justification for the existence of the state is that government can use coercion to secure preexisting rights. Government does not create rights, in this view, but rather the government is created solely for the purpose of using coercion to secure these rights.

A contractarian view[5] might rest on the claim that all members of society recognize that they find themselves in a Hobbesian prisoner's dilemma. Of course, if such a process is infinitely repeated, cooperation might emerge naturally and spontaneously. However, if defection is common and the number of players is large, then punishment is a public good and likely to be

---

[4] The quote is attributed to Jeremy Bentham (1907).

[5] Of course, Hobbes was a contractarian. I mean *contractarian* in the more limited sense of choosing a specific form of government through a constitution. See, for example, Narveson (1988) or Brennan and Buchanan (2000).

underprovided. The solution could be specialized third-party enforcement, voluntarily contracted for with unanimous consent *ex ante* (although, of course, welchers would try to escape punishment *ex post*). As Hobbes puts it:

> For he that performs first has no assurance the other will perform after; because the bonds of words are too weak to bridle men's ambition, avarice, anger, and other Passions, without the fear of some coercive Power.... But in a civil estate, where there is a Power set up to constrain those that would otherwise violate their faith, that fear is no more reasonable; and for that cause, he which by the Covenant is to perform first, is obliged so to do. (Hobbes 1651/1996, 96)

Buchanan and Tullock (1962, 2–5) make something like this argument in their "exchange theory" of government origin.

Hardin (1989) is quite explicit about the idea of creating specialized enforcement agents ("government") with a specific list of justified triggers for the use of coercion. However, he is also skeptical of either the Hobbesian "mutual advantage" account or the Lockean "contractarian" account. The problem with the Hobbesian account, as Hardin puts it, is:

> What justifies an instance of coercion *by this particular government?* This is a much more complex issue than the in-principle justification of coercion by *some* government. Any credible and compelling answer to it must address alternatives *other than* the state of nature. If our initial motivating value is welfarist, then we must compare the effects of other possible forms of government to the effects of *this* one. (Hardin 1989, 82; emphasis in original)

This is an important point, and one often confused by Hobbes enthusiasts. The Hobbesian logic justifies an amount of coercion greater than zero, in principle. However, because in the Hobbesian view literally any government is better than the state of nature, there is no means of saying whether a government that imposes coercion of type A or coercion of type B is better, only that either is better than nothing. How then to choose *between* A and B?

It makes a significant difference whether one is trying to *justify* coercion or trying to *limit* coercion through the artifice of the "contract." Consider the language of the American Declaration of Independence, which has elements of each:

> We hold these truths to be self-evident, that all men are created equal, that they are endowed by their Creator with certain unalienable Rights, that among these are Life, Liberty and the pursuit of Happiness. That to secure these rights, Governments are instituted among Men, deriving their just powers from the consent of the governed. (1776)

The first sentence is the natural rights claim, asserting that certain rights are both self-evident and unalienable, implying that no signing of a contract could legitimately divest a person of those rights. The second sentence first justifies an amount of coercion greater than zero, provided that coercive power is used to "secure these rights," but then circles back, limiting the amount of coercion to whatever the governed consent to.

It is on these rocky shoals that many theories of justification for coercion run aground. Is residence "consent"? No explicit agreement to the contract itself is required for a person born and raised in a nation to be subject to its laws, right?[6] "Consent" in this setting requires no act of endorsement by the new citizen other than residence and the opportunity to participate in collective decision making, on the basis of whatever rules of election and recall are laid out in the founding or constituting document.

However, this means that the idea of consent and contract have been watered down from the robust tonic of the Declaration to a very thin gruel. The justification for coercion in the first instance was my explicit agreement that I, like everyone else, would be punished for certain transgressions that all agreed were harmful. I agreed, too; I consented. In the second instance, the practical working of a democracy, I may well be punished for acting, or failing to act, when I never consented to the agreement. I am coerced simply because a majority desires that these actions be punished, or obliged. Enfranchisement may be universal and choice majoritarian, but coercive enforcement is imposed on all, not just the majority that consented. All are ruled by most, which makes the notion of consent organic and collective rather than individual. However, "we" cannot consent. Each "I" has to consent.

For this reason, a consent theory must be focused on changes, rather than inherited obligations. We can only make changes in the distribution of power, wealth, or other valued tokens if everyone consents.[7] In other words, the ideal solution would be to require actual unanimity.

An argument for utilitarian justifications, founded only on majority "consent" for initiation of coercion violates any possible conception of consensual contractarianism. Again, to be binding, consent must be real. Further, as I will argue in the next section, such an approach fails on the practical ground that it cannot generate information that is both sufficient and unbiased enough to imply a determinate outcome, unless we allow that utility is cardinal and interpersonally comparable.

---

[6] Hume (1752) offers serious objections to any full blown theory of consent as a source of moral obligation. Much more context about the problem of authority, and theories of obligation, can be found in Huemer (2013).

[7] This is a slightly extended version of the argument made by Wicksell (1896). Consent can be a justification, but only if there is real consent. Potential Pareto is not enough.

In the next section I will seek to identify and contrast the key underlying assumptions of KHS and CB, with the burden of my argument being
that KHS requires information that only CB can generally provide. Thus,
in conditions where Kaldor-Hicks-Scitovsky and Coasian Bargaining are
otherwise equivalent, we should be indifferent between them, because they
produce identical results. And, in conditions of low information, Coasian
Bargaining is preferable.

3. Comparing Kaldor-Hicks-Scitovsky Compensation and Coasian Bargaining

It is useful to review the five steps of the argument of this section: First, I
examine the KHS compensation principle. Second, the CB process is considered, and its euvoluntary features examined. Third, the outcomes of KHS
and CB processes are compared and shown to be computationally identical.
Fourth, the underlying assumptions if both approaches are considered, and
the role of transactions costs explained. Finally, it is argued that Coasian
Bargaining has a key advantage: it is voluntary and requires that compensation actually be paid. That is, Coasian Bargaining is an actual means of
achieving unanimity, whereas the KHS approach is only *potentially* Pareto
superior and under narrow utilitarian assumptions.

3.1. The Kaldor-Hicks-Scitovsky Compensation Principle Is Coercive

Intuitively, KHS is very close to cost-benefit analysis, which, as I have claimed
elsewhere,[8] has the following features. The underlying assumptions of KHS
are as follows:

1. *The costs and benefits to individuals can be measured in dollars by
   an outside observer.* This is not the same as saying that utilities of
   different individuals are being compared. Instead, the problem is one
   of converting into dollars the effects of a proposed policy change from
   an identifiable status quo to a new policy. This blurs the problems
   of interpersonal utility comparisons ethically and puts the quantities
   to be compared into identical units practically. The foundations of
   the KHS approach were two papers (Kaldor 1939, Hicks 1939) that
   were in part a response to the intellectual cul-de-sac in which welfare

---

[8] See Munger (2000); for background and technical underpinnings, see Chipman and Moore
(1978) and Gaus (2008).

economics found itself. Just one year earlier, Harrod (1938, 396–397; quoted in Chipman and Moore 1978, 547) asked the question this way:

> Consider the Repeal of the Corn Laws. This tended to reduce the value of a specific factor of production – land. It can no doubt be shown that the gain to the community as a whole exceeded the loss to the landlords – but only if individuals are treated in some sense as equal. Otherwise how can the loss to some – and that was a loss can hardly be denied – be compared with the general gain?

The defense that KHS offered (Scitovsky's paper was published in 1941) was that policy recommendations were generally impossible without some metric that goes beyond the simple Pareto criterion. What if some are benefitted, and some harmed, by the proposed policy change from the status quo to the new policy? It might well be true that each of the policies being compared is a Pareto optimum in its own right. What then?

The KHS answer is simple: utilitarianism, with a dollar metric. Add up the net losses to the losers, and the net gains to the winners. If the sum of the gains to the gainers exceeds the losses to the losers, then it is possible to transform the comparison of two Pareto optima to the standard Pareto improvement structure. That is, because the gains to the gainers exceed the losses to the losers, the gainers can compensate the losers their net losses, satisfying at a minimum the weak Pareto criterion.

2. *The risks of failure, and chances of success, can be captured through probability discounting.* The problems of risk discounting can be solved by appropriate manipulations of the streams of losses and gains. This means that the results may exhibit a sensitive dependence on assumptions about discount rates, but so long as the analyst is transparent about those assumptions then the degree of sensitivity can be gauged by any trained observer.

3. *The future value of an asset, and the present value of a future cost or benefit, can be measured using compound interest and discount rates.* Just as with risk discounting, present value calculations allow the comparison of streams of costs and benefits that may not match up in time.

Overall, it is clear why KHS was taken to be a significant advance in welfare economics, particularly as a template for public cost-benefit analysis. Requiring that economic experts be mute in any setting other than pure Pareto improvement leaves the passage of many potentially beneficial policy changes up to voting. Voting simply adds up the number of people for and against, rather than looking at the intensity of preferences as KHS claims to be able to do.[9]

Still, there are two troubling things about the KHS approach, as have been pointed out by many scholars. The first is the question of *standing*.[10] We want to count gains and losses, but which gains and losses count? Putting locks on doors clearly hurts the earnings potential of robbers; should we credit this very real cost in choosing public policy? The problem is that the idea of externalities is a complicated thing to put into practice. If something you do upsets me, that is a loss. If it upsets me a lot, it might take millions of dollars to "compensate" me for the loss. However, should we credit subjective, self-reported losses, or gains, with all the potential for irrationality and strategic misrepresentation? Should we instead rely on "objective" measures of gains and losses, made by a third person?

The second problem is the question of *distribution*: the KHS approach is often called the "compensation principle" because there is no requirement that the compensation actually be effected. So long as net gains are positive, and compensation is *possible*, the policy action is correct. Stokey and Zeckhauser (1978, 279; quoted at the beginning of this essay) characterize this approach as: "Make a change when total income increases; don't worry about how it is distributed." This advice accords with a standard axiom of policy analysis: focus on efficiency, and leave distribution aside as a political question.

That is not to say that distribution is an unimportant question; it is just a different question. The Kaldor-Hicks-Scitovsky approach simply separates the creation of the surplus created by a policy choice and the distribution of that surplus. Distributional questions are relegated to the larger question of equity within the entire system of taxes and subsidies, and inequities created by the choices of particular policies should be addressed in that context, not in pairwise comparisons of the policies themselves. KHS suggests that officials should try to get policies right, at the margin, for many different

---

[9] Bentley (1908) and Truman (1951) argue that voting processes are able to account for intensity of preference through interest group politics. See Becker (1983) and Mitchell and Munger (1991) for reviews of this literature.

[10] The issue of standing is quite complex. For a review of the issues, and some important arguments about who should "count," see Whittington and MacRae (1986). They note that entities may be given standing by participating directly in decisions, by having their preferences counted, by having their welfare counted, or by representation by others whom they do not choose. As the reader may recall, the Lorax presumed to "speak for the trees."

decisions, and then address the inequities with redistribution on a more granular scale.

Inescapably, however, the KHS is coercive. The question of standing is decided by qualifying in some legal entitlement process rather than a preexisting property right. The "losers" have no veto over decisions, only a claim to compensation – at best conjectural, on the basis of some top-down legal process judging entitlement claims that are based on need, not the taking of property or value.

3.2. Coasian Bargaining Is Euvoluntary in an Existing Property Rights Regime

The process of Coasian Bargaining can be described as follows: CB is a situation in which a dispute over a property right is resolved by internalizing the externality that is causing the dispute. Externalities, according to Coase, are "reciprocal." If a tree falls in the forest, there may be a sound, but there is no noise nuisance, because no one hears it. An example may help illustrate how CB works.

On the TV show *Seinfeld*, there was a character named Jacopo Peterman.[11] On the show, he owned the catalog clothing company J. Peterman. Many people knew him as the owner of J. Peterman, although only in the fictional world of *Seinfeld*.

After the show ended, there was discussion of the actor who played J. Peterman on the show working in advertising the clothing line. However, there was no immediate agreement on how to compensate him and negotiations stalled. The company entered bankruptcy.

So, the actor who played J. Peterman on *Seinfeld* decided he would solve the problem by buying the real clothing company J. Peterman from the real John Peterman. The actor, John O'Hurley, underwrote much of the financing of the new J. Peterman after it came out of bankruptcy and now owns a substantial portion of the company. This solution is a classic example of CB: internalizing a problem by capturing the gains from cooperation.

Again, imagine a concrete company creates a lot of truck traffic, and loud noises, disturbing a neighboring home and its residents. The residents sue, asking that the cement company be forced to move, or cease operations. However, it might well be much cheaper for the cement company to buy out the neighbor's house. If the neighbors are not there, there is no externality. So, again, the externality is internalized.

---

[11] Thanks to Tim Groseclose for suggesting this example.

Under Coasian bargaining, both parties have incentives to represent their willingness to pay, and willingness to accept, accurately. And the transaction can only go forward if both parties agree to it. CB requires, however, that a set of assumptions be met. It is useful to describe those assumptions, or preconditions, at some length:

1. *Property rights are clearly and exclusively specified.* Coase (1960) clearly conceives of a situation in which property rights are in the hands of individuals and are exclusive, rather than common property or state property.

2. *The consequences of distribution can be ignored, and transactions costs are negligible. In particular, the number of actors is small, and they can easily communicate with each other.* As we shall see, the "distributional consequences can be ignored" portion of this is strikingly similar to the claim by KHS advocates. On the one hand, this is an important technical assumption for Coase, because it means that changes in resource allocations because of wealth effects can be ignored. However, it also means that the award of the rights, presumably the core issue from the perspective of the litigants, is of essentially no interest to the analyst, or even to the judge, because it has no impact on the efficiency of the system. In the case of the concrete facility, suppose that the owner of the facility owns the rights to make noise. Then the neighbors would sell the property and move. Now suppose that the homeowner has the right to force the concrete plant to cease operations. The answer is that the owner would buy the property, and the homeowner would move. The actual decision, of course, matters a lot to the litigants. However, it has zero impact on the distribution of resources.[12] In other words, *both allocations, where rights go to the plaintiff or rights go to the defendant, are Pareto optima.*

These are the two conditions most conducive to private bargaining solutions. Coase (1960) concludes that the actual assignment of rights is of no practical consequence if the two conditions are met. The resulting allocation of resources will be both efficient and invariant to changes in property right

---

[12] It is possible that the cement plant is operating at a loss, or just breaking even, of course. In that case, even a small judgment of damages against it will drive it bankrupt, if the homeowner has the property rights. If the concrete factory owner has the rights, he will sell them relatively cheaply to the homeowner, who will buy the concrete plant and then close it. Either way, the concrete plant closes, regardless of the assignment of rights.

assignments. This claim has been restated as the famous Coase Theorem, although Coase himself never made it.[13]

3.3. Isomorphism of Results of KHS and CB

For some reason, KHS and CB are thought of as being unrelated, even opposed. In fact, however, they are identical in nearly every respect if one recognizes that there is an "externality" involved in choosing in groups. That is, if we choose to remain at the status quo, all those who preferred to move to the new policy are harmed. If we choose instead to move to the new policy, all those who preferred the status quo are harmed. This "externality" aspect of collective decisions has been long recognized as a problem of coercive collective choice.

Let us be clear. There is nothing inherent in majority rule that restricts the domain of choice to goods that are technically "public." In fact, the creation of a collective choice mechanism based on majority rule obliterates the line between public and private, as the preferences of some affect the welfare of all. As Buchanan and Tullock point out in *The Calculus of Consent*, "many individuals may prefer to accept the expected costs of private decision-making... rather than to undergo the expected costs of collectivization, which represent yet another kind of *externality*" (Buchanan and Tullock 1962, 51–52; emphasis in original).

Once this is accepted, the difference between Kaldor-Hicks-Scitovsky and Coasian bargaining lies in the details of implementation. Consider the following example. There are two people, 1 and 2, and two alternatives, α and β. Person 1 likes α better and would be willing to pay up to $1,000 if α rather than β were selected. Person 2 likes β better and would be willing to pay up to $5,000 if β were selected rather than α.

Notice that we have placed no restrictions on what α and β are. They could be road projects or liability assignments for damages caused by a

---

[13] The Coase Theorem actually derives from Stigler (1974). Coase was not trying to analyze economics in the absence of transactions costs. In fact, as he says in Coase (1988, 174–175): "The world of zero transaction costs has often been described as a Coasian world. Nothing could be further from the truth. It is the world of modern economic theory, one which I was hoping to persuade economists to leave.... Economists [have] been engaged in an attempt to explain why there are divergences between private and social costs and what should be done about it, *using a theory in which private and social costs were necessarily always equal*. It is therefore hardly surprising that the conclusions reached were often incorrect,... their theoretical system did not take into account a factor which is essential of one wishes to analyze the effect of a change in the law on the allocation of resources. *This missing factor is the existence of transactions costs*" (emphasis added).

Table 5.1. *Example with two alternatives*

	A	β
Person 1	$1,000	(−$1,000)
Person 2	(−$5,000)	$5,000
Net benefit	(−$4,000)	$4,000

confectioner's mortar and pestle. All that is required is that there are two people faced with two alternatives and that the choice between them is either-or and binding on both. The preceding information can be summarized as follows (see Table 5.1).

The Kaldor-Hicks-Scitovsky Approach: Assume that our government analyst has access to the preceding information and that this information is accurate and reliable. The gains to moving to β from α are $5,000, enjoyed by person 2; the losses of moving to β from α are $1,000, imposed on person 1. The net benefit to the "society" is $4,000 (assume everyone else is indifferent), and there is also in effect a transfer of $1,000 from person 1 to person 2. Because this transfer has no welfare impact, all we look at is the $4,000 net increase in GDP, and β is implemented.

The Coasian Bargaining Approach: Assume in the first instance that person 1 has the right to veto a change in policy, perhaps because he owns some property or some other valuable right necessary to move from α to β. Assume further that no one has seen the preceding table and that all information is private, with each bargainer knowing only his own preferences.

Person 2 makes 1 an offer. Would you consider $500 to sell the right to make this unanimous and move to β? Person 1 demurs. Person 2 makes additional offers. The actual outcome is indeterminate, of course, as in any bilateral bargaining problem, but somewhere at or more than $1,001 person 1 agrees to sell the right to person 2. Person 2 makes the payment and then implements the change from α to β. The outcome (move from α to β) is the same as with KHS, but this time the potential Pareto is actual Pareto, because person 1 receives compensation rather than suffering a taking. GDP increases by $4,000 exactly, with the increase being the sum of the benefit to person 2 of moving from α to β and the rent earned by person 1 for selling the right necessary to make that move possible. In other words, if person 1 drove a hard bargain and got $2,000 from person 2, the increase in GDP would be person 2's $5,000 from moving from α to β, minus the $2,000 paid to person 1, plus any rents earned by 1. However, because person 1 sold a right worth $1,000 to him for $2,000, for a rent of $1,000, the increase in GDP is the $3,000 benefit to person 2 plus the $1,000 rent earned by person 1, for a total of $4,000. Again, this result is precisely the same as in the KHS problem, and that is not an accident. It is exactly the same problem, and no matter how we change the numbers it would always come out this way if person 1 owned the required right.

Assume instead that person 2 owns the necessary right. Person 2 announces his intention to move from α to β but invites person 1 to make offers if he wants. Person 1 offers $500 and is turned down, because person 2 values the move at $5,000. Person 1 offers $1,000, and is turned down again. At this point the bargaining stops, and the move from α to β is implemented. This means that GDP is increased by $4,000, with person 2 deriving a benefit of $5,000 and person 1 suffering a harm of $1,000. This outcome is even closer to the KHS outcome; the numbers are exactly the same. The difference is that under KHS the harm is imposed as a result of a new collective decision, one that person 1 might not have expected. In the case of CB the outcome results from the ownership of the key property right by person 2, and person 1 had no reason to expect anything else. The allocation is the same, but KHS is coercive and CB is not, unless one believes that property is theft.

It is also worth pointing out that neither of the bargainers had the full information possessed by the KHS analyst, but managed to work things out on their own, as values were revealed through private bargaining. This result is important, as we shall see in the case in which the KHS analyst tries to deal with the problem of private information. Remember, in the preceding example the KHS analyst was presented with a table of information – a table which by assumption contains complete and accurate information about willingness to pay. In the absence of such information, the analyst must either estimate values or use surveys to obtain the information.

Further, the participants all know that if the outcome they like less is chosen, they receive no compensation, because KHS has no requirement that the compensation must actually be paid. If the analyst asks person 2 first, and person 2 is honest, he says, "I prefer β to α, and I would pay $5,000 to ensure that."

Person 1 is not so honest, although the analyst has no way of knowing this. Person 1 says he prefers α to β and that he would be willing to pay $6,000 to ensure that α is chosen. The analyst does the computations and concludes (wrongly) that α is potentially Pareto preferred to β. Person 1 gains $1,000 relative to a move to β, person 2 loses $5,000, and GDP declines by $4,000. In addition, person 2 receives no compensation for his politically forced loss, simply suffering from the externality of being forced to accept collective choices.

We could do the CB example over again, but we already did it. There is no assumption, and no need, of complete information in the CB setting, so long as transactions costs are negligible (a large assumption, admittedly). In any setting with small numbers and low transactions costs, CB dominates KHS. The two approaches have identical results under full information, and CB is superior if there is private information.

4. The Breach of the Low Transactions Cost Assumption

It might well be objected that the "test" conducted in the previous section was not fair. No one would likely propose that KHS be applied to a two-person bargaining problem. However, many problems that cities and counties deal with for zoning and other policy changes have small numbers of agents who clearly deserve standing, unless "I like to see green space when I drive by once a month" should have a voice in how a parcel of land is used.

That is the point. Collective decision making, as Buchanan and Tullock (1962) suggest, is a violent producer of uncompensated externalities. The state acts on small amounts of pollution to protect the weak; why should not a single-property owner faced with a mass of angry neighbors be able to seek the same protection? The fact that I want to develop a parcel of land that is now undeveloped, but which produces an "external" effect on my neighbors who would prefer it to remain undeveloped, is a profound negative externality. In a democracy, all voters automatically have "standing," regardless of whether property rights might dictate otherwise.

Remember, as Coase (1960) argued, externalities are reciprocal. It is the proximity of the two uses that produces the externality, not the agent who is proposing a change from the status quo. The only question should be whether the move from α to β, from status quo to new policy, increases GDP.

Therefore, if the owner of an undeveloped plot of land seeks to have the land rezoned to allow development of houses and the 100 neighboring parcels that have already been developed object, who is creating the externality? If all the land were undeveloped, there would be no externality. So is the cause of the externality (new development reducing surrounding land values) the green space or the existing development that abuts it?

Coase would say the answer is yes. The cause or fault is of little interest. The problem is to obtain the information necessary to assign the rights to

Table 5.2. *New example*

	A	B
Persons 1–99	$1,000	(−$1,000)
Person 100	(−$125,000)	$125,000
Net benefit	(−$26,000)	$26,000

the party (ies) that will use it to increase GDP maximally. As we saw in the previous section, this is what both KHS and CB try to do, in principle.

Which is likely to be more successful? There are actually two distinct problems. The first is to find some means of eliciting accurate information. The second is to get everyone involved to accept the outcome, without coercion.

4.1. Kaldor-Hicks-Scitovsky with No Compensation

Suppose that the ninety-nine neighbors all oppose the development, at a "willingness to accept" of $1,000 each, and the increase in GDP is $125,000, as posited in Table 5.2. Then under full information the KHS analyst will recommend that the project be built. The sum of the costs is $99,000, and the benefit is $125,000, for a net benefit of $26,000.

Of course, under KHS there is no compensation paid. That means that in a democracy the correct outcome under KHS is impossible to implement for two reasons. First, because they know that the dollar amount is a fiction anyway, each neighbor will report a minimum willingness to accept that is much higher than what they would in fact accept. If each of them reports a willingness to accept that is, for example, $2,000 on average, then the total is $198,000, larger than the $125,000 benefit, leading the KHS analyst to deny the project.

However, second, even if the analyst sees through the misrepresentation and gives the project the go-ahead, the analyst will immediately be fired by the elected city council. The developer will be denied by force the chance to build a project that is a potentially Pareto improving transaction. Paradoxically, the only way that force will not be applied to stop the project is if the community is a dictatorship. A dictatorship would still face the preference revelation problem but would be free to approve the project even though it is unpopular. Either way, KHS is inherently and irreducibly coercive, because it relies on (a) involuntary and coercive restrictions in democracies or (b) involuntary and coercive impositions in authoritarian regimes.

4.2. Coasian Bargaining with Varying Rights Assignments

Under Coasian bargaining, the project might be built. However, the likelihood of the project being built depends on the initial assignment of rights because transactions costs are high with so many participants. If the property right to build is assigned to the owner of the undeveloped land, he will build. He may receive a visit from the neighbors, who have taken up a collection to try to persuade him not to build, but the collection will be, at most, $99,000, the sum of the aggregate willingness to pay on the part of the all the neighbors combined. And, because some neighbors will likely free ride, or underpay their donation, the amount offered might be considerably less than $99,000.

The key point is that it will always be less than $125,000, the amount required to buy out the developer and keep the land green and undeveloped. So if the right is assigned to the developer, the project will be built.

However, suppose the right is assigned to the surrounding neighbors – that is, the developer must obtain unanimous consent (the Pareto criterion) to build. He can do that by making side payments to each neighbor, until the neighbor agrees. Now, by assumption, $1,000 makes each neighbor indifferent between development and no development. Therefore, if the developer offers each neighbor, for example, $1,100, that is a total of $108,900, which is less than $125,000. So development is Pareto superior to nondevelopment, and not because of coercion. Each member of the community genuinely prefers development to nondevelopment, if CB with realized side payments is the decision rule.

Of course, the transactions costs of discovering this outcome are significant. If the ninety-nine neighbors have just a few hard bargainers, or stubborn hold-outs, hoping for a better deal, then no transaction may result. However, the reason the transaction is defeated is transactions costs, or in effect a kind of friction in the system, not explicit coercion.

This is a very important point, one that has been made by several scholars. As O'Driscoll (1980, 359) points out, those who advocate KHS are "actually grappling with the calculation problem." That is, the problem of the socialist calculation debate is precisely the same problem that blocks KHS from achieving Pareto efficiency. As Stringham (2001) argues at some length, the problem of trying to estimate values without prices is not just hard – it is impossible, for reasons made clear by Hayek (1945).

To summarize, KHS lacks any mechanism for accurately measuring either willingness to pay or willingness to accept. CB does have such a mechanism, as the result of self-interested bargaining, in which each participant has incentives to reveal correct information about prices. However, in a high transactions cost setting CB is also likely to fail, because of collective action problems in even moderately large groups of bargainers.[14]

This result is quite different from the usual account of public welfare economics. In general, CB is relegated to a kind of curiosity – a conjuror's trick that works only in extreme conditions and under silly assumptions. And, it is true that CB works perfectly only with zero transactions costs. However, KHS also assumes zero transactions costs, in the sense that it assumes costless elicitation of accurate information about willingness to pay and willingness to accept. If anything, CB is more likely to solve this problem than KHS, because at least the participants in CB still have some incentive for accurate revelation, since the side payments that are the subject of bargaining actually have to be made.

Otherwise, KHS and CB are not just similar, but identical. They imply exactly the same outcomes, and for the same reasons, under full information, and both of them set aside the consideration of ethics and distribution. KHS does this by assuming away the need for actual compensation, and CB does this by assuming that wealth effects are negligible, which ensures that willingness to pay and willingness to accept are identical. Both approaches assume away the problem that is of most interest to the actual participants: who, specifically, wins and loses? Am I better off or worse off? Both KHS and CB obscure this aspect of outcomes, which may explain why they are more popular among economists than politicians.

5. CB Is Voluntary, and KHS Is Coercive

In this essay I have argued that the KHS compensation principle and the CB principle are identical, except that CB is voluntary and KHS is coercive.

The reasons that the two approaches are identical is that each seeks to measure, through different means, the aggregate costs and benefits of different activities. As Coase himself said:

It would clearly be desirable if the only actions performed were those in which what was gained was worth more than what was lost. But in choosing between social arrangements within the context of which individual decisions are made, we have to bear in mind that a change in the existing system which will lead to an improvement in some decisions may well lead to a worsening of others. Furthermore we have to take into account the costs involved in operating the various social arrangements

---

[14] There is a solution I had missed: one that was pointed out by Kevin Munger. The Coasian solution is clearly for the 99 neighbors to incorporate: each contributes 1/99 of the cost and buys the land, and then develops it. They would each earn maximal profit, and the land would be developed. So, in the zero transactions cost condition, Coasian Bargaining might work even here.

(whether it be the working of a market or of a government department), as well as the costs involved in moving to a new system. In devising and choosing between social arrangements we should have regard for the total effect. This, above all, is the change in approach which I am advocating. (1960, 44)

If that sounds like Coase was thinking of cost-benefit analysis, perhaps he was. However, CB proposes a different means of obtaining information about preferences, as well as a voluntary mechanism for implementing the solution.

I have argued that KHS might never be implementable in a democracy, because it does not require that side payments actually be made. That means that large numbers of people who are slightly opposed to a project can kill that project, even if in the aggregate terms proposed by both KHS and CB, the project should be built. Perhaps the most paradoxical claim I have made is that KHS is only implementable in autocracies. In democracies, KHS will generally be used as a smoke screen to provide cover for coercively imposed obstacles that block Pareto improvements, because side payments are not possible.

References

Becker, Gary (1983). "A Theory of Competition Among Pressure Groups for Political Influence." *Quarterly Journal of Economics* 98: 371–400.

Bentham, Jeremy (1907). *Introduction to the Principles of Morals and Legislation.* Oxford: Oxford University Press.

Bentley, Arthur (1908). *The Process of Government.* Chicago: University of Chicago Press.

Brennan, Geoffrey and James Buchanan 2000. *The Reason of Rules: Constitutional Political Economy.* Indianapolis: Liberty Fund.

Buchanan, James and Gordon Tullock (1962). *The Calculus of Consent.* Ann Arbor: University of Michigan Press.

Chipman, John and James Moore (1978). "The New Welfare Economics." *International Economic Review* 19: 547–584.

Coase, R. H. (1960). "The Problem of Social Cost." *Journal of Law and Economics* 3: 1–44.

Coase, R. H. (1988). *The Firm, The Market, and the Law.* Chicago: University of Chicago Press.

Gaus, Gerald F. (2008). *On Philosophy, Politics, and Economics.* Belmont, CA: Thompson/ Wadsworth.

Guzmán, Ricardo and Michael Munger. (2014). "Euvoluntariness and Just Market Exchange: Moral Dilemmas from Locke's Venditio." *Public Choice* (forthcoming).

Hardin, Russell (1989). "Rationally Justifying Political Coercion." *Journal of Philosophical Research* 15: 79–91.

Harrod, R. F. (1938). "Scope and Methods of Economics." *Economic Journal* 48: 383–412.

Hayek, Friedrich (1945). "The Use of Knowledge in Society." *American Economic Review* 35(4): 519–530.

Hicks, John (1939). "The Foundations of Welfare Economics." *Economic Journal* 49(196): 696–712.

Hobbes, Thomas (1651/1996). *Leviathan.* New York: Cambridge University Press.

Huemer, Michael (2013). *The Problem of Political Authority: An Examination of the Right to Coerce and the Duty to Obey.* New York: Palgrave – Macmillan.

Hume, David (1752/1953). "Of the Original Contract." In C. W. Hendel (ed.), *David Hume's Political Essays.* Indianapolis: Bobbs-Merrill Co, 465–487.

Kaldor, Nicholas (1939). "Welfare Propositions in Economics and Interpersonal Comparisons of Utility." *Economic Journal* 49(195): 549–552.

Mitchell, William and Michael Munger (1991). "Economic Theories of Interest Groups: An Introductory Survey." *American Journal of Political Science* 35: 512–546.

Munger, Michael (2000). *Analyzing Policy.* New York: W.W. Norton and Company.

Munger, Michael (2011). "Euvoluntary or Not, Exchange is Just." *Social Policy and Philosophy* 28: 92–211.

Narveson, Jan (1988). *The Libertarian Idea.* Philadelphia: Temple University Press.

O'Driscoll, Gerald (1980). "Justice, Efficiency, and Economic Analysis of Law." *Journal of Legal Studies* 9: 355–366.

Schmidtz, David (2001). "A Place for Cost-Benefit Analysis." *Philosophical Issues* 11: 148–171.

Scitovsky, Tibor (1941). "A Note on Welfare Propositions in Economics." *Review of Economic Studies* 9(1): 77–88.

Stigler, G. J. (1974). "Free Riders and Collective Action: An Appendix to Theories of Economic Regulation." *Bell Journal of Economics and Management Science* 5(2): 359–365.

Stokey, Edith and Richard Zeckhauser (1978). *A Primer for Policy Analysis.* New York: W.W. Norton and Co.

Stringham, Edward (2001). "Kaldor Hicks Efficiency and the Problem of Central Planning." *Quarterly Journal of Austrian Economics* 4: 41–50.

Truman, David (1951). *The Governmental Process.* New York: Alfred A. Knopf.

Whittington, Dale and Duncan MacRae, Jr. (1986). "The Issue of Standing in Cost-benefit Analysis." *Journal of Policy Analysis and Management* 5(4): 665–682.

Wicksell, Knut (1896). *Finanztheoretische Untersuchungen.* Jena: Gustav Fischer Verlag. Partially reprinted as Wicksell, Knut (1958). "A New Principle of Just Taxation." In Richard A. Musgrave and Alan T. Peacock (eds.), *Classics in the Theory of Public Finance.* London: Macmillan, 72–118.

Discussion

A Sociological Perspective on Coercion
and Social Welfare

Edgar Kiser

The essays by Roger Congleton and Michael Munger and are examples of analytically precise and insightful analyses of some of the most fundamental issues in contemporary political economy. Congleton uses matrix representations to provide clear definitions of voluntary and coercive associations and exchanges, and Munger provides a very detailed comparison of the Kaldor-Hicks Compensation principle and Coasian Bargaining, showing that they are more similar than previously thought, but still differ in important ways. Both of these essays, like the other chapters in this book, make significant contributions to our understanding of the meaning of coercion, the conditions under which its use is justified, and its effects on social welfare. Instead of addressing the specifics of the arguments by Congleton and Munger in detail, I will outline an alternative sociological perspective on these general issues and contrast it briefly to the perspective underlying their essays.

Sociology and the Rational Choice models that have dominated the disciplines of economics and, more recently, political science have become much more similar lately. Rational Choice theory has made some inroads in sociology (Coleman 1990; Hechter and Kanazawa 1997), and institutional and behavioral economics (North 1990; Thaler 1994) have brought it closer to traditional sociological concerns. However, there are still important differences between the disciplines, and these two essays illustrate them. First, the branch of political economy addressed in these two essays tends to be philosophical and prescriptive, focusing on the question of what the relationship between the state and individuals should be. Sociologists who have focused on these issues tend to be more descriptive and empirical, interested in analyzing relations between states and individuals in particular existing states. Second, Rational Choice models have tended to make simple assumptions regarding the preferences of actors and have rarely been interested in the determinants of preference formation and transformation.[1] Sociologists, on the other hand, especially those interested in culture and ideology, have spent a great deal of effort trying to understand the origins of preferences (which they generally refer to as values).

My comments will come from the sociological perspective on both of these issues, and I will attempt to use some sociological ideas to elaborate on the arguments made by Congleton and Munger. I will admit at the outset that there is a significant cost to my approach. A third important difference between the disciplines is that economists tend to value theoretical parsimony and precision, whereas sociologists generally prefer theories that are broader and more descriptively realistic. My comments will reflect this difference in tastes in that they will suggest the addition of many messy and imprecise elements to the elegant arguments presented by Munger and Congleton, and I fully understand why they might not view these changes as improvements.

Coercion, like the related concept of power, is notoriously difficult to define. It is easy to see when police officers draw their guns, generals roll in their tanks, or wardens lock their prison cells – but a definition including only the use of force would be much too narrow. Coercion is broader than this, and often much more subtle, but it is exactly this breadth and subtlety that creates definitional difficulties. The term *voluntary* carries the same ambiguities and definitional difficulties. To make matters even more complicated, as Munger notes, rational actors will voluntarily choose some types of coercion, because the threat of *ex post* coercion is a necessary condition for most *ex ante* agreements. Even with these difficulties, the authors of both of these essays (and others in this volume) are able to provide precise definitions by using objective criteria – either the use of force to change actions or a situation in which majoritarian politics result in some actors contributing more to the state than they receive from it (see the nice summary of this perspective in the Introduction to this volume).

The problem with objective definitions of voluntariness and coercion is that the actions of the individuals involved will be based on their subjective views of what is voluntary and what is coercive, and these may not match these models of objective conditions. All of the authors in this volume are, of course, aware of this issue. Munger discusses the problem of subjectivity in assessments of adequate compensation, Congleton discusses both the subjective nature of proposals and the use of ideal (instead of objective)

---

[1] This has begun to change with the advent of behavioral economics and neuro-economics, but these are still minority positions in the discipline.

baselines as counterfactuals to judge coercion, and Tea Party activists might view appropriate levels of coercion by the state very differently than most Europeans. However, none of them take this problem seriously enough to take the next theoretical step: if ideas about coercion are fundamentally subjective, what determines differences in the level or type of coercion that individuals will deem necessary, appropriate, and fair?[2]

Unfortunately, sociologists cannot answer this difficult question with a parsimonious formal model, but they do have some useful ideas about the determinants of these preferences. As Lukes (1974) notes, one of the most ubiquitous ways in which power is exercised is through the shaping of preferences. This is also one of the most effective ways of exercising power, because by the time choices are made, no explicit form of coercion is necessary. Marxists have long argued that elites usually control not only the means of production of material goods and services but also most of the means of production of ideas as well and use that to disseminate ideas and values that support their interests. Although most Marxist arguments are out of favor these days for quite good reasons, in an age of Fox News and Silvio Berlusconi, that particular argument does not seem unreasonable. To the extent to which state rulers and economic elites do control important media outlets,[3] they can use that control to shape and alter median voters' (or subjects in autocratic states) preferences about what counts as coercion and the conditions in which it should be used.

Another line of sociological argument comes from Weber (1923/1978) in work related to his theory of the state referred to in the Introduction to this volume. He notes that a state that relied only on coercion (or positive incentives) to achieve compliance (by both citizens and the staff of the state) would be prohibitively expensive and thus very inefficient because the costs of monitoring and sanctioning would be so high – a conclusion echoed and reinforced by the analysis in the essays by Wallis and Skaperdas. All states thus use some mix of coercion and attempts to attain legitimacy – essentially to convince individuals that rulers have the right to control some of their behavior, and they have the responsibility to comply. Different types of states do this in different ways. In systems of traditional authority, current state policies are justified by reference to past state policies (this is

---

[2] Munger addresses the important issue of which models force individuals to reveal their preferences through bargaining but not the prior question of what determined their preferences in the first place.

[3] That extent varies significantly across both historical and contemporary cases and is probably declining in the contemporary world as a result of the increasing importance of more democratically controlled outlets such as the Internet and its social networking sites.

the way things have always been done). In these cases, current preferences regarding coercion would be a function of the extent and conditions in which coercion had been used in the past. Preferences about coercion would thus be determined by history. Another important type relies on what Weber calls charismatic authority. In this case, people comply because they believe the current ruler has unique personal features (intelligence, bravery, descent from some deity) that make him/her especially qualified to rule. Rulers with this sort of charisma (Napoleon and Hitler would be two examples) are often able to use much more coercion than rulers lacking it. To take a more recent, and more democratic example, John F. Kennedy was the sort of charismatic leader who could demand sacrifice from citizens in a way that most leaders, lacking such charisma, could not.

I do not have the space in these short comments to elaborate on these sociological arguments about the formation and transformation of preferences regarding coercion, but I do hope I have said enough to convince readers that exploring the subjective dimension of this issue is important. I have probably also convinced you that it is difficult and that current ideas about it lack the formality and precision of most of the arguments in the two essays I am discussing, a state of affairs that does not make the issue I am raising less deserving of further study.

References

Coleman, James (1990). *Foundations of Social Theory*. Cambridge: Harvard University Press.

Hechter, Michael and Satoshi Kanazawa (1997). "Sociological Rational Choice Theory." *Annual Review of Sociology* 23: 191–214.

Lukes, Stephen (1974). *Power: A Radical View*. London: MacMillan.

North, Douglass (1990). *Institutions, Institutional Change and Economic Performance*. Cambridge: Cambridge University Press.

Thaler, Richard (1994). *Quasi Rational Economics*. New York: Russell Sage.

Weber, Max (1923/1978). *Economy and Society*. Berkeley: University of California Press.

PART III

COERCION IN PUBLIC SECTOR ECONOMICS:
THEORY AND APPLICATION

6

Non-Coercion, Efficiency and Incentive
Compatibility in Public Goods

John O. Ledyard

1. Introduction

Based on Wicksell's principles of unanimity and voluntary consent in tax-ation, Lindahl (1919) proposed a market-like equilibrium for public goods economies. Foley (1970) provided proof that Lindahl equilibrium alloca-tions are in the core of a private ownership economy. Given those results, it would not be unreasonable to think that efficient and non-coercive public goods decisions should be possible through some process yielding Lindahl equilibria. Efficiency comes from the fact that the coalition of the whole cannot block such allocations. Non-coercion, at least at a minimal level, comes from the fact that individuals cannot block such allocations.

However, in Lindahl markets, each consumer is effectively a monopsonist in the market for her own consumption of the public good. Thus, it is unlikely that she would behave like a price taker, and as a result, in practice the Lindahl allocation would not obtain. Samuelson (1954) actually went further and suggested that, in public goods economies, no decentralized process could produce an allocation that was efficient. We now know that he was too pessimistic. Nevertheless, he made a good point. In considering social decisions, we need to be aware of the incentives created for the actors in the economy. Normative considerations need to be tempered by reality.[1]

One way to incorporate reality into the discussion is through incentive compatibility constraints. This is the approach of mechanism design. Accept the fact that the system one puts in place to decide on allocations will be inhabited by purposive agents. Then choose the social decision process you want so that it is compatible with the incentives of the consumers. This is the

---

[1] Wicksell himself seemed too aware of this. He wrote: "How much of this . . . may be of practical use in the near future, men of affairs may decide" (1896, 730).

approach I will take in this essay as I explore the trade-offs between social welfare and coercion in the presence of incentive compatibility constraints.

2. Some Basics

To begin with, I introduce notation and ideas that may be familiar to the readers.

2.1. Public Goods Economies

There are n consumers, each with an initial endowment of a private good, $w^i \in \Re$. Consumer i will consume x^i of the private good. There is also a public good that each i consumes in the amount $y \in \Re$. Consumer i has a utility function $u^i(y, x^i, v^i)$. The parameter $v^i \in V^i$ is the consumer's type. There is also a production side to the economy. I keep this simple and model it with a cost function $c(y)$, which is the amount of the private good necessary to produce y. I call $e = \{c(y), v^1, \ldots, v^n, w^1, \ldots, w^n\}$ an environment, and let E be the set of environments under consideration.

We will be interested in allocation-tax plans, $a = (y, t^1, \ldots, t^n)$. Here, t^i is the amount of the tax paid by consumer i. I will often refer to these simply as allocations. The utility that i attains in e from the allocation a is $U^i(a, v^i, w^i) = u^i(y, w^i - t^i, v^i)$. A couple of definitions will be useful.

Definition 1 *An allocation is feasible (in e) if and only if the sum of the taxes collected from all the consumers is at least equal to the cost of the public good – that is, $\sum_{i=1}^{N} t^i \geq c(y)$.*

We will let F be the set of feasible allocations for e.

Definition 2 *An allocation a' is efficient (in e) if and only if it is feasible and there is no other feasible allocation a^* such that $U^i(a^*, v^i, w^i) \geq U^i(a', v^i, w^i)$ for all i and $U^i(a^*, v^i, w^i) > U^i(a', v^i, w^i)$ for some i.*

2.2. Mechanisms and Their Performance Functions

A mechanism is a process through which disparate individuals in an economy can communicate and arrive at an allocation. Market equilibria and social choice functions are examples of mechanisms. We model a mechanism as a game form[2] (M, g). Here $M = M^1 \times \cdots \times M^n$, where M^i is i's

---

[2] In this paper I will stick with normal form games. We could consider extensive form games to deal with iteration, etc., but normal forms will be sufficient for our purposes.

language of communication – the set of messages that i can send to others. The *outcome function* $g : M \to F$ describes the allocations that arise, where $g(m)$ is the allocation that occurs if each i sends the message m^i.

Given a mechanism (g, M) and an environment $\{c(y), v^1, \ldots, v^n, w^1, \ldots, w^n\}$, we get a game $(M, \rho^1(m), \ldots, \rho^n(m))$ where M^i is i's strategy space and $\rho^i(m) = U^i(g(m), w^i, v^i)$ is i's payoff function. Given a game, we can consider its game-theoretic equilibria. For now we use Nash equilibria. For the game $G = (M, \rho^1, \ldots, \rho^n)$, the strategy $m^* \in M$ is a Nash equilibrium of G if and only if $\rho^i(m^*) \geq \rho^i(m^*/m^i)$ for all $m^i \in M^i$ for all i.[3]

We are ultimately interested in the allocations that result from a mechanism in an environment for a particular equilibrium concept.

Definition 3 *The performance function of the mechanism* $\mu = (M, g)$ *in the environments E for Nash- equilibrium is* $P : E \to F$, *where* $P(e) = g(m^*(e))$ *and* $m^*(e)$ *is the Nash equilibrium of the game derived from the mechanism* μ *in the environment e.*

It should be noted that a performance function is simply an *allocation function* $a : E \to F$, which specifies an allocation for each environment in E.

3. Efficient, Non-Coercive, Incentive Compatible Allocations

In spite of Samuelson's conjecture, we now know that it is indeed possible to find mechanisms, or decentralized processes, such that the performance function of the mechanism in public goods environments produces a Lindahl equilibrium in each environment.

Theorem 1 *Hurwicz (1979a), Walker (1981)*

Let $L : E \to F$ be the Lindahl equilibrium correspondence for the environments E – that is, $L(e)$ is the set of Lindahl equilibria for $e \in E$. There exists a mechanism $\mu^* = (M^*, g^*)$ such that the performance function $P : E \to F$ of the mechanism μ^* in the environments E for Nash equilibrium satisfies $P(e) = L(e)$ for all $e \in E$.

Thus, it would seem that, even if we take into account the incentives of the consumers, there is no conflict between efficiency and non-coercion as long as we are happy with Lindahl allocations. However, there is a priori nothing

---

[3] The expression $(m^*/m^i) = (m^{*1}, \ldots, m^{*i-1}, m^i, m^{*i+1}, \ldots, m^{*n})$.

John O. Ledyard

particularly special about Lindahl equilibrium allocations. Why stop there? There are many more allocations that are both efficient and non-coercive. We know from Muench (1972) that even in large economies, the core can be much larger than the set of Lindahl equilibria. Might not these core allocations be candidates for non-coercive, efficient allocations?

I will use the concept of voluntary participation to identify allocations that are not blocked by individuals. The idea is that, in a private ownership economy, a consumer can always take her endowment and just not participate in whatever process is being used. Voluntary participation seems to me to be a necessary condition for non-coercion.[4]

Definition 4 *A feasible allocation a in an economy e satisfies voluntary participation for consumer i if and only if*

$$u^i(y, w^i - t^i, v^i) \geq u^i(0, w^i, v^i). \tag{1}$$

It may of course be possible for the consumer to "not participate" by not paying taxes and still consume the public good if it is not excludable. Or, the consumer could take her resources and the technology to produce the public good when she does not participate. Each of these would provide a higher value for the right-hand side and a smaller set of allocations satisfying nonparticipation. However, I will stay with the definition we have because it is the weakest and sufficient for the result of interest. For ease in notation, from this point forward, I will normalize each i's utility so that $u^i(0, w^i, v^i) = 0$.

I want to identify all allocations that are efficient and satisfy voluntary participation. However, I also want these allocations to be achievable in the sense that there is a mechanism whose Nash equilibria will yield those allocations. Such allocations are called incentive compatible.

Definition 5 *Given a set of environments E we say that the allocation function $a : E \to F$ is Nash incentive compatible on E if and only if there is a mechanism $\mu = (M, g)$ such that the performance function $P : E \to F$ for μ in E for Nash equilibrium satisfies $P(e) = a(e)$ for all $e \in E$.*

I am now equipped to state a rather remarkable theorem.

Theorem 2 *Hurwicz (1979b)*

---

[4] It does assume that private property rights are enforced. We discuss this assumption in Section 7.2.

Given a set of public goods environments, E, that is rich enough,[5] suppose there is an allocation function $a : E \to F$ such that a is efficient (for all $e \in E$), is Nash incentive compatible, and satisfies voluntary participation. Then, $a(e) \subseteq L(e)$ for all $e \in E$. That is, the only allocation function that is efficient, non-coercive, and Nash incentive compatible is the Lindahl equilibrium allocation function.[6]

One might wish to stop at this point because it seems that Lindahl has been validated. However, there is problem from a strict game-theoretic point of view. Nash equilibrium is a complete information concept. It is an appropriate game-theoretic equilibrium only when all of the consumers know all of the details of the environment. We are usually interested in situations in which each consumer knows only his own type (w^i, v^i) and not the types of the others. For that, I need a new game-theoretic model of behavior.

4. Incomplete Information

In this section I examine the trade-offs between efficiency and non-coercion when consumers have incomplete information about the environment. Because we are now in a world of uncertainty, I will assume that consumers are von Neumann-Morgenstern decision makers who act as if they have beliefs and maximize expected utility. To model this, I add one concept to the previous complete information model: a prior distribution over possible types,[7] $\pi(v^1, \dots, v^n)$. To make things simpler, I will assume consumers have quasi-linear preferences – that is, $u^i(y, w^i - t^i, v^i) = \phi^i(y, v^i) + w^i - t^i$.

To make things interesting, I will assume that there is always a public goods problem. That is, I assume (a) sometimes it is efficient to produce the public good: if $a(v)$ is efficient for all $v \in V$, then $\int y(v) d\pi(v) > 0$; and (b) some types get no benefit from the public good: for each i there is $v_0^i \in V^i$ such that $u^i(y, w^i, v_0^i) \leq u^i(0, w^i, v^i) = 0$.

As is standard, I distinguish two different incomplete information situations: one in which consumers know their own type but know nothing else

---

[5] A sufficient condition for "rich enough" is that all Constant Elasticity of Substitution utility functions are in E. Weaker conditions are possible.

[6] In a comment on the Hurwicz results, Thomson (1979) proves for private goods economies if one replaces voluntary participation with fairness (non-envy), then one gets that the allocation function must be Walrasian from equal endowments. I am sure that the same type of result holds in public goods economies where Walrasian is replaced with Lindahl.

[7] We could include endowments, w^i, in the type but that just adds notation.

(called the interim situation) and one in which consumers know nothing, not even their own type (called the *ex ante* situation).

4.1. Interim Information

In the interim information condition, when the consumer knows her own type v^i, her (expected) utility for an allocation is

$$U^i(a(\cdot)|v^i) = \int_{V^{-i}} u^i(a(v), v^i)d\pi(v|v^i), \tag{2}$$

where $V^{-i} = V^1 \times \cdots V^{i-1} \times V^{i+1} \times \cdots \times V^n$ and $\pi(v|v^i)$ is the conditional distribution on V^{-i} given v^i.

A mechanism (M, g) and an incomplete information environment (π, E), where π is the prior beliefs and E is a set of complete information environments, combine to create a game with incomplete information, $(M, \rho^1(m, v^1), \ldots, \rho^n(m, v^n), \pi)$. In these games, a strategy for i is a function $\beta^i : V^i \to M^i$. The relevant game-theoretic equilibrium for incomplete information is Bayes equilibria.

Definition 6 *For the game* $G = (M, \rho^1, \ldots, \rho^n, \pi)$, *the strategy* β^* *is a Bayes equilibrium of* G *if and only if for all* $v \in V$, $m^i \in M^i$, i,

$$\int_{V^{-i}} u^i(g(\beta^*(v)), v^i)d\pi(v|v^i) \geq \int_{V^{-i}} u^i(g(\beta^*(v/m^i)), v^i)d\pi(v|v^i). \tag{3}$$

I am interested in the allocations that arise from a mechanism. By the revelation principle, P is the performance function of some mechanism (M, g) in the environment (π, E) for Bayes equilibrium, where $P(e) = g(\beta^*(v))$, if and only if $P(\cdot)$ is interim incentive compatible in (π, E).

Definition 7 *A feasible allocation (or a performance function),* $a : v \to F$, *is interim incentive compatible (IIC) in* (π, E) *if and only if for all* $v^i \in V^i$ *and for all* i,

$$U^i(a(\cdot)|v^i) \geq \int_{V^{-i}} u^i(a(v/v^{*i}), v^i)d\pi(v|v^i), \tag{4}$$

where $(v/v^i) = (v^1, \ldots, v^{i-1}, v^{*i}, v^{i+1}, \ldots, v^n)$.

Because of the incomplete information, I also need a new concept for non-coercive allocations. In the interim situation, a feasible allocation $a(\cdot)$

is (individually) non-coercive only if it satisfies an interim voluntary participation constraint.

Definition 8 *A feasible allocation a : V → X × Y satisfies interim voluntary participation (IVP) if and only if* [8]

$$U^i(a(\cdot)|v^i) \geq 0 \quad \text{for all } v^i \in V^i, \text{ for all } i. \tag{5}$$

Given these concepts, I can now explore whether in the interim information situation we can find a social choice rule or mechanism that is interim incentive compatible, interim non-coercive, and efficient. Unfortunately the general answer is no.

Theorem 3 *Güth-Hellwig (1986), Mailath and Postlewaite (1990), Hellwig (2003)*

There is no mechanism (M, g) whose performance function in (π, E) for Bayes equilibrium is efficient, incentive compatible (IIC), and satisfies interim voluntary participation (IVP).

The idea is that with positive production in some environments required by efficiency, those unlucky enough to be very low types, near v_0, will be worse off (in interim utility) than if they could exit, avoid taxation, and live off their endowments. There is an unavoidable conflict between non-coercion and efficiency under the interim information condition.

The conflict becomes extreme in larger economies. To see this, let us give up efficiency and only ask which non-coercive, incentive compatible mechanisms are possible. The answer is not good. In large economies if per capita costs are not infinitesimal, then any allocation that is interim incentive compatible and satisfies interim voluntary participation has the property that the probability of producing the public good is infinitesimal.

Theorem 4 *Mailath and Postlewaite (1990)*

Let $\mu^n = (M^n, g^n)$ and (E^n, π^n) be a sequence of mechanisms and sets of economies as $n \to \infty$. Let $a^n(v) = (y^n(v), t^n(v)$ be the performance function of μ^n in (E^n, π^n). Suppose that, for all n, there is a positive constant, δ such that $c^n(y^n(v)) > n\delta + \sum_i u^i(y^n(v), w^{ni} + t^{ni}(v), v^i)$ for some $v \in V^n$. Then, $\int_V y^n(v)d\pi^n(v) \to 0$ as $n \to \infty$.

---

[8] Remember that I normalized utility so that $u^i(0, w^i, v^i) = 0$.

The reason is very intuitive and worth repeating. As the group grows large, if $y(v)$ is an efficient allocation for all $v \in V$, then i's report about v^i has less and less effect on the choice. Therefore by IIC, i's tax must depend less and less on i's report. In the limit this means i's tax is constant no matter what i says. If that is true for everyone, then his or her taxes are equal to the per capita cost of the public good. Therefore, when i has very low utility for the public good, when their value v^i is less than the per capita cost, they will be worse off than if they did not participate at all. That is, IVP can not hold unless the probability of producing the public good is very small. Thus, in the limit there can be no production of the public good.[9]

This is really bad news. It says that in very large groups if we impose individual interim voluntary participation constraints, we are doomed to zero public good production. The conflict between non-coercion and efficiency is as bad as it gets in interim information situations in large economies.[10] To sidestep the interim conflict, some argue that mechanisms should not be chosen in the interim information situation but instead in the *ex ante* information situation. That is, one should go behind Rawl's veil of ignorance. Let us see what happens when we do that.

4.2. *Ex Ante* Information

In the *ex ante* situation, are there mechanisms, or allocations, that are feasible, incentive compatible, non-coercive, and efficient? We need to use the relevant information concept for each. We will use interim incentive

---

[9] A formal argument can be easily made in linear environments, where $u^i(y, x^i, v^i) = v^i y + x^i$, $v^i \in [v_0, v_1]$, $c(y) = nky$, and $k \in (v_0, v_1)$. Efficiency requires that $y(v) = 1$ if and only if $\frac{\sum v^i}{n} \geq k$; $y(v) = 0$ otherwise. Let $Q(v^i) = \text{prob}\{\frac{\sum_{-i} v^i}{n} \geq k - \frac{v^i}{n} | v^i\}$ and $T(v^i) = \int_{V-i} t^i(v) d\pi (v|v^i)$. Then, $\partial Q(v^i)/\partial v^i \to 0$ as $n \to \infty$. Interim incentive compatibility requires, assuming continuity, $v^i \partial Q(v^i)/\partial v^i - \partial T(v^i)/\partial v^i = 0$, $\forall v^i$. Therefore, $T(v^i) = T^i$ where by feasibility $\sum T^i = kn \int y(v) d\pi (v) = kY$. That is, incentive compatibility and feasibility combine to require per capita taxation for all i. Assume symmetry and let $t^i(v) = k$, $\forall i, v$. Remember i's utility is then $U^i(a(\cdot), v^i) = (v^i - k)\text{prob}[y(v) = 1]$. For some i, $v_0 \geq v^i < k$. Thus, IVP is violated unless $\text{prob}[y(v) = 1] = 0$.

[10] Hellwig (2003) provides a more optimistic result by changing the assumption on costs. He assumes that costs are independent of the size of the economy so that if the efficient level of the public good is bounded, as it is in the linear economy where $y \in [0, 1]$, then per capita costs will become infinitesimal in large economies. Then the solution to $\max \int_V \sum u^i(y(v), w^i - t^i(v), v^i) - c(y(v)) d\pi''(v)$ subject to $a(\cdot)$ is IVP and IIC and will have the property that in large economies $a(\cdot)$ is approximately efficient. Of course, this is because in Hellwig's large economies the maximum amount of the good should almost always be produced.

compatibility because that is the information state when the mechanism is deployed. However, I want an *ex ante* concept for voluntary participation.

In the *ex ante* information condition, when a consumer does not know her type, her (expected) utility for an allocation is

$$U^i(a(\cdot)) = \int_V u^i(a(v), v^i)d\pi(v). \tag{6}$$

Definition 9 *A feasible allocation a(·) satisfies* ex ante *voluntary participation (EVP) if and only if*

$$U^i(a(\cdot)) = \int_V u^i(a(v), v^i)d\pi(v) \geq 0, \forall i. \tag{7}$$

Is there a mechanism that is efficient, interim incentive compatible, and satisfies *ex ante* voluntary participation? Perhaps surprisingly, in light of the results in the previous section, the answer is yes. Following Bierbrauer (2009), I take this in two steps.

First, d'Aspremont and Gérard-Varet (1979) and Arrow (1979) have shown us there are mechanisms whose performance functions are efficient and interim incentive compatible. These AGV mechanisms are VCG mechanisms[11] (Vickrey 1961, Clarke 1972, Groves 1973), using the prior beliefs in a clever way to balance the budget. They are generally referred to as expected externality mechanisms because everyone is taxed the expected externality they cause for the rest of the group through their participation.

Second, remember that, in quasi-linear environments, efficient allocations balance the budget (that is, $\sum t^i(v) = c(y(v))$ and maximize surplus (that is, $y(v) \in \arg\max_y \sum \phi^i(y, v^i)$). If, as I have assumed, when y is efficient $\int y(v)d\pi(v) > 0$, then the expected surplus of an efficient allocation function, $\int_V \max_y[\sum \phi^i(y(v), v^i) - c(y(v))]d\pi(v)$, will be positive. Take any AGV mechanism and add lump sum taxes so that every consumer shares the expected surplus equally. This gives a new mechanism that remains incentive compatible and efficient and now satisfies *ex ante* voluntary participation.

Proposition 1 *Bierbrauer (2009)*

There are mechanisms whose performance functions are efficient, interim incentive compatible, and satisfy *ex ante* voluntary participation. That is,

---

[11] VCG stands for Vickrey-Clarke-Groves who independently and simultaneously discovered this class of mechanisms. For a more formal definition, please consult their cited publications.

there is no conflict between efficiency and non-coercion in the *ex ante* information condition even if we impose incentive compatibility constraints. However, what do these allocations look like?

4.3. Efficiency, Non-Coercion, and Voting

What do *ex ante* non-coercive, efficient allocations look like? Could they come from any institutions that we already know? For example, are they Lindahl equilibria? For now I leave this as an open question and, instead, look at a special case.

It turns out that for large electorates in linear public goods economies[12] these *ex ante* non-coercive, efficient mechanisms do look like something we know. In particular they can be approximated by q-referenda. A q-referendum begins with individuals voting yes or no on whether to produce the public good. The good is produced if the percentage of yes votes is greater than or equal to q. If the good is produced, everyone pays k in taxes. If the good is not produced, no one pays. Using results from Ledyard and Palfrey (2002), one can show:

Theorem 5 *Let q satisfy $qE[v|v > k] + (1 - q)E[v|v < k] = k$.[13] Let a^o be the surplus maximizing allocation, and let a^q be the performance function of the q-referendum. Then, $\lim_{n \to \infty} \sum \int u^i(a^o(v), v^i)d\pi(v) - \sum \int u^i(a^q(v), v^i)d\pi(v) = 0$.*

There is a q-referendum that generates allocations that are interim incentive compatible and, in large economies, approximately efficient. If the types are distributed symmetrically, then the q-referendum allocations also satisfy *ex ante* voluntary participation.

In fact, there is an even stronger result. These q-referenda are *ex post* incentive compatible in the sense that, even after all voters know everything, no one wants to change their vote. q-referenda are dominant strategy mechanisms. Thus, they do not depend on the existence of a common prior or common knowledge of information and rationality. The only place that the beliefs play a role is in the determination of q.[14]

---

[12] Linear economies have $u^i = v^i y + w^i - t^i$, $c(y) = kny$, $y \in \{0, 1\}$, π has full support on $V = [v_0, v_1]^n$ and $v_0 < k < v_1$.

[13] If $k = (E[v|v > k] + E[v|v < k])/2$, then $q = 1/2$.

[14] I must admit this result is not so interesting for independent values because then, as $n \to \infty$, it becomes certain whether to always produce the public good or to never produce the good so $q = 0$ or 1. However, if values are correlated, this becomes a lot less trivial.

5. Future Possibilities?

In the previous section, I have relied heavily on the model of Bayes equilibrium for economies with incomplete information. Many, including myself, view the required underlying assumptions of common knowledge of information and rationality as unrealistic. Often, as an alternative, one redirects the search to try to find mechanisms in which individuals can act rationally without any common knowledge. One class of such mechanisms contains those whose games have dominant strategy equilibria.

Definition 10 *For the game* $G = (M, \rho^1, \ldots, \rho^n)$, *the strategy* β^*, *where* $\beta^i : V^i \to M^i$, *is a dominant strategy equilibrium of G if and only if for all* $v \in V$, $m^i \in M^i$, i,

$$u^i(g(\beta^*(v)), v^i) \geq u^i(g(\beta^*(v)/m^i), v^i). \tag{8}$$

I am particularly interested in the allocations that arise from mechanisms with dominant strategy equilibria. By the revelation principle, $P : V \to F$ is the performance function of such a mechanism if and only if P is *ex post* incentive compatible.

Definition 11 *A feasible allocation* $a(\cdot)$ *is* ex post *incentive compatible (EIC) in E if and only if for all* $v \in V$, $m^i \in V^i$, i

$$u^i(a(v), v^i) \geq u^i(a(v/m^i), v^i). \tag{9}$$

This is called *ex post* incentive compatible because it is an equilibrium of the game played in the *ex post* information situation when all information is known. It should be noted that *ex post* incentive compatibility is stronger than interim incentive compatibility. If a mechanism is *ex post* incentive compatible, then it is also interim incentive compatible, but not the reverse. Further, unlike the interim approach, *ex post* incentive compatibility requires neither common knowledge of information nor common knowledge of rationality.

Are there allocations that are efficient, *ex post* incentive compatible, and satisfy voluntary participation? It is well known that, no matter what type of voluntary participation constraint is considered, the answer is no.

Theorem 6 *If the class of environments, E, is rich enough, there is no mechanism* (M, g) *whose performance function on E in efficient and* ex post *incentive compatible.*

Does this mean we need to give up our search for allocations that are efficient, non-coercive, and *ex post* incentive compatible? Maybe not. In a recent paper, Krajbich et al. (2009) suggest that future technology may be able to significantly change the incentive compatibility constraints we have been using. Based on research in neuro-economics, they first show for a very special case that it is possible to observe a neuro-signal using MRI that is correlated with the consumer's value of the public good. Then, they show that if the tax paid by consumers depends appropriately on both the consumer's claimed value for the public good and the signal, the consumer will have an incentive to correctly report their true value for the good. This possibility has some interesting implications for our discussion of efficiency and non-coercion.

The signal technology can be represented by a conditional probability function where $f(s, v)$ is the probability that we will observe the signal s if the agent's true type is v. Using the revelation principle, we need only consider direct mechanisms, where $M^i = V$, augmented with the signal so that $h(m, s) = [y(v), t(v) + r(v, s)]$. The game-theoretic equilibrium we will use is that of dominant strategies in m before the observation of s.[15]

Definition 12 *The augmented mechanism (V, h) is* ex post *incentive compatible in E if and only if for all $v \in V$, $m^i \in V^i$, and for all i,*

$$\phi^i(y(v), v^i) + w^i - t^i(v) - \int_S r^i(v, s)dF(s, v) \geq, \tag{10}$$

$$\phi^i(y(v/m^i), v^i) + w^i - t^i(v/m^i) - \int_S r^i(v/m^i, s)dF(s, v). \tag{11}$$

Definition 13 *The augmented mechanism (V, h) satisfies* ex post *voluntary participation in E if for all $v \in V$, and for all i,*

$$\phi^i(y(v), v^i) + w^i - t^i(v) - \int_S r^i(v, s)dF(s, v) \geq 0. \tag{12}$$

Krajbich et al. (2010) are able to establish that if the signal technology satisfies a condition originally identified by Cremer and McLean (1985, 1988),[16] then

---

[15] This timing is crucial to all of the discussion that follows. I discuss this in more detail in Section 7.1.

[16] The condition is that, for all $v \in V$, the vector $f(\cdot, v) \in \Delta(S)$ is not in the interior of the convex hull of all such vectors.

Theorem 7 *Krajbich et al. (2010)*

Let $a(\cdot)$ be an allocation function that is efficient and satisfies voluntary participation $(u^i(a(v), v^i) \geq 0, \forall v)$. Then, there is an augmented mechanism that is *ex post* incentive compatible and satisfies *ex post* voluntary participation and whose performance function, $a^a(\cdot)$, yields the same expected outcome.[17]

With the availability of a signal technology, even if we require dominant strategies, incentive compatibility imposes no constraints on the choice of efficient and non-coercive allocations. In particular there is an *ex post* incentive compatible mechanism satisfying *ex post* voluntary participation whose performance function is the Lindahl equilibrium allocation function.

6. Summary to Here

My goal in this essay is to explore options for efficient and non-coercive public good decisions when the choices are constrained to be incentive compatible. We have seen that the answers depend crucially on which concept of incentive compatibility I use. This, in turn, depends on which behavior model of consumers I use and what I assume about their state of information.

In a world of complete information in which consumers are price takers, Lindahl equilibrium allocations are an option. Further, if consumers are more strategic and act in accord with Nash equilibrium, Lindahl equilibrium allocations become the only option.

In a world of incomplete information, with Bayes equilibrium behavior, the options depend on the state of information. In the interim information situation, there is an impossibility theorem. There are no allocations that are efficient, non-coercive, and incentive compatible. Worse yet, in large economies, the only allocations that are non-coercive and incentive compatible involve virtually no production of the public good.

In *the ex ante* information situation, there is an existence theorem. There are efficient, non-coercive, and incentive compatible allocations. Further, for the very special case of linear public goods economies, these allocations are approximated by voting mechanisms called q-referenda.

Finally, in a world with a technology generating signals correlated with individual values, even if one asks for mechanisms that have dominant strategies, incentive compatibility puts absolutely no constraint on our

---

[17] That is, $y^a(v) = y(v)$ and $t^a(v) = t^a(v) + \int_S r^a(v, s)dF(s, v)$.

choice of efficient and non-coercive allocations so long as decisions are made before the signals are generated. However, we are still left with a number of open questions. In the remainder of this essay, I want to mention two of these.

7. Commitment and Enforcement

7.1. Timing

It is tempting to think of the *ex ante* and interim situations not as information conditions but as a sequence in time. In this view, decisions are first made in the *ex ante* stage and then they are played out, with perhaps more decisions, in the interim stage. If one thinks like this, it raises a host of new questions, most of which remain open.

First, if the mechanism chosen in the *ex ante* stage is efficient, interim incentive compatible, and satisfies *ex ante* voluntary participation, then by theorem 3, there is a positive probability that at the interim stage, some consumer will not satisfy the interim voluntary participation constraint[18] – that is, they will want to take their endowments and not participate.

Suppose, at the *ex ante* stage, someone anticipates the interim stage and proposes that decisions be made subject to interim voluntary participation. This would, of course, mean giving up efficiency, but one could still maximize expected surplus subject to the constraints. The problem is:

Theorem 8 *Bierbrauer (2009: Let $a(\cdot)$ be an allocation that is interim incentive compatible and satisfies interim voluntary provision. Then, at the* ex ante *stage, there is an efficient, interim incentive compatible allocation satisfying* ex ante *voluntary participation, $\hat{a}(\cdot)$ such that*

$$U^i(\hat{a}(\cdot)) > U^i(a(\cdot)) \forall i. \tag{13}$$

Any proposal to impose interim voluntary participation at the *ex ante* stage would be defeated unanimously. The issue is commitment. With commitment on the part of everyone not to defect when and if the interim voluntary participation constraint is violated at the interim stage, implementing the efficient, incentive compatible allocation satisfying voluntary participation goes smoothly. If there is no such possible commitment, then from a game-theoretic point of view, we should introduce something like a sub-game

---

[18] By theorem 4, as $n \to \infty$ this probability becomes a certainty.

perfection constraint at the *ex ante* stage. This would certainly involve interim voluntary participation. However, undoubtedly there is more. For example, we may want to rule out choosing mechanisms in the *ex ante* stage that will be unanimously voted out in the interim stage. A minimal requirement for this would be that the mechanisms be interim incentive efficient.[19] What else is involved in sub-game perfection for mechanisms remains an open question.

Notice that the same issue arises if we introduce a third stage, generally called the *ex post* stage, at the time when everyone knows everything. Then, even if interim voluntary participation is satisfied, *ex post* voluntary participation may not be – that is, it is possible that $u^i(a(v), v^i) < u^i(0, w^i, v^i)$. This happens, for example, if one is on the losing side of a referendum.

The same issue is involved in the mechanisms of Section 5 in which decisions are made before observing the signal. There is no guarantee that consumers would, given the opportunity, be willing to voluntarily participate after their signal is known, because it is possible that $u^i(y(v), w^i - t^i(v) - r^i(v, s), v^i) < u^i(0, w^i, v^i)$. The consumer is willing to make the bet on participation before the signal is known but may be unhappy and regret the decision after. This is true even if the consumer is risk neutral as I have assumed earlier. It is also true that if the consumers can report their value after the signals are known, then there is no mechanism for which it will be a dominant strategy to report truthfully. With a commitment to live with the result of the signal, we can get efficiency, incentive compatibility, and voluntary participation. Without that commitment, we do not.

We really need a better model that takes into account the timing and repeated nature of the public goods decision problem. However, that might be good news. Up to now we have been considering a single (perhaps multidimensional) decision along with a sequence of times to get to that decision and beyond it. However, what if the group of consumers is going to be confronted by a series of public good decisions over time, then sometimes an individual would want the public good, ... $^1v > k$, and sometimes they may not, $^2v^i < {}^2k$. Taken over a long time, this is like being in the *ex ante* stage. Losing one election is not so bad if, on average, the winning compensates for the losing. However, again, the possible problem is the inability of a group to commit. Anyone who has been involved in faculty decisions over time knows how hard it is to enforce inter-temporal agreements. Even

---

[19] That is, there is no other mechanism for which it is common knowledge – at the interim stage – that everyone would be at least as well off and some would be better off.

the U.S. Congress has this problem. Some form of sub-game perfection will need to be incorporated into incentive incompatibility to deal with this.

7.2. The Guardians

One question always lurking in the background of any mechanism design paper is "But who will guard the guardians?"[20] There is always, at some point in the analysis, a reliance on explicit or implicit enforcement of the rules of the game. The voluntary participation constraints I have been using rely heavily on the explicit commitment to enforce property rights. If endowments can be confiscated, then voluntary participation constraints can be ignored. The incentive compatibility constraints I have been using rely heavily on the implicit commitment of the mechanism to actually implement the public good levels and taxes required by the reports of the consumers. If those implementing the rules can change their minds after seeing the reports of the consumers, then our positive analysis is wrong. Anticipating the lack of commitment, consumers will behave differently than we have modeled. For example, in the augmented mechanism of Section 5 our dominant strategy model predicts consumers will report their true value when asked. However, if they anticipate that the managers of the mechanism process will do something other than advertised, the consumers would be rational to report other than truthfully.

In all of our analysis, there is an intended game form, and there is, what Hurwicz (2007) called, a true game. Are the intended game and its equilibria self-enforcing in the context of the true game? How does this affect the revelation principle? I have some thoughts on these and other relevant questions, but that is for a future paper.

References

Arrow, K. (1979). "The Property Rights Doctrine and Demand Revelation Under Incomplete Information." In M. Boskin (ed.), *Economics and Human Welfare*. New York: Academic Press, 23–39.

Bierbrauer, F. (1972). "On the Legitimacy of Coercion for the Financing of Public Goods." Preprints of the Max Planck Institute for Research on Collective Goods, Bonn 2009/15 (2009).

Clarke, E. (1972). "Multi-part Pricing of Public Goods." *Public Choice* 11: 17–33.

Cremer, J. and R. P. McLean (1985). "Optimal Selling Strategies under Uncertainty for a Discriminating Monopolist When Demands Are Interdependent." *Econometrica* 53: 345–361.

---

[20] This question from the Roman author Juvenal is the title of Leo Hurwicz's Nobel Prize Lecture (Hurwicz 2007).

Cremer, J. and R. P. McLean (1988). "Full Extraction of the Surplus in Bayesian and Dominant Strategy Auction." *Econometrica* 56: 1247–1257.

d'Aspremont, C. and L.-A. Gérard-Varet (1979). "Incentives and Incomplete Information." *Journal of Public Economics* 11:25–45.

Foley, D. (1970). "Lindahl's Solution and the Core of an Economy with Public Goods." *Econometrica* 38(1): 66–72.

Groves, T. (1973). "Incentives in Teams." *Econometrica* 41: 617–631.

Güth, W. and M. Hellwig (1986). "The Private Supply of a Public Good." *Journal of Economics* 5: 121–159.

Hellwig, M. (2003). "Public Good Provision with Many Participants." *Review of Economic Studies* 70: 589–614.

Hurwicz, L. (1979a). "Outcome Functions Yielding Walrasian and Lindahl Allocations at Nash-equilibrium Points." *The Review of Economic Studies* 46(2): 217–224.

Hurwicz, L. (1979b). "On Allocations Attainable through Nash-Equilibria." In J. J. Laffont (ed.), *Aggregation and Revelation of Preferences*. Amsterdam: North-Holland.Publishing, 397–419.

Hurwicz, L. (2007). "But Who Will Guard the Guardians?" Nobel Prize Lecture, http://nobelprize.org/nobel_prizes/economics/laureates/2007/hurwicz-lecture.html.

Krajbich, I., C. F. Camerer, J. Ledyard, and A. Rangel (2009). "Using Neural Measures of Economic Value to Solve the Public Goods Free-Rider Problem." *Science* 326: 596–599.

Krajbich, I., C. F. Camerer, J. Ledyard, and A. Rangel (2010). "Neurometrically Informed Mechanism Design." Working paper. Pasadena, CA: Caltech.

Ledyard, J. and T. Palfrey (2002). "The Approximation of Efficient Public Good Mechanisms by Simple Voting Schemes." *Journal of Public Economics* 83: 153–172.

Lindahl, E. (1919/1967) "Die Gerechtigkeit der Besteurung," translated (in part) as "Just Taxation: A Positive Solution." In R. Musgrave and A. Peacock (eds.), *Classics in the Theory of Public Finance*. New York: St. James's Press, 168–176.

Mailath, G. and A. Postlewaite (1990). "Asymmetric Information Bargaining Problems with Many Agents." *Review of Economic Studies* 57: 351–367.

Muench, T. (1972)."The Core and the Lindahl Equilibrium of an Economy with a Public Good: An Example." *Journal of Economic Theory* 4(2): 241–255.

Samuelson, P. (1954). "The Theory of Public Expenditure." *Review of Economic Studies* 36: 387–389.

Thomson, W. (1979). "Comment." In J. J. Laffont (ed.), *Aggregation and Revelation of Preferences*. Amsterdam: North-Holland.Publishing, 420–432.

Vickrey, W. (1961). "Counterspeculation, Auctions, and Competitive Sealed Tenders." *Journal of Finance* 16: 8–37.

Walker, M. (1981). "A Simple Incentive Compatible Scheme for Attaining Lindahl Allocations." *Econometrica* 49: 65–71.

Wicksell, K. (1896). "A New Principle of Just Taxation." In R. Musgrave and A. Peacock (eds.), and J. Buchannan (trans.), *Classics in the Theory of Public Finance*. London: Macmillan, 72–118.

7

Social Welfare and Coercion in Public Finance

Stanley L. Winer, George Tridimas, and Walter Hettich

1. Introduction

In their introductory essay, the editors of this volume analyze a stylized social choice situation to illustrate how coercion inevitably arises in any democratic state. It is useful to begin by recalling that example here: There is a group of people who have come together in a room for a common purpose and who must collectively set the temperature on a thermostat and then pay for the resulting use of energy. Inevitably, some end up too hot or too cold, and even those for whom the temperature is just right are generally unhappy with the balance between what they pay and what they get.[1] Individuals were able to escape the situation only if they moved out of the building. However, if they stayed, they had to put up with the coercion implied by their assent to the collective decision.

The example embodies several essential aspects of coercion in the public economy. Although we shall only deal with one of these in this essay, it is useful to review all of them briefly to provide a broader context for our discussion. Individuals will voluntarily participate in a collectivity despite its coercive nature if joining makes them better off. This suggests a first focus, namely the analysis of why communities form, under what circumstances people will join or leave them, and the nature and determinants of coercion that may persist in the equilibria of different types of societies. A separate body of work has developed on this topic, including the essays in the first part of this volume.[2] A second focus deals with the choice of decision

---

[1] If Lindahl pricing was feasible and implemented, at *given* tax prices everyone would vote for the same setting on the thermostat (or level of the public good). Disagreement over the setting of tax prices may remain however.

[2] See also Hirschman (1970), Skaperdas (1992), Usher (1993), and Alesina and Spolaore (2003).

rules once a community has been formed. Here the classic work in a public finance context is by Wicksell (1896) and Lindahl (1919). As pointed out in the editors' introductory essay, Wicksell's proposal for approximate unanimity stems from his desire to minimize coercion exercised via the public finances for members of a community while providing for their welfare. The mechanism design literature discussed in the previous essay by John Ledyard extensively studied the question of the existence under various conditions of the Wicksell-Lindahl solution, in which marginal tax prices are equal to individual marginal evaluations of the public good that is provided at its Pareto efficient level.

Buchanan and Tullock (1962) made a further contribution to this line of work by adding efficiency as a criterion in the choice of the decision rule and by considering the trade-off between decision costs and coercion associated with alternative rules, while Breton (1996) examined the relationship between coercion and budgetary institutions. One should note, however, that these authors did not provide a definition of coercion that could serve as a basis for welfare comparisons among different fiscal systems or institutional forms of government.

After collective decision rules have been put in place, participants in any community are inevitably faced with coercion arising from policies chosen in an externally fixed decision framework. This third aspect of coercion, which has received the least attention in the public finance literature so far, is the major focus of this essay. One should note that in contrast to the previous essay, we assume that exit from the community is not a viable option.

The usual approach in such a context has been to assume the existence of a planner who chooses public outputs and imposes taxes so as to maximize a social welfare function. In the preceding example, he or she would set the temperature in the room and fix tax rates for all the participants under the assumptions that there is agreement on the nature of the welfare function to be optimized and that there is sufficient information to do so. Although the analysis of specific policies, such as taxation, in the social welfare tradition has been extensive and highly successful, the existing literature has not so far dealt with the measurement and evaluation of coercion implicit in the possible actions of a planner.

In this essay, we examine the nature and measurement of coercion in a planning context by focusing on the extent to which individuals are unhappy with the balance between what they pay in taxes and what they get from the public sector. In Section 2 we ask whether and how such coercion can be formally defined, why it is different from redistribution, and how it can be explicitly taken into account in the design of social plans by incorporating specially designed constraints into the planner's problem. We then proceed in Section 3 to reexamine the well-known problem of linear income taxation with a public good if coercion constraints are imposed.

A special concern of fiscal analysis is the trade-off between social objectives. Introduction of coercion constraints allows us to formally explore the implications for social welfare of varying the degree of coercion in policy design. We pursue this topic in Section 4 by considering the trade-off between social welfare and coercion, both in a general framework and in a more restricted model in which a trade-off curve is explicitly constructed. Here the degree of coercion implied by traditional social planning is calculated.

Although the essay emphasizes policy analysis in a planning framework, it is important to realize that the use of coercion constraints also has applications in alternative institutional settings. Accordingly, in Section 4 we also compare a social plan with the outcome of a competitive electoral system by locating both on the same welfare-coercion trade-off curve. The analysis provides conditions under which electoral competition may lead society to a position on the downward sloping part of the trade-off, where social welfare is lower and the degree of coercion is higher than in the corresponding (coercion-unconstrained) social plan.

1.1. Intellectual Antecedents

Because the combination of social planning and a concern with coercion is unusual, it will be useful to consider the underlying ideas and literature somewhat further before beginning the formal analysis. In this regard, it should be noted that the design and implementation of constraints on the state has a long and distinguished history (see, for example, Gordon 1999 and Riker 1982). A concern with coercion has often arisen in the analysis of collective choice because individuals do not usually agree on the nature of the social objectives to be sought.

For this reason at least, participation in communal affairs is often predicated on the preservation of rights that limit the scope of collective action. Concern with coercion also arises because of the desire to cope with the agency of politicians, bureaucrats, or the military and because of the possibility that some groups of citizens may coerce (or take advantage of) others using the collective choice process even in the absence of agency control problems. In this essay, we accept the premise that constraints on the ability of a collectivity to coerce individual citizens are desirable and explore how such constraints *ought to* influence the structure of the public finances.

A precursor to such an inquiry in public finance can be found in the work of Simons (1938), who was concerned with establishing tax rules that limit interference in the lives of citizens and the private economy while also serving distributional ends. Buchanan and Congleton (1998, chapter 8) have more recently developed this approach further, calling for imposition of a very simple proportional tax system without a demogrant as a way to limit possible coercion. However, these authors do not provide a measure of the coercion implied by their proposals.

One should note that coercion can also be imposed in ways other than through the balance between what citizens get and what they pay in taxes, including, for example, through public administration (Alm, McClelland, and Schulze 1992), conscription (Levy 1997), regulation of access to and limitation of the scope of private markets (Wiseman 1989), as well as through the legal system (Anderson 2006, Leiser 2008). In this essay, we set administration and other non-fiscal dimensions of public policy aside and confine the analysis to coercion arising from the balance between collectively provided goods, services or transfers received, and taxes paid.

We realize that imposing constraints on a planner derived from a concern with coercion extends the analysis beyond criteria generally accepted in the planning literature. It also takes us outside of traditional public choice analysis. There have been other attempts to explicitly link collective choice concerns with the planning approach to policy analysis by imposing appropriate constraints. Acemoglu, Golosov, and Tsyvinski (2008) have explored the nature of optimal fiscal policy rules when one acknowledges the existence of incentive compatibility constraints of politicians.[3] Here we deal with a different aspect of normative political economy: coercion of some citizens by others exercised through collective choice and public policy – a problem that would arise even if somehow agency problems were absent.

The approach we take to acknowledging the importance of coercion in public finance differs from that of mechanism design in an interesting and important manner. A mechanism design approach, such as that employed

---

[3] They argue that optimal policy then requires the distortionary taxation of both capital and labor to reduce the amount of rents that need to be paid to the politician. One may note here that incentive compatibility constraints are themselves dependent on the nature of threats and force that is permitted in society, an issue taken up by the editors in their introductory essay. They are not given entirely by the state of nature. What is known about individual politicians or taxpayers depends on the range of actions that may be legitimately applied in uncovering individual characteristics and in preventing socially undesirable behavior. See also Acemoglu and Robinson (2013) who argue for generally taking conflicts between economic and political forces into account in the design of public policy.

by John Ledyard in the previous essay, starts with imposition of voluntary participation constraints for individuals, thus, requiring that people voluntarily assent to the fiscal conditions they are faced with, because they always have the option of leaving the community. However, many people do not want to leave, often because it is costly to do so, and may still object to coercive arrangements. What is at stake in this essay, then, is the nature of the community when citizens are committed for whatever reason to staying at "home."

In an earlier contribution that implicitly acknowledges the coercive aspects of collective fiscal choices, Boadway (2002) proposes to break the formulation of optimal policy into four stages: constitutional, legislative, implementation, and market response. At each step the analyst takes the results of previous stages, which will include aspects of collective choice, as given in the design of a social plan. The approach in this essay is consistent with such a framework, but it goes further by explicitly incorporating coercion constraints into an analysis that could be used at any relevant stage.

2. A Formal Definition of Coercion in Public Finance

We shall define coercion for an individual as the difference between this person's utility under what he or she regards as *appropriate* treatment by the public sector and the utility that he or she actually enjoys as a result of its operation. To make this definition concrete, it is necessary to explain what appropriate treatment means. In the public finance setting, there are two polar approaches to this issue, each corresponding to a particular view of the relationship between the individual and the state.[4] The one we shall emphasize is what we shall call the *individual-in-society* definition in which, in terms of our original example, the individual citizen remains in the room submitting to, but critically judging, the outcome of the collective choice process.[5]

Formally, let the individual's actual tax share be $\tau_j = \frac{T_j}{PG}$, where T_j is his or her total tax payment, with $T_j = t_j Y_j$ where t_j is the income tax rate and

---

[4] Buchanan (1968, 145–146) stresses the importance of the nature of the social situation in doing public finance.

[5] Hart (1961) argues, as we see it, that to accept coercion as a result of a collective choice process, the individual must be assured that law-abiding citizens in society will not be taken advantage of. Or, in other words, that the situation must involve the threat of legal sanction backed by force to deal with possible tax evasion. The individual-in-society definition of coercion we shall use and that in the legal tradition may thus be seen as having a common basis. On coercion in the legal tradition, see also Anderson (2006).

Y_j is income, and P is the (assumed) constant supply price of the public good G, and assume, as in Buchanan (1968) and Breton (1974, 1996), that the individual believes he would pay this tax share if quantity adjustment were possible. Let V_j be the actual indirect utility of individual j, and V_j^* his maximum utility when he is free to choose the level of the public good G_j^* at the individual tax price $\tau_j P$. Then in the individual-in-society approach, an individual's coercion is defined as

$$[V_j^*(G_j^*, W_j, \tau_j P) - V_j], \quad \text{where} \quad G_j^* = \arg\max_{\{G\}} V_j(G, W_j, \tau_j P) \quad (1)$$

where W_j is the person's wage or ability. This definition is implicit in the work of Buchanan (1968) and Breton (1974, 1996).[6] In a private competitive market, an individual takes price as given, and quantity adjusts so that he or she is always satisfied with what he or she pays for. The definition in (1) is motivated by this private market analogue. Here, the individual accepts that the tax price is determined by collective choice and would like to, but cannot, quantity adjust.[7]

It should be noted that the definition in (1) implies that, in general, the amount of coercion is simultaneously determined along with the parameters of the fiscal system. This holds whenever the extent of coercion is taken into account in deciding on the fiscal system and its implied tax prices, unless the counterfactual is specified independently of contemporaneous policy choices.

Figure 7.1 illustrates the individual-in-society definition. Here indifference curves in the (t, G) space are constructed from the individual utility function $U = U(X, G)$ where X is the sole private good, and G is the actual level of public good, and the individual budget constraint is $X = Y(1 - t)$ with t the actual proportional tax rate levied on this citizen.[8] Then, the slope of the indifference curves in (t, G) space is $dt/dG = \left(\frac{\partial U}{\partial G} / \frac{\partial U}{\partial X}\right) / Y = (MRS_{GX}/Y) > 0$. Given his tax share τ_j the price

---

[6] Breton (1974) defines coercion as depending on the deviation of marginal evaluations of public services from tax prices. Although the total amount of coercion defined in (1) varies with this difference, it is not coercion itself.

[7] One might also fix the level of the public good and then ask what tax price the individual would like to pay, as is perhaps suggested by Lindahl's (1919) analysis. We rely on the private market analogue in this essay. Sehili and Martinez-Vazquez use Lindahl's approach in the next essay.

[8] With a proportional tax (a linear income tax with no lump sum component), the point (t, G) must lie on the dotted tax-share line. With a demogrant, the relationship between the tax rate and the individual tax share is more complicated.

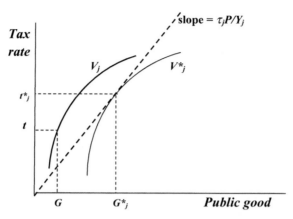

Figure 7.1. Coercion using the individual-in-society counterfactual.

Legend:

t : actual tax rate paid

$t_j^* = G_j^*(\tau_j P / Y_j)$: the implied income tax rate tax at which the *individual-in-society* is assumed to be able to quantity adjust the level of the public good, given his tax share τ_j, the price of the public good P and income Y_j

G: actual level of the public good

G_j^*: level of the public good that the individual would like the community to provide at his given tax price

V_j^*: maximum desired utility at the individual's given tax price if that person could quantity adjust the level of the public good

$V_j^* - V_j$: coercion when the individual-in-society counterfactual is adopted

of the public good P and income Y_j, the individual would like G_j^* rather than G at an implied tax rate of $t_j^* = G_j^*(\tau_j P / Y_j)$ Coercion (1) is shown as the resulting difference in utility between the counterfactual and actual situations, $[V_j^* - V_j]$.

There is an alternative definition of coercion based on a counterfactual that is a polar opposite to the individual-in-society approach illustrated in the figure. One could think of individuals as judging social outcomes from a perspective in which they alone decide what is best for them *and* for others. In this individual-as-dictator approach (not shown in Figure 7.1), the counterfactual utility would be determined by maximizing the person's indirect utility subject to the government budget restraint that shows all feasible combinations of tax rates and actual public good levels. Because the counterfactual then involves a choice directly from the government budget constraint, there is never any simultaneity between the counterfactual and the actual operation of the public sector. In effect, then, as can be seen by looking at the optimization problems introduced later, the problem simplifies to optimizing social welfare with different weights on certain individuals.

The individual-as-dictator approach is more appropriate in studying situations in which individuals consider whether to join a group rather than for the third aspect of the coercion problem in which a community is already assumed to have formed. Moreover, it is interesting to confront the role of the counterfactual level of welfare in the definition of coercion throughout the analysis. For these reasons, we comment only briefly on the implications of adopting the individual-as-dictator approach in what follows.

2.1. Coercion Versus Redistribution by a Social Planner

To understand the definition of coercion in (1), it is helpful to ask at this point why standard social planning does not take it into account, even though the difference between benefits and costs of public provision for each individual is reflected in individual indirect utilities and, therefore, in the social objective. The reason lies in the fact that the social planning approach posits no limits on the loss or gain in utility for particular individuals or groups occurring as part of a social plan. Any amount of redistribution required in the course of maximizing social welfare is implicitly regarded as acceptable – that is, as a matter of social solidarity with the planner's objective, regardless of the degree of coercion implied. (We shall return to the difference between coercion-constrained and socially optimal redistribution in Section 4, where a coercion-constrained social planner's optimization problem is formally compared to a traditional plan.)

It might be argued that application of the Pareto criterion – that only reallocations leaving every one better off are permissible – can attenuate concern with coercion. Strict application of the Pareto criterion limits the degree of individual coercion for moves from the status quo. It does not, however, alleviate any mismatch between benefits received and taxes paid that is embedded in the status quo itself. Moreover, much applied work using social welfare analysis goes beyond the strict Pareto criterion, which is too weak to allow for most social action, using the Kaldor-Hicks-Scitovsky potential compensation criterion instead. In that case, reallocations are considered desirable even if some people become worse off, as long as gainers could *in principle* more than compensate losers. For this reason, an explicit concern with coercion is justified and needed in most practical instances.

To see in general terms that coercion in public life is widely viewed as distinct from income redistribution, it is also instructive to consider the Bill of Rights in the United States and similar documents or unwritten constitutional rules in other countries. The rights afforded by these documents are intended to apply equally to the poor and rich; they were not created with reference to income levels but rather with reference to individual lives. There may, of course, be an interaction of redistribution as traditionally defined and coercion, but this only reinforces the insight that redistribution is not the sole origin of coercion.[9] A similar point is emphasized by Wicksell (1896), who reminds us that an imperfect correspondence between what people pay in taxes and what they receive in a democratic society providing public services and collecting taxes differs from voluntary redistribution and should be a cause for concern.[10]

2.2. Using Constraints to Model the Role of Coercion

To develop a normative approach that allows us to compare and evaluate specific fiscal policies and electoral mechanisms in terms of the coercion and welfare they imply, we shall proceed by imposing coercion constraints on maximization of social welfare as usually defined. The use of constraints in this way may be defended on both conceptual and practical grounds.

We have already noted the long history of attempts to limit the power of politicians and coercion of some citizens by others through the fiscal system. The most important way in which limits on such activities have been introduced into political arrangements is by written or unwritten

---

[9] In an interesting paper complementary to the current one – the perspective is that of the first issue identified earlier – Perroni and Scharf (2003) develop a positive theory of the self-enforcing fiscal system. The problem they begin with is that there is no external power to enforce the power to tax so that ultimately, in their view, all fiscal systems must be self-enforcing equilibria in which the continual consent of the public is sought. They search for efficient, self-enforcing equilibria that are robust to renegotiation among groups of citizens. As a consequence, they claim (result 4) that when citizens have identical preferences, efficiency and renegotiation proofness requires horizontal equity in taxation. However, as they explicitly state, this is "fully unrelated to any distributional goal" (p. 9). Rather, in their approach, it is a matter of ensuring the stability and viability of society as a whole.

[10] "From the point of view of general solidarity . . . parties and social classes should . . . share an expense from which they receive no great or direct benefit. Give and take is a firm foundation of lasting friendship. . . . It is quite a different matter, however, to be forced so to contribute" Wicksell (1896/1958, 90).

constitutional provisions restricting the power of government to abridge individual rights. Such provisions do not in principle allow for a trade-off between the rights that are given and other policy objectives. They may, of course, be subject to interpretation by the courts but always with the understanding that the rights take precedence over other public aims. The setting of boundaries or constraints on public action thus represents a well-known and tested approach to dealing with coercion in public life.

A strict welfarist might argue that if it matters to an individual that he is being coerced, then this should be reflected in his or her utility function. And if it is, then social welfare maximization will take this concern into account. However, introducing coercion into a utility function is obviously a shorthand for a complicated social situation.[11] It is hardly clear that this is the best way to proceed, even if using constraints appears to involve the introduction of a non-welfarist criterion.

Consider an analogy to modeling the social role of money. Macroeconomists have tried to come to grips with the role of money in society either by putting money into the utility function following Patinkin (1965) – an obvious approximation to the complex social role of money – or by adding constraints to the specification of the economy while continuing to model individual economic agents in a more or less traditional fashion (e.g., the cash-in-advance constraints of Clower 1967). Our approach is analogous to the second method. We add coercion constraints to a planning problem to incorporate an important aspect of collective choice in a simple and (we think) revealing manner. Although justification on the basis of the way in which boundaries on collective action are actually set seems to us sound, to an extent the approach we develop also reflects our judgment that it is a useful way to proceed in an important area of research in which little progress has so far been made. Our investigation remains essentially welfarist in intention, although in a broader context where a concern with limits on the degree of coercion is regarded as important for the social welfare of the community.[12]

Before we can specify the coercion constraints that are to be imposed on the planner, there are two additional matters to consider. First, there is the issue of whether we apply coercion constraints at the level of each individual, as implied by the use of the subscripts in definition (1), or at a

---

[11] The same is true if coercion is put into the welfare function but outside of individual utilities.

[12] See Kaplow (2008) for an extensive comparison of the Pareto principle and criteria that formally depart from standard social welfare maximization, but which may nonetheless serve welfarist ends.

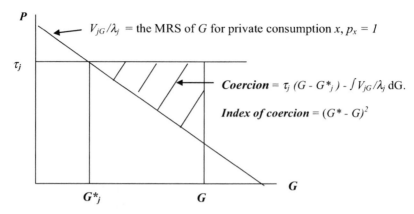

Figure 7.2. Coercion measured by the level of the public good.

group level. Although applying constraints to each individual is consistent with the tradition initiated by Wicksell, we also want to explore an approach that allows for stronger policy judgments and a greater degree of coercion. Although there is not a complete parallel, defining coercion over a group of individuals is similar to the use of the Kaldor-Hicks-Scitovsky (KHS) potential compensation criterion. In what follows, we mainly employ a constraint on aggregate coercion (its sum across individuals), which is analogous to the application of the KHS criterion. The corresponding analysis with individual constraints is provided in an Appendix.

Second, because the simultaneity of coercion and the actual (or planned) operation of the public sector can lead to considerable mathematical complexity, it proves useful for working out examples to approximate coercion by using levels of the public good – a method that follows Buchanan and Breton. The argument is illustrated in Figure 7.2. Because the marginal evaluation of the public good declines with the size of the public sector, the difference in utility in (1) is monotonically related to the difference between the level of the public good in the counterfactual and that provided by the operation of the public sector, $(G^* - G)$. To allow for cases in which the difference between G and G^* is sometimes negative and sometimes positive, we may use the square of the difference in public good levels as an index of coercion.[13] Thus, people who want less of the public good in the

---

[13] It should be noted that it may be the case that only one of these two types of individuals will arise in a fiscal system. The reason is that coercion depends on what individuals *think* is appropriate treatment *for themselves*, not what is actually feasible for society as a whole.

Table 7.1. *Alternative coercion constraints based on the individual-in-society definition of coercion*

Counterfactual or its proxy used in the definition	Type of coercion constraint	
	Individual ($j = 1 \ldots N$)	Aggregate
Utility if the individual could adjust the level of the public good at the prevailing tax-price	Case 1: $(V_j^* - V_j) \leq K_j$	Case 2: $\sum_j (V_j^* - V_j) \leq K$
Desired level of the public good given the prevailing tax-price	Case 3: $(G_j^* - G)^2 \leq K_j$	Case 4: $\sum_j (G_j^* - G)^2 \leq K$

Legend:

G_j^*: level of the public good that the individual would like the community to provide at his given tax price

G: actual level of the public good provided

K_j: the degree of coercion for citizen j. We note that the Greek word for coercion is *katanagasmos*

K: (unsubscripted) an aggregate level of coercion

V_j^*: maximum desired utility at the individual's given tax price if that person could adjust the level of the public good

V_j: actual level of utility

counterfactual (illustrated in Figure 7.2) are treated symmetrically with those who would like more. This is so because in either case, the actual utility at given tax prices must be less than what it would be in the individual's preferred counterfactual.

The different ways of specifying coercion constraints that have been pointed to are conveniently summarized in Table 7.1, in which we use K_j to denote the "degree" of coercion applied to individual j (and, later, κ for the associated shadow price) because the Greek word for coercion is *katanagasmos*. The constraints are specified in the table as inequalities, although in the following analysis we assume for mathematical convenience that coercion is applied up to the maximum allowed, so that in practice we deal only with equalities.

In specifying how coercion will enter the analysis, in addition to coercion constraints one may want to acknowledge that coercion may serve as a method of reducing the costs of policy actions, such as that associated with the excess burden of taxation, thus having a productive as well as a harmful social role. We do not incorporate this possibility into the analysis. Excess burdens are defined in the usual manner, independently of the degree of coercion.[14] The emphasis here is on defining coercion arising from the collective provision and financing of public goods and services, on investigating how limits to such coercion *ought* to alter the structure of optimal policy, and on comparing the degree of coercion implied by optimal policy with coercion that results from a collective choice process.

3. Coercion-Constrained Optimal Linear Income Taxation with a Public Good

Having offered a formal definition of coercion, we can now show how the introduction of coercion constraints alters the welfare analysis of a fiscal system in which a pure public good is financed with a linear income tax of the form $T_j = t Y_j - a$.[15] We choose this application because it permits easy comparison with accepted results in the literature.

This investigation differs from that of earlier pioneers Simons (1938) and Buchanan and Congleton (1998). In one sense it is less general: they derive the nature of a fiscal system they regard as most efficient given the satisfaction of their concern to limit coercion. This is the genesis of Simons's advocacy of the broad base income tax, which by its breadth prevents governments from "dipping into great incomes with a sieve." By starting with a fiscal system of a particular type, we cannot replicate this sort of investigation. On the other hand, we shall be able to proceed with greater analytical depth with regard to the definition of coercion and its role in determining parameters of the fiscal system, allowing careful comparison of the coercion-constrained system with the traditional social plan as well as an investigation of the trade-off between coercion and social welfare.

Assume then that there are N individuals indexed by j, each maximizing utility defined over a private good X_j, leisure L_j, and a public good G and receiving a fixed wage W_j. The individual's optimization problem is

$$\text{Max } U_j = U_j(X_j, L_j, G) \quad \text{subject to} \quad X_j = (1 - t) W_j(1 - L_j) + a;$$
$$j = 1, \ldots N \qquad (2)$$

---

[14] For example, we do not explicitly allow the planner to force independent evaluations of ability on taxpayers, or to coercively uncover economic activity, thereby relaxing incentive compatibility constraints.

[15] Here neither the tax rate t nor the lump sum component a varies across individuals, thus providing a simple way of introducing the excess burden of taxation while also ruling out a Lindahl voluntary exchange equilibrium in which taxes are raised without any welfare loss. With $a = 0$ the tax is proportional to income, with $a > 0$ it is progressive, and with $a < 0$ regressive. For comparability with the literature, we follow Sandmo's (1998) notation.

where, in addition to previous definitions, H_j is the supply of labor, with $L_j + H_j = 1$.[16]

To establish the counterfactual, we consider the individual when he is free to choose the level of the public good G_j, given his (average) tax share τ_j, which is assumed by the individual to be constant with respect to the level of the public good. This tax share is given by the ratio of the tax paid by j to total tax revenue: $\tau_j = T_j / \Sigma_j T_j$. We note for later use that with the linear tax system this tax share is

$$\tau_j = \frac{t Y_j - a}{t \Sigma_j Y_j - Na}. \tag{3}$$

Because the marginal cost of the public good P is constant, the actual tax price per unit of G, $\tau_j P$ is also the one that applies to marginal changes in public services when viewed from the perspective of each individual. The individual's optimization problem we can use to define his or her counterfactual then can be stated as

$$\text{Max } U_j = U_j(X_j, L_j, G_j) \quad \text{subject to} \quad X_j + \tau_j PG_j = W_j(1 - L_j). \tag{4}$$

Solving the first order conditions, $U_{jX} = \lambda_j^*$, $U_{jL} = \lambda_j^* W_j$ and $U_{jG} = \lambda_j^* \tau_j P$, yields the *counterfactual* indirect utility V_j^* in (1), where the (*) reflects the fact that the individual is considered to be choosing his most preferred level of G at the *given* tax price.

3.1. Social Welfare Maximization under an Aggregate Coercion Constraint

In choosing fiscal policy instruments, the coercion-constrained planner chooses G, t, and a to solve the problem of maximizing social welfare subject to a budget restraint:

$$\text{Max } S = \sum_j V_j \quad \text{subject to} \quad t \sum_j W_j H_j - Na = PG. \tag{5}$$

In addition, the planner faces one or more coercion constraints. In this respect, for simplicity we consider case 2 in Table 7.1, in which coercion is

---

[16] To help the reader follow later derivations, we note here that solving this problem yields the usual condition $U_{jL}/U_{jX} = (1 - t)W_j$, the final demand for the private good $X_j = X_j[(1 - t)W_j, a, G]$, the labor supply $H_j = H_j[(1 - t)W_j, a, G]$, and the indirect utility function $V_j = V_j[(1 - t)W_j, a, G]$. Denoting the marginal utility of income by λ_j, the partial derivatives of utility with respect to the fiscal variables for person j are $V_{jt} = -\lambda_j Y_j$, with $Y_j = W_j(1 - L_j)$; $V_{ja} = \lambda_j$ and $V_{jG} = U_{jG}$, and the marginal willingness to pay for the public good is $m_j = U_{jG}/U_{jX} = V_{jG}/\lambda_j$.

defined using utility levels and aggregated across individuals. As we have
already pointed out, this case is analogous to the use of the Kaldor-Hicks-
Scitovsky criterion in cost-benefit analysis. The corresponding Lagrangean
for the constrained social planning problem is

$$L = \sum_j V_j + \mu \left[t \sum_j W_j H_j - Na - PG \right] + \kappa \left[K - \sum_j (V_j^* - V_j) \right] \quad (6)$$

In solving this problem, V_j^* and the shadow price of coercion κ are
determined simultaneously along with policy instruments, so the coercion
constraint cannot be simply collapsed into a part (V_j) that can be added to
the social welfare function and a remainder that is constant and so can be
ignored. In other words, as we pointed out earlier, acknowledging coercion
does not amount to simply placing added weight on the utility of some
individuals in a social plan. The reason is that a concern with coercion
requires that weight be given to the *counterfactual* level of utility for each
individual V_j^*.[17]

By the envelope theorem, the shadow price of coercion κ is equal to
dS^*/dK, where the star denotes an optimal value. Social welfare will reach
its maximum when this derivative is zero, at a corresponding and generally
non-zero level of aggregate coercion K (to be derived in the next section
for a particular case). Welfare will then be equal to what it would be in the
unconstrained or traditional social plan. Accordingly, we may say that when
the shadow price is high, there will be a large payoff (in terms of social welfare) from solidarity with the aims of the unconstrained social planner. We
shall consider the shadow price of coercion further in what follows, noting
at this point only that the formulation of the coercion constraint in (6) does
not ensure that it will always be positive, because K may exceed the level of
coercion that is consistent with the traditional social welfare optimum.

Using the definition of V_j^*, we have the first order conditions for the
coercion – constrained planner's problem:

$$(1 + \kappa) \sum_j \lambda_j W_j H_j$$

$$= \mu \left[\sum_j W_j H_j + t \sum_j W_j \left(\frac{\partial H_j}{\partial t} \right) \right] + \kappa \sum_j \lambda_j^* P G_j^* \left(\frac{\partial \tau_j}{\partial t} \right) \quad (7.1)$$

---

[17] One may also note that if there is only one person, or if everyone is identical, there will
be no difference between V^* and V at an optimum, and any coercion constraint will be
irrelevant. Coercion as defined here has no meaning in a single agent planning model.

$$(1 + \kappa) \sum_j \lambda_j = \mu \left[N - t \sum_j W_j \left(\frac{\partial H_j}{\partial a} \right) \right] - \kappa \sum_j \lambda_j^* PG_j^* \left(\frac{\partial \tau_j}{\partial a} \right)$$

(7.2)

$$(1 + \kappa) \sum_j \lambda_j m_j = \mu \left[P - t \sum_j W_j \left(\frac{\partial H_j}{\partial G} \right) \right]$$ (7.3)

where m_j is the marginal rate of substitution between public and private goods for person j, and λ_j is his or her marginal utility of money. These equations feature two important new elements that are absent from traditional optimal taxation but that are always present in the analysis of coercion:

1. the translation of tax structure into the tax price – appearing earlier as $\left(\frac{\partial \tau_j}{\partial t} \right)$ and $\left(\frac{\partial \tau_j}{\partial a} \right)$; and
2. the translation of the tax price into welfare via the demand for G – shown as $\lambda_j^* PG_j^*$

To explore the implications of these equations for fiscal structure, we first use them to characterize optimal coercion-constrained policy in a general manner. We begin with (7.3), which characterizes the coercion-constrained size of government. Define the covariance between the λ_j and m_j by $\sigma_{\lambda m}^2 = (\Sigma_j \lambda_j m_j / N) - (\Sigma_j \lambda_j / N)(\Sigma_j m_j / N)$. Also define the means $\lambda = \Sigma_j \lambda_j / N$ and $m = \Sigma_j m_j / N$, and the normalized covariance between λ_j and m_j, $\delta = \sigma_{\lambda m}^2 / \lambda m$. The latter reflects the distributional characteristics of the public good.

Then substituting these definitions into (7.3) and manipulating yields a characterization of the optimal coercion-constrained level of the public good:

$$(\Sigma_j m_j)(1 + \delta)(1 + \kappa) = \frac{\mu}{\lambda} \left(P - t \Sigma_j W_j \frac{\partial H_j}{\partial G} \right).$$ (8)

Equation (8) is a generalization of the Samuelson condition as amended by Atkinson and Stern (1974) to acknowledge a concern with coercion of some citizens by others through the fiscal system. The right-hand side is the familiar (coercion-unadjusted) social marginal cost of the public good net of the induced revenue effects of public provision on labor supply.[18] The

---

[18] It is equal to the product of the marginal valuation of government revenue, μ/λ and the net (of induced revenue) rate of transformation of the public good, $P - t \Sigma_j W_j (\partial H_j / \partial G)$.

left-hand side represents the social marginal benefit from public provision in the presence of the coercion constraint. The first two terms here are also familiar: the sum of the marginal rates of substitution between private and public goods $\Sigma_j m_j$, and the term $1 + \delta$, which adjusts the marginal rates of substitution for the distributional characteristics of public good. The new term $(1 + \kappa)$ reflects the effect of the coercion constraint and combines with $(1 + \delta)$ to represent the average effect of coercion.

The traditional planning solution in the absence of a coercion constraint is derived by setting $\kappa = 0$ in (8). Comparison of the implications for fiscal structure of (8) with those of the traditional formula is not straightforward however, as the solution depends on the level of coercion as well as on the relationship between K and its shadow price, which is endogenous. We discuss the $\kappa - K$ relationship, the size of government, and the welfare-coercion trade-off in the next section, where an extended example is explored.

Condition (8) also shows that the coercion-adjusted marginal cost of funds (MCF) appropriate for policy analysis is $\mu/[\lambda(1 + \kappa)]$. This coercion-adjusted MCF will tend to be low when κ is high – that is, when increasing K to relax the coercion constraint has a large payoff in terms of social welfare. Again, the traditional formula is derived simply by setting the shadow price to zero. And although comparison with the two formulas is complicated by the endogeneity of κ, it should be noted that the MCF remains relevant in the present context as an analytical concept.

3.2. The Optimal Coercion-Constrained Tax Rate

To derive the optimal income tax rate in the presence of coercion, we proceed as follows.

Multiplying (7.1) by $(1/N)$ and (7.2) by $\left(\sum_j W_j H_j/N^2\right)$, subtracting the latter from the former, and using the Slutsky decomposition, $\partial H_j/\partial t = s_j - W_j H_j(\partial H_j/\partial a)$, yields

$$(1 + \kappa)\sigma_{\lambda Y}^2 = t\left[\frac{\mu}{N}\Sigma_j W_j s_j - \sigma_{Ya}^2\right] + \frac{\kappa}{N}\Sigma_j \lambda_j^* PG_j^*\left(\frac{\partial \tau_j}{\partial t} + \frac{\partial \tau_j}{\partial a}\overline{Y}\right), \quad (9)$$

where $Y_j = H_j W_j$ and the negative covariance $\sigma_{\lambda Y}^2$ shows the relationship between the marginal utility of income and income from work and reflect the distributional effects of income taxation. Covariance $\sigma_{\lambda Y}^2$ is negative because the higher the level of income, the lower the marginal utility. The term $\overline{WS} = \Sigma_j W_j s_j / N$ is the mean substitution effect of taxation on labor supply, which is also negative. The covariance term in (9),

$$\sigma_{Ya}^2 = \frac{1}{N}\left[\Sigma_j W_j \frac{\partial H_j}{\partial t} W_j H_j - \left(\Sigma_j W_j \frac{\partial H_j}{\partial a}\right)\left(\frac{\Sigma_j W_j H_j}{N}\right)\right]$$

shows the relationship between income and the income effect of taxation; it is non-negative when the effect of income on labor supply is small for those with high incomes.

The quantity $q_j \equiv \partial\tau_j/\partial t + (\partial\tau_j/\partial a)\overline{Y}$ in (9) is the change in the tax share of j when the tax rate and the lump-sum transfer both change, where a bar above Y denotes its mean. If we let $\psi_j \equiv V_{j\tau}^* = -\lambda_j^* PG_j^*$, we can write $\Sigma_j \lambda_j^* PG_j^*\left(\frac{\partial\tau_j}{\partial t} + \frac{\partial\tau_j}{\partial a}\overline{Y}\right) = \Sigma_j \psi_j q_j$. Using the covariance formula, the right side of this last expression is $\Sigma_j \psi_j q_j = N\sigma_{\psi q}^2 + N\overline{\psi}\,\overline{q}$, where $\overline{\psi}$ and $\overline{q}$ denote the mean values of ψ_j and q_j, respectively. Here $\sigma_{\psi q}^2$ captures the relationship between the marginal utility of the tax share and the marginal tax share and is an important determinant of how coercion is spread across the community. The value of $\sigma_{\psi q}^2$ depends on the size of the parameters of the utility function and is therefore an empirical matter. If taxpayers who experience a large increase in their tax shares will also experience a significant fall in utility, $\sigma_{\psi q}^2$ will be negative. In addition, by differentiating the tax share we obtain $\Sigma_j \partial\tau_j/\partial t = \Sigma_j \partial\tau_j/\partial a\ \overline{Y} = 0$ and thus $\overline{q} = 0$.[19]

This last result and the definition of $\sigma_{\psi q}^2$ in (9) leads to the coercion-constrained optimal income tax rate:

$$t = \frac{(1+\kappa)\sigma_{\lambda Y}^2 + \kappa\sigma_{\psi q}^2}{\mu(\overline{WS} - \sigma_{\psi q}^2)}. \tag{10}$$

When the shadow price is positive and the $\sigma_{\psi q}^2$ covariance is negative, the optimal rate t rises with κ because the $\sigma_{\lambda Y}^2$ covariance is negative and so is the denominator. That is, the higher is the payoff to solidarity with the aims of the unconstrained social planner, the higher the optimal coercion-constrained income tax rate. However, note that the size of government and of tax rates may still be lower in the constrained situation than in the traditional social plan.[20]

---

[19] To derive this expression, we differentiate τ_j in (3) with respect to t and a and recognize that a change in t and a affects the level of income.

[20] If the *individual-as-dictator* counterfactual had been used to define coercion, the counterfactual utility would no longer depend on the choice of the fiscal system, and the resulting formula for the tax rate would be simpler, omitting the second term in the numerator

By comparing equation (10) with its traditional counterpart, obtained by setting $\kappa = 0$ (which need not be stated explicitly here), one can see that the more general formulation of the optimal tax rate features four new terms in comparison to the standard formula: the shadow price of coercion κ; the covariance $\sigma^2_{\psi q}$ between the marginal utility of the tax share and the marginal tax share; and via $\sigma^2_{\lambda Y}$, the translation of the tax system into tax shares $\partial \tau_j / \partial a$ and the translation of the tax price into welfare via the demand for G, $\lambda^*_j PG^*_j$.

The analogue to conditions (8) and (10) when individual coercion constraints are imposed on the planner is worked out in the Appendix. The solutions are much more complicated, involving also the distributional pattern of coercion as one should expect. It turns out to be the case that in comparison to the Kaldor-Hicks-like situation, government size and tax rates may be larger or smaller when coercion is specified at the individual level.

4. The Trade-Off between Social Welfare and Coercion

The existence of the trade-off in the present framework allows us to explore some of the implications for public finance of the clash of social objectives with individual rights embedded in the coercion constraints. We begin by considering the relationship of the shadow price of coercion and the degree of coercion in the case of the linear income tax and the welfare-coercion trade-off implied by this relationship. In the linear income tax case, maximization of social welfare subject to the government budget and an aggregate coercion constraint involves solving a system of five equations: first order conditions (7.1)–(7.3), the government budget constraint $t \sum_j W_j H_j = Na + PG$, and the coercion constraint $\sum_j (V^*_j - V_j) = K$. The five unknowns are the three fiscal parameters, t, a, and G, and the two Lagrange multipliers, κ and μ. This means that the solution for the shadow price of coercion (along with the rest of the endogenous variables) is a function of the distribution of individual tastes for work, leisure, and consumption, captured by the parameters of the utility function and denoted by $\mathbf{\Gamma}$; the characteristics of the distribution of earning abilities captured by the wage rates and denoted by $\mathbf{W}$; the marginal cost of the public good P; and the level of coercion K.

We may write the implied solution for the shadow price of coercion (as well as that for all other endogenous variables) as $\kappa = \kappa(\mathbf{\Gamma}, \mathbf{W}, P, K)$,

---

of (10). (The general form of the solution for G given by equation (8) is the same with both counterfactuals, although the level of G will differ in each case.)

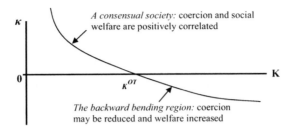

K^{OT} = the degree of aggregate coercion corresponding to the traditional (coercion-unconstrained) social plan

Figure 7.3. A possible relationship between the shadow price of coercion κ and the aggregate degree of coercion K.

and the general solution for coercion-constrained social welfare as $S^* = F(\mathbf{\Gamma}, \mathbf{W}, P, K)$. As noted earlier, these are linked by the envelope theorem $dS^*/dK \equiv \Sigma_j(dV_j/dK) = \kappa$. If κ is positive (negative), coercion-constrained social welfare is rising (falling) with the level of coercion K, and when κ is zero, social welfare is at its maximum and policy instruments will conform to their traditional optimal tax values. $k(\mathbf{\Gamma}, \mathbf{W}, P, K) = 0$ thus defines implicitly the value of $k(K^{OT})$ that is implied by traditional social planning.

Figure 7.3 illustrates one possible relationship between the shadow price and the aggregate degree of coercion. The part of the $\kappa - K$ curve labeled the "consensual society" is where welfare and coercion are positively correlated. This part is where any society that positively values both social welfare and the absence of coercion would like to be. Such a society would not want to be at the point associated with a traditional social plan, where $K = K^{OT}$.

The part of the $\kappa - K$ curve to the right of K^{OT} corresponds to the downward sloping part of the welfare-coercion trade-off, where welfare increases as coercion declines. This part is to be avoided without compensating virtues.

In the example illustrated, the implied trade-off between social welfare and coercion would be concave with its peak at K^{OT}. However, this is a hypothetical relationship. What does the welfare-coercion trade-off look like for the linear income tax case we have explored? This turns out to be a difficult question to answer. As shown in the Appendix, in the linear income tax model with an aggregate coercion constraint, we cannot even sign the slope of the shadow price – coercion relationship, the derivative $d\kappa/dK$, without further assumptions.

In the next section, we provide an explicit derivation of the trade-off between social welfare and the degree of coercion in a more simplified setting. Here we shall also compare the point on the trade-off chosen by a traditional social planner with the outcomes that result from the operation of exogenously determined collective choice processes.

5. The Welfare-Coercion Trade-off in a Simplified Setting

To proceed further, we assume that taxation is strictly proportional to income, utility is Cobb-Douglas, and aggregate coercion is measured using levels of the public good as in case 4 of Table 7.1. The utility function of voter j is defined over private consumption X_j and a public good G; $U_j = \alpha_j \ln X_j + \gamma_j \ln G$, $\alpha_j + \gamma_j = 1$. Income Y_j is assumed to be exogenous, and there are N individuals in the society. Because the tax system is proportional at rate t, for each citizen, $X_j = (1 - t)Y_j$. Normalizing the unit price of the public good to unity, the budget constraint of the government is $t \sum_j Y_j = G$. Aggregate coercion will be defined by the level of the public good, so that the coercion constraint is

$$K = \sum_j \left(G - G_j^* \right)^2, \ j = 1, \dots, N. \tag{11}$$

Because there are only two policy instruments linked by the government budget restraint in the simplified setting, the coercion constraint is sufficient to determine the level of the public good in the coercion-constrained planning problem once the counterfactual, G_j^*, is specified. The latter is determined by maximizing U_j subject to the budget constraint $Y_j = X_j + \tau_j G_j$, where τ_j is the ratio of the tax paid by j to the total tax revenue, $\tau_j = T_j / \sum_j T_j$. With a proportional income tax system, the latter is simply $\tau_j = Y_j / \sum_j Y_j$. Indirect utility of j can then be written as $V_j = (1 - \gamma_j)\ln(1 - (\frac{G_j}{\Sigma_j Y_j})Y_j) + \gamma_j \ln G_j$, and maximization of this with respect to G_j yields

$$G_j^* = \gamma_j \sum_j Y_j. \tag{12}$$

Thus in the simplified model, the counterfactual demand for the public good depends only on the individual taste for the good and total income and is independent of what the planner does.[21]

---

[21] Thus the assumptions of Cobb-Douglas utility, defined over two goods only (with no labor-leisure choice), and exogenous income result in the same counterfactual level of G_j^*. under both the individual-in-society and the individual-as-dictator approaches.

It will be helpful at this point to outline the outcome of coercion-unconstrained or traditional social planning, as a benchmark for what is to follow. This planner chooses G and t to maximize the weighted sum of individual utilities, $S = \sum_j z_j V_j$, $\sum_j z_j = 1$, subject to the government budget restraint. (The introduction of the weights z_j will facilitate later comparison of social planning with collective choice processes.) Using the covariance formula $\sum z\gamma = N(\sigma_{z\gamma}^2 + \bar{z}\bar{\gamma})$, where a bar denotes the mean value of a variable, and exploiting the equality $N\bar{z} = 1$, maximization of welfare S subject (only) to the government budget constraint yields the optimal policy:

$$G^{OT} = \left(\bar{\gamma} + N\sigma_{z\gamma}^2\right)\Sigma Y \quad \text{and} \quad t^{OT} = \bar{\gamma} + N\sigma_{z\gamma}^2. \tag{13}$$

The aggregate degree of coercion associated with this standard fiscal system is not zero. Using G^{OT} in (11) shows that the degree of coercion in traditional social planning is positive and equal to

$$K^{OT} = N(\Sigma Y)^2 \left[\sigma_\gamma^2 + \left(N\sigma_{z\gamma}^2\right)^2\right]. \tag{14}$$

Intuitively, coercion in a social plan rises with the magnitude of demands for the public good, because the welfare losses from departures from preferred counterfactuals are larger then, with heterogeneity of tastes for the public good, because it is harder to satisfy a more heterogeneous community with the same restricted set of policy instruments, and with the covariance between the intensity of preferences for the public good and the weights of individuals in the social welfare function, because the social planner attaches a higher priority to the satisfaction of those with high preference for the public good. (When individuals with intense preference for the public good, high value of γ, enter the social welfare function with a large weight, high value of z, the covariance $\sigma_{z\gamma}^2$ is positive, and so K^{OT} is rising with the latter.)

5.1. The Trade-off

Observing the coercion constraint generally requires that a nonlinear relationship be maintained between aggregate coercion and public sector size. Substituting from (12) into the coercion constraint (11) and using formulas for mean and variance indicates that

$$K = N\left[G^2 - 2\bar{\gamma}(\Sigma Y)G + \left(\sigma_\gamma^2 + \bar{\gamma}\right)(\Sigma Y)^2\right] \tag{15}$$

where implicitly, $dG/dK = 1/2N(G - \overline{\gamma}\Sigma Y)$. Therefore, G increases with K as long as its initial size is greater than $\overline{\gamma}\Sigma Y$, the standard optimal tax value when $\sigma_{z\gamma}^2 = 0$, and it decreases with K when G is less than this value. This is a complicated pattern, showing the difficulty of making comparisons of the fiscal system in a coercion-constrained fiscal system and in a traditional social plan using general formulas like (8) and (10).

To derive coercion-constrained social welfare, S, we substitute G implicitly defined by (15) into the indirect utility functions in S and aggregate across citizens. The result yields the welfare-coercion trade-off. Differentiating S so derived with respect to K, we see that

$$\frac{dS}{dK} = \frac{G^{OT} - G}{2N(G - \overline{\gamma}\Sigma Y)(\Sigma Y - G)G} \quad \text{and} \quad \frac{d^2S}{dK^2}$$

$$= \frac{G\left(G - G^{OT}\right)\left[(1 + \overline{\gamma})\sum Y - 2G\right] + \left(\sum Y - G\right)G^{OT}\left(\overline{\gamma}\sum Y - G\right)}{4N^2 G^2 \left(\sum Y - G\right)^2 \left(G - \overline{\gamma}\sum Y\right)^3}.$$

$$(16)$$

Then, using (13) and the definition of aggregate private consumption, $\sum_j X_j = \sum_j Y_j - G$, shows that[22]

$$\frac{dS}{dK} = 0 \quad \text{and} \quad \frac{d^2S}{dK^2} = \frac{-G^{OT}}{4N^4 G^{OT}\left(\sum X\right)\left(\sigma_{z\gamma}^2\right)^2} < 0.$$

We can conclude that when the standard social plan is employed, welfare reaches its unconstrained maximum and that the trade-off between social welfare and the degree of coercion is globally concave. This concave trade-off is illustrated in Figure 7.4. The upward sloping part of the trade-off corresponds to what we referred to as the "consensual society" in Figure 7.3.

In Figure 7.4, K^{OT} is again the degree of coercion corresponding to social planning. K^{MR} is the degree of coercion corresponding to majority rule in a competitive political system, which we shall analyze shortly. The origin ($K = 0$) is blanked out because the Lindahl solution may not be feasible, and

---

[22] PROOF. Differentiation of $S(K)$ yields $dS/dK = \Sigma z(1 - \gamma)[-1/(\Sigma Y - G)]dG/dK + \Sigma z\gamma(1/G)dG/dK$. Substituting from (15) we have $dS/dK = (\Sigma z\gamma \Sigma Y - \Sigma zG)/2N(G - \overline{\gamma}\Sigma Y)(\Sigma Y - G)G$. Recalling that $G^{OT} = \Sigma z\gamma \Sigma Y$ and using the covariance formula yields the first derivative in (16). Differentiating this with respect to K, we obtain the following expression for the numerator of the second derivative in (16): [numerator d^2S/dK^2] $= [-(dG/dK)(-G^3 + \Sigma Y(1 + \overline{\gamma})G^2 - (\Sigma Y)^2\overline{\gamma}G) - (dG/dK)(-3G^2 + 2\Sigma Y(1 + \overline{\gamma})G - (\Sigma Y)^2\overline{\gamma})(\Sigma Y\Sigma z\gamma - G)]$. Substituting for dG/dK and rearranging then yields the second derivative, QED.

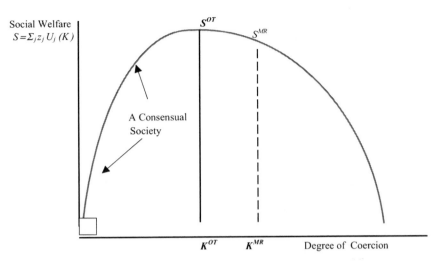

Figure 7.4. The welfare-coercion trade-off.

if so, the planner's coercion-constrained social welfare planning problem is then not defined. (This matter was considered in the previous essay.)

6. Collective Choice Versus Social Planning

The use of coercion constraints represents a general approach of analysis that is also applicable in other settings of fiscal decision making, thus allowing for a new type of comparison among systems for reaching collective choices. To explore this important extension of the approach, we now inquire as to how democracy compares to the traditional social plan in terms of their implied trade-off between welfare and coercion. We shall consider a competitive electoral system in which policy outcomes represent a balancing of the heterogeneous economic interests of citizens, as in a probabilistic spatial voting model. This model is well described in the literature (see, for example, Hettich and Winer 1999, Persson and Tabellini 2000, Tridimas and Winer 2005, Adams, Merrill, and Grofman 2005, and Schofield and Sened 2006) and will be outlined quickly here. Variants of this model can be used to describe equilibria in proportional or majoritarian electoral systems, but we shall retain a more general viewpoint.

There are two expected vote-share-maximizing parties, A and B, whose policy platforms converge in the competitive political equilibrium. Voting behavior of individual citizens differs according to their economic interests including tastes for the public good, as well as according to individual political sensitivities, or propensities to switch support between parties if one of them offers the voter a more preferred fiscal system. Parties are assumed to have the same knowledge of the stochastic distribution of the characteristics of voters.

Whether a voter votes for party A depends on two components: a policy component and a non-policy component. The policy component depends on the indirect utility of the voter (specified earlier) when party A rather than B implements its proposed policy. The non-policy component, or valence, depends on how the voter evaluates the ideology or other personal characteristics of the competing politicians.[23] Formally, voter j supports party A if $V_j(G_A, t_A) > V_j(G_B, t_B) + \rho + s_j$, where V is again indirect utility. The valence term $(\rho + s_j)$ has two components: ρ common to all voters and uniformly distributed on $[-1/2\xi, 1/2\xi]$, and a term s_j, which is an idiosyncratic preference uniformly distributed on $[-(1/2)\zeta_j + h_j, (1/2)\zeta_j + h_j]$.

The expected vote share that party A maximizes by choice of a fiscal system is

$$P_A = \frac{\xi}{\zeta_j} \Sigma_j \left\{ \zeta_j \left[V_j(G_A, t_A) - V_j(G_B, t_B) \right] \right\} + \frac{1}{2} \frac{\xi}{\Sigma_j \zeta_j} \qquad (17)$$

Here, ζ_j represents the voter's political sensitivity – that is, the effect on the probability that he will support party A of a change in his well-being (that results from a proposed change in A's platform.) Analogously, B maximizes $P_B = 1 - P_A$.

Because the parties converge in the Nash electoral equilibrium, to characterize the equilibrium without loss of generality we maximize P_A with respect to G_A and t_A subject to the budget constraint facing any successful party, with G_B and t_B constant, which requires

$$\frac{dP_A}{dG} = \sum_j \zeta_j \frac{dV_j}{dG} = 0.$$

Since utility is Cobb-Douglas, this implies that the political equilibrium values of G and t are

$$G^{MR} = \frac{\Sigma_j \zeta_j \gamma_j}{\Sigma_j \zeta_j} \Sigma_j Y_j \quad \text{and} \quad t^{MR} = \frac{\Sigma_j \zeta_j \gamma_j}{\Sigma_j \zeta_j}$$

---

[23] Adding the stochastic valence term, which has a continuous probability distribution, introduces continuity into the expected vote-share functions of the opposing parties and by so doing eliminates the possibility of a vote cycle. Equilibrium also requires concavity of these objective functions, which here is assured by the form of the utility function.

Denoting the relative political sensitivity of voters j by $\theta_j \equiv \zeta_j / \Sigma_j \zeta_j$, $\Sigma \theta_j = 1$ and using the covariance formula, equilibrium fiscal structure can then be written in a convenient form easily compared to the policy (13) chosen by the unconstrained planner:

$$G^{MR} = \left(\overline{\gamma} + N\sigma_{\theta\gamma}^2 \right) \Sigma Y \quad \text{and} \quad t^{MR} = \overline{\gamma} + N\sigma_{\theta\gamma}^2. \tag{18}$$

The corresponding degree of coercion is

$$K^{MR} = N(\Sigma Y)^2 \left[\sigma_\gamma^2 + \left(N\sigma_{\theta\gamma}^2 \right)^2 \right] \tag{19}$$

That is, similarly to (14), the degree of coercion will be higher with the size of demands for the public good (captured by the level of income), the heterogeneity of tastes for the public good (captured by σ_γ^2), and the covariance between the intensity of preferences for the public good and the political sensitivity of voters ($\sigma_{\theta\gamma}^2$), because voters with high intensity of preference for the public good are politically more influential.

A comparison of planning and democratic political competition shows that

$$K^{MR} - K^{OT} = N^3 \left[\left(\sigma_{\theta\gamma}^2 \right)^2 - \left(\sigma_{z\gamma}^2 \right)^2 \right] (\Sigma Y)^2. \tag{20}$$

If the planner weighs all citizens equally ($\sigma_{z\gamma}^2 = 0$), coercion in the competitive political system will always *exceed* that imposed by the social planner. The essential reason for this is that majority rule introduces fiscal discrimination according to political influence, in addition to that according to narrowly defined individual economic preferences. And, because K^{OT} corresponds to the point of maximum welfare, social welfare in the democracy will be lower, at some point on the backward bending part of the trade-off.

One possibility that this conclusion opens up is that of reducing coercion while raising social welfare, either by imposing additional constraints on the nature of fiscal instruments (as Simons [1938] and Buchanan and Congleton [1998] suggest) or by changing the nature of the collective choice mechanism (as suggested by Wicksell [1896] and many others since).[24] Another possibility is that the constraints on state action imposed by globalization may serve as effective constraints on coercion. However, exactly what each proposed or actual institutional change implies in terms of a

---

[24] On the other hand, if society is on the upward sloping part of the trade-off, additional constraints on public policy of this sort may reduce social welfare along with coercion.

well-defined welfare-coercion trade-off remains to be formally investigated in future research.

7. Conclusion

Although coercion is a central fact in the design and operation of the public sector, normative public economics based on the planning model has not made it an explicit element of the analysis. In this essay, we formally introduce coercion into normative analysis by adding constraints that limit allowable coercion caused by tax and expenditure programs. We focus on situations that arise when citizens experience a mismatch between what they receive in public goods and services and what they pay in taxes. The essay demonstrates that it is possible to conduct formal analysis of the structure of public policy taking coercion into account even without knowing the optimal degree of coercion. In particular, one can delineate the welfare-coercion trade-off and ask what policies are consistent with attainment of the frontier and where particular institutions lead in relation to coercion-unconstrained social planning.

To make the concept of coercion operational, a counterfactual specifying what individuals regard as appropriate treatment by the public sector is required. We have employed a counterfactual that assumes that the individual accepts some coercion by society, along with a socially determined tax price. One may then specify coercion constraints either in terms of individual or aggregate utility or by using a convenient approximation that relies on a reference level of government expenditure. The aggregate definitions are analogous to the use of the Kaldor-Hicks-Scitovsky criterion and impose a less severe constraint on decision making than those having an individual basis.

Coercion constraints have important and complex effects on a social plan. Using both aggregate (KHS-like) and individual coercion constraints, we work out these effects for a fiscal system that uses an optimal linear income tax to provide a public good. These cases were chosen because they permit straightforward comparisons with standard optimal tax results, including the size of government, the pattern of average rate progressivity, and the marginal cost of funds. A novel aspect of the analysis relates to the trade-off between social welfare as traditionally defined and coercion. Using a Cobb-Douglas formulation, we derive a trade-off function, as well as the degree of coercion implied by unconstrained social planning. The analysis allows us to examine how to achieve the highest level of traditionally defined welfare for a given degree of coercion or, in other words, how to be coercion efficient. The trade-off between narrowly defined welfare and aggregate coercion raises the possibility that collective choice in a democracy will tend to lead us to a point on the downward sloping part of the trade-off, opening up the possibility that coercion may be reduced and social welfare increased by appropriate institutional reform.

Extensions of the analysis are possible in several directions. One could, for example, explicitly account for the interaction of incentive compatibility and coercion constraints. Such interaction would occur in situations in which the coercion of individuals in different income groups is relevant to decision making by those who may find it advantageous to mimic the behavior of others. In addition, coercion will have relevance for the structure of the fiscal system. Although we have considered coercion when only an income tax is employed, the analysis could be extended to situations in which a full mix of direct and indirect taxes exists.[25] More generally, the relationship between complexity of tax structures and the coercion-welfare trade-off also deserves investigation. One suspects that more complex fiscal systems, which are also administratively more costly, may involve less coercion for a given level of welfare.[26]

The trade-off analysis can also be used to investigate how coercion can be reduced at given levels of social welfare through institutional means. Work on the scope of the public sector suggests that the boundary between private and public sectors matters in this regard and that the welfare-coercion frontier may be shifted favorably by removing certain types of economic activity from the public sphere. The trade-off function could be used to formalize this argument.

Public goods coercion also has relevance for the discussion of federalism. Following Tiebout (1956), the literature on optimal assignment in federations has been concerned with balancing the welfare gains from decentralization with the loss of efficiency from fiscal externalities that arise under decentralized decision making. One may expect decentralization to reduce coercion, but this connection has not yet been formally acknowledged or

---

[25] See, for example, Boadway and Marchand (1995) on incentive compatibility and public expenditure and Hettich and Winer (1988, 1999) on the formation of tax structure. Compared to the existing literature, a new element in the work on tax structure will be preferences for public goods, because coercion depends in part on such preferences.

[26] Yitzhaki (1979) and Hettich and Winer (1999) have dealt with tax complexity, but not in a framework that explicitly acknowledges coercion.

analyzed in the optimal assignment literature.[27] (The connection between coercion and decentralization is addressed in Chapter 9.)

Finally, the welfare-coercion frontier also allows us to extend the analysis of collective choice in an important way. The concept provides a new basis for comparing political equilibria under alternative institutional arrangements or voting rules and for the ranking of such equilibria with respect to the implied trade-off between welfare and coercion.

APPENDIX

1. Linear Income Taxation with Individual Coercion Constraints

When the planner is constrained by how much he or she can coerce each *individual* taxpayer separately (as in case 1 of Table 7.1), the Lagrangean for the planning problem becomes

$$L = \Sigma_j V_j + \mu[t\Sigma_j W_j H_j - Na - PG] + \Sigma_j \kappa_j [K_j - (V_j^* - V_j)]. \quad (A1)$$

Although the situation is considerably more complex than before, the corresponding first order conditions are generalizations of equations (7) and are not stated here. Working as before, the condition for the optimal coercion-constrained size of government (analogous to condition (8)) becomes[28]

$$\left(\sum_j m_j\right)[(1+\delta)(1+\kappa) + \kappa\phi] = \frac{\mu}{\lambda}\left(P - t\sum_j W_j \frac{\partial H_j}{\partial G}\right) \quad (A2)$$

where in addition to previous definitions, $s_{\kappa\lambda} = \sigma_{\kappa\lambda}^2/\lambda\kappa$ is the covariance between coercion and the marginal utility of income; $s_{\kappa m} = \sigma_{\kappa m}^2/\kappa m$ is

---

[27] For reviews of the literature, see Wildasin (2006) and Wilson (1999). Pennock (1959) analyzed the relationship between majority rule and federalism, arguing that decentralization increases the total number of citizens in a majority coalition. However, although this suggests that decentralization reduces coercion, he did not measure coercion formally nor integrate efficiency into his argument.

[28] To derive (A2), note that the analogue to first order condition (7.3) when coercion constraints apply to individuals is $\sum_j(1+\kappa_j)\lambda_j m_j = \mu[P - t\sum_j W_j(\partial H_j/\partial G)]$. The left-hand side of this can be written as $\sum_j(1+\kappa_j)\lambda_j m_j = \sum_j \lambda_j m_j + \sum_j \kappa_j \lambda_j m_j$. Recall that κ, λ, and m are the means of κ_j, λ_j, and m_j, respectively: $cov(\kappa_j\lambda_j) = (1/N)\sum_j(\lambda_j - \lambda)(m_j - m)$ and $cov(\kappa_j\lambda_j m_j) = (1/N)\sum_j(\kappa_j - \kappa)(\lambda_j - \lambda)(m_j - m)$. Manipulating the covariances and using the new first order condition yields intermediate steps: $\sum_j \lambda_j m_j = N\sigma_{\lambda m}^2 + \lambda\sum_j m_j$ and $\sum_j \kappa_j \lambda_j m_j = [\kappa\lambda\sum_j m_j + N(\kappa\sigma_{\lambda m}^2 + \lambda\sigma_{\kappa m}^2 + m\sigma_{\lambda\kappa}^2 + \sigma_{\kappa\lambda m}^2)$.

the covariance between coercion and the marginal rate of substitution; $s_{\kappa\lambda m} = \sigma^2_{\kappa\lambda m}/\kappa\lambda m$ is the covariance between coercion, the marginal utility of income, and the marginal rate of substitution; and finally, where

$$\phi \equiv s_{k\lambda} + s_{km} + s_{k\lambda m}.$$

The right-hand side of equation (A2) is already familiar. It is the product of the marginal valuation of government revenue times the net marginal rate of transformation of the public good. The left-hand side of (A2) again shows the marginal benefit from the public good. However, now it is the product of the sum of marginal rates of substitution multiplied by the adjustment for the combined effect of the distributional characteristics of the public good *and* the effects of coercion. In the present case of individual coercion constraints, the adjustment for coercion contains two new elements relative to standard social planning, (a) the average effect of coercion $(1 + \delta)(1 + \kappa)$, a term that also appears in the previous case of aggregate coercion, and (b) the term $\kappa\phi$, which corrects the aggregate term for the "distributional characteristics of coercion."

We use the term "the distributional characteristics of coercion" advisedly here, for want of a better one. Because concern with coercion arises out of concern with individual rights or, alternatively, with the degree of social solidarity individuals have with the objectives of the planner, it is not clear that we ought to think about it the same way that we do redistribution in the traditional planning model.

Now the benefit from public provision increases in the following cases, assuming κ is positive: (a) if the rich (low λ_j) view the payoff from solidarity with the planner less favorably (low κ), so that $\sigma^2_{\kappa\lambda} > 0$ and $s_{\kappa\lambda} > 0$; (b) if those who value public goods less (low m_j) "have less social solidarity" (low κ), then $\sigma^2_{\kappa m} > 0$ and $s_{\kappa m} > 0$; and (c) if the rich (low λ_j) also value public goods less (low m_j), so that $\sigma^2_{\kappa\lambda m} > 0$ and $s_{\kappa\lambda m} > 0$, because the previous two effects are compounded.

If all these conditions apply, ϕ is positive. Then, on comparing (8) and (A2), one can also say that the KHS-like solution for a coercion-constrained optimum (8) will involve *less* spending and a lower tax rate than when coercion is defined on an individual basis. However, either of these comparisons could in principle go the other way, and it will be interesting to determine in practice what situation is likely to apply.

To derive the optimal income tax rate under individual coercion constraints, we require additional covariances (normalized again by the means of the indicated variables): $\sigma^2_{\kappa\lambda Y} =$ the covariance of κ_j, λ_j and Y_j; $\sigma^2_{\kappa\psi q} =$ the covariance of κ_j, ψ_j, and q_j; $\sigma^2_{\kappa Y} =$ the covariance of κ_j and Y_j;

$\sigma_{\psi q}^2$ = the covariance of ψ_j and κ_j; $\sigma_{\kappa q}^2$ = the covariance of κ_j; and q_j. Also, let κ, λ, ψ, and q be the mean values of κ_j, λ_j, ψ_j, and q_j, respectively. Then, using these definitions and the Slutsky equation, and working as before, we obtain the formula for the coercion-constrained optimal income tax rate[29]:

$$
t = \frac{(1+\kappa)\,\sigma_{\lambda Y}^2 + \kappa\sigma_{\psi q}^2 + \lambda\sigma_{\kappa Y}^2 + \psi\sigma_{\kappa q}^2 + \sigma_{\kappa\lambda Y}^2 + \sigma_{\kappa\psi q}^2}{\mu\left(\overline{WS} - \sigma_{Ya}^2\right)} \tag{A3}
$$

This optimal income tax rate depends as usual on the income distribution effect of taxation, captured by $\sigma_{\lambda Y}^2$, and the efficiency effect of taxation on labor (shown again by the denominator). In common with the case of aggregate coercion, it also depends on the relationship between the marginal utility of the tax share and the marginal tax share $\sigma_{\psi q}^2$. In addition, the optimal tax rate depends on the distributional effects of coercion, as the remaining four covariance terms make clear. It should be noted that little is presently known about the sign or size of the covariances involved.

2. Derivation of $d\kappa/dK$ in Section 4, Showing that in the Case of Linear Income Taxation and an Aggregate Coercion Constraint, the Sign of This Derivative is Ambiguous

Maximization of the welfare function subject to the government budget and the coercion constraint generate a system of five equations with five unknowns: the three first order conditions (7.1), (7.2), and (7.3), the government budget restraint (5), and the aggregate coercion constraint $\sum_j(V_j^* - V_j) = K$.

Here there are five unknowns: the three fiscal parameters, t, a, and G, and the two Lagrange multipliers, μ (for the budget constraint) and κ (for the coercion constraint). Solving the preceding system gives us the formulas for, t, a, and G that we discuss in the text, as well as the solutions for μ and κ.

As noted in the text, the equilibrium values of the endogenous variables are a function of the distribution of individual tastes for work, leisure,

---

[29] To proceed, one multiplies the analogue to (7.1) for individual constraints by $(1/N)$ and that for (7.2) by $(\sum_j W_j H_j/N^2)$ and subtracts the latter from the former. The left-hand side of the result involves the distributions of three variables: the individual coercion constraint κ_j, the marginal utility of income λ_j, and income Y_j. Similarly, the right-hand side features the individual coercion constraint κ_j, the marginal utility of the tax share $\psi_j = -\lambda_j^* P G_j^*$, and the marginal tax share, $q_j = [(\partial\tau_j/\partial t) + (\partial\tau_j/\partial a)Y]$, as well as the effect of income taxation on labor supply. Applying the definitions of covariances in the text then yields (A3).

and consumption, captured by the parameters of the utility function and denoted by Γ; the characteristics of the distribution of earning abilities captured by the wage rates and denoted by W; the price of the public good P; and the degree of (aggregate) coercion K. We may write the system of reduced-form equations:

$$t = t(\Gamma, W, P, K); \quad a = a(\Gamma, W, P, K); \quad G = G(\Gamma, W, P, K);$$

$$\kappa = \kappa(\Gamma, W, P, K); \quad \mu = \mu(\Gamma, W, P, K). \tag{A4}$$

Using the assumptions of the linear tax model in Section 4, totally differentiating the system of equations (A4), using subscripts to denote derivatives and rearranging gives the following:

$$
\begin{bmatrix}
A_{tt} & A_{ta} & A_{tG} & -\alpha_{t\mu} & \alpha_{t\kappa} \\
B_{at} & B_{aa} & B_{aG} & -\beta_{a\mu} & \beta_{a\kappa} \\
C_{Gt} & C_{at} & C_{GG} & -\gamma_{G\mu} & \gamma_{G\kappa} \\
\alpha_{t\mu} & -\beta_{a\mu} & -\gamma_{G\mu} & 0 & 0 \\
\alpha_{t\kappa} & -\beta_{a\kappa} & -\gamma_{G\kappa} & 0 & 0
\end{bmatrix}
\times
\begin{bmatrix}
dt \\
da \\
dG \\
d\mu \\
d\kappa
\end{bmatrix}
=
\begin{bmatrix}
0 \\
\mu\,dN \\
\mu\,dP + a\,dN \\
G\,dP \\
dK
\end{bmatrix}
\tag{A5}
$$

where:

$$A_{tt} \equiv (1+\kappa)\Sigma(\lambda_t Y + \lambda Y_t) - \mu(2\Sigma Y_t + t\Sigma Y_{tt}) - \kappa\Sigma\lambda^* PG^* \tau_{tt};$$

$$A_{ta} \equiv (1+\kappa)\Sigma(\lambda_a Y + \lambda Y_a) - \mu(\Sigma Y_a + t\Sigma Y_{ta}) - \kappa\Sigma\lambda^* PG^* \tau_{ta};$$

$$A_{tG} \equiv (1+\kappa)\Sigma(\lambda_G Y + \lambda Y_G) - \mu(\Sigma Y_G + t\Sigma Y_{tG});$$

$$\alpha_{t\mu} \equiv \Sigma Y + t\Sigma Y_t; \quad \alpha_{t\kappa} \equiv \Sigma\lambda Y - \Sigma\lambda^* PG^* \tau_t$$

$$B_{at} \equiv (1+\kappa)\Sigma\lambda_t + \mu(\Sigma Y_a + t\Sigma Y_{at}) + \kappa\Sigma\lambda^* PG^* \tau_{at};$$

$$B_{aa} \equiv (1+\kappa)\Sigma\lambda_a + \mu t\Sigma Y_{aa} + \kappa\Sigma\lambda^* PG^* \tau_{aa};$$

$$B_{aG} \equiv (1+\kappa)\Sigma\lambda_G + \mu\Sigma Y_{aG}; \quad \beta_{a\mu} \equiv N - t\Sigma Y_{at};$$

$$\beta_{a\kappa} \equiv \Sigma\lambda + \Sigma\lambda^* PG^* \tau_a$$

$$C_{Gt} \equiv (1+\kappa)\Sigma U_{Gt} + \mu(\Sigma Y_G + t\Sigma Y_{Gt});$$

$$C_{Ga} \equiv (1+\kappa)\Sigma U_{Ga} + \mu t\Sigma Y_{Ga};$$

$$C_{GG} \equiv (1+\kappa)\Sigma U_{GG} + \mu t\Sigma Y_{GG}; \quad \gamma_{G\mu} \equiv P - t\Sigma Y_G; \quad \gamma_{G\kappa} \equiv \Sigma U_G$$

By Cramer's rule, $\dfrac{d\kappa}{dK} = \dfrac{|D|}{|\Omega|}$ where $|D| = \begin{vmatrix} A_{tt} & A_{ta} & A_{tG} & -\alpha_{t\mu} \\ B_{at} & B_{aa} & B_{aG} & -\beta_{a\mu} \\ C_{Gt} & C_{Ga} & C_{GG} & -\gamma_{G\mu} \\ \alpha_{t\mu} & -\beta_{a\mu} & -\gamma_{G\mu} & 0 \end{vmatrix}$

and $|\Omega|$ is the determinant of the matrix of coefficients in (A5). This derivative cannot be signed unambiguously even with the assumptions of the simple linear income tax model, because none of the individual terms in the determinants of D and Ω can be signed without making further assumptions.

References

Acemoglu, Daron, Michael Golosov and Aleh Tsyvinski (2008). "Dynamic Mirrlees Taxation under Political Economy Constraints." Working paper 08–08, February 15. Cambridge, MA: MIT.

Acemoglu, Daron and James A. Robinson (2013). "Economics versus Politics: Pitfalls of Policy Advice." *Journal of Economic Perspectives* 27(2): 173–192.

Adams, J. F., S. Merrill III and B. Grofman. (2005). *A Unified Theory of Party Competition. A Cross-National Analysis Integrating Spatial and Behavioural Factors.* New York: Cambridge University Press.

Alesina, Alberto and Enrico Spolaore (2003). *The Size of Nation.* Cambridge, MA: MIT Press.

Alm, James, Gary H. McClelland and William D. Schulze (1992). "Why Do People Pay Taxes?" *Journal of Public Economics* 48(1): 21–38.

Anderson, Scott (2006). "Coercion. Stanford Encyclopedia of Philosophy." http://plato.stanford.edu/entries/coercion.

Atkinson, Anthony B. and Nicholas H. Stern (1974). "Pigou, Taxation and Public Goods." *Review of Economic Studies* 41: 119–128.

Atkinson, Anthony B. and Joseph E. Stiglitz (1980). *Lectures on Public Economics.* New York: McGraw-Hill.

Becker, Gary (1983). "A Theory of Competition among Pressure Groups for Political Influence." *Quarterly Journal of Economics* 98: 371–400.

Boadway, Robin (2002). "The Role of the Public Choice Considerations in Normative Public Economics." In Stanley L. Winer and Hirofumi Shibata (eds.), *Political Economy and Public Finance.* Cheltenham: Edward Elgar, 47–68.

Boadway, Robin and Maurice Marchand (1995). "The Use of Public Expenditures for Redistributive Purposes." *Oxford Economic Papers,* New Series, 47(1): 45–59.

Breton, Albert (1974). *The Economic Theory of Representative Government.* Chicago: Aldine.

Breton, Albert (1996). *Competitive Governments: An Economic Theory of Politics and Public Finance.* Cambridge: Cambridge University Press.

Buchanan, James M. (1964). "Fiscal Institutions and Efficiency in Collective Outlay." *American Economic Review, Papers and Proceedings* 54(May): 227–235.

Buchanan, James M. (1968). *The Demand and Supply of Public Goods: Chicago.* Chicago: Rand McNally.

Buchanan, James M. and Roger Congleton (1998). *Politics by Principle, Not Interest.* New York: Cambridge University Press.

Buchanan, James M. and Gordon Tullock (1962). *The Calculus of Consent. Logical Foundations of Constitutional Democracy.* Ann Arbor: University of Michigan Press.

Clower, Robert (1967). "A Reconsideration of the Microfoundations of Monetary Theory." *Western Economic Journal* 6: 1–8.

Dalton, Thomas (1977). "Citizen Ignorance and Political Activity." *Public Choice* 32: 85–99.

Escarrez, D. R. (1967). "Wicksell and Lindahl: Theories of Public Expenditure and Tax Justice Reconsidered." *National Tax Journal* 20: 137–148.

Gordon, Scott (1999). *Controlling the State: Constitutionalism from Ancient Athens to Today*. Cambridge, MA: Harvard University Press.

Hart, H. L. A. (1961). *The Concept of Law*. Oxford: Oxford University Press.

Hettich, Walter and Stanley L. Winer (1985). "Blueprints and Pathways: The Shifting Foundations of Tax Reform." *National Tax Journal* 38(4): 423–445.

Hettich, Walter and Stanley L. Winer (1988). "Economic and Political Foundations of Tax Structure." *American Economic Review* 78(4): 701–712.

Hettich, Walter and Stanley L. Winer (1999). *Democratic Choice and Taxation: A Theoretical and Empirical Investigation*. Cambridge, MA: Cambridge University Press.

Hirschman, Albert O. (1970). *Exit, Voice and Loyalty: Responses to Declines in Firms, Organizations and States*. Cambridge, MA: Harvard University Press.

Kaplow, Louis (2008). Pareto Principle and Competing Principles, in Steven Durlauf and Laurence E. Blum (eds.), *The New Palgrave Dictionary of Economics*, 2nd Edition, Vol. 6. Basingstoke: Palgrave Macmillan, 295–300.

Leiser, B. M. (2008). "On Coercion." In D. Reidy and W. Riker (eds.), *Coercion and the State*. Berlin: Springer, 31–43.

Levy, Margaret (1997). *Consent, Dissent, and Patriotism*. Cambridge, MA: Cambridge University Press.

Lindahl, Eric (1919/1958). "Just Taxation. A Positive Solution." In Richard Musgrave and Alan Peacock, *Classics in the Theory of Public Finance*. London: Macmillan, 168–176.

Mirrlees, James A. (1971). "An Exploration in the Theory of Optimum Income Taxation." *Review of Economic Studies* 38: 175–208.

Mueller, Dennis (2003). *Public Choice III*. New York: Cambridge University Press.

Patinkin, Don (1965). *Money, Interest and Prices: An Integration of Monetary and Value Theory*, 2nd edition. New York: Harper and Row.

Pennock, Roland (1959). "Federal and Unitary Government – Disharmony and Frustration." *Behavioral Science* 4: 147–157.

Perroni, Carlo and Kimberley Scharf (2003). "Viable Tax Constitutions." CEPR Working Paper DP 4210. University of Warwick.

Persson, Torsten and Guido, Tabellini (2000). *Political Economics, Explaining Economic Policy*. Cambridge MA: MIT Press.

Ramsey, Frank P. (1927). "A Contribution to the Theory of Taxation." *Economic Journal* 37: 47–61.

Reidy, David A. and Walter J. Riker (eds.) (2008). *Coercion and the State*. Berlin: Springer.

Riker, William H. (1982). *Liberalism Against Populism: A Confrontation Between the Theory of Democracy and the Theory of Social Choice*. San Francisco: W.H. Freeman & Company.

Sandmo, Agnar (1998). "Redistribution and the Marginal Cost of Public Funds." *Journal of Public Economics* 70: 365–382.

Schofield, N., and Itai Sened (2006). *Multiparty Democracy: Parties, Elections and Legislative Politics in Multiparty Systems*. New York: Cambridge University Press.

Simons, Henry C. (1938). *Personal Income Taxation: The Definition of Income as a Problem of Fiscal Policy*. Chicago: University of Chicago Press.

Skaperdas, Stergios (1992). "Cooperation, Conflict, and Power in the Absence of Property Rights." *American Economic Review* 82: 720–739.

Tiebout, Charles (1956). "A Pure Theory of Local Expenditures." *Journal of Political Economy* 64: 416–424.

Tridimas, George and Stanley L. Wine (2005). "The Political Economy of Government Size." *European Journal of Political Economy* 21: 643–666.

Usher, Dan (1993). *The Welfare Economics of Markets, Voting and Predation.* Ann Arbor: University of Michigan Press.

Wicksell, Knut (1896/1958). "A New Principle of Just Taxation." In R. Musgrave and A. Peacock, *Classics in the Theory of Public Finance.* London: Macmillan, 72–118.

Wildasin, David (2006). "Fiscal Competition." In Barry R. Weingast and Donald A. Wittman (eds.), *The Oxford Handbook of Political Economy.* Oxford: Oxford University Press 502–520.

Wilson, John (1999). "Theories of Tax Competition." *National Tax Journal* 52: 269–304.

Wiseman, Jack (1989). *Cost, Choice and Political Economy.* Cheltenham: Edward Elgar.

Yitzhaki, Shlomo (1979). "A Note on Optimum Taxation and Administrative Costs." *American Economic Review* 69: 475–480.

Discussion

The Role of Coercion in Public Economic Theory

Robin Boadway

Coercion is by definition a feature of public economics – that is, the study of the economics of government intervention, from either a normative or positive perspective. Even the so-called minimal-government allocation involves coercion because it involves at a minimum the enforcement of property rights. If those property rights are considered inviolate, so that government policy focuses solely on achieving gains from trade via overcoming the free-rider problem, coercion in a different sense is involved. The gains from trade must be somehow be allocated among persons, and this amounts to a zero-sum game that presumably would not command unanimous consent. If the government, viewed as either planner or political policy maker, is also able to redistribute among persons, coercion is potentially all the more pronounced.

All this begs the questions of what is an appropriate definition of coercion, to what extent it should be considered a criterion or a constraint in evaluating public economic outcomes, and how such a concern should be operationalized. These two essays by Winer, Tridimas and Hettich (WTH) and Ledyard provide differing perspectives on these issues and very useful starting points for future studies of coercion and public economics.

Coercion in Ledyard involves being required to accept outcomes that are inferior to some default option, thought of as nonparticipation. Although it is hard to conceive of nonparticipation in society as a viable option in the strict sense, it nonetheless serves as a useful benchmark for analysis. Ledyard takes an absolutist approach. The participation constraint must be satisfied: there is no room for trading off coercion versus, for example, social welfare or efficiency.

The interpretation of coercion as violating a participation constraint is a relatively weak one compared with that of WTH. To them, coercion involves outcomes that deviate from individuals' most preferred ones. It is virtually certain that collective decision making, whether by a benevolent planner government or a politically motivated one, will entail some coercion in that sense. The extent of coercion then becomes endogenous, and the question becomes how to characterize admissible or preferred amounts of coercion.

The procedure used by WTH exemplifies how they think this question should be addressed. Consider some collective decision being taken by the government, such as fiscal decisions involving the choice of public goods' levels and/or the choice of a tax system. A welfare-optimizing planner would choose policies to maximize social welfare subject to a revenue constraint, and perhaps information constraints in an optimal income tax setting. Individuals might also have their most preferred allocations, obtained by maximizing their own welfare subject to the same constraints. Coercion would exist to the extent that utilities obtained under social welfare maximization differed from individuals' utilities in their most preferred allocations.

To give coercion some weight on social decision making, WTH propose adding one or more coercion constraints to the planner's social welfare maximizing problem. These constraints specify maximum levels of coercion, either for each individual or aggregated over individuals. Their analysis considers how such coercion constraints affect the policy choices made by the planner. This procedure is an effective way of indicating the trade-off between social welfare and coercion, because the effect of relaxing the coercion constraints on social welfare can be studied.

They illustrate their method using a special example. The government chooses the level of a public good to supply, using a linear progressive tax to finance it. However, the parameters of the income tax are restricted such that each person's tax share of the cost of the public good is fixed, as in the famous Bowen (1943) median-voter analysis of voting over a public good. This effectively restricts government decision making to be one dimensional because the choice of public good implies a level of individual taxation through the government budget constraint. Each individual has single-peaked preferences over the level of the public good, so their most preferred value is well defined. The planner chooses the level of public good subject to a revenue constraint and an aggregate coercion constraint. The solution to the problem is nicely characterized and shows in an intuitive way how coercion affects the public good decision rule and the constrained optimal linear progressive tax. WTH use this analysis to explore (a) the trade-off between coercion and social welfare and (b) the extent of coercion that would be obtained under a majority voting system of decision making.

The analysis is meant to be exploratory, and as such, it is very suggestive. At the same time, a number of questions can be raised about the methodology.

The first is the way in which coercion is incorporated into the social welfare maximizing problem – that is, by adding aggregate or per person coercion constraints. An alternative procedure, which would be in keeping with welfarist approaches to normative collective decision making, is to treat coercion as an element of individual utility functions that go into the social welfare function. Arguably, this would be more appealing on normative grounds because it preserves the welfarist approach and recognizes that one's well-being depends on the extent to which one is being coerced. The issue is analogous to the problem of horizontal equity. The coercion constraint is like a horizontal equity constraint, which limits the extent to which policies can make one worse off. Authors such as Kaplow (2001) have argued that treating horizontal equity as an additional consideration over and above social welfare can lead to Pareto inferior outcomes. A similar concern might arise here.

Second, the definition of coercion is not unambiguous. Instead of defining it with respect to one's preferred level of personal utility, it is as reasonable to define it with respect to one's preferred social outcome, what might be called an individual-as-planner approach as opposed to an individual-in-society approach. This approach has been used in a number of other contexts, either to condition individual behavior in social contexts or to influence individual voting. Thus, voluntary contributions to public goods might be conditioned by what one thinks is fair (Bordignon 1990), as experimental evidence suggests (Andreoni 1995). Tax evasion might be influenced by one's judgment about the fairness of one's tax liabilities (Bordignon 1993). Similarly, tax avoidance (reducing one's labor supply in the face of redistributive taxes) may be limited to the extent that one thinks redistributive policy is fair (Boadway, Marceau, and Mongrain 2007). Socially driven behavior may be driven by what one thinks is fair (Baron 2010), and voting may be based on one's social values (Brennan and Hamlin 1998; Cervellati, Esteban, and Kranich 2010). It might be reasonable to think of coercion in the same light. Indeed, the whole notion of a social welfare function might be rationalized by a consensus in society regarding redistribution – a consensus that might differ from one country to the next.

The example used in the essay to illustrate coercion as a constraint is a very special one. It focuses entirely on preferences for a public good, given tax shares, and ignores preferences over redistribution. Once one allows individual's most preferred outcomes to include both the size of the public sector and the extent of redistribution, the approach becomes more problematic. For example, suppose instead of analyzing the choice of a public good, given tax shares, one analyzes a pure redistribution problem such as the choice of a linear progressive tax structure given revenue requirements. If all persons choose their preferred outcome selfishly, individual preferences are in fundamental conflict and the limited coercion constraints become difficult to interpret. The social welfare maximization is presumably going to appear more coercive to high-income persons than to low-income persons. Should all persons then still get equal weight in the coercion constraint? The formulation of the coercion constraint itself must incorporate some interpersonal weights that necessarily have social welfare content.

Indeed, this issue of specifying the coercion constraints presents a more general problem with the approach. What is the appropriate way to limit the amount of coercion to which different persons can be exposed? There seems no easy answer to that question. The procedure of simply adding coercion into a single aggregate may seem reasonable when the decision is simply how much public good to provide. It is not as reasonable when the collective decision is over how much redistribution there should be.

Finally, a couple of more detailed questions arise about the extensions to the basic analysis. The voting analysis is a natural extension to the social welfare maximization approach. Similar questions arise. It is assumed that voters vote on the basis of their private utilities, along with party preferences. Should they not take coercion into account in their voting choice if coercion is a problem? If so, political parties would presumably take coercion into account in selecting their platforms. As well, voting is assumed to be over the level of the public good only. This is a nicely behaved single-peaked voting problem for which one supposes a Condorcet winner arises. If the voting had been over redistribution as well, there may not be a Condorcet winner, so the extent of coercion would not be well defined.

These problems do not vitiate the analysis and the valuable original contribution of this essay. They do, however, suggest some issues that should be taken into account in developing the approach further. Such further development would be welcome.

Ledyard's essay is also a very fine paper. It is written fairly tersely and draws on literature and results that are not spelled out. This makes it difficult to grasp fully the implications of the analysis and its results, so my comments will be quite speculative and some may be off the mark.

Rather than studying normative social welfare maximizing allocations or political economy allocations, Ledyard focuses on incentive compatible mechanisms and considers the possibility of efficient, incentive compatible allocations that satisfy a participation constraint. The participation, or no-coercion, constraint requires that an individual not be better off by keeping their endowment and not participating in the market economy. Perhaps not surprisingly, Lindahl mechanisms satisfy these properties, although they may be restrictive on other grounds, especially redistributive. More important, the Lindahl mechanism is the only one that will always satisfy these properties, at least in a complete information setting. The results become much more agnostic when information is imperfect – that is, when person's preference types are private but not public information. This agnosticism is undone when preference types are not even known privately, so the participation (no-coercion) constraint applies before individuals know their type, so are behind the veil of ignorance.

Therefore, it seems that coercion need not be a problem in principle either under full information, or *ex ante* information. That is, mechanisms can be found that will achieve efficiency, incentive compatibility, and participation in these cases. Alas, if the mechanism applies *ex post*, after information is revealed, such outcomes can no longer be guaranteed.

It is not easy to pose reasonable questions in the context of this highly general analysis. Nonetheless, some naïve ones come to mind. The participation constraint is what rules out coercion in this analysis, and the interest is in finding efficient allocations that do not violate it. How big a problem is this likely to be? The incentive compatibility constraint contributes to satisfying the participation constraint. Presumably, it is the possibility that the mechanism is highly redistributive that generates the possibility that participation is violated. One wonders if this is likely to be a major problem for most reasonable applications. Taking one's endowment and withdrawing from the market economy is a very drastic move because one loses access to all markets. It is hard to imagine it being binding.

More generally, mechanisms of necessity will have redistribution built into them. Potential violations of the participation constraint presumably depend on the mechanism being punitively redistributive against particular persons. This begs the question of who gets to decide on the mechanism.

From another perspective, it is not obvious how one would want to define a participation constraint in principle. In Tiebout models of community choice, there is a natural participation constraint. However, choosing not to participate in the market economy seems like a very weak concept of non-coercion. Nonparticipation would be very bad indeed, worse than being in a laissez-faire setting.

Once one moves to incomplete information cases, some other conceptual questions arise. For one, the meaning of efficiency in the interim information case is not spelled out. One supposes that it refers to *ex ante* efficiency, which may be different from *ex post* efficiency.

The *ex ante* information problem is an interesting one from a normative point of view, given that it corresponds with the Rawlsian notion of putting persons behind the veil of ignorance. However, does *ex ante* voluntary participation really correspond with an absence of coercion? That is, it is hard to imagine one having to commit to participate in society behind the veil of ignorance. Moreover, *ex ante* information seems only to be with respect to preference types, and not with respect to endowments. What happens if endowments are not known *ex ante*, which would correspond with behind the veil of ignorance in the usual normative sense? Finally, combining *ex ante* participation with interim incentive compatibility seems to me to be a bit odd.

As mentioned, these are naïve questions that betray a lack of familiarity of the literature underlying the results in this essay. The Ledyard essay remains a formidable piece of analysis that fruitfully explores one notion of coercion, albeit one that is complementary to that preferred by WTH.

References

Andreoni, J. (1995). "Cooperation in Public Goods Experiments: Kindness or Confusion?" *American Economic Review* 85: 891–904.

Baron, David B. (2010). "Morally-Motivated Self-Regulation." *American Economic Review* 100: 1299–329.

Boadway, Robin, Nicolas Marceau, and Steeve Mongrain (2007). "Redistributive Taxation under Ethical Behaviour." *Scandinavian Journal of Economics* 109: 505–529.

Bordignon, Massimo (1990). "Was Kant Right? Voluntary Provision of Public Goods under the Principle of Unconditional Commitment." *Economic Notes* 3: 342–372.

Bordignon, Massimo (1993). "A Fairness Approach to Income Tax Evasion." *Journal of Public Economics* 52: 345–362.

Bowen, Howard R. (1943). "The Interpretation of Voting in the Allocation of Resources." *Quarterly Journal of Economics* 58: 27–48.

Brennan, Geoffrey and Alan Hamlin (1998). "Expressive Voting and Electoral Equilibrium." *Public Choice* 95: 149–175.

Cervellati, Matteo, Joan Esteban, and Laurence Kranich (2010). "Work Values, Endogenous Sentiments Redistribution" mimeo. *Journal of Public Economics* 94: 612–627.

Kaplow, Louis (2001). "Horizontal Equity: New Measures, Unclear Principles." In Kevin Hassett and Glenn Hubbard (eds.), *Inequality and Tax Policy*. Washington: American Enterprise Institute, 75–97.

8

Lindahl Fiscal Incidence and the Measurement
of Coercion

Saloua Sehili and Jorge Martinez-Vazquez

1. Introduction

This essay presents measures of the distribution or incidence of net fiscal
benefits, when net benefits are generally defined as the difference between
the willingness to pay for public services and the actual tax price paid by
individuals. This difference can be regarded as a measure of fiscal coercion,
and the results can be seen as providing the distribution of a welfare-based
measure of gains or losses from a coercive fiscal system across household
groups.

Alternatively, we may think of the results as showing the net incidence
of the fiscal system when each individual's, group's, or household's net
benefits are measured relative to a situation in which there is no coercion.
In this sense, the analysis is of the differential incidence type, because we are
estimating what happens to the distribution of net benefits when an actual
fiscal system is replaced with another, ideal and non-coercive Lindahl-
like one (Lindahl 1919). In the Lindahl-like counterfactuals used in our
calculations, we consider situations in which the supply of public goods is
efficient (and satisfies the Samuelson condition) as well as ones in which
public goods supply is not at the level where the sum of marginal benefits
equals the marginal cost of public goods supply.

The essay uses an interregional applied general equilibrium model to
actually measure the distribution of net benefits or losses (relative to the
Lindahl solution) across households from government services and taxes,
at the subnational level. We build on Piggot and Whalley's (1987) study at
the national level to allow for the existence of excess burden losses from
state and local taxes and the consumer surplus gains from state and local
public goods. This improves on existing measures of net fiscal incidence
at the subnational level based on the Aaron and McGuire (1970) and

Martinez-Vazquez (1982) methodology, which compares only actual tax prices to marginal willingness to pay.[1]

In addition, we make two modifications to Piggot and Whalley's approach that are particularly relevant to the definition and measurement of net fiscal incidence at the subnational level. First, we allow for the effect of tax exporting (i.e., of exploitation of nonresidents) on the demand for public goods and net fiscal incidence at the subnational level. The conventional view in the tax exporting literature is that by shifting some of the tax burden to nonresidents, local jurisdictions tend to overspend on public goods. Wildasin (1987), however, has shown that income effects from the excess burden of taxes imposed by several jurisdictions may actually reduce local public expenditure and welfare in each of the jurisdictions. Second, we allow for the effect of the potential inefficiency in the supply of public goods arising from the political decision process at the subnational level. In particular, we assume that the actual quantity of the public good supplied is decided by the median voter. Although other approaches to public good supply decisions can be adopted, the objective in our measure of net fiscal incidence is to account for any inefficiency the public good decision process may produce.

Our mathematical model is similar to that of Fullerton and Rogers (1993) but is a single-period, two-region model of the state of Georgia and the Rest of the United States (ROUS), and of course uses the Lindahl solution as a standard of reference.[2]

We obtain three main sets of results. First, under a fairly standard set of assumptions for the main parameters in the model, we find that the distribution of net fiscal benefits (or the coercive effect of the fiscal system) across income groups in Georgia is regressive. This is true for three increasingly comprehensive measures of net fiscal incidence that include (a) excess burdens of taxes and consumer surplus from public goods a la Piggot and Whalley (1987); (b) tax exporting/importing across regions, and; (c) the welfare effects of the inefficient supply of public goods as a result of the political process. Second, from an exclusively Georgia perspective, state-local taxes are welfare improving in that the income effects from exporting taxes to nonresidents dominate those introduced by distortionary taxation. However, tax exporting by both Georgia and the ROUS results in welfare

---

[1] For references to the fiscal incidence literature, see, for example, Bird and Slack (1983), Zimmerman (1983), and Zodrow and Mieszkowski (1986).

[2] For interregional applied general equilibrium models, see, for example, Ballentine and Thirsk (1978) and Morgan, Mutti, and Rickman (1996) and references therein.

losses to both regions from the distortionary effects of taxation, which supports the Wildasin (1987) hypothesis. Third, the distribution of net fiscal incidence is quite sensitive to the assumed distribution of preferences between private and public goods among taxpayers of different income levels. In particular, if we allow the elasticity of substitution between public and private goods in the preferences of taxpayers to increase enough from its estimated level for Georgia, net fiscal incidence in Georgia turns from regressive into progressive.

The rest of the essay is organized as follows. Section 2 briefly restates the concept of net fiscal incidence and the theoretical derivation of the demand for public goods. Section 3 describes the model. Section 4 presents the results and sensitivity tests, and Section 5 concludes.

2. Lindahl Net Fiscal Incidence

Net fiscal incidence analyses evaluate how individual welfare is affected by government budgets through paying taxes and receiving benefits from public services. These changes in welfare have been measured in the literature by quantifying to different degrees what households in different income categories receive in benefits and pay in taxes to the public sector on a net basis (benefits less taxes).[3] In some of the earlier studies, both taxes and government expenditures are fully allocated by income class, thus ignoring welfare effects of variations in taxation and public good provision.[4] More recent studies have allowed for the possibility that public goods may not be provided efficiently and that therefore the benefits to taxpayers from public goods may differ from their cost of provision. However, these studies have also ignored the marginal welfare costs associated with different tax structures and changes in consumer surplus arising from changes in the supply of public goods.[5] The significant contribution of Piggot and Whalley (1987) was to set the question and measurement of net fiscal incidence in an applied general equilibrium framework and emphasize the importance of deadweight losses from taxes and consumer surplus benefits from public goods in any measure of net fiscal incidence.

---

[3] Examples of such studies are Gillespie (1965), Tax Foundation (1965), Aaron and McGuire (1970), Maital (1973), Musgrave, Case and Leonard (1974), Greene, Neenan and Scott (1976), Musgrave and Musgrave (1980), Martinez-Vazquez (1982), and Chaudry-Shah (1989).

[4] Gillespie (1965); Tax Foundation (1965); Musgrave, Case, and Leonard (1974); Greene, Neenan, and Scott (1976); and Musgrave and Musgrave (1980).

[5] Aaron and McGuire (1970); Maital (1973); and Martinez-Vazquez (1982).

Following Aaron and McGuire (1970) and Martinez-Vazquez (1982), we rely on the Lindahl market analogue pricing rule to define a household's benefits from state-local public goods. In this sense, net fiscal incidence is first approximated by the difference for each taxpayer between the Lindahl price or willingness to pay for the public good and the actual tax price paid.[6] We assume taxpayers' preferences as represented by a Constant Elasticity of Substitution (CES) utility function of a composite private good C_i and a composite state-local public good G_i,[7]

$$U_i = \left[\alpha^{1/\sigma} G_i^{(\sigma-1)/\sigma} + (1-\alpha)^{1/\sigma} C_i^{(\sigma-1)/\sigma} \right]^{\sigma/(\sigma-1)}, \qquad (8.1)$$

where σ is the elasticity of substitution between C_i and G_i, and α is the share parameter. This utility function implies unit income elasticity of demand for the composite public good, G_i. This means that the Lindahl price or willingness to pay for the public good is assumed to rise in proportion to income.

Each taxpayer attempts to maximize U_i subject to a budget constraint,

$$I_i = P_{Gi} G_i + P_{Ci} C_i, \qquad (8.2)$$

where P_{Ci} is the price of the composite private good, C_i; P_{Gi} is the consumer's personalized price of the public good, equal to the consumer's tax share τ_i

---

[6] Instead of using the Lindahl market analogue pricing rule as the counterfactual, net fiscal incidence can be defined with a counterfactual of a world without government (public goods and taxes); we do not pursue that avenue in this essay. What we call net fiscal incidence in this essay based on the Lindahl counterfactual has been called by others "coercion" or "fiscal coercion." See, for example, Winer, Tridimas, and Hettich in Chapter 7 of this volume.

[7] The assumption of a single state-local public good is not too limiting when analyzing the incidence of the entire budget, and it is also convenient to avoid the potential problem of multiple equilibria. Sato (1972) has shown that double-log form demand equations, such as those used to estimate demands for public goods (Bergstrom and Goodman 1973 and Borcherding and Deacon 1972) are based on additive utility functions of the CES form. However, the assumption of a single state-local public good hides a variety of sub-distributional effects for the different categories of state-local public goods and services. Expenditures on general education, health, and welfare are likely to be largely redistributive in nature. Although they may also benefit the rich because the rich care about access to those services by the poor; those services, it can be argued, are likely to benefit the poor more. See Bahl, Martinez-Vazquez, and Wallace (2002). On the other hand, there are other categories of public spending that are likely to benefit the rich more than the poor – higher education, parks and recreation, justice and police, maybe roads, and so on. The assumption of a single state-local composite public good averages all these things together. Future research will need to be conducted with a disaggregated approach to public spending.

times the marginal cost of the public good, P_G; and I_i is the consumer's gross (before state and local taxes) income.[8]

Consumer i's tax share, τ_i, is defined as state-local taxes paid by consumer i divided by the expenditures on the state-local public good. Thus, the first order Lindahl equilibrium conditions yield:

$$MRS_{CiGi} = \frac{MU_{Gi}}{MU_{Ci}} = \left(\frac{\alpha}{1-\alpha}\right)^{1/\sigma} \left(\frac{C_i}{G_i}\right)^{1/\sigma} \tag{8.3}$$

and

$$MRS_{CiGi} = \frac{P_{Gi}}{P_{Ci}}. \tag{8.4}$$

We assume that the political decision process on public good supply can be represented by the median voter model (Bergstrom and Goodman 1973, Borcherding and Deacon 1972). In this framework, equations (3) and (4) hold true only for the median voter who obtains the amount of public good G that he wants and pays for. To parameterize the model, we solve for α using the median income group of taxpayers and assume that α is the same for all taxpayers. This leads to the following demand equation for the public good:

$$G_i = \frac{\alpha I_i}{P_{Gi}^{\sigma} \left[\alpha P_{Gi}^{(1-\sigma)} + (1-\alpha)P_{Ci}^{(1-\sigma)}\right]}. \tag{8.5}$$

Because they have a different income and tax price than the median voter, consumers demand different quantities of the state-local public good, but they are forced to consume the quantity most preferred by the median voter. Income is thus redistributed from those who demand a smaller quantity than that actually provided to those who demand a larger quantity. Figure 8.1 illustrates a median voter equilibrium for three consumers, each one with his demand or marginal benefit curve for the public good, MBi. The crossing of the marginal cost curve and the vertical summation of the three MBi curves, illustrate the Samuelson-efficient quantity of the public good. The height of each MBi curve at this quantity defines the (first-best) Lindahl prices. The equilibrium in Figure 8.1 assumes that the tax system imposes on consumer 1 a higher tax price (P_{Gi}) than his Lindahl price (corresponding to the quantity of the public good actually provided), on consumer 3 a lower tax price than his Lindahl price, and on consumer 2 a tax price exactly

---

[8] The model presented in the next section allows consumers to choose between leisure and income.

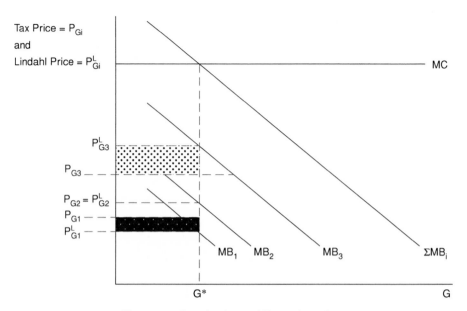

Figure 8.1. Coercion in a public goods setting.

equal to his Lindahl price. Whereas consumer 2 is in equilibrium exactly paying what he desires to pay, the system is charging consumer 1 (the low demander) more than he is willing to pay and consumer 3 (the high demander) less than he is willing to pay. The amounts that are overcharged to consumer 1 and undercharged to consumer 3 are represented by the respective shaded rectangles in Figure 8.1. These measures of net fiscal incidence could also be interpreted as alternative measures of coercion to those offered by Winer, Tridimas, and Hettich in their essay in this volume. In their approach, coercion arises from individuals having to consume quantities of the public good that are less than or more than the amount they most prefer at the set tax price. In our approach in this essay, coercion would arise from individuals having to pay a price that is less than or more than their willingness to pay for the set quantity of the public good. Being forced to pay a tax price that is higher than the marginal willingness to pay offers an intuitive interpretation of coercion. However, being "forced" to pay a tax price that is less than the marginal willingness to pay is not a so clearly appealing interpretation of coercion.

For a median voter equilibrium to be a Lindahl equilibrium, it must satisfy two conditions: (a) the public good quantity actually provided must be Pareto optimal, that is, efficiently provided according to the Samuelson

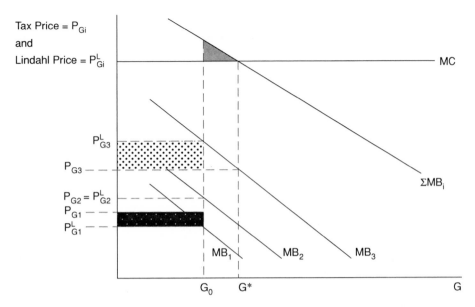

Figure 8.2. Voting equilibrium with inefficiency in public goods supply.

rule, and (b) there must be unanimity, that is, each taxpayer demands the Pareto optimal quantity of the public good at their current tax price.[9] In terms of Figure 8.1, this would happen at quantity G^* and with a tax price for each consumer equal to his Lindahl price. In general, there is no guarantee that the median voter equilibrium will produce the Pareto optimum or Samuelson quantity of the public good. Figure 8.2 illustrates a voting equilibrium that reproduces a similar net fiscal incidence as the one in Figure 8.1, but in this case the quantity of the public good provided Go is inefficient and less than the Pareto optimum quantity of the public good G^*. The shaded area between the marginal cost curve and the vertical summation of the three MBi curves represents the welfare losses as a result of the underprovision of the public good.

In the following simulation model, we experiment with several tax and public expenditure scenarios that allow us to address the two conditions for a median voter equilibrium to be a Lindahl equilibrium separately and simultaneously. In particular, we compare the benchmark net benefit distribution arising from current tax prices and public good provision to six different alternatives of tax-public good provision. These alternatives

[9] In the presence of distortionary taxation, efficient public good provision requires the tax-modified Samuelson rule (Atkinson and Stern 1974).

Table 8.1. *Six-tax public good provision alternatives*

Alternative I: Aaron & McGuire	Adjust Georgia consumer's actual tax prices to Lindahl-equivalent tax prices through lump-sum taxes or subsidies.
Alternative II: A-M with excess burden of taxes	Remove all Georgia state-local taxes and replace them with lump-sum taxes to obtain a Lindahl tax structure.
Alternative III: Piggott & Whalley	Change public good provision rule to Samuelson rule. Use proportional tax/subsidy to maintain budget balance.
Alternative IV (I and III): A-M and Piggott & Whalley	Adjust Georgia consumer's actual tax prices to Lindahl-equivalent tax prices through lump-sum taxes or subsidies. Change public good provision rule to Samuelson rule. Use proportional tax/subsidy to maintain budget balance.
Alternative V (II and III): A-M and Piggott & Whalley	Remove all Georgia state-local taxes and replace them with lump-sum taxes to obtain a Lindahl tax structure. Change public good provision rule to Samuelson rule. Use proportional tax/subsidy to maintain budget balance.
Alternative VI: Wildasin	Remove all Georgia and ROUS state-local taxes and replace them with lump-sum taxes. Median voter rule of public good provision.

are summarized in Table 8.1. Each of the alternative scenarios provides a different measure of net fiscal incidence by allowing for different aspects of the impact of the tax-public good packages on taxpayers' welfare analyzed in the literature. We also use the simulation model to assess the sensitivity of our results to the assumed value of the elasticity of substitution between the public good and the composite private good.

3. The Model

The mathematical specification of the model and the level of detail are similar to that of Fullerton and Rogers (1993). The full mathematical specification of the model is presented in the Appendix.[10] Our model, however, differs from that in Fullerton and Rogers (1993) in several respects. It is a single-period, two-region model of the state of Georgia and the ROUS.[11]

---

[10] Specifically, in the Appendix we model in some detail the treatment of taxes, the production side, the consumption side for public and private goods, the labor-leisure choice, the foreign sector, and the equilibrium conditions. We also summarize the simulation steps in the Appendix.

[11] The model does not incorporate any Tiebout sorting, whereby different income groups sort into different relatively homogenous communities, between Georgia and the ROUS. This is because the two regions are large enough to allow for that sorting within each region.

Table 8.2. *Producer goods*

1	Agriculture, forestry, and fisheries
2	Mining
3	Crude petroleum and gas
4	Contract construction
5	Food and tobacco
6	Textiles, apparel, and leather
7	Paper and printing
8	Petroleum refining
9	Chemicals, rubber, and plastics
10	Lumber, furniture, stone, clay, and glass
11	Metals, machinery, instruments, and other manufacturing
12	Transportation equipment and ordinance
13	Motor vehicles
14	Transportation, communications, and utilities
15	Trade
16	Finance and insurance
17	Real estate
18	Services
19	State and local government enterprises
20	Federal government enterprises

For Georgia, the model includes three factors (labor, capital, and land), twenty sectors (see Table 8.2), seventeen private commodities (see Table 8.3), one composite public good, and nineteen income groups aggregated in population quantiles.

For the ROUS, the model includes the same factors, sectors, and private commodities, but only one income group. Each private industry in each region comprises a corporate sector and a noncorporate sector.[12] The state-local composite public good in Georgia is measured as the level of total public expenditures. This public good is financed with revenues generated by Georgia's state and local taxes.[13] The production of the public good is modeled as a composite of regional producer goods through a

---

[12] However, the housing industry consists of owner housing and rental housing rather than corporate and noncorporate sectors.

[13] Georgia State taxes include income (personal and corporate) taxes, sales taxes, and fuel taxes. Local taxes include property taxes and charges and fees. Property taxes paid by homeowners are deductible from the income tax. Owner-occupied housing receives special tax treatment in addition for mortgage interest deductions, whereas rental housing receives the same treatment as the noncorporate sector. See the Appendix for a description of how these taxes are modeled.

Table 8.3. *Consumer goods*

1	Food
2	Alcohol
3	Tobacco
4	Households fuels and utilities
5	Shelter
6	Furnishings
7	Appliances
8	Apparel
9	Public transportation
10	New and used cars, fees, and maintenance
11	Cash contributions and personal care
12	Financial services
13	Reading and entertainment
14	Household operations
15	Gasoline and motor oil
16	Health care
17	Education

Cobb-Douglas specification. The regional (state-local) government in the ROUS returns all its revenues to the ROUS single consumer. The federal government collects revenues by imposing identical taxes on both regions.[14] This revenue is then distributed directly to the consumers in both regions as lump-sum transfers proportional to their income.

In Georgia, as reviewed in the previous section, consumers are assumed to have uniform preferences. Consumers are grouped into nineteen population quantiles on the basis of annual gross income to capture differences in consumption patterns and tax and benefit incidence (see Table 8.4). The treatment of the single consumer in the ROUS is similar to the treatment of Georgia consumers, except that the ROUS representative consumer does not formulate explicit demand for public goods.

Each consumer group is assumed to consume leisure, own-region private commodities, and the state-local public good. The nested utility function consists of a Cobb-Douglas combination of private commodities at the lowest level, a CES combination of the state-local public good, and composite private commodities at the second level (as in equation (1)), and a CES composite of leisure and composite public good and private commodities at the upper level.

---

[14] Federal taxes include personal income, corporate income, payroll, and fuel taxes. See also the Appendix for a description of how these taxes are modeled.

Table 8.4. *Consumer's factor income in Georgia*

Income group[a]	Labor income[b]	Capital income[b]	Total income[b]	Average income[c]
1	214	355	569	3,524
2	533	304	837	5,186
3	688	386	1,074	6,654
4	1,097	352	1,449	8,978
5	1,206	712	1,918	11,889
6	1,639	762	2,401	14,881
7	2,254	702	2,956	18,321
8	2,957	469	3,426	21,230
9	3,149	674	3,823	23,694
10	3,357	1,109	4,466	27,673
11	4,375	761	5,136	31,831
12	4,530	1,204	5,734	35,535
13	5,296	1,134	6,430	39,848
14	6,166	1,063	7,229	44,799
15	6,520	1,759	8,279	51,307
16	6,986	2,636	9,622	59,628
17	9,379	2,059	11,438	70,881
18	10,472	3,764	14,236	88,220
19	17,430	9,277	26,707	165,506

[a] Each group consists of 161,365 households.
[b] 1993 U.S. $millions.
[c] Per person in U.S. dollars.

When calibrating this model, it is assumed that in the benchmark equilibrium, the median voter maximizes his utility subject to market prices and his personal tax price for the public good. The public good therefore enters as a common argument in each household's preference function, with the level of provision chosen by the median voter (median income group).

Production factors in each region consist of capital, assumed to be perfectly mobile between regions and sectors, and interregionally immobile land and labor. Interregional trade is modeled through an estimated interindustry interregional input-output matrix. Thus interregional trade is captured through intermediate demands of other-region's outputs.[15]

Our tax treatment also follows that in Fullerton and Rogers (1993), except that we separate federal and state-local taxes. Furthermore, we model the state-local and federal income taxes paid by each group as two linear

[15] See Round (1978) for estimating interregional input-output matrices.

tax functions, each with an intercept that captures the various personal deductions in the tax code and a slope that reflects the marginal tax rate for each group on all labor and capital income, with adjustment for industry differentials.[16]

The theoretical model is translated into an empirical model using the 1993 consistent benchmark equilibrium data for Georgia and the ROUS. The Georgia wage rate is arbitrarily chosen as the numeraire, and we use the same elasticity parameters for the production and utility functions as in Fullerton and Rogers (1993). The most critical parameter in our model is the elasticity of substitution between the public good and the composite private good in household preferences, σ. Initially, we set this parameter at 0.5 on the basis of 1990 tax price elasticity estimates for Georgia and report sensitivity analyses in Section 4.[17] The base case solution to the model is presented in Table 8.5.

In Georgia, the patterns of personalized tax prices and public good quantities demanded across income groups satisfy the median voter assumption of public good provision.[18] Household tax prices increase more than proportionally as income increases, indicating a progressive statutory overall state-local tax structure. Buchanan (1964) and Bergstrom and Goodman (1973) have shown that a Lindahl equilibrium tax structure can be derived from the income and price elasticities of demand for public goods. Thus, the elasticity of the Lindahl equilibrium tax prices with respect to income is equal to negative the ratio of income elasticity to price elasticity of demand for public goods. Therefore, given that the income and price elasticity of demand for public goods are set to 1 and -0.5, respectively, the elasticity of the Lindahl tax prices with respect to income at the benchmark quantity of public goods is $-(1/-0.5) = 2.0$. A regression of the natural log of tax prices on the natural log of income for the nineteen income groups shows that the elasticity of actual tax prices with respect to income is 0.90 ($p < 0.001$). This indicates that the actual tax structure should be made more progressive to attain a Lindahl equilibrium.

As a result, given their actual tax prices, lower income households demand a lower quantity of the public good than provided in the benchmark, higher

---

[16] See Ballard et al. (1985).

[17] See Piggott and Whalley (1987).

[18] We must note that there is certain arbitrariness in how one can draw the boundary between tax and expenditure policy. Cash transfers, and even perhaps in-kind transfers that are means tested, can be viewed as tax price reductions for the low income groups. In this sense, tax prices for the poor in Table 8.5 would be overstated. In the calculations we make no such adjustments to the tax prices, and transfers of all kinds are incorporated into the composite public good.

Table 8.5. *Benchmark equilibrium pattern of tax prices and public good demand*

Income group	Personalized price of the public good[a]	Quantity demanded of the public good[b]	QSPG[c]
1	0.032	1,757	3,990
2	0.034	2,374	3,990
3	0.041	2,467	3,990
4	0.044	2,808	3,990
5	0.072	2,867	3,990
6	0.081	3,105	3,990
7	0.087	3,535	3,990
8	0.090	3,757	3,990
9	0.106	3,866	3,990
10	0.138	3,990	3,990
11	0.142	4,171	3,990
12	0.171	4,336	3,990
13	0.185	4,599	3,990
14	0.201	4,812	3,990
15	0.251	4,982	3,990
16	0.315	5,249	3,990
17	0.341	5,788	3,990
18	0.471	6,225	3,990
19	0.946	8,262	3,990

Note: All quantities are in 1993 U.S. millions of dollars.
[a] Personal price of the public good.
[b] Personal quantity demanded of the public good.
[c] Quantity supplied of the public good.

income households demand a higher quantity, and the median income household (income group 10), demands the amount of public good actually provided in the benchmark. Lower income households are thus forced to pay a tax price, which is higher than their marginal willingness to pay at the benchmark public good level of provision, whereas higher income households are willing to pay a higher tax price than they are actually paying. This implies that a Lindahl tax structure at the benchmark level of public good provision would reduce tax prices for the lower income groups and increase tax prices for the higher income groups. In the previous literature (Aaron and McGuire 1970, Martinez-Vazquez 1982), this result was interpreted as net fiscal incidence being regressive. However, this measure ignores the impact on net fiscal incidence of the excess burden of taxation, the potential inefficiency of public good supply, and tax exporting.

The following section reports the expanded measurements of net fiscal incidence by looking at the welfare impacts of changes in the tax structure and public good provision. Income class welfare measures are based on the equivalent variation evaluated at prices in the base case solution to the model. Aggregate welfare changes correspond to a utilitarian social welfare function in which the equivalent variation measures are summed across income groups.[19]

4. Empirical Results and Sensitivity Tests

The most comprehensive measure of net fiscal incidence, one capturing all welfare effects of government taxation and public good provision, can be obtained by comparing the benchmark equilibrium to a full Lindahl equilibrium characterized by lump-sum taxation (no excess burdens and no tax exporting) and the efficient Pareto optimal quantity of the public good. However, before we estimate this comprehensive measure of net fiscal incidence, we isolate the effects of its various components. This allows for a better understanding of net fiscal incidence and also for a better comparison to previous approaches in the literature. In total we perform six experiments to isolate the effects of non-Lindahl pricing, the potential inefficiency of public good provision under median voter rule, and the excess burden of taxes and tax exporting. Table 8.1 summarizes the six alternative tax-public good provision experiments that we perform to analyze net fiscal incidence in Georgia, and the results to each alternative are presented in Tables 8.6 through 8.11. Alternatives I and II produce two different measures of the conventional approach to net fiscal incidence given that actual taxes are not Lindahl taxes. Alternative III measures the welfare impact of producing an inefficient quantity of the public good. Alternatives IV and V produce different measures of comprehensive net fiscal incidence in which the quantity of public good is at its efficient optimal level and the taxation system is Lindahl-equivalent, as corresponding to alternatives I and II. In alternative VI we use lump-sum taxes not only in Georgia but also in the ROUS to isolate the public good demand and welfare impact of tax exporting.

Alternative I. Lindahl-equivalent tax prices: *Adjust Georgia consumer's actual tax prices to Lindahl-equivalent tax prices through lump-sum taxes or subsidies.*

The measurement of net fiscal incidence in alternative I is similar to Martinez-Vazquez's (1982) measure of net fiscal incidence. It compares

---

[19] Other social welfare functions with different weights for the poor and rich could be used, of course. For simplicity we stick with the utilitarian social welfare function.

Table 8.6. *Welfare effects of Lindahl-equivalent tax prices: Adjust Georgia consumer's actual tax prices to Lindahl-equivalent tax prices through lump-sum taxes or subsidies*

Household	% PPPG[a]	% QDPG[b]	EV[c]	EV[d]
1	−78	127	634	20
2	−62	68	638	13
3	−59	62	758	12
4	−47	42	790	9
5	−45	39	1,039	9
6	−36	28	1,058	7
7	−19	13	917	5
8	−9	6	913	4
9	5	3	838	4
10	0	0	677	2
11	9	−4	657	2
12	16	−8	276	1
13	29	−13	−166	−0
14	40	−17	−574	−1
15	46	−20	−1,474	−3
16	57	−24	−2,955	−5
17	86	−31	−4,799	−7
18	102	−36	−8,801	−10
19	184	−52	−30,664	−20

Note: Percent changes are relative to the benchmark equilibrium.
[a] Personal price of the public good.
[b] Personal quantity demanded of the public good.
[c] Average equivalent variation per household in dollars.
[d] Equivalent variation as a percentage of income.

actual tax prices to the marginal willingness to pay or Lindahl-equivalent tax prices.[20] This measure, however, does not take into account the excess burden or exporting of taxes, nor does it correct for the potential inefficiency of the public good quantity supplied. The change in tax prices to Lindahl-equivalent tax prices leads to two effects. First, income is effectively redistributed, in this case from higher income groups to lower income groups. Second, a surplus or deficit of state-local government revenue is generated. In this case there is a surplus. To maintain budget balance, this excess

[20] The name *Lindahl-equivalent* is used here to imply that the new tax prices are still distortionary but coincide with taxpayers' marginal willingness to pay for the amount of the public good actually provided. The Lindahl-equivalent prices and the quantity of the public good provided do not constitute a Lindahl equilibrium because the supply of the public good is likely not Pareto optimal.

revenue is distributed to households proportionately to their income.[21] Note that previous partial equilibrium analyses such as Martinez-Vazquez (1982) or Aaron and McGuire (1970) did not address the issue of excess or shortage of tax revenues under a Lindahl tax structure at the benchmark public good provision but instead compared the actual net benefit distribution to the one that would prevail in the presence of a Lindahl tax structure, assuming no change in tax revenues or public good provision. In a general equilibrium framework adjustments arising from income redistribution to lower income groups lead to a reduction in the prices of producer goods and, thus, a reduction in the marginal cost of the public good. Therefore, the same amount of public good provision requires less tax revenue at the state-local level, hence the budget surplus. The lower marginal cost of the public good is not the only reason for the excess revenues. In the process of adjusting consumer tax prices to Lindahl-equivalent tax prices, the additional taxes imposed on the high income groups outweigh the subsidies distributed to the low income groups. Thus, the bulk of excess revenues are mainly a result of the wide discrepancy between Lindahl-equivalent tax prices and actual tax prices for higher income groups. The general equilibrium adjustments are further reflected in the behavior of the median voter (income group 10). Income effects from the rebated excess revenues and the reduction in the marginal cost of the public good lead the median voter to demand a higher quantity of the public good. To maintain his initial public good demand, his tax price has to be increased by 0.3 percent.[22] The equivalent variation measure in Table 8.6 shows that net fiscal incidence in Georgia is regressive.[23]

Alternative II. Lindahl-equivalent tax prices with no excess burden and no tax exporting: *Remove all Georgia state-local taxes and replace them with lump-sum taxes to obtain a Lindahl tax structure.*

Tax-public good alternative II is only different from alternative I in that it removes the excess burden and exporting of state-local taxes in Georgia by introducing lump-sum taxes. In Georgia, the net returns to capital and land increase by 9 and 7 percent, respectively. The composite price of private goods decreases by 5 percent, and the price of leisure for consumers

---

[21] This is a quite commonly used assumption in the literature. Of course, there are other ways of distributing excess revenues, and the results could be affected by the distribution rule that is chosen.

[22] This result also represents a significant difference between the general equilibrium approach used in this essay and previous partial equilibrium measures of net fiscal incidence using Lindahl-equivalent tax prices. Under partial equilibrium the tax price of the median voter is assumed unchanged.

[23] If the equivalent variation relative to income decreases (increases) as income increases, the benchmark net fiscal incidence is said to be regressive (progressive).

Table 8.7. *Welfare effects of Lindahl tax prices: Remove all*
Georgia state-local taxes and replace them with lump-sum taxes
to obtain a Lindahl tax structure

Household	% PPPG[a]	% QDPG[b]	EV[c]	EV[d]
1	−80	127	376	11
2	−64	68	365	7
3	−61	62	415	7
4	−49	42	418	5
5	−48	39	426	4
6	−39	28	383	3
7	−22	13	183	1
8	−11	6	264	1
9	−6	3	62	0
10	−2	0	−364	−1
11	8	−4	−291	−1
12	13	−8	−921	−3
13	25	−13	−1,503	−4
14	36	−17	−1,991	−4
15	41	−20	−3,280	−7
16	50	−24	−5,310	−9
17	79	−31	−7,320	−11
18	93	−36	−12,112	−14
19	167	−52	−35,954	−23

Note: Percent changes are relative to the benchmark equilibrium.

[a] Personal price of the public good.
[b] Personal quantity demanded of the public good.
[c] Average equivalent variation per household in dollars.
[d] Equivalent variation as a percentage of income.

increases on the basis of their marginal tax rate. Results in Table 8.7 show that state-local net fiscal incidence is still regressive in Georgia. However, all income groups are worse off relative to alternative I. The overall effect for Georgia is a welfare loss of 9 percent. Although one would expect efficiency gains from the elimination of state-local distortionary taxes, lump-sum taxes also remove the ability of Georgia consumers to export taxes to the ROUS.[24] Our results thus indicate that Georgia state-local taxes are (from Georgia's viewpoint exclusively) welfare improving overall and by income class in that the beneficial tax-exporting effect dominates efficiency costs of distortionary taxes. Note that Lindahl tax prices are lower than in

[24] In our model, state-local taxes are exported through three channels: capital mobility, intermediate input sales, and off-setting reductions in federal tax liabilities. Intermediate input sales are modeled using an interregional input-output matrix between Georgia and the ROUS.

alternative I. For instance, relative to the benchmark, the median voter's tax price decreases by 2 percent in alternative II as opposed to an increase of 0.3 percent in alternative I. Because income effects from tax exporting dominate those arising from distortionary taxation, consumers' real income does not increase as much as it did in alternative I, hence the lower tax prices. The marginal cost of the public good decreases less in alternative II than in alternative I (-1.4% as opposed to -1.7%), and the excess revenues generated are 3.5 percent lower than in alternative I.

Alternative III. Samuelson provision of the public good: *Change public good provision rule to Samuelson rule. Use proportional tax/subsidy to maintain budget balance.*

In the absence of distortionary taxes, efficient provision of public goods requires compliance with the Samuelson (1954) condition: the sum of the marginal rates of substitution between the public and private goods over households equals the marginal rate of transformation between these goods.[25] Political processes such as the median voter model, however, do not in general result in an optimal allocation of public goods (see, for example, Buchanan 1964 and Barlow 1970). Thus, in tax-public good alternative III, the public good provision rule is changed from the median voter rule to the Samuelson rule. Budget balance is preserved through lump-sum taxes levied on consumers in proportion to their income. These additional taxes are also incorporated in consumers' tax prices when they formulate their public good demand. Results show that relative to the Samuelson quantity, there is a 30-percent undersupply of the public good in the benchmark. This is because of the fact that, in the benchmark, tax prices for high income groups are low relative to their marginal rates of substitution at the benchmark quantity of the public good, outweighing the opposite effect for low income groups, and resulting in an undersupply of the public good in the benchmark equilibrium. Table 8.8 shows that providing the public good according to the Samuelson rule would improve welfare in Georgia for all income groups, with lower income groups benefiting proportionally more. Thus, relative to an equilibrium in which the Samuelson public good quantity is provided, the benchmark net fiscal incidence is regressive.[26] Aggregate welfare gains in Georgia amount to 2.4 percent.

---

[25] We use the Samuelson quantity, although it is no longer optimal in the presence of distortionary taxes, as pointed out by Atkinson and Stern (1974).

[26] Tax prices change because of the additional revenues needed to supply 30% more of the public good and because of changes in resource supply and consumption behavior. Thus, consumers demand a different public good quantity than they did in the benchmark, but they receive the Samuelson quantity.

Table 8.8. *Welfare effects of Samuelson public good provision: Change public good provision rule to Samuelson rule. Use proportional tax/subsidy to maintain budget balance*

Household	% PPPG[a]	% QDPG[b]	EV[c]	EV[d]
1	1	5	521	16
2	11	−2	450	9
3	9	−1	537	8
4	13	−4	502	6
5	4	0	806	7
6	5	−1	822	6
7	8	−3	738	4
8	12	−5	683	3
9	10	−4	771	3
10	5	−2	963	4
11	8	−4	899	3
12	6	−3	1,007	3
13	8	−4	933	2
14	9	−5	893	2
15	5	−4	1,067	2
16	1	−3	1,246	2
17	4	−5	961	1
18	0	−4	1,183	1
19	−2	−7	1,819	1

Note: Percent changes are relative to the benchmark equilibrium.
[a] Personal price of the public good.
[b] Personal quantity demanded of the public good.
[c] Average equivalent variation per household in dollars.
[d] Equivalent variation as a percentage of income.

Alternative IV. Lindahl-equivalent tax prices and Samuelson public good quantity: *Adjust Georgia consumer's actual tax prices to Lindahl-equivalent tax prices through lump-sum taxes or subsidies. Change public good provision rule to Samuelson rule. Use proportional tax/subsidy to maintain budget balance.*

In tax-public good alternative IV, consumers are taxed according to the benefit principle, and the public good is provided according to the Samuelson rule. Under these conditions, the public good quantity is only 14 percent higher than the benchmark quantity. Because public good demands by higher income households dominate those by lower income households, increasing tax prices for the rich results in a smaller undersupply of the public good relative to alternative III. As Table 8.9 shows, net fiscal incidence is still regressive, with lower income groups gaining more than they did in alternative III, and the highest income group experiencing a welfare

Table 8.9. *Welfare effects of Lindahl-equivalent tax prices and Samuelson public good provision: Adjust Georgia consumer's actual tax prices to Lindahl-equivalent tax prices through lump-sum taxes or subsidies. Change public good provision rule to Samuelson rule. Use proportional tax/subsidy to maintain budget balance*

Household	% PPPG[a]	% QDPG[b]	EV[c]	EV[d]
1	−83	162	704	22
2	−71	94	707	14
3	−69	87	847	13
4	−60	64	871	10
5	−58	61	1,248	11
6	−52	49	1,302	9
7	−39	31	1,208	7
8	−31	23	1,200	6
9	−28	19	1,246	5
10	−23	16	1,321	5
11	−17	11	1,295	4
12	−11	6	1,176	3
13	−2	0	909	2
14	7	−4	669	1
15	12	−7	262	1
16	21	−12	−546	−1
17	43	−20	−1,905	−3
18	58	−26	−4,392	−5
19	126	−44	−19,653	−12

Note: Percent changes are relative to the benchmark equilibrium.
[a] Personal price of the public good.
[b] Personal quantity demanded of the public good.
[c] Average equivalent variation per household in dollars.
[d] Equivalent variation as a percentage of income.

loss. There is an aggregate welfare loss of 2 percent in Georgia, as opposed to an aggregate welfare gain of 2.4 percent in alternative III.

Alternative V. Lindahl tax prices with no excess burdens and no tax exporting and the efficient quantity of the public good: *Remove all Georgia state-local taxes and replace them with lump-sum taxes to obtain a Lindahl tax structure. Change public good provision rule to Samuelson rule. Use proportional tax/subsidy to maintain budget balance.*

Tax-public good alternative V is a Lindahl equilibrium in which Georgia state-local taxes are no longer distortionary or exportable, and the public good is provided at its efficient level according to the Samuelson rule. This

Table 8.10. *Welfare effects of Lindahl tax prices and Samuelson public good provision: Remove all Georgia state-local taxes and replace them with lump-sum taxes to obtain a Lindahl tax structure. Change public good provision rule to Samuelson rule. Use proportional tax/subsidy to maintain budget balance*

Household	% PPPG[a]	% QDPG[b]	EV[c]	EV[d]
1	−84	155	436	14
2	−71	89	425	9
3	−69	82	491	8
4	−60	60	491	6
5	−58	56	603	5
6	−51	44	593	4
7	−37	27	435	2
8	−29	19	519	2
9	−25	16	418	2
10	−21	12	186	1
11	−14	7	265	1
12	−9	3	−150	−0
13	1	−2	−584	−1
14	10	−7	−925	−2
15	14	−10	−1,812	−4
16	22	−14	−3,297	−6
17	45	−22	−4,886	−7
18	58	−28	−8,440	−10
19	123	−46	−26,809	−17

Note: Percent changes are relative to the benchmark equilibrium.
[a] Personal price of the public good.
[b] Personal quantity demanded of the public good.
[c] Average equivalent variation per household in dollars.
[d] Equivalent variation as a percentage of income.

alternative provides the most comprehensive measure of net fiscal incidence. The results are similar to those obtained with other tax-public good alternatives but with some revealing differences. The efficient public good quantity is 12 percent higher than that in the benchmark equilibrium, but lower than the quantity demanded in alternative IV (14 percent). This indicates that tax exporting dominates the income effects from distortionary state-local taxes and results in an oversupply of the public good, a result anticipated in the tax exporting literature. With respect to net fiscal incidence, Table 8.10 shows that relative to the Lindahl equilibrium, the distribution of net fiscal benefits in Georgia is regressive. The elasticity of this Lindahl tax structure with respect to income obtained from a regression of the natural log of

Lindahl tax prices on the natural log of income for the nineteen income groups is 1.50 (p < 0.001). Aggregate welfare decreases by 6 percent compared to the 2-percent loss in alternative IV, which indicates that tax exporting has a significant impact on Georgia welfare.

Alternative VI. The impact of tax exporting in a system of jurisdictions:
Remove all Georgia and ROUS state-local taxes and replace them with lump-sum taxes. Median voter rule for public good provision.

All the simulations discussed so far have maintained the ROUS state-local taxes at their benchmark level. The present model, however, allows us to investigate an issue raised by Wildasin (1987, 598). He states: "[T]ax exporting may, but does not necessarily, stimulate local government spending . . . it is possible that tax exporting by a *system* of jurisdictions might actually reduce local public spending through the negative income effects associated with the deadweight loss from the distortion of trade." Our results so far have shown that from the perspective of the state of Georgia alone, tax exporting does stimulate state-local government spending.[27]

To our knowledge, there have been no empirical investigations so far of Wildasin's conjecture on the effect of tax exporting on the supply of public goods in a system of jurisdictions. Our interregional numerical general equilibrium model seems to offer the appropriate framework for this analysis. Thus, in tax-public good alternative VI, we remove all state-local taxes (in Georgia and the ROUS), replace them with lump-sum taxes, and provide the median voter's most preferred public good quantity. We find that all income groups demand more of the public good, with the median voter in Georgia demanding 12 percent more than in the benchmark. This increase is because of not only the removal of the distortion of trade between the two regions but also the removal of the excess burden of state-local taxes. Thus, we perform two more simulations: First, we remove only Georgia's state-local taxes and replace them with lump-sum taxes. This eliminates exporting of Georgia taxes and excess burdens only in Georgia. However, Georgia taxpayers still pay for the exported taxes from the ROUS. We find that the median voter demands 3 percent less of the public good than in the benchmark. This is consistent with our previous results and indicates that the effects of tax exporting in Georgia dominate the excess burden of locally borne distortionary taxes. Second, we replace all state-local taxes only in the

---

[27] An important determinant of this effect is the distinction between traded and non-traded goods, which is not addressed in our model. Allowing for traded and non-traded goods could affect our finding on the stimulative effect of tax exporting in Georgia.

Table 8.11. *Welfare effects of tax exporting and median voter public good provision: Remove all Georgia and ROUS state-local taxes and replace them with lump-sum taxes. Median voter rule for public good provision*

Household	% PPPG[a]	% QDPG[b]	EV[c]	EV[d]
1	−11	16	1,230	39
2	−12	12	1,341	27
3	−12	13	1,621	26
4	−12	12	1,815	21
5	−12	13	2,531	22
6	−12	13	2,883	20
7	−12	12	3,042	17
8	−12	12	3,207	15
9	−12	12	3,615	16
10	−12	12	4,268	16
11	−12	12	4,393	14
12	−12	12	4,946	14
13	−12	11	5,059	13
14	−12	10	5,287	12
15	−12	10	5,942	12
16	−12	9	6,361	11
17	−12	8	5,908	8
18	−12	6	6,542	8
19	−11	1	5,755	4

Note: Percent changes are relative to the benchmark equilibrium.
[a] Personal price of the public good.
[b] Personal quantity demanded of the public good.
[c] Average equivalent variation per household in dollars.
[d] Equivalent variation as a percentage of income.

ROUS with lump-sum taxes, thus eliminating tax exporting from ROUS to Georgia, and find that the median voter demands 13 percent more of the public good than in the benchmark. Therefore, although tax exporting by Georgia leads to an oversupply of the public good, tax importing from the ROUS leads to an undersupply of the public good, together resulting in an overall undersupply of the public good in the benchmark. The 12-percent increase in public good demand is primarily a result of the elimination of the distortion of trade between the two regions. These findings provide strong support for Wildasin's (1987) conjecture. Table 8.11 shows that eliminating distortionary and exportable taxes from both regions would result in a welfare gain for all income classes and the ROUS consumer. Aggregate welfare gain in Georgia amounts to 11 percent, with the lowest income groups gaining the most. The ROUS consumer's welfare in turn increases by 1.3 percent. Furthermore, we find that there is a higher welfare gain (smaller welfare loss) if any of the tax-public good alternatives described incorporated the replacement of all state-local taxes in both regions with lump-sum taxes.

4.1. Sensitivity of the Results to the Elasticity of Substitution

A key parameter in model computations is the elasticity of substitution between the composite public good and the composite private good in household preferences, σ. The simulations thus far have used a value of 0.5, which implies an uncompensated elasticity of demand with respect to the tax price of -0.5, if the public good expenditure shares are small (Piggott and Whalley 1987).[28] Econometric estimates of the tax price elasticity in the median voter literature have varied from -1.15 to $+0.25$.[29] We estimated demand curves for public goods using Georgia counties with populations of more than 15,000 in 1990. The results in Table 8.12 show that the tax price elasticity is estimated at $-.547$ for general expenditure and varies between $-.706$ for "correction" to $-.286$ for "highway." Given this range of econometric estimates, we assess the sensitivity of our results to the estimated value of σ and present them in terms of alternative V, which is the most comprehensive measure of net fiscal incidence.[30]

Table 8.13 shows that as σ increases, benchmark equilibrium net fiscal incidence becomes less regressive and turns progressive, welfare gains (losses) by income class become smaller and eventually turn into losses (gains), and the undersupply of the public good becomes smaller and eventually turns into an oversupply. These results suggest that there is an elasticity of substitution between public and private goods that would imply that the actual state-local tax structure in Georgia is equivalent to a Lindahl tax structure (which is distributionally neutral) with Samuelson public good provision. This value for σ turns out to be 0.82, which is slightly higher than the elasticity of substitution corresponding to "corrections" expenditures.

---

[28] There is no easy intuition on what may determine the elasticity of substitution. For example, when public goods take the form of cash transfers, they become perfectly substitutable with private goods.

[29] See, for example, Borcherding and Deacon (1972), Bergstrom and Goodman (1973), and Pommerehne and Schneider (1978).

[30] When public goods take the form of cash transfers, they become perfectible substitutable with private goods. We do not consider this case here.

Table 8.12. *Demand curves for public goods (counties in Georgia with population more than 15,000 in 1990) (with tax share adjusted for no. of households)*

Equation (log of)	Constant	Log of tax share	Log of M. income	Log of no. households	Crowding parameter	R^2	F	No. of obs.
General	2.412	−.547**	.253	1.184**	1.406	0.902	252.07	86
expenditure		(.083)	(.253)	(0.058)				
Welfare	−12.931	−.553**	1.351*	1.099**	1.221	0.683	56.7	83
		(0.209)	(.578)	(.126)				
Hospital	15.405	−.610	−1.700	1.514**	2.320	0.637	19.26	37
		(.361)	(1.256)	(0.235)				
Health	19.900	−.055	−1.881**	1.462**	1.489	0.680	58.04	86
		(.174)	(.546)	(.121)				
Highway	2.221	−.286*	.361	.889**	0.844	0.702	64.32	86
		(.126)	(.394)					
Police	−7.277	−.166	1.118**	1.049**	1.058	0.888	216.38	86
		(.089)	(.280)	(.062)				
Correction	6.449	−.706*	−.786	1.552**	2.878	0.606	39.40	81
		(.280)	(.831)	(.177)				
Parks &	−20.221	−.507	2.104**	1.140**	1.284	0.621	44.23	85
recreation		(.272)	(0.745)	(.164)				
Sewerage	−11.374	−.258	1.254*	1.246**	1.332	0.734	75.39	86
		(.178)	(.557)	(.124)				

* Significant at .05 level; ** Significant at .01 level.

Source: 1992 Census of Government; 1990 Census of Population and Housing; 1988–1989 Georgia Statistical Abstract; Georgia Department of Revenue's Statistical Report for 1990; 1990 Sales/Assessment Study Summary.

Table 8.13 shows that when σ equals 0.82, welfare losses are approximately proportional at 4 percent. These welfare losses are only a result of the elimination of tax exporting, which dominates the excess burden effects of state-local taxation, and therefore imply that Georgia state-local taxes are welfare improving at a proportional rate of 4 percent.

The distribution of marginal rates of substitution between the public good and the composite private good across income classes depends on the assumed value of σ (see equation (3)). As σ changes from 0.82 in either direction, the tax price adjustments necessary to attain a Lindahl-equivalent tax structure become larger, which in turn implies a higher regressivity (for $\sigma < 0.82$) or progressivity (for $\sigma > 0.82$) of the benchmark state-local tax structure. The benchmark distribution of net benefits changes from regressive to progressive simply because when σ is less (more) than 0.82, the poor demand less (more) than the benchmark public good quantity. Those who demand less lose because their tax prices are too high.

Table 8.13. *Sensitivity analysis of net fiscal incidence to changes in the elasticity of substitution between private and public goods, σ*

	$\sigma = 0.4$			$\sigma = 0.82$			$\sigma = 1.5$		
% QSPG[d]	12			0			−19		
Income group	% PPPG[a]	% QDPG[b]	EV[c]	% PPPG[a]	% QDPG[b]	EV[c]	% PPPG[a]	% QDPG[b]	EV[c]
1	−93	195	15	−35	42	1	69	−57	−23
2	−84	117	12	−11	7	−3	99	−66	−20
3	−82	104	11	−13	10	−3	79	−60	−17
4	−74	78	9	−2	−1	−4	88	−63	−14
5	−67	66	8	−16	13	−3	38	−41	−11
6	−62	52	7	−11	8	−3	35	−39	−10
7	−48	32	5	0	−2	−4	41	−42	−9
8	−38	24	5	7	−7	−3	45	−43	−8
9	−32	19	4	4	−5	−4	32	−35	−7
10	−24	12	2	−3	0	−4	13	−18	−6
11	−13	7	2	2	−3	−3	15	−20	−5
12	−4	1	1	−0	−1	−3	5	−8	−4
13	10	−6	−1	3	−5	−4	3	−6	−4
14	24	−10	−2	5	−6	−4	0	−2	−4
15	34	−15	−4	0	−3	−4	−11	18	−3
16	50	−22	−8	−3	−1	−5	−21	40	−3
17	85	−29	−9	6	−8	−5	−20	37	−3
18	109	−36	−13	2	−5	−5	−32	76	−2
19	212	−55	−19	7	−10	−7	−48	168	0

Note: All amounts are in percent changes relative to the benchmark equilibrium.
[a] Personal price of the public good.
[b] Personal quantity demanded of the public good.
[c] Equivalent variation as a percentage of income.
[d] Quantity supplied of the public good.

The relationship between σ and whether there is an under- or oversupply of the public good in the benchmark is mostly a consequence of the large jump in income for the highest income class. Because of this group's high income (relative to their tax price), their demand for the public good tends to dominate all other groups' demands. Thus, a different benchmark tax structure could have yielded an oversupply of the public good at low values of σ.

5. Conclusion

This essay presents different definitions and measurements of Lindahl net fiscal incidence defined as the difference between the willingness to pay and the actual tax price paid by individuals for a set quantity of the public good determined by a voting equilibrium. These measures of net fiscal incidence can also be interpreted as the incidence of the net benefits of a coercive fiscal system, or as the distribution of a welfare-based measure of coercion analogous to that studied by Winer, Tridimas, and Hettich in their essay in this book, where individuals are forced to consume quantities of the public good that are more than or less than the level they would like at the tax price they have to pay.

We investigate net fiscal incidence at the state-local level in a numerical general equilibrium framework allowing for explicit demands for public goods, median voter rule of public goods provision, and interregional tax exporting. We have compared the benchmark equilibrium to a full Lindahl equilibrium (which is the most comprehensive measure of net fiscal incidence) as well as to other equilibria incorporating various non-comprehensive approaches followed in the literature when measuring net fiscal incidence. We find that all these measures yield the same characterization of the distributional impact of the state-local tax and expenditure package, although the exact magnitudes are different. What is critical, however, is the elasticity of substitution between public and private goods in household preferences. The distribution of net benefits across income groups at the regional level (state of Georgia) is regressive, and the public good is undersupplied if the elasticity of substitution between public goods and private goods is less than 0.82, which, according to our estimates for Georgia, it is. The distribution is progressive and the public good is oversupplied if the elasticity of substitution is more than 0.82. Net fiscal incidence is neutral and the public good is efficiently provided if the elasticity of substitution is 0.82. We also find that Georgia state-local taxes are welfare improving in that the income effects from tax exporting dominate those of distortionary taxation. However, tax exporting by both Georgia and the ROUS results in welfare losses to both regions from the distortion of trade.

The main goal of this essay has been to expand on our understanding of how governments' tax and expenditure policies affect the distribution of individual welfare and the level of aggregate welfare. Using a computable general equilibrium approach expands our understanding of net fiscal incidence by allowing for the excess burdens of taxes, the exporting of taxes across jurisdictions, and the welfare effects of the inefficient supply of the public goods through the political system. Net fiscal incidence or the value taxpayers put to a tax public expenditure package depends clearly on the preferences of taxpayers and in particular how much they value public goods against the private goods they have to forgo in taxes to finance the public good. Therefore, it is not surprising that the progressivity or regressivity of government budgets depends on the preferences of taxpayers as reflected in the elasticity of substitution between public and private goods. What is surprising is that net fiscal incidence in this case is not very sensitive to the comprehensiveness of the approach used to measure it. This is of course a direct consequence of the fact that the distortionary effects of state-local taxes are dwarfed by the distribution of benefits across consumers.

From a policy point of view, our analysis implies that, given a state's budget, the scale of the distributional impact of state-local taxes is more important than the scale of their excess burden. However, because there is still considerable uncertainty regarding the true value of the elasticity of substitution between public and private goods, the essay does not lead to specific policy implications and how much redistributive tax and spending policies should be at the regional level, in our case Georgia. The determination of the actual elasticity of substitution is left for future research. Also, future research should tackle the composition of public spending, especially allowing for the explicit separate modeling of those expenditures that have a direct redistributive impact, such as welfare spending, and should be more discriminating in the computations of actual tax prices based on the final economic incidence of the various taxes among different income groups. It is our hope that this essay has contributed a useful framework to conduct that further analysis.

APPENDIX

Treatment of Taxes

The personal income tax has graduated marginal rates that differ among income groups. Regional and federal income taxes paid by each group j are thus modeled as two linear tax functions,

$$T_j^{lg} = B_j^g + \tau_j^g P_L L_j + \tau_j'^g P_K K_j, \qquad (A.1)$$

where g is the type of government (regional or federal), B_j^g is the intercept that captures the various personal deductions in the tax code, τ_j^g is the marginal tax rate for group j on all labor and capital income, and $\tau_j'^g$ is the marginal tax rate for group j, adjusted for industry differentials (debt versus retained earnings and new shares investment financing). Expanded income,

I_j, equals labor and capital income, plus the value of leisure, minus income taxes. Income spent on private commodities can then be written as

$$I_j - P_{le}le_j = P_L L_j + P_K K_j - T_j^I, \tag{A.2}$$

where P_{le} is the price of leisure, and T_j^I is the sum of regional and federal income taxes paid by group j.

On the production side, taxes on capital income are modeled using the cost-of-capital approach. Each sector uses three sources of finance: debt, retained earnings, and new shares. Nominal discount rates for each sector are calculated using the appropriate weights for the sources of finance and the required rate of return on each type of finance. The required rates of return are different because of taxes, but no risk is involved. It is further assumed that arbitrage leads to equal net-of-tax rates of return earned from these financial instruments. The net real return to debt holders is $r = i(1 - \tau_d) - \pi$, where i is the nominal interest rate, π is the expected inflation rate, and τ_d is the personal marginal income tax rate of debt holders.

In the corporate sector, interest costs are deducted at the statutory corporate income tax rate u. This statutory corporate income tax rate is a function of the federal and the state corporate income tax rates, u^f and u^s, such that $u = u^f + u^s - u^f u^s$. A debt-financed investment must therefore earn a net-of-corporate-tax return of $r_d = i(1 - u)$. The net return on retained earnings, r_{re}, is taxed at the personal marginal tax rate on accrued capital gains, τ_{re}. Because of arbitrage, the nominal net return $r_{re}(1 - \tau_{re})$ has to be equal to the nominal net return, $i(1 - \tau_d)$. This leads to a discount rate on retained earnings of $r_{re} = i(1 - \tau_d)/(1 - \tau_{re})$. Similarly, the discount rate on new shares is $r_{ns} = i(1 - \tau_d)/(1 - \tau_{ns})$, where τ_{ns} is the personal marginal tax rate on dividend income. The corporate sector's overall discount rate is therefore a weighted average of these three discount rates in which the weights depend on the proportions of corporate investment financed by debt, retained earnings, and new shares,

$$r_C = c_d r_d + c_{re} r_{re} + c_{ns} r_{ns}, \tag{A.3}$$

where c_d, c_{re}, and c_{ns} are the proportions of corporate investments financed by the three types of mechanisms.

In the noncorporate sector, entrepreneurial income is taxed at the personal marginal tax rate, τ_{NC}. Noncorporate investment can be financed through debt or equity, and because of arbitrage, these two instruments must earn the same net rate of return on investment. The overall discount rate for the noncorporate sector is thus a weighted average of the discount rates on debt-financed investment and equity-financed investment:

$$r_{NC} = n_d[i(1 - \tau_{NC})] + n_e[i(1 - \tau_d)], \qquad (A.4)$$

where n_d and n_e are the shares of noncorporate investment financed by debt and equity, respectively.

In the housing industry, the distinction is between rental housing and owner-occupied housing rather than between corporate and noncorporate sectors. Owner-occupied housing receives special tax treatment whereas rental housing receives the same treatment as the noncorporate sector. For homeowners, interest expenses are deductible at the personal marginal tax rate τ_h, so the appropriate discount rate on debt is $i(1 - \tau_h)$. Because of arbitrage, the return on homeowner equity must equal the net return to holding debt, $i(1 - \tau_d)$. Therefore, the overall discount rate in the owner-occupied housing sector is

$$r_h = h_d[i(1 - \tau_h)] + h_e[i(1 - \tau_d)], \qquad (A.5)$$

where h_d and h_e are the debt and equity shares of owner-occupied housing investment, respectively.

The gross-of-tax costs of capital facing the corporate, noncorporate, and housing sectors can be written as

$$\rho_i^{NC} = \frac{r_{NC} - \pi + \Delta_i}{1 - \tau_{NC}} \left(1 - \tau_{NC} a_i^{NC}\right) + \upsilon_i - \Delta_i, \quad i = k, l, \quad (A.6)$$

$$\rho_i^C = \frac{r_C - \pi + \Delta_i}{1 - u} \left(1 - u a_i^C\right) + \upsilon_i - \Delta_i, \quad i = k, l, \quad (A.7)$$

$$\rho^h = r_h - \pi + (1 - \lambda\tau_h)\upsilon_h, \qquad (A.8)$$

where k is capital, l is land, π is the expected rate of inflation, Δ_i is the economic depreciation rate of factor i, u is the statutory corporate income tax rate, a_i^C and a_i^{NC} are present values for depreciation allowances for corporate and noncorporate factors of type i, υ_i is the property tax rate on factor i, λ is the fraction of property taxes deducted by homeowners, and υ_h is the property tax rate on homes.

THE PRODUCTION SIDE

Each industry's value added is modeled as a CES function of labor and composite capital and land,

$$VA = \varphi[\delta L^{(\sigma_1 - 1)/\sigma_1} + (1 - \delta)K^{(\sigma_1 - 1)/\sigma_1}]^{\sigma_1/(\sigma_1 - 1)}, \qquad (A.9)$$

where L is labor used in the industry, K is a composite of capital and land used in the industry, σ_1 is the elasticity of substitution between labor and composite capital, φ is a production scale parameter, and δ is an input-weighting parameter.

Producers choose labor and composite capital to minimize factor costs, subject to the constraint that the value-added in equation (A.9) equals one. Therefore, demand for labor and capital per unit of value added are

$$L/VA = \varphi^{-1}\left[(1-\delta)\left(\frac{\delta P_K}{(1-\delta)P_L^*}\right)^{1-\sigma_1} + \delta\right]^{\sigma_1/(1-\sigma_1)}, \quad (A.10)$$

$$K/VA = \varphi^{-1}\left[\delta\left(\frac{(1-\delta)P_L^*}{\delta P_K}\right)^{1-\sigma_1} + (1-\delta)\right]^{\sigma_1/(1-\sigma_1)}, \quad (A.11)$$

where P_K is the gross of tax cost of composite capital and land, and $P_L^* = P_L(1+t_L)$ is the gross wage paid by producers. The minimized cost of value added is therefore $P_L^*L + P_K K$, and the price per unit of value added is $P^v = P_L^*L/VA + P_K K/VA$ for each industry in each region.

Composite capital and land, K, is specified as a CES function of capital and land,

$$K = \left[\psi_k^{1/\sigma_2}\, k^{(\sigma_2-1)/\sigma_2} + \psi_l^{1/\sigma_2}\, l^{(\sigma_2-1)/\sigma_2}\right]^{\sigma_2/(\sigma_2-1)}, \quad (A.12)$$

where k is capital, l is land, and σ_2 is the elasticity of substitution between land and capital. Producers minimize the total cost of land and capital, $\rho_l l + \rho_k k$, subject to the constraint that the quantity of composite capital and land in equation A12 be equal to K. This optimization results in the following demands for capital and land:

$$k = \frac{\psi_k(P_K K)}{(\rho_k)^{\sigma_2}\left[\psi_k(\rho_k)^{1-\sigma_2} + \psi_l(\rho_l)^{1-\sigma_2}\right]} \quad (A.13)$$

$$l = \frac{\psi_l(P_K K)}{(\rho_l)^{\sigma_2}\left[\psi_k(\rho_k)^{1-\sigma_2} + \psi_l(\rho_l)^{1-\sigma_2}\right]}, \quad (A.14)$$

In each region, consumer goods are produced from producer goods through the fixed coefficient transition matrix Z. Each coefficient in this matrix gives the amount of producer good i needed to produce one consumer good m.

The Consumption Side

Consumption of Public Goods
Utility, X, is specified as a CES function of the regional public good, G, and a composite of private goods, C,

$$X = (\alpha^{1/\sigma} G^{(\sigma-1)/\sigma} + (1 - \alpha)^{1/\sigma} C^{(\sigma-1)/\sigma})^{\sigma/(\sigma-1)}, \qquad (A.15)$$

which the consumer maximizes subject to

$$I = P_X X = P_G G + P_C C, \qquad (A.16)$$

where I is gross income less federal taxes paid, G is the regional public good, C is the composite private good, α is a share parameter, σ is the elasticity of substitution between the public good and the composite private good, and P_G is the consumer's tax price (share of state and local taxes paid times the marginal cost of the public good). First order conditions yield

$$MRS_{CG} = \frac{MUX_G}{MUX_C} = \left(\frac{\alpha}{1-\alpha}\right)^{1/\sigma} \left(\frac{C}{G}\right)^{1/\sigma} = \frac{P_G}{P_C} \qquad (A.17)$$

or

$$MRS_{CG} = \frac{P_G}{P_C}, \qquad (A.18)$$

where P_C is the price of the composite private good C. It follows then that for each consumer group, demand functions are

$$G = \frac{\alpha I}{(P_G)^\sigma \left[\alpha (P_G)^{(1-\sigma)} + (1-\alpha) P_C^{(1-\sigma)}\right]} \qquad (A.19)$$

and

$$C = \frac{(1-\alpha) I}{(P_C)^\sigma \left[\alpha (P_G)^{(1-\sigma)} + (1-\alpha) P_C^{(1-\sigma)}\right]}. \qquad (A.20)$$

Given that the quantity G actually provided is the one chosen by the median voter, the value α can be determined as

$$\alpha = \frac{(P_{G_m})^\sigma G_m}{(P_{G_m})^\sigma G_m + (P_{C_m})^\sigma C_m}, \qquad (A.21)$$

where m refers to the median voter. The value G_m chosen by the median voter is then imposed on all consumer group representatives.

Labor-leisure Choice

At the upper level, utility is modeled as a CES function of leisure, *le*, and the composite of public good and composite private commodities *X*. Each consumer group maximizes a CES utility function

$$U = [\beta^{1/\varepsilon} X^{(\varepsilon-1)/\varepsilon} + (1-\beta)^{1/\varepsilon} le^{(\varepsilon-1)/\varepsilon}]^{\varepsilon/(\varepsilon-1)}, \qquad (A.22)$$

where β is a weighting parameter, and ε, is the elasticity of substitution between the composite *X* and leisure *le*. Leisure is labor endowment (*E*) less time spent working (*L*). Each consumer maximizes this utility (equation (A.22)) subject to the constraint,

$$GEI = P_X X + P_{le} le, \qquad (A.23)$$

where *GEI* is expanded income gross of state and local taxes but net of federal taxes, P_X is the price of the composite private commodities and public good *X*, and P_{le} is the price of leisure. The price of leisure, P_{le}, is taken to be the after-tax return to labor of each income group. Because a unit of labor earns P_L after factor taxes, $P_{le} = P_L (1 - \tau_j)$, where τ_j is the *jth* consumer's personal income marginal tax rate. This marginal tax rate is a combination of federal and state marginal tax rates, τ_j^F and $\tau_j^S (\tau_j = \tau_j^F + \tau_j^S - \tau_j^F \tau_j^S)$. Constrained maximization of this utility function leads to the following demand functions:

$$X = \frac{\beta GEI}{P_X^\varepsilon \left[\beta P_X^{(1-\varepsilon)} + (1-\beta) P_{le}^{(1-\varepsilon)} \right]};$$

$$le = \frac{(1-\beta)(GEI)}{P_{le}^\varepsilon \left[\beta P_X^{(1-\varepsilon)} + (1-\beta) P_{le}^{(1-\varepsilon)} \right]}. \qquad (A.24)$$

Consumption of Private Commodities

Private consumption is modeled as a Cobb-Douglas function of the seventeen private commodities. Each consumer thus maximizes a utility function,

$$C = \Pi_i c_i^{\gamma_i}; \sum_{i=1}^{N} \gamma_i = 1, \qquad (A.25)$$

where *N* is the number of private commodities, c_i is the amount purchased of commodity *i*, and γ_i is the expenditure share parameter for commodity *i*.

Each consumer maximizes equation (A.25) subject to the budget constraint

$$\sum_{i=1}^{N} P_{c_i} c_i = P_C C, \tag{A.26}$$

where P_{ci} is the gross of tax price of commodity i. The resulting demands for each consumer good i are then

$$c_i = \frac{\gamma_i(P_C C)}{P_{c_i}}; \quad i = 1, \ldots, 17. \tag{A.27}$$

Each producer output is specified as a CES composite of corporate and noncorporate outputs Y^C and Y^{NC},

$$Y_i = \left[\zeta_i^{1/\xi} \left(Y_i^C \right)^{(\xi-1)/\xi} + (1 - \zeta_i)^{1/\xi} \left(Y_i^{NC} \right)^{(\xi-1)/\xi} \right]^{\xi/(\xi-1)}, \tag{A.28}$$

where $.\zeta_i$ is the preference weight parameter, and ξ is the elasticity of substitution between corporate and noncorporate outputs in consumption.

Consumer groups maximize equation (A.28) subject to the budget constraint

$$p_i^C Y_i^C + p_i^{NC} Y_i^{NC} = p_i^Y Y_i, \tag{A.29}$$

where p_i^C is the price of the corporate good i, p_i^{NC} is the price of the noncorporate good i, and p_i^Y is the price of the composite corporate-noncorporate output Y_i. This optimization leads to the following demand functions for the corporate and noncorporate outputs of industry i:

$$Y_i^C = \frac{\zeta_i \left(p_i^Y Y_i \right)}{\left(p_i^C \right)^\xi \left[\zeta_i \left(p_i^C \right)^{(1-\xi)} + (1 - \zeta_i) \left(p_i^{NC} \right)^{(1-\xi)} \right]};$$

$$Y_i^{NC} = \frac{(1 - \zeta_i) \left(p_i^Y Y_i \right)}{\left(p_i^{NC} \right)^\xi \left[\zeta_i \left(p_i^C \right)^{(1-\xi)} + (1 - \zeta_i) \left(p_i^{NC} \right)^{(1-\xi)} \right]}. \tag{A.30}$$

The Foreign Sector

For each of the twenty producer goods, a foreign export demand function and a foreign import supply function are specified as exponential functions,

$$M_i = M_i^o (P_{Mi}^w)^\mu, \quad i = 1, \ldots, 20$$

$$E_i = E_i^o (P_{Ei}^w)^\nu, \quad i = 1, \ldots, 20; \tag{A.31}$$

where M_i and E_i are the import demand and export supply functions, M_i^o and E_i^o are constants, P_{Mi}^w and P_{Ei}^w are the world price of imports and the world price of exports. The parameters μ and v are the price elasticity of imports and the price elasticity of exports.

For each region, a trade balance constraint is imposed so that

$$\sum_{i=1}^{20} P_{Mi}^w M_i = \sum_{i=1}^{20} P_{Ei}^w E_i. \tag{A.32}$$

Using the exchange rate to translate world prices of exports and imports into domestic prices of exports and imports, import supply functions and export demand functions for each producer good, i, and each region, R, can be written as

$$M_i^R = M_i^{oR}(P_{Mi}^R)^\mu \left(\frac{\Omega_2^R}{\Omega_1^R}\right)^{\frac{\mu}{\mu-v}},$$

$$E_i^R = E_i^{oR}(P_{Ei}^R)^v \left(\frac{\Omega_2^R}{\Omega_1^R}\right)^{\frac{v}{\mu-v}}, \tag{A.33}$$

where Ω_1 and Ω_2 are given by

$$\Omega_1 = \sum_{i=1}^{20} (P_{Mi})^{\mu+1} M_i^o,$$

$$\Omega_2 = \sum_{i=1}^{20} (P_{Ei})^{v+1} E_i^o, \tag{A.34}$$

and the exchange rate e is defined as

$$e = \left(\frac{\Omega_2}{\Omega_1}\right)^{\frac{1}{v-\mu}}. \tag{A.35}$$

Equation (A.33) can be interpreted as foreign import supply and export demand functions, each written as a function of each region's prices and satisfying the condition of zero trade balance for each region.

Equilibrium Conditions

General equilibrium in this model is characterized by four conditions: equality of demand and supply in the labor, land, and capital markets in each region; equality of demand and supply in each private goods market in each region; provision of the regional public good according to the Georgia's median voter's preference; and equality of each government's spending and its revenue. The model thus searches for a vector of prices that satisfies all four conditions. Because capital is specified as mobile between regions, the net-of-tax rate of return to capital is the same for each region. Each region, however, uses its own land and labor.

Given the costs of land and capital, the cost of composite capital and land can be written as

$$P_{Kj} = \left[\psi_{kj} \rho_k^{(1-\sigma_2)} + \psi_{lj} \rho_l^{(1-\sigma_2)} \right]^{\frac{1}{(1-\sigma_2)}}, \tag{A.36}$$

for each industry, j, and each sector (corporate, noncorporate, and owner-occupied housing).

The wage rate, P_L^*, is net of industry-level (payroll) taxes but gross of personal taxes. Given the cost of composite capital, P_{Kj}, and the gross wage rate, P_L^*, the price per unit of value-added can be computed as

$$P_j^v = \frac{P_L^* L_j}{VA} + \frac{P_{Kj} K_j}{VA}, \tag{A.37}$$

for each sector of each industry, j. The price per unit of final output for each sector of industry j, is thus

$$P_j^s = \sum_i P_i^{sv} a_{ij}, \quad s = C, NC, \tag{A.38}$$

where a_{ij} is the use of output i in the production of output j, and where the summation runs across all industries and regions.[31]

The price of composite output Y_j in each industry is based on the prices of the corporate and noncorporate outputs of the industry. The price of this output can be written as

$$p_j^Y = \left[\zeta_j (p_j^C)^{1-\xi} + (1 - \zeta_j)(p_j^{NC})^{1-\xi} \right]^{1/(1-\xi)}, \tag{A.39}$$

---

[31] There are two sectors in each private industry, as well as two government enterprises in each region. Any sector of any industry can use the output of any other sector of any other industry in their region and other regions as an intermediate input. Equation (A.38) thus sums more than seventy-six producer outputs.

for each producer good, j. The prices of the seventeen private consumer goods are related to these producer prices through the coefficients of the transition matrix, Z,

$$P_{ci} = \sum_{j=1}^{20} p_j^Y Z_{ji}, \tag{A.40}$$

where Z_{ji} is the amount of producer good j involved in the production of consumer good i. The price of the composite private good C is calculated as:

$$P_C = \Pi_i \left(\frac{p_{ci}}{\gamma_i} \right)^{\gamma_i}. \tag{A.41}$$

Given the personalized tax price P_G, the price of the composite of private goods and regional public good, X, is

$$P_X = \left[\alpha P_C^{1-\sigma} + (1-\alpha) P_G^{1-\sigma} \right]^{1/(1-\sigma)}. \tag{A.42}$$

Simulations Steps

Alternative I. Lindahl-equivalent tax prices: *Adjust Georgia consumer's actual tax prices to Lindahl-equivalent tax prices through lump-sum taxes or subsidies.*

Define BB_j^S and BBB_j^S added in equation (A.1). BB_j^S is the lump-sum tax or subsidy that adjusts the tax equation for group j,

$$T_j^{Is} = B_j^s + BB_j^s + BBB_j^s + \tau_j^s P_L L_j + \tau_j^{'s} P_K K_j,$$

where s is the regional government. This variable is fixed to zero in the benchmark equilibrium and allowed to vary under this simulation, such that each consumer's tax price changes to satisfy equation (A.18) at the benchmark quantity of the public good provided – that is, as determined by the median voter. This in turn affects government revenues. For the benchmark quantity of the public good to be provided, excess or shortages of revenues are in turn redistributed to, or imposed on, consumers in proportion to their incomes. Hence, BBB_j^S also added to equation (A.1), set to zero at the benchmark, and allowed to vary under this simulation such that the regional government budget is balanced, and the quantity of the public good provided is the benchmark quantity provided.

Alternative II. Lindahl-equivalent tax prices with no excess burden and no tax exporting: *Remove all Georgia state-local taxes and replace them with lump-sum taxes to obtain a Lindahl tax structure.*

All state and local taxes are set to zero; BB_j^S and BBB_j^S are solved for as in simulation alternative I.

Alternative III. Samuelson provision of the public good: *Change the public good provision rule to Samuelson rule. Use proportional tax/subsidy to maintain budget balance.*

Here, equations (A.17) and (A.18) are adapted to define the Samuelson public good quantity:

$$\sum_i MRS_{C_iG} = \frac{P_G}{P_C},$$

$$\sum_i MRS_{C_iG} = \sum_i \left(\frac{\alpha}{1-\alpha}\right)^{1/\sigma} \left(\frac{C_i}{G}\right)^{1/\sigma}.$$

And the Samuelson quantity is solved for using these equations. BBB_j^S is allowed to adjust to maintain budget balance while providing the Samuelson quantity of the public good.

Alternative IV. Lindahl-equivalent tax prices and Samuelson public good quantity: *Adjust Georgia consumer's actual tax prices to Lindahl-equivalent tax prices through lump-sum taxes or subsidies. Change public good provision rule to Samuelson rule. Use proportional tax/subsidy to maintain budget balance.*

This simulation is defined as alternative III, but also adjusts BB_j^S to obtain Lindahl tax prices – that is, consumers demand the Samuelson quantity of the public good at the tax price they pay.

Alternative V. Lindahl tax prices with no excess burdens and no tax exporting and the efficient quantity of the public good: *Remove all Georgia state-local taxes and replace them with lump-sum taxes to obtain a Lindahl tax structure. Change public good provision rule to Samuelson rule. Use proportional tax/subsidy to maintain budget balance.*

This is simulated in the same way as alternative IV, except all state and local taxes are set to zero.

References

Aaron, H., and M. McGuire (1970). "Public Goods and Income Distribution." *Econometrica* 38: 907–920.

Atkinson, A. B., and N. H. Stern (1974). "Pigou, Taxation and Public Goods." *Review of Economic Studies* 41: 19–128.

Bahl, R., J. Martinez-Vazquez, and S. Wallace (2002). "State and Local Choices in Fiscal Redistribution." *National Tax Journal* 4: 723–742.

Ballard, C. L., D. Fullerton, J. B. Shoven, and J. Whalley (1985). *A General Equilibrium Model for Tax Policy Evaluation.* Chicago: University of Chicago Press for National Bureau of Economic Research.

Ballentine, J. G., and W. R. Thirsk (1978). *The Fiscal Incidence of Some Experiments in Fiscal Federalism: Technical Report.* Ottawa: Canada Mortgage and Housing Corporation.

Barlow, R. (1970). "Efficiency Aspects of Local School Finance." *Journal of Political Economy* 78(5): 1028–1040.

Bergstrom, T. C., and R. P. Goodman (1973). "Private Demands for Public Goods." *American Economic Review* 63(3): 280–296.

Bergstrom, T. C., D. Rubinfeld, and P. Shapiro (1982). "Micro-based Estimates of Demand Functions for Local School Expenditures." *Econometrica* 50(5): 1183–1205.

Bird, R., and E. Slack (1983). *Urban Public Finance in Canada.* Toronto: Butterworth's.

Borcherding, T. E., and R. T Deacon (1972). "The Demand for the Services of Non-Federal Governments." *American Economic Review* 62(3): 891–902.

Buchanan, J. M. (1962). "Politics, Policy, and the Pigouvian Margins." *Economica* 29: 17–28.

Buchanan, J. M. (1964). "Fiscal Institutions and Efficiency in Collective Outlay." *American Economic Review* 54(2): 227–235.

Chaudry-Shah, A. M. (1989). A Capitalization Approach to Fiscal Incidence at the Local Level. *Land Economics* 65(4): 359–375.

Fullerton, D., and D. L. Rogers (1993). *Who Bears the Lifetime Tax Burden?* Washington, DC: Brookings Institution.

Gillespie, I. H. (1965). "Effect of Public Expenditures on the Distribution of Income." In R. A. Musgrave (ed.), *Essays in Fiscal Federalism.* Washington, DC: Brookings Institution, 51–84.

Greene, K. V., W. G. Neenan, and C. Scott (1976). "Fiscal Incidence in the Washington Metropolitan Area." *Land Economics* 52(1): 13–31.

Lindahl, E. (1919/1967). "Die Gerechtigkeit der Besteurung," translated (in part) as "Just Taxation: A Positive Solution." In R. Musgrave and A. Peacock (eds.), *Classics in the Theory of Public Finance.* New York, St. James's Press 168–176.

Maital, S. (1973). "Note and Comments on Public Goods and Income Distribution: Some Further Results." *Econometrica* 41(3): 561–568.

Martinez-Vazquez, J. (1982). "Fiscal Incidence at the Local Level." *Econometrica* 50(5): 1207–1218.

Morgan, W., J. Mutti, and D. Rickman (1996). "Tax Exporting, Regional Economic Growth, and Welfare." *Journal of Urban Economics* 39: 131–159.

Musgrave, R. A., and P. Musgrave (eds.) (1980). *Public Finance in Theory and Practice.* New York: McGraw Hill.

Musgrave, R. A., K. E. Case, and H. B. Leonard (1974). "The Distribution of Fiscal Burdens and Benefits." *Public Finance Quarterly* 2: 259–311.

Neenan, W. B. (ed.) (1972). *Political Economy of Urban Areas.* Chicago: Markham Publishing Company.

Piggott, J., and J. Whalley (1987). "Interpreting Net Fiscal Incidence Calculations." *Review of Economics and Statistics* 69: 685–694.

Pommerehne, W. W., and F.S. Schneider (1978). "Fiscal Illusion, Political Institutions, and Local Public Spending." *Kyklos* 31: 381–408.

Romer, T., and H. Rosenthal (1979). "Bureaucrats vs. Voters: On the Political Economy of Resource Allocation by Direct Democracy." *Quarterly Journal of Economics* 93: 563–587.

Round, J. I. (1978). "On Estimating Trade Flows in Interregional Input-Output Models." *Regional Science and Urban Economics* 8: 289–302.

Samuelson, P. A. (1954). "The Pure Theory of Public Expenditure." *Review of Economics and Statistics* 36: 387–389.

Sato, K. (1972). "Additive Utility Functions with Double-Log Consumer Demand Functions." *Journal of Political Economy* 80(1): 102–124.

Shoven, J. B., and J. Whalley (1984). "Applied General Equilibrium Models of Taxation and International Trade: An Introduction and Survey." *Journal of Economic Literature* 22: 1007–1051.

Tax Foundation, Inc. (1961 and 1965). *Tax Burdens and Benefits of Government Expenditures by Income Class.* New York: Tax Foundation Inc.

Wildasin, D. (1987). "The Demand for Public Goods in the Presence of Tax Exporting." *National Tax Journal* 40: 591–601.

Zimmerman, D. (1983). "Resource Misallocation from Interstate Tax Exportation: Estimates of Excess Spending and Welfare Loss in a Median Voter Framework." *National Tax Journal* 36(2): 183–201.

Zodrow, G., and P. Mieszkowski (1986). "Pigou, Property Taxation and the Underprovision of Local Public Goods." *Journal of Urban Economics* 19: 356–370.

Discussion

State-Local Fiscal Incidence and the Tiebout Model

George R. Zodrow

Fiscal incidence studies almost always focus on differential tax incidence, as they measure the effects of alternative tax systems holding the levels of government services constant. Such an approach is certainly reasonable, especially if the goal of the analysis is simply to measure the effects of tax reforms in isolation; moreover, focusing solely on differential tax incidence avoids the difficult conceptual problem of allocating the benefits of public services across households. Nevertheless, at some level, it is net fiscal incidence – that is, the difference between taxes paid and some measure of the benefits of public services received for each household – that is of primary concern in many instances, especially if one is attempting to evaluate the progressivity or regressivity of government policy. To cite just one example that is a subject of current discussion, arguments against the introduction of a value-added tax in the United States on the grounds that it is a regressive tax may be misplaced if the revenues from the tax are used to finance expenditures (e.g., health care benefits) that are distributed either roughly uniformly or accrue primarily to the poor. In addition, fiscal incidence studies are often – although less so than in the past – conducted within the context of a simple partial equilibrium framework that focuses on statutory incidence. However, as is well known, the incidence of many taxes differs considerably from their statutory incidence once tax shifting is analyzed within the context of a general equilibrium model, and such an analysis is also able to capture the relative efficiency effects, or excess burdens, of alternative tax structures.

The analysis presented in the essay in this volume by Sehili and Martinez-Vazquez thus represents an important and useful contribution to the literature, as it analyzes the net fiscal incidence of state and local taxes and expenditures in the state of Georgia, using a fully specified general equilibrium model that includes state and local public services explicitly in individual utility functions. In particular, the paper provides a much richer analysis than the early partial equilibrium net fiscal incidence studies, such as those of Aaron and McGuire (1970) and Martinez-Vazquez (1982), and also significantly extends the general equilibrium framework of net fiscal incidence constructed by Piggott and Whalley (1987). Specifically, with respect to the latter model, Sehili and Martinez-Vazquez consider explicitly the impact of tax exporting to nonresidents, an issue that is often prominent in popular discussions of tax incidence – although the extent of tax exporting is often seriously overstated, especially in modern economies characterized both by national or international competition and significant factor mobility (Zodrow 1999); moreover, they do so in a rich general equilibrium context that considers not only the effects of the exporting of state and local taxes in Georgia but also the effects of tax exporting from other states in the union to the residents of Georgia. And, rather than simply assuming a fixed level of public services, the authors determine the level of public services endogenously, using the standard median voter model (although their assumption of a unitary income elasticity for public services may be problematical for services such as education in which private substitutes are available to high income households). Finally, their general equilibrium analysis also includes endogenous revenue changes, with surpluses or deficits having feedback effects on tax rates.

In addition to constructing a rich model for analyzing net fiscal incidence in Georgia, Sehili and Martinez-Vazquez provide a wide range of simulation results that examine the effects of various changes to their model. This provides considerable detail regarding (a) the effects on net fiscal incidence of numerous variations in their model, such as the use of lump-sum taxes to augment or replace actual state and local taxes to yield "Lindahl-equivalent tax prices" under which taxes paid equal the valuation of benefits received, and (b) the effects of the provision of public services under both the median voter rule and the alternative Samuelson efficiency rule (under which individual demands for a pure public good are aggregated to obtain a single measure of social demand). These multiple simulations also provide the reader with considerable intuition regarding the operation of the model, which is useful in interpreting the results of any complex computable general equilibrium modeling exercise.

In keeping with the theme of this volume, Sehili and Martinez-Vazquez cast their analysis as a measure of the use of coercion by the state. As recognized by the authors, however, this interpretation is somewhat strained for low income individuals, as it is difficult to describe the payment of taxes that fall short of the valuation of benefits received as "coercion." Nevertheless, the comparison of the actual tax system with a "non-coercive, Lindahl-like one" to identify those who benefit and those who lose from the coercion implicit in the taxing authority of the state is an interesting application of the concepts examined in this volume and highlights another way in which the paper extends the existing literature.

Although Sehili and Martinez-Vazquez obtain a wide variety of results, they are all consistent with the same general message, which is that for what they believe to be plausible values of the key parameter in the analysis – the elasticity of substitution between public and private goods – the net fiscal incidence of the state and local tax system in Georgia is regressive. However, they also find that the extent of regressivity is quite sensitive to this elasticity and that a sufficiently large value implies that the fiscal system in Georgia is progressive. One striking result of the analysis concerns the effects of tax exporting. The conventional wisdom is that tax exporting results in an over-supply of public services, as the residents of a jurisdiction perceive that the tax price of public services is low as a result of the potential for tax exporting and thus choose to over-consume public services. However, as pointed out by Wildasin (1986), in a general equilibrium context all other jurisdictions are also simultaneously engaging in tax exporting, and the negative income effects of these activities may result in a net reduction in demand for public services. Sehili and Martinez-Vazquez show that this latter effect is quite important quantitatively, as eliminating all tax exporting in the model gives rise to a 12 percent increase in the demand for public services, accompanied by an aggregate welfare gain of 11 percent for the residents of Georgia because of the expansion of public services from an inefficiently low level attributable to the general equilibrium effects of simultaneous tax exporting by all jurisdictions. Their analysis thus provides yet another example of a situation in which the intuition regarding the economic effects of a particular policy developed from a partial equilibrium perspective is reversed when the interactions among various jurisdictions are taken into account using a general equilibrium perspective.

Although the use of general equilibrium analysis to examine net fiscal incidence in a model that considers tax exporting and endogenous public good determination is compelling and the analysis in this essay is comprehensive and insightful, one potentially serious problem lurks underneath the surface. Throughout their analysis, Sehili and Martinez-Vazquez assume that the public good that enters individual utility functions is a single pure (uncongested) public good, which consists of the aggregate level of state and local public services that is provided to all residents of the state of

Georgia. Although perhaps a reasonable rough approximation for state-level services, there are two reasons why this approach seems inappropriate for local services – which account for about 60 percent of state and local expenditures in Georgia. First, most analyses of the provision of local public goods, drawing on empirical evidence on the per capita costs of local service provision, assume that such services are highly congestible rather than pure uncongested public goods; indeed, the standard assumption in the local public finance literature is that local public services, especially primary and secondary education, are "publicly provided private goods." The second and closely related point is that all residents of a state do not consume the same level of local public services, which can vary significantly across local jurisdictions. Indeed, the classic Tiebout (1956) model of local public goods argues that competition among local jurisdictions in the provision of local public services coupled with perfect individual mobility results in an efficient local public goods equilibrium, as consumers reveal their public goods preferences by "voting with their feet" and sorting themselves into jurisdictions that are perfectly homogeneous with respect to resident household demands for local public services. Note that under this scenario, the voting mechanism is irrelevant, because households are segregated by tastes for public services so that there is no conflict regarding the optimal level of service provision. Moreover, if local public goods are financed with head taxes, then the Tiebout mechanism effectively results in a Lindahl-type equilibrium in which each resident pays for the identical level of public services, which are modeled as publicly provided private goods that are produced at constant per capita cost and provided uniformly to residents. (The latter assumptions are necessary to ensure that migration incentives are efficient, as the marginal cost of public services faced by an immigrant equals the average cost; see Mieszkowski and Zodrow (1989) for further discussion.)

In reality, head taxes are of course not available, as the property tax is the primary revenue instrument for local governments. However, the Tiebout model has been extended to accommodate property taxation under two sets of circumstances. In the first case, all communities are homogeneous with respect to both demands for government services and demands for housing so that house values and thus property taxes are identical (and binding fiscal zoning constraints preclude the construction of smaller homes by potential residents who would like to take advantage of the jurisdiction's public services at a relatively low tax price), replicating Tiebout's head tax equilibrium (Hamilton 1975). In the second case, some communities are heterogeneous with respect to house values, but all communities are fully developed and alternative homogeneous housing communities are available, in which case the capitalization of fiscal differentials – the difference in present values of future taxes and the value of benefits received – into house values again converts the property tax into the head tax envisioned by Tiebout; in this case, the combination of property taxes paid and capitalization effects ensures that all residents of the jurisdiction effectively make the same payment for the identical level of public services provided to each (Hamilton 1976).

My point is not that the Tiebout model necessarily describes reality perfectly. Indeed, as discussed in Zodrow (2001a,b), the model rests on numerous stringent assumptions, especially (as suggested by the partial list of assumptions noted earlier) when the model is extended to include the property tax as a pure benefit tax for the local public services provided by the jurisdiction. Nevertheless, many observers believe that the model provides important insights into the operation of the local public sector. For example, Fischel (2001) argues that the empirical evidence supporting fiscal capitalization is overwhelming and that this is consistent with the view that the property tax is a benefit tax for local public services; similarly, Oates (2006, 27) notes that "many studies now take full capitalization as a premise" and stresses that capitalization is the essential feature of the second and more plausible version of the benefit view of the property tax described earlier. More generally, Fischel, Oates, and Youngman (2011, 121) argue that the "Tiebout model, and the associated benefit view [of the property tax], have long been taken by scholars in local public finance to provide a description of the working of the local public sector in metropolitan areas."

Note that the implications of the Tiebout model for the analysis of Sehili and Martinez-Vazquez are potentially quite important – and indeed suggest that fiscal federalism at the local level, coupled with household mobility across jurisdictions, acts to limit coercion, as discussed in the essay by Brosio in this volume. Indeed, if the model described reality perfectly and all local public services were financed with residential property taxes, then net fiscal incidence in all jurisdictions would be zero, as local property taxes would exactly equal the value of benefits received in each jurisdiction. In this case, the property tax is an efficient benefit tax and coercion – as defined by Sehili and Martinez-Vazquez, as well as in the essay by Winer, Tridimas, and Hettich in this volume, as the difference between what households pay for public services and how they value them (although the discussion by Boadway raises some concerns about this definition) – simply disappears. Net fiscal incidence is thus zero, despite the significant variation in the level of public services across jurisdictions that is the hallmark of the Tiebout model, given variations in public service demands because of the difference in incomes or tastes. The key point is that, in such a Tiebout equilibrium, the Sehili and Martinez-Vazquez methodology would incorrectly indicate a wide variation in net fiscal incidence. This result is inevitable, because the methodology compares tax payments across all jurisdictions to a single level of public services determined at the state level, thus ignoring the variations in service levels across local jurisdictions, which, according to the Tiebout model, exactly match the variations in taxes paid and thus result in an efficient local public goods equilibrium in which net fiscal incidence is zero.

The implications of this point of course depend on the relevance of the Tiebout model for local jurisdictions in Georgia. The Sehili and Martinez-Vazquez analysis assumes that state and local public services can be treated as a single good that is provided at a uniform level and thus appears to assume that the Tiebout mechanism is inoperative or relatively unimportant for local public services. The analysis would be much improved if it were able to capture and analyze in some way the possibility that some of the differences between taxes paid and the level of public services desired by the median voter that are defined as net fiscal incidence instead reflect differences in local public services provided across jurisdictions. In any case, it would be useful for the authors to discuss explicitly their views regarding the potential importance of the variation in public services expected under the Tiebout mechanism for their estimates of net fiscal incidence.

References

Aaron, Henry J., and Martin C. McGuire (1970). "Public Goods and Income Distribution." *Econometrica* 38(6): 907–920.

Fischel, William A. (2001). "Homevoters, Municipal Corporate Governance, and the Benefit View of the Property Tax." *National Tax Journal* 54(1): 157–173.

Fischel, William A., Wallace E. Oates, and Joan Youngman (2011). "Are Local Property Taxes Regressive, Progressive, or What?" Unpublished manuscript.

Hamilton, Bruce W. (1975). "Zoning and Property Taxation in a System of Local Governments." *Urban Studies* 12(2): 205–211.

Hamilton, Bruce W. (1976). "Capitalization of Intrajurisdictional Differences in Local Tax Prices." *American Economic Review* 66(5): 743–753.

Martinez-Vazquez, Jorge (1982). "Fiscal Incidence at the Local Level." *Econometrica* 50(5): 1207–1218.

Mieszkowski, Peter and George R. Zodrow (1989). "Taxation and the Tiebout Model: The Differential Effects of Head Taxes, Taxes on Land Rents, and Property Taxes." *Journal of Economic Literature* 27(3): 1098–1146.

Oates, Wallace E. (2006). "The Many Faces of the Tiebout Model." In William A. Fischel (ed.), *The Tiebout Model at Fifty*. Cambridge MA, Lincoln Institute of Land Policy, 21–45.

Piggott, John, and John Whalley (1987). "Interpreting Net Fiscal Incidence Calculations." *Review of Economics and Statistics* 69(4): 685–694.

Tiebout, Charles M. (1956). "A Pure Theory of Local Expenditures." *Journal of Political Economy* 64(5): 416–424.

Wildasin, David (1986). *Urban Public Finance.* New York: Harwood.

Zodrow, George R. (1999). *State Sales and Income Taxes.* College Station: Texas A&M University Press.

Zodrow, George R. (2001a). "Reflections on the New View and the Benefit View of the Property Tax." In Wallace E. Oates (ed.), *Property Taxation and Local Government Finance.* Cambridge MA: Lincoln Institute of Land Policy, 79–111.

Zodrow, George R. (2001b). "The Property Tax as a Capital Tax: A Room with Three Views." *National Tax Journal* 24(1): 139–156.

9

Fiscal Coercion in Federal Systems, with Special Attention to Highly Divided Societies

Giorgio Brosio

1. Introduction

This essay explores the connection between federalism and coercion that arises through the design and operation of federal systems of government. Coercion stems from applying the same treatment – by means of a public policy, or a tax-expenditure combination – to every individual when preferences differ. It derives from uniformity of publicly produced goods and services and from the fiscal rules used for their financing. Coercion is inevitable with public goods. With publicly provided private goods financed with compulsory payments, uniformity is a matter of policy choice. Although coercion is an inevitable consequence of public actions, it can be reduced or constrained with appropriate political and constitutional arrangements, such as qualified majorities, separation of powers, and, it is often asserted, with decentralization.

Coercion at lower levels of government is usually considered to be lower than at higher levels. In the fiscal federalism literature, coercion is often referred to as a lack of preference matching. Pennock (1959) in an article that predated the analyses of Oates (1968, 1972) used the phrase "disharmony and frustration," which had been coined earlier by Riker and Schaps (1957). Coercion is, in general, a loss of utility individuals experience when they are not treated according to their preferences by the public sector. Winer, Tridimas, and Hettich provide a definition in Chapter 7 of this volume, one that will be used in diagrammatic analysis later, which depends on the difference between what citizens get in services and what they think they deserve at the socially determined tax price that they pay. An alternative definition, used in the following Sehili-Martinez-Vazquez essay (Chapter 8 in this volume), considers the difference between the tax price paid for the public services actually received and what citizens think they should pay. Coercion in either sense can derive from a choice of policies with no appreciable cost for their provision, such as determining the duration of the hunting season, or from policies requiring public revenues for their financing, as in the case of the typical public good analyzed in the public finance literature. Coercion may be particularly strong when, for some individuals, publicly provided services are public "bads" – that is, they require compensation for being forced to consume them. This is especially likely to be the case for societies deeply divided by ethnic, cultural, or religious preferences, a situation that will be explored later in the case of Macedonia.

Decentralization is traditionally regarded as a fundamental means by which coercion or lack of preference matching can be reduced, because of the expected higher homogeneity of preferences within small-sized jurisdictions, and because people can increase spatial homogeneity by sorting themselves according to their preferences for locally produced goods. At the local level citizens can also keep their government in check by exiting and using locally available information. This consideration acknowledges that coercion arises because not only of a lack of preference matching and for reasons related to the costliness of providing different public services to people with varying tastes, but also from differentiation, or discrimination that can arise through policy choices.

Are these commonly held views about the links between decentralization and coercion correct, and are they complete? We shall consider these matters in this essay, showing that answers to questions of whether, and to what extent, it is possible to reduce coercion by altering the structure of governance are more complex than is often thought. Section 2 provides a short review of the theoretical and empirical literature that (effectively, if not explicitly) deals with coercion when the degree of decentralization varies. Section 3 makes use of a simple stylized model to explore the possibility of reducing coercion using decentralized governance, with somewhat ambiguous results. A discussion of the case of Macedonia after the breakup of Yugoslavia illustrates several of the ideas in the preceding sections – this is done in Section 4. Section 5 introduces and considers the interplay between coercion and redistribution, and a Conclusions section completes the essay.

2. The Advantages of Decentralization over Centralization

The superiority of decentralized or federal systems to cater to the preferences of their citizens, and thus their higher potential to reduce coercion, lies in large measure in the presumed incapacity of the central government to provide spatially differentiated policies. In the traditional fiscal federalism literature (see Boadway and Tremblay 2012 for a recent review), higher uniformity of levels of service provision and of taxes at upper levels of government than at lower levels is usually a maintained hypothesis that provides an important, if not the main, rationale for the existence of federal/decentralized systems. This is so, for example, in the analysis of Oates (1972), which shows that decentralized provision of public services that matches local preferences Pareto-dominates centralized uniform provision.

If upper level governments were as able as lower level governments to diversify territorially their policies, there would no more need for the latter, if they were equally efficient in supplying the good and had the same level of good governance. In fact, if both governments were equally good in preference matching, there would in practice be no need for decentralization because a single, large, and efficient government would have the additional advantage of better coordination among subunits and better internalization of regionalized external effects when they exist (Lockwood 2006).[1]

Uniformity of central government policies has never been empirically demonstrated convincingly in the literature on fiscal federalism. On the contrary, observations of nonuniformity of central government policies are easier to find than references to uniformity (see for example, Treisman 2007, Chapter 2).[2] Oates has in his recent works (2005, 2006) clarified the instrumental purpose of equating centralized provision with uniformity of levels of service provision. For example, in his review of the second generation theory of fiscal federalism Oates (2006, 10) writes: "This obviously served my purposes quite well in the theorem by providing a benchmark against which to compare (favorably) a varied, decentralized pattern of outputs of public goods."

Additional arguments about decentralization arise when one allows for alternative modes of governance in the debate. In one of two major streams of this literature, government is assumed to be predatory, attempting to exploit citizens by taxing them more than they would wish (see, for example,

---

[1] Breton (1996) argues that the main rationale for federalism and decentralization is intergovernmental competition, both vertical and horizontal. While this competition clearly provides benefits, one wonders if it cannot be replaced by other competitive mechanisms working within a single-layered system of government.

[2] Breton and Salmon (2007) remark, quite interestingly, that even in France, a country with a deeply entrenched tradition of centralization of government and uniformity of policies, one can observe substantial regional differences in the levels of provision of services by the central government. They result from the explicit delegation of discretionary powers to the Prefects.

Brennan and Buchanan 1980). Here central governments are worse than localized ones because of the absence of constraints on their power that come from the ability of citizens to move between jurisdictions.

A second and more recent stream of thought concerning the role of governance – for example, Lockwood (2002, 2006) and Besley and Coate (2003) – attributes the mismatching of local preferences and fiscal systems to the incapacity of individual legislators at the national level to form winning coalitions without spreading pork barrel expenditure over a large set of electoral districts while funding them with national taxation. Cross-subsidization across local jurisdictions with varying preferences is the result. The obvious policy suggestion coming from this literature dealing with governance, like that of the more traditional public finance literature, is that (coordination costs aside) decentralization of public goods provision should be preferred. However, the arguments can go either way: for example, Brosio, Cassone, and Ricciuti (2002) advance the hypothesis that the observed, more widespread tax evasion in the poorer regions of Southern Italy is the result of an informal agreement with the authorities by which higher and semi-officially sanctioned tax evasion in these regions is allowed as a way to reduce coercion stemming from higher than desired, uniform, and centrally imposed taxes.

Of course, it is possible to replicate the same national to regional exercise downwards, confronting this time regional legislatures that are not perfectly homogenous (but more homogeneous than the national legislature) with local legislatures that are (more) homogeneous, obtaining a higher level of preference matching. Again, better local performance derives basically from higher homogeneity in smaller than in larger jurisdictions. Here preference homogeneity comes from appropriate drawing of the borders of local jurisdictions, as well as from self-sorting through migration.

Citizens can also actively constrain governments using their electoral voices, thereby reducing coercion. Hill (2009) provides a good review of this branch of the literature, listing four factors inducing better local governance: (a) lower costs of subnational electoral activities; (b) greater interest of local populations in the results of local policies; (c) greater information in decentralized, federal systems; and (d) a greater capacity of local government to facilitate cooperation between groups with different identities.

However, such arguments concerning the ability of federalism to reduce the "distance" between governments and citizens are not especially robust when it comes to institutional design and are often context specific, and the case for decentralization remains unclear especially when political economy issues are considered. Even in the *Federalist Papers* (1788, Number 10[3]), concern about capture of local governments by "factions" induced James Madison to argue for retention of powers at the federal level.

Following on from this concern, Feeley and Rubin (2008) argue that in a decentralized setting political identity can be based on some shared economic interest, or mode of life, and not necessarily on shared language, religion, or ethnicity. Political identity can create loyalties sufficient to hold together a political alliance against the usual pressures of self-interested defection. Subgroups united by a common political identity can, therefore, form a stable winning coalition if they capture control of the government. This can reduce *their* coercion.[4] At the same time, however, other subgroups may suffer exploitation at the hands of this coalition and could be excluded from political power. Hence, in the Feeley-Rubin view, there can be no general conclusion to the effect that decentralized arrangements can reduce coercion in divided societies.

The literature so far considered is largely theoretical in nature. There is also a small but growing empirical literature on preference matching, which is more or less concerned with coercion by another name and which is also ambiguous in its conclusions. Ahmad, Brosio and Tanzi (2008) provide an extensive review of this literature as it applies to decentralized systems, in which the focus of attention is on differences before and after decentralization occurs.

The results are not conclusive: first because preference matching is not generally well defined – in fact, in many studies it is simply equated with growth, as if it were the dominant all-catching goal – and, secondly, because the studies make assumptions about the nature of preferences before decentralization but are not able to provide convincing evidence for them. For example, in two widely quoted and interesting works, Faguet (2004) and Faguet and Sanchez (2008) assess how decentralization affects the composition of local expenditure by type of expenditure and whether this is in line with citizens' preferences.

The studies show that with decentralization, investment priorities shift from services such as water, sewerage, and roads to education and health,

---

[3] The essays appeared anonymously in New York newspapers in 1787 and 1788 under the pen name "Publius." A bound edition of the essays was first published in 1788, but only in the 1818 edition published by the printer Jacob Gideon were the authors of each essay identified by name.

[4] The argument by Pauly (1973) that redistribution can be a local public good because of links between rich and poor at the local level may also fit here.

which, *they suggest*, should better correspond to local preferences. However, suggestions are not proof of actual preference patterns.

Possibly the best structured analysis of preference matching is provided by Strumpf and Oberholzer-Gee (2002), who study the regulation of the liquor sales in the United States between 1934 and 1970. The study refers to the repealing of the Prohibition Act in the United States in 1933 when the states were made responsible for liquor control. States then had the choice between centralized, statewide regulation and devolution of regulation to their local governments (counties, municipalities, and towns). The authors predict, and show with their empirical analysis, that decentralization of regulation was chosen in states with relatively large heterogeneity of preferences for liquor sales, whereas centralization tended to prevail where less extreme disparities between localities existed. (How coercion as calculated in earlier essays was affected is not known.)

One should note that there has been little empirical research on the homogeneity of policies at the local level. There is, instead, a lot of casual observation for many cities concerning differentiation in public infrastructure and concerning levels of service provision between rich and poor residential areas, for which there are many explanations, including differences in the political influence of rich and poor people.[5] One should note also that cities could be considered as a centralized form of government vis-à-vis its constituent neighborhoods. If autonomous, the neighborhoods might adapt their policies to their citizens' preferences, but also the central government (the city) may do it. We do not have general empirical results about these possibilities.

3. Coercion and Decentralization: A Simple Stylized Model

There are many options to consider in the design of decentralized institutions. In this section we consider the matter conceptually and from a perspective in which the goal is to reduce coercion through decentralization while preserving or enhancing efficiency.

The simplest way to decentralize is to devolve a function and its financing from a higher to a lower level of government. We can distinguish between

---

[5] Such differences could be ascribed also to preference-matching policies. In this interpretation, local governments provide better services to rich neighborhoods, increasing the value of their property and the taxes they pay, whereas in poorer neighborhoods taxes and services remain lower. Obviously, residents of poor jurisdictions will complain, but their complaints cannot be interpreted as evidence of being coerced – they are getting what they pay for.

two alternative situations/solutions. The first one is when the lower level governments do not yet exist and are carved out from a higher level jurisdiction. In this case, the creation of the new units could be executed with the aim of minimizing coercion according to some criterion. The second alternative is when the function is devolved to already existing local units. In this case, the heterogeneity of preferences is common knowledge before devolution and cannot be modified immediately by the latter. This is a more realistic option to the extent it has to take into consideration the existing constraints.[6]

The general expectation – on which the suggestion that decentralization may reduce coercion is based – is that with smaller territorial size (in terms of the population) of jurisdictions preferences become more homogeneous, and therefore the creation of smaller units of government can reduce coercion, or better, the number of persons coerced will get smaller. Pennock (1959) put this argument more than fifty year ago,[7] and this is the argument at the core of Oates' work. It is also possible that communities will become more homogenous, because of higher mobility induced by the smaller cost of relocating, as in a typical Tiebout (1956) process.

With no mobility, and thus with preferences remaining nonhomogeneous at the lower level where the policy has been assigned, a median voter decision-making framework will lead to less coercion. It can, however, create a higher volume of total coercion measured by the aggregate change in consumer surplus. This happens when the level of public good chosen with decentralization is farther away – with reference to the level under centralization – from the preferences of citizens with distant/extreme preferences. It may be a realistic case in ethnically divided societies like that of Macedonia considered later, or in local jurisdictions that have become the recent destination of substantial flows of migrants. This is not a new idea: the argument has been presented almost thirty years ago (see, for example, Casahuga 1978, 1982b) and is illustrated later.

---

[6] Both options can be implemented either on a general basis, in which all lower level governments receive the new responsibility, or on piecemeal basis with asymmetric arrangements. With asymmetry, some lower level governments will be assigned/or request the devolution of (a) new responsibilities (and their financing), whereas the other still stay with the upper/central government. When all local governments request the new responsibility, asymmetric arrangements become simple devolution.

[7] "[F]rom the point of view of maximizing voter satisfaction with government, indeed of achieving a greater harmonization of conflicting demands, it is a major advantage of federalism that the decentralization of voter decision makes for the satisfaction of more of the voters more of the time than if they acted as a single unit" (Pennock 1959, 140).

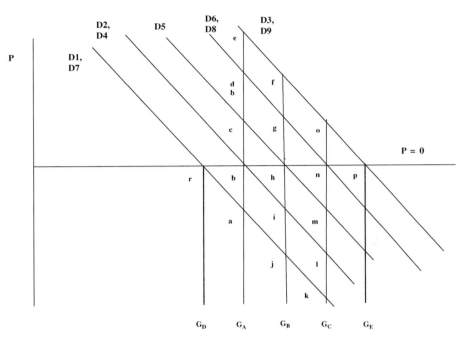

Figure 9.1. Decentralization with widely diverging preferences.

Consider Figure 9.1 in which the demand curves express the preferences of nine individuals concerning a publicly provided good that has no cost of production, as in an earlier example about the duration of the hunting season. To simplify things there are four couples of individuals with identical preferences, plus one, represented simply by five distinct demand curves. (The zero cost function is superimposed on the horizontal axis.) Coercion derives from the difference between each individual's preferred quantity at the given tax price (set equal to $P = 0$ with loss of generality) and the quantity that is effectively provided.

In a median voter framework, the quantity provided will be chosen that corresponds to the median voter's preferences, thus maximizing her or his surplus. For all other individuals this quantity will be higher or lower than the preferred one, and there is no exact preference matching. Their surpluses will consequently be lower than in the situation in which they were the strategic voter.

With centralization, the quantity G_B will be produced corresponding to the preferences of the national median voter who is individual 5.

Alternatively, with decentralization the nine individuals are assumed to be assigned to three newly created local jurisdictions. Individuals 1, 2, and 9 are assigned to jurisdiction A, and 4, 5, and 6 to jurisdiction B, with the remaining individuals 3, 7, and 8 assigned to jurisdiction C. In this decentralized system, under simple majority voting jurisdiction A will choose G_A, jurisdiction B will choose G_B, and jurisdiction C will choose G_C.

Let us now consider the differences between the centralized and decentralized solutions. For jurisdiction B, there is no difference, given the coincidence of the national and local median voter. In jurisdiction A, individuals 1 and 2 suffer with centralization a loss of welfare being forced to consume more than what they value given the tax. Specifically, the preferred quantity of individual 2 is G_A, which is smaller than what she is forced to consume, which is G_B. Hence, she is forced to consume more than she prefers. Area *bch* shows her loss of consumer surplus. On the other hand, with decentralization she gets exactly what she prefers, and coercion disappears.

Individual 9 has extreme preferences: he would like to have a large quantity of the public good, G_E. With centralization he was getting G_B with a loss of surplus of *hpf*. With decentralization he is assigned to jurisdiction A that will produce G_A. His loss of surplus is now *bpe*, with an increase of *befh*.

We are left with individual 1, who wants little. Decentralization allows him to gain *rba*. Two individuals, 1 and 2, gain and one individual, 9, loses, but his loss is bigger than the aggregate gain of the other two, as it can easily be checked by construction in the figure, where demand curves are parallel. Therefore, in this subcase, decentralization is unable to pass the aggregate Kaldor-Hicks test, although more persons are satisfied from it.

A general conclusion of this section is that any reduction in coercion with decentralization, as well as the change in economic welfare, depends on the way and extent to which heterogeneity of preferences is affected. There are a large number of possibilities.

4. Reducing Coercion through Decentralization: The Case of Macedonia

Consideration of the breakup of Yugoslavia provides an illustration of some of the ideas introduced earlier, with Macedonia being a particularly interesting case.[8] It also hints at the importance of alternative modes of governance for the relationship between decentralization and coercion.

---

[8] In fact, Macedonia has two names. The provisional name is "Former Yugoslav Republic of Macedonia (Fyrom)" that was adopted as a compromise because of Greece's strong objection to the use of Macedonia. The constitutional name is "Republic of Macedonia," and it is recognized by a considerable number of countries. The name dispute is blocking Macedonia's membership with NATO and the EU.

Macedonia was the second Yugoslav republic to secede and to create an independent state (Judt 2005). Macedonia is an ethnically divided society with a population of about two million people. According to the last census in 2002, its population is composed of 64.2 percent ethnic Macedonians. A quarter of its population (25.2%) declares themselves to be ethnic Albanians. There are also other small ethnic groups: Turks (3.9%), Roma (2.7%), Serbians (1.8%), and Vlachs.

During the old regime, Albanians and the other smaller nationalities were economically marginalized as a result of the policy of addressing at first the deepest regional inequalities across the whole country. This policy led to the neglect of smaller ethnic populations, particularly those who lived in mountainous and remote areas. As a consequence, Macedonia as a whole received industrial investment that was located mostly in the urban and low-level areas that were inhabited mainly by ethnic Macedonians, to the detriment of the Albanians and of the other, smaller, minorities who lived elsewhere.

With independence, the ethnic Macedonians continued to constitute the majority of the population and came to control the central government, in partnership with one of the Albanian political parties through a power-sharing scheme. One should note that Albanian politics itself was quite fractious, with a high number of small political parties pretending to represent the whole ethnic constituency, and that the arrangement with the Macedonians was not stable.

Albanian and other minorities became concerned that the previous politics of neglect could turn, after independence, into a policy of further marginalization. In terms of the arguments in the paper, the Albanian Macedonians feared that the distance between their preferred and the actual policies would become larger after the independence of the country, or in other words that preference mismatching would involve substantial coercion.

Between March and June of 2001 a civil war was fought between the government and groups of ethnic Albanian insurgents, mostly in the north and west areas of the country. According to most interpretations (see Buzar 2006, Ethnobarometer 2009, and Lebamoff and Ilievsky 2008), the war was not ignited solely or mainly by conflicts between ethnic groups. Loss of control by the government of the areas at the border with Kosovo to the advantage of organized crime contributed also to the outbreak of the war. The war ended with the intervention of a NATO cease-fire monitoring force.

Under the terms of the Ohrid Agreement, reached under strong pressure exerted by the international community, the government agreed to devolve greater political power and cultural recognition to its Albanian minority. A number of steps have been taken thereafter. Following and completing the devolution in 1997 to local governments of the responsibility for infrastructure for education, culture, and social services – three areas that are quite sensitive to ethnic cleavages. In 2005 the responsibility to manage personnel, including teachers, in these areas was also devolved.

In addition, the right to study in one's mother tongue that is enshrined in the constitution was enforced with more determination. Any language spoken by at least 20 percent of the population was recognized as an official language. This applies also to the municipal level, implying that municipalities with a linguistic minority of at least 20 percent of the population have to use officially the language of this minority.

To enhance the protection of the "larger" minorities – those representing at least 20 percent of the population – in 2003 the central government proceeded in the restructuring of municipalities, whose number was reduced from 123 to 84, as well as the restructuring of the capital city of Skopje. The restructuring aimed at creating more ethnically homogeneous municipalities, meaning – above all – the increase of the number of municipalities with an Albanian share of the population of at least 20 percent, where the provisions concerning language and culture and other areas of interest to minorities could be applied. As a consequence of this provision, it is now estimated that the Albanian language is used as an official language in twenty-five of the eighty-four municipalities, the Turkish language in three municipalities, and Serbian and Roma in a municipality each.

Finally, mention has to be made of two consocional-type arrangements – where no group can form a majority – applied at all levels of government. The first of these is the "Badinter majority system" that requires a double majority vote, both a majority of all members of parliament and a majority of representatives of each ethnic community.[9] At the national parliament level this system applies to laws relating to right of communities – namely laws affecting culture, education, language, use of symbols, and the like. It also applies to laws on local finances, local elections, and the boundaries of municipalities. At the municipal level, again when a greater than 20-percent minority exists, the Badinter system applies to regulations referring to culture, use of languages, and alphabets.

---

[9] An example should clarify. Suppose there are seventy MPs of community A and thirty MPs of community B. The Badinter majority system requires, for the concerned laws, first at least fifty-one votes of the all parliament, and secondly, thirty-six votes of community A, plus sixteen votes of community B.

The second arrangement is the creation, also at the local level, of the Inter-Community Relations Committees (CICRs), or more commonly known as commissions for improving interethnic relations.[10] They are again established in every ethnic-mixed municipality in the Republic of Macedonia, where at least 20 percent of the citizens are of ethnic background different than the majority of the citizens. These CICRs are part of the local government and are in charge of monitoring ethnic relations and of advancing proposals aimed at their improvement.

The result of all these arrangements and policies has been a differentiation of policies at the local government that has clearly eased coercion of the Albanian minority in those local governments, where it has not become straight out a majority following the redrawing of municipal borders. It is possibly that this development has also created more fiscal coercion of the predominant ethnic Macedonian population that has surely to bear some of the cost of the new policies and arrangements. It has at the same time increased frustration, if not more coercion, for the smaller minorities that feel they are now more relegated than before to the margins of policy making and policy implementation (Ethnobarometer 2009).

Vis-à-vis the Albanian minority, some experts lament that differentiation of policies in its favor may create unnecessary segregation. For example, as a result of the lack of school buildings, teaching takes place in separate shifts making it impossible for students of different ethnic groups to meet during school time, thus nullifying the positive impact on political life deriving from a creation of identity of interests. Everybody, and in particular the international community that is behind many of these changes, is expecting more results from the improvements in governance that should derive from decentralization per se. These are late to come, partly because of lack of capacity and of financial resources. As an Albanian politician has recently declared: "Decentralization is no longer an Ethnic issue, but a State one" (International Crisis Group, 2011, 20). At the same time, there is little competition between political parties at the local level in ethnic municipalities. This does not improve local governance, and it is a risk that ethnically divided jurisdictions generally have to face.

---

[10] A similar institution operates at the national level, namely the Inter-Community Relations Committee. It is a standing body of the national assembly. The committee consists of seven MPs from among the Albanian and Macedonian community each, and one MP from the Turkish, Vlach, Roma, Serbian, and Bosnian ethnic communities. The basic competence refers to examining the issues relating to the intercommunity relations and giving proposals for their solution.

5. The Interplay of Coercion and Redistribution

Coercion may be mixed with redistribution when the publicly provided good or policy is financed with an income tax or a set of taxes that are related to income or wealth. In this section we consider the interplay of coercion and redistribution under centralized and decentralized solutions. To fix ideas, we analyze a case in which the disappearance of coercion does not lead to an increase in utility because the redistribution associated with coercion also disappears.

In the standard model, the citizens' preferences over a publicly provided good, g, and a composite private good, x, are represented by

$$u = u(g) + v(x). \tag{9.1}$$

The total cost C of supplying the publicly provided good is $C = c(N)$, while $p = C/N$ is the average, per individual, cost for the population of size N.

The cost of providing g is financed through an income tax that is proportional to individual income, y. Total tax payments by individual voters are therefore ty, where t is the tax rate. For individuals, the budget constraint is

$$x = y - ty, \tag{9.2}$$

whereas the government budget constraint is $cg = tY$, where Y is aggregate income.

Letting $y = Y/N$ be the per capita tax base, the government budget constraint becomes

$$pg = ty. \tag{9.3}$$

Individuals maximize their utility, U, by choosing the level of g, subject to equations (9.2) and (9.3), which can then combined into a single constraint

$$x = y - (pg/y)y. \tag{9.4}$$

In Figure 9.2, this last constraint is represented by the straight line from the origin, and preferences are represented by indifference curves whose level increases as they move southeast. Note that the slope of the indifference curve is

$$R(y, t, g) = dt/dg \quad U = u'(g)/v'(x) \tag{9.5}$$

and the slope of the budget constraint is

$$dt/dg = p/t. \tag{9.6}$$

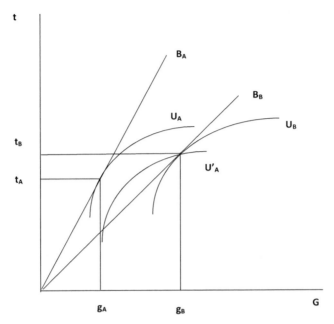

Figure 9.2. Coercion and redistribution with a publicly provided good financed with an income tax.

At the individual optimum the slopes of the two curves U_A and U_B are equal. If free, individuals would choose a level of the public good corresponding to the point of tangency. Given the budget constraint, determined by average income and by the cost of provision of the public good, the choice of a level of the public good implies, automatically, the choice of the tax rate.

Before decentralization, individual A has a level of utility shown by indifference curve U'_A. The level of public good g_B is chosen by somebody else – for example, the national median voter – and does not correspond to his preferred one (there is no tangency with the budget line).

With decentralization, A, who is assumed to then become the strategic voter, gets a level of public good g_A that corresponds exactly to his preferences, and so coercion disappears. However, it is also assumed that A happens to live now in a community that is poorer than before: the budget line is steeper and the point of tangency is on an indifference curve, U_A, that corresponds to a lower level of utility. Coercion has disappeared, but utility is smaller. Clearly, in these circumstances, there is trade-off between coercion and the benefits coming from redistribution.

The same figure could also be used to show that an individual may prefer centralization because the positive impact on their welfare from redistribution is higher than the negative impact of increased coercion.[11] Suppose the representative resident of region A faces budget line B_A and has a level of utility of U_A. He or she joins region B, which is richer and where its residents choose g_B and consequently pay t_B and have a level of utility of U_B. The person from region A feels now that they are coerced because this combination does not correspond to their preferred one. However, before joining region B – that is, under decentralization – he faced a much less steep budget curve, B_A. Hence with centralization – that is, after joining B – he ended up with a higher level of utility ($U'_A > U_A$) than before, although he has to pay a higher tax rate.

These results are not general: if the difference in preferences between the two regions is very large, residents of A who join with those in B could find themselves with a lower level of utility because the impact of coercion cannot be compensated for by the redistributive impact of joining the richer region.

Coming back to the case of divided societies such as Macedonia discussed in the previous section, it is useful to point out that decentralization can be a source of disappointment because of the interplay of coercion and redistribution. After decentralization, ethnic minorities may not feel anymore that they are being coerced, but they may not be as well off. To make them fully happy would require the payment of transfers aimed at offsetting the loss in welfare.

Analogously, the interplay of coercion and redistribution may also pose problems in the case of (re)unification of countries. Consider, for example, the Korean peninsula, where two jurisdictions with extremely different economic conditions, North and South Korea, could merge into a single unified jurisdiction. If the preferences of the richer jurisdiction impact on the level of service provision after reunification, this would likely produce coercion in the much poorer one and make unification less attractive, assuming that the financing rule does not differentiate according to where people live (Wildasin, 2003). Compensation and differential taxation may alleviate the problem, as well as reducing the threat of destabilizing migration flows from poor to rich regions. As a matter of fact, the government of South Korea

---

[11] To be precise the figure would need to be slightly modified to take into account the fact that in region B the average income is now lower because of the merging with poorer region A. This will make the budget line a little steeper and induce the choice of a lower level of the public good.

announced recently (*Economist*, August 21, 2010) a unification tax to be paid only by its citizens of an unspecified amount if that event should come about.

6. Conclusions

Robust conclusions about coercion and decentralization are hard to come by, as they are in the case for decentralization solely on the basis of efficiency (see Treisman 2007). Obviously decentralization, if it consists of creating new local units that are each a perfect replica of the distribution of preferences existing at the central government level, each using the same governance structure, cannot reduce coercion. From an analytical point of view, decentralization can reduce coercion if it is accompanied, or followed through mobility, by a lower dispersion of preferences in the local units. Lower dispersion of preferences is, however, a context-specific result and cannot provide a general, a priori argument in favor of decentralized government as a coercion-reducing instrument. Further complicating matters is the fact that changes in the degree of coercion because of decentralization (or of unification) will usually be associated with redistribution of income, which will also have to be taken into account.

Coercion is an important part of life in a federal system. Although the task of reaching general conclusions about the relationship between decentralization and coercion is a challenging one, it is also one that is worthy of further study.

References

Ahmad, E., G. Brosio, and V. Tanzi (2008). "Local Service Provision in Selected OECD Countries: Do Decentralized Operations Work Better?" In G. Ingram and Yu-Hung Hong (eds.), *Fiscal Decentralization and Land Policies.* Cambridge, MA: Lincoln Institute of Land Policy, 73–104.

Bardhan, P., and D. Mookherjee (1999). "Relative Capture of Local and National Governments: An Essay in the Political Economy of Decentralization." Working Paper. Berkeley: University of California, Department of Economics.

Bardhan, P., and D. Mookherjee (2000). "Capture and Governance at Local and National Levels." *American Economic Review* 37(2): 135–139.

Besley, T., and S. Coate (2003). "Centralized versus Provision of Local Public Goods: A Political Economy Approach." *Journal of Public Economics* 87(12): 2611–2637.

Boadway R., and J.-F. Tremblay (2012). "Reassessment of the Tiebout Model." *Journal of Public Economics* 96(11–12): 1063–1078.

Breton A. (1996). *Competitive Governments: An Economic Theory of Politics And Public Finance.* New York: Cambridge University Press.

Breton, A., and P. Salmon (2007). "France: Forces Shaping Centralization and Decentralization in Environmental Policymaking." In A. Breton, G. Brosio, S. Dalmazzone, G. Garrone (eds.), *Environmental Governance and Decentralization: Country Studies.* Cheltenham: Edward Elgar, 457–494.

Brosio, G., A. Cassone, and R. Ricciuti (2002). "Tax Evasion across Italy: Rational Noncompliance or Inadequate Civic Concern?" *Public Choice* 112(3–4).

Brennan, J., and J. Buchanan (1980). *The Power to Tax: Analytical Foundations of a Fiscal Constitution.* New York: Cambridge University Press.

Buzar, S. (2006). *Geographies and Ethnopolitics: Unravelling the Spatial and Political Economies of 'Ethnic Conflict.* Oxford: SEESOX.

Casahuga, A. (1978). "Aspectos de la descentralization fiscal: una vision critica del enfoque de Musgrave." *Hacienda Publica Española* 50: 311–324.

Casahuga, A. (1982). "La invalidez general del teorema de la descentralización." Cuadernos *Economicos de ICE* 20: 37–52.

"Ethnobarometer." (2009). *Macedonia 2009.* http://www.ethnobarometer.org.

Faguet, J. P. (2004). "Does Decentralization Increase Government Responsiveness to Local Needs?" *Journal of Public Economics* 88: 667–693.

Faguet, J. P., and Sánchez, F. 2008. "Decentralization's effect on educational outcomes in Bolivia and Colombia". *World Development* 36(7): 1294–1316.

"Federalist Papers." (1788). http://www.constitution.org/fed/federa00.htm.

Feeley, M., and E. Rubin (2008). *Federalism: Political Identity and Tragic Compromise.* Ann Arbor: University of Michigan Press.

Hills R. (2009). "Federalism and Public Choice." New York University Law and Economics Working Papers.

International Crisis Group (2011). *Macedonia: Ten Years after the Conflict.*

Judt, T. (2005). *Postwar. A History of Europe Since 1945.* London, Penguin Press.

Lebamoff, M. F., and Z. Ilievsky (2008). "The Ohrid Framework Agreement in Macedonia: Neither Settlement nor Resolution of Ethnic Conflicts?" International Studies Association Conference.

Lockwood B. (2002). "Distributive Politics and the Costs of Centralization." *Review of Economic Studies* 69(2): 313–337.

Lockwood, B. (2006). "The Political Economy of Decentralization." In E. Ahmad and G. Brosio (eds.), *Handbook of Fiscal Federalism.* Cheltenham, UK: Edward Elgar, 33–60.

Oates, W. (1968). "The Theory of Public Finance in a Federal System." *Canadian Journal of Economics* 1: 37–54.

Oates, W. (1972). *Fiscal Federalism.* New York: Harcourt-Brace.

Oates, W. (2005). "Toward a Second-Generation Theory of Fiscal Federalism." *International Tax and Public Finance* 12: 349–374.

Oates, W. (2006). "On the Theory and Practice of Fiscal Decentralization." Working Paper, No. 2006–05. IFIR.

Pauly, M. (1973). "Redistribution as a Public Good." *Journal of Public Economics* 21: 35–58.

Pennock, R. (1959). "Federal and Unitary – Disharmony and Frustration." *Behavioral Science* 4(2): 147–157.

Riker, W., and R. Schaps (1957). "Disharmony in Federal Government." *Behavioral Science* 2(4): 276–290.

Strumpf, K., and F. Oberholzer-Gee (2002). "Endogenous Policy Decentralization: Testing the Central Tenet of Economic Federalism." *Journal of Political Economy* 110: 1–36.

Tiebout, C. (1956). "A Pure Theory of Local Expenditures." *Journal of Political Economy* 64: 416–424.

Treisman, Daniel (2007). *The Architecture of Government: Rethinking Political Decentralization.* New York: Cambridge University Press.

Wildasin, D. (2003). "Liberalization and the Spatial Allocation of Population in Developing and Transition Countries." In J. Martinez-Vasquez and J. Alm (eds.), *Public Finance in Developing and Transition Countries: Essays in Honor of Richard Bird.* Cheltenham, UK: Edward Elgar Publishing, 63–100.

Discussion

On Coercion in Highly Divided Societies

Bernard Grofman

Economics is all about how people make decisions; sociology is all about why they don't have any real decisions to make.
    – James Dusenberry, Professor of Economics

Although much of microeconomics is, at its heart, about mutually beneficial transactions such as gains from trade and there is a vast literature on public goods provision that looks at incentives for cooperation versus the likelihood of free riding, there is also a large segment of the political economy literature that emphasizes the potential mismatch between the goods and services provided by government and what (some or all of) the citizens want. When there is such a mismatch, there is particular problem with coercion. If citizens are not getting the bundle of goods from government they want, but are yet compelled to provide taxes to pay for it, it may be very difficult to gain tax compliance. In the more extreme case, there may be incentives for immigration or, if large enough segments of the society are affected, secession.

One way to end up with a mismatch between output and preferences is simply the combination of preference heterogeneity and the alleged difficulty of "narrowcasting." Here the problem is that government is supposedly only capable of producing goods, including public goods, which fall into the "one-size-fits-all" category. Another route to mismatch is the likelihood of "pork-barrel" coalitions behind inefficient projects that are supported by a log-rolling majority that shifts taxes onto the general public (Shepsle and Weingast 1981) Still another problem is the fundamentally coercive nature of government, for example, the "government as leviathan" approach associated with the work of James Buchanan (see, e.g., Buchanan 1975; Brennan and Buchanan 1980), in which the state is a tax collection machine operating in the interests of elected officials who engage in "predatory taxation."

In this brief comment on George Brosio's essay, I will only look at the first of these three ways to generate a mismatch between citizens' want and what government provides – namely, preference heterogeneity.

In the public choice framework there are two key routes to dealing with the problem of preference heterogeneity in the context of group decision making: super-majoritarianism (special cases of which are unanimity and veto rules) and segmentation of control over outcomes.

The first stream of literature looks at how increases in the size of the majority needed to make decisions affect the likelihood of the average citizen seeing the collective goods s/he wishes to see produced get produced, on the one hand, and the likelihood that the average citizen will be faced with collective decisions that s/he disapproves of, on the other. What is needed is a way of assessing trade-offs with benefits and losses associated with different decisions rules. The key idea is that requiring more than simple majorities yields greater protection for voters against costs being imposed on them but also makes it harder to get agreement on potentially mutually beneficial policies (see, e.g., Rae 1969). The *locus classicus* of this literature is chapter 1 of Buchanan and Tullock (1962) in their discussion of k/N rules, although the further complication of transaction costs of reaching decisions with a given quorum rule is also introduced.

A second stream of literature worries less about the size of the majority and more about exactly who it is who will be given decision-making power over particular types of decisions. There are several different substreams of relevant literature. One deals with the normative delineation of individual and group rights. Sen's (1970) work on the dilemma of the "Paretian Liberal" is a classic in this vein, done from a social choice perspective. Another, related substream deals with how to partition a set of voters into subsets of (presumably) more preference-homogenous voters, as judged, for instance, by lower variance. As Brosio (this volume) notes, the central idea (see especially Oates 1972) is that the greater the preference heterogeneity, the greater, *ceteris paribus*, the gains from decentralizing choices so as to be able to tailor policies to local tastes (if we are dealing with the more usual territorial forms of federalism), or to tailor policies to the preferences of specific groups (if, for example, we were providing separate family law courts for members of different religious communities, as was found in the Ottoman Empire's *millet* system). From this "efficiency" result comes the empirical testable hypothesis that the greater the preference heterogeneity, the more likely are federal/decentralized forms of decision making to be employed.

There are two extensive subsets of this literature that provide complementary bottom-up and top-down methods for creating homogeneity. One is associated with voluntary sorting processes (migration), such as in the Tiebout model (Tiebout 1956), that lead to greater homogeneity within jurisdictions and greater heterogeneity across jurisdictions in, for instance, tax and amenity bundles. The other is associated with the framing of governmental jurisdictional boundaries to generate a reduced variance in the descriptive/ascriptive characteristics of the citizens already included within them.

Of course, as Brosio also points out, this hypothesis assumes that localized decision making does create more preference homogeneity. However, that assumption seems empirically well substantiated, at least if we treat homogeneity in ascriptive/descriptive characteristics as a proxy for preference homogeneity. Consider, for example, the differences between the U.S. House and the U.S. Senate in descriptive representation of minorities. Black population nationwide is 12.3 percent in 2010. There are no majority black states and currently no black U.S. senators, but as of 2010, around 10 percent of U.S. House districts elect a black representative – almost entirely from black majority or black plurality districts shared with other minorities.

However, Brosio also points out the possibility that, even if localities are more preference homogeneous, the Oates model has some perhaps unrealistic assumptions in it that give rise to the result of how homogeneity is necessarily better. For example, imagine that the national level uses some proportional allocation rule such that every jurisdiction is given a share of some public good equal to its population share. If, at the local level, the majority group in each district monopolizes the public good, but there still are sizeable minority blocs in most jurisdictions, then, from an efficiency standpoint, the utility loss will still be large with a localized rule. Arguably this is the situation that prevailed in the U.S. South under Jim Crow laws. When there were federal allocations – for instance, for farm subsidies – to the southern states during the Great Depression, because of local control, with the states as the unit of allocation, those were disproportionately if not entirely "captured" by whites, that is, by the majority voting bloc in the state. As Brosio notes, this problem is a classic one in the literature on constitutional design, going back at least as far as Federalist Paper No. 10. Of course, for a centralized rule to do better, the national government would have to have a way to direct resources very precisely to individual targets; however, then, of course, the U.S. government does exactly that, in for example, Social Security and Medicare payouts.

On the other hand, Brosio also identifies a (noneconomic) factor that will advantage local decision making, namely the notion of a greater "sense of community" at the local level, so that people are more willing to treat their "neighbors" as persons of moral and social worth, whatever their religious, racial, or economic characteristics, then they might be willing to accord the same treatment to "strangers" with similar characteristics. The flip side of this is that heterogeneous communities over a larger area may be unable to generate a sense of community and thus have suboptimal levels of public spending. Alesina and Glaeser (2004), in work not cited by Brosio, provide compelling evidence for this effect in terms of diminished mean levels of welfare spending levels across nations and across the fifty U.S. states as a product of greater ethnic heterogeneity. When there is such ethnic heterogeneity, we expect, for a given level of taxes and welfare spending, that the majority community feels greater coercion because it sees "its" money being spent on people not like itself. This feeling of coercion is likely to be greater if one group is also economically more advantaged than another.

The classic Madisonian idea of checks and balances, when combined with the concept of a bill of rights, reflects a combination of these two notions of super-majoritarianism and segmentation. Here there are multiple governmental entities that must reach agreement, each with a somewhat different constituency base – some of which may operate under super-majoritarian rules – thus forcing compromise among those with different preferences and/or blocking changes to the status quo that would discommode any of the veto players (Tsebelis 2002), and there may also be domains where any collective action is, in effect, prohibited (or at least rendered suspect) as an encroachment on individual rights.

In Macedonia, as Brosio tells the compelling story, after a small-scale civil war, international intervention led to devolution of powers (over education, culture, and social services) to local governments, which meant that portions of the country that were largely ethnically Albanian had rights to self-control. And minority language rights were now to be more strongly protected, so that multiple languages at the local level could be recognized as "official." However, because ethnic concentration levels mattered, there was a top-down reorganization of municipalities that led to a higher proportion of municipalities having a substantial enough Albanian population to be given special language protections. Also part of the concessions was a Calhoun-style *concurrent majority* (Calhoun 1849), here called the *Badinter majority system,* a rule closely related to what Lijphart (1999), in the terminology most familiar to political scientists, would call a *minority veto.* The combination of these various provisions, along with elections based on proportional representation, give rise to what political scientists would call (here following Lijphart 1977), *consociational* arrangements.

However, as is almost always the case with consociational arrangements, as Brosio points out, those who look at Macedonia worry about the
hardening of ethnic differentiation there with increased support for both
self-segregation of the minority community and state support for arrangements that minimize contacts across ethnic lines. Here it is important to
emphasize, in a point that I think is not as clear as it could be in Brosio's otherwise excellent presentation, that, when it comes to public goods,
ethnic divisions often have a dichotomous (binary) or polychotomous
(n-ary) oppositional nature to them, where n is the number of ethnic
groups, that economic differences, which can be viewed along a continuum, do not. Thus, there are reasons to be especially worried about both
the degree of enforcement needed for tax contributions and the dangers
of political conflict and fissiparous activities when we have a society whose
ethnic cleavage lines are reinforced by economic inequalities across ethnic
groups.

References

Alesina, Alberto and Edward L. Glaeser (2004). *Fighting Poverty in the U.S. and Europe:
A World of Difference.* Oxford: Oxford University Press.

Brennan, James and James M. Buchanan (1980). *The Power to Tax: Analytic Foundations
of a Fiscal Constitution.* New York: Cambridge University Press.

Buchanan, James M. (1975). *The Limits of Liberty: Between Anarchy and Leviathan.*
Chicago: University of Chicago Press.

Buchanan, James M. and Gordon Tullock (1962). *The Calculus of Consent: Logical
Foundations of Constitutional Democracy.* Ann Arbor, MI: University of Michigan
Press.

Calhoun, John C. (1849). *Disquisition on Government.* (Reprinted by the Constitution
Society, http://www.constitution.org/jcc/disq_gov.htm)

Lijphart, Arend. (1977). *Democracy in Plural Societies: A Comparative Exploration.* New
Haven: Yale University Press.

Lijphart, Arend (1999). *Patterns of Democracy: Government Forms and Performance in
Thirty-Six Countries.* New Haven: Yale University Press.

Oates, W. (1972). *Fiscal Federalism.* New York: Harcourt-Brace.

Rae, Douglas W. (1969). "Decision-Rules and Individual Values in Constitutional
Choice." *American Political Science Review* 63(1): 40–56.

Sen, Amartya (1970). "The Impossibility of a Paretian Liberal." *Journal of Political
Economy* 78(1): 152–157.

Shepsle Kenneth A. and Barry Weingast (1981). "Political Preferences for the Pork
Barrel – A Generalization." *American Journal of Political Science* 25(1): 96–111.

Tiebout, C. A. (1956). "Pure Theory of Local Expenditures." *Journal of Political Economy*
64(5): 416–424.

Tsebelis, George (2002). *Veto Players: How Political Institutions Work.* Princeton; Princeton University Press.

PART IV

COERCION IN THE LABORATORY

10

Cooperating to Resist Coercion

An Experimental Study

Lucy F. Ackert, Ann B. Gillette, and Mark Rider

1. Introduction

Liberal-democratic states often pursue coercive policies. In their essays in this book, Wallis, Skaperdas, and Congleton all describe ways other than actual physical force in which coercion may be imposed in such regimes through tax, expenditure, and regulatory policies. For example, the collective decision to supply a given quantity of a public good, which lies at the very heart of public policy, involves coercion whenever a uniform tax price is used to finance this good in the presence of heterogeneous preferences.[1] Individuals with varying tastes for the public good will demand different quantities of it at any given tax price. Because of the nature of a public good, however, everyone must consume the same amount. Therefore, the government is bound to coerce some people, forcing them to consume more (or less) of the good than they would like.[2]

In authoritarian regimes, liberal-democratic regimes, and totalitarian regimes alike, people may seek to overturn government actions with which they disagree – that is, coercive government actions. The manner in which citizens can legitimately express resistance to government action and the

---

[1] More specifically, Winer, Tridimas and Hettich (in Chapter 7) discuss one definition of coercion following Buchanan and Breton that could be used in theoretical studies, and Sehili and Martinez-Vazquez (in Chapter 8) suggest a different definition based on the work of Lindahl and apply it using a general equilibrium model.

[2] In economics, a pure pubic good is non-rival in consumption and is non-exclusive. Therefore, everyone must consume the same quantity of it. An example of a pure public good is national defense. The assumption that everyone pays a uniform tax price for the public good is made to simplify the discussion. This assumption could be relaxed to allow for a variety of tax prices. Technically speaking, Winer et al. (Chapter 7, this volume) contend that there is coercion if a person's marginal rate of substitution for the public good is different from the tax price that they must pay to the government to provide it.

criteria for determining successful resistance depends on, among other things, the nature of the regime. Generally speaking, however, resisting government action is costly to individuals in terms of time, money, and possibly one's very well-being. To succeed, typically resistance must exceed a threshold – a tipping point. There may be formal and explicit rules describing the threshold for successful resistance (i.e., majority rule in liberal-democratic regimes) or arbitrary and implicit rules (i.e., intolerable level of social unrest), particularly in authoritarian and totalitarian regimes.

In any event, the threshold, whatever it may be, can be achieved either through large contributions of time, money, and effort by a few individuals or through small contributions of the same by many. Because a commitment device is typically not available, a substantial coordination problem arises when trying to rally public support to resist unpopular government actions. In short, cooperating to resist government action is similar to cooperating to provide a public good. With this highly stylized description of resisting coercive government action in mind, we adapt a public goods game to investigate whether people are able to cooperate to resist coercion. For this purpose, we use a resistance game, similar to the one used by Mertins (2008) to examine procedural justice.

In our version of a resistance game, a randomly chosen, anonymous, decision maker (DM) is given the opportunity to expropriate all or part of the experimental endowments of four experimental subjects, henceforth referred to as "Others." Others can resist a DM's transfer demand by making voluntary contributions to a resistance fund, and the sum of these contributions is called the resistance fund balance (RFB). If the RFB equals or exceeds a predetermined, common knowledge threshold, the Others are not required to pay the DM's transfer demand. If, however, the RFB does not equal or exceed the resistance threshold, then resistance is unsuccessful, and the Others are required to pay the DM's transfer demand. Whether or not resistance is successful, the Others lose their contributions to the resistance fund.

Presumably one's contribution to the resistance fund is the result of the interplay between (a) the intensity of one's desire to resist a given transfer demand and (b) one's subjective beliefs regarding the amount that the remaining members of the group will contribute to the fund. As in the real world, allowing participants to make differing contributions to the resistance fund reflects the fact that the cost of resistance is typically a continuous choice variable in terms of time, money, and perhaps physical risk, and not a simple binary choice variable.

Because of the non-exclusive nature of successful (or unsuccessful) resistance, cooperating to resist government action creates a social dilemma, as in the case of voluntary contributions to a public good. In the context of our game, Others are collectively better off when "out-of-equilibrium" transfer demands by a DM are successfully resisted.[3] However, a subject in this game can gain a private advantage from not contributing to the resistance fund and free riding on successful resistance financed by the remaining members of the group. The inability to exclude those who do not contribute to the resistance fund from enjoying the benefit of successful resistance creates a social dilemma and thus exacerbates the coordination problem in our resistance game.

The goal of this essay is to investigate the ability of subjects to cooperate to resist coercive expropriation of their experimental endowments by a randomly selected, anonymous DM. Specifically, we examine the interplay between increasing the resistance threshold on the size of a DM's transfer demand and the ability of Others to cooperate in resisting expropriation of their experimental endowments. Summarizing our main results, DMs generally pursue out-of-equilibrium strategies, and Others only enjoy partial success in resisting these transfer demands. Consequently, the observed average earnings of DMs are substantially greater than that predicted by the theory. We also find evidence that the probability of resistance decreases in later rounds of a session as compared to the probability of resistance in the initial rounds. Finally, increasing the resistance threshold from 13 francs to 29 francs has a substantial positive effect on a DM's average transfer demand; a substantial negative effect on the probability of resistance; and a positive (negative) effect on the earnings of DMs (Others).

The remainder of the essay is organized as follows. In the next section, we describe the resistance game in greater detail. In the subsequent section, we provide a detailed discussion of our empirical findings. The final section concludes.

2. Experimental Design and Method

This experiment consists of two resistance level treatments, and five sessions in total. Each session consists of fifteen university students for a total

---

[3] An out-of-equilibrium transfer demand is one that exceeds the resistance threshold divided by the number of Others. More specifically, suppose the resistance threshold is 13 francs, and there are four Others. As discussed in greater detail below, the equilibrium transfer demand in this example is 3 francs. Others should not contribute to resist a transfer demand less than the equilibrium value of 3 francs because successful resistance would cost them more than simply paying the DM's transfer demand.

of seventy-five subjects in the entire experiment.[4] All trading is in francs, an experimental currency, which is converted into U.S. dollars at a rate of 1 franc = $0.20 or 5 francs = $1.00 for purposes of paying the subjects. Subjects are undergraduate and graduate students with a variety of majors. All are inexperienced subjects, in that none participated in a previous experiment with similar design, and each subject participated in only one session of our experiment. Participants earned from $12.40 to $130.80 in the experiment, with average earnings of $49.40.[5] Each session took approximately two hours to complete. Based on our observations, the participants appeared to be motivated by the monetary rewards.

On arrival at the designated time and place of the experiment, subjects receive a set of instructions that the experimenter reads aloud.[6] Subjects are encouraged to ask clarifying questions, and the experimenters conduct a few practice periods to make sure everyone understood the instructions. Each session consists of ten (8) decision periods.[7] The fifteen participants in a given session are randomly and anonymously assigned to one of three groups of five subjects each. One member of each group is randomly designated the DM; the remaining four group members are henceforth referred to as Others. As explained in the instructions, the membership of each group of five and their respective roles in each group are pre-randomized by the experimenter. The membership of the three groups and their respective roles in each group remain the same throughout a session. Members of a group do not know the identity of the members of their group, and they do not know one anothers' roles – that is, DM or Other.

At the beginning of each decision period, all subjects are endowed with 25 francs ($5.00). As mentioned earlier, our experimental design is most similar to a more complex procedural justice design used by Mertins (2008). Little resistance occurred in that study. Although there are other design differences, we believe the primary reason that there is more resistance in our experiment is the reference frame of the DM. The DM in Mertins' study has no initial endowment and thus no earnings from the experiment unless the DM solicits and receives funds from the Others. If the Others are averse

---

[4] Two DMs and two Others do not report their marital status, so they are excluded from the regression analysis.

[5] A participant's total compensation includes a $2 bonus for being on time and $4 for completing a post-experiment questionnaire. All seventy-five participants received the additional compensation of $6.

[6] The instructions are included in an appendix to this paper.

[7] Although our intention was to include ten rounds in each session, the first session consists of only eight rounds because we ran short of time.

to such inequities, then they may not resist transfer demands by DMs, which make the distribution of payoffs among the members of a group more equal. To avoid this induced reference frame, we gave our DMs the same initial endowment as the Others.

The DM of each group then announces a transfer demand to the Others in his group; the DM's proposed transfer demand is the same for all four Others. For example, suppose the DM makes a transfer demand of 5 francs. Ignoring for the moment the ability of Others to resist such demands, 5 francs would be subtracted from the endowment of each of the four group members thus resulting in a total transfer demand of 20 francs. On receiving the DM's transfer demand, the Others then decide whether and how much to contribute to the resistance fund. Others can pay any number of francs from their initial endowment into the group's resistance fund. To resist paying a DM's transfer demand, the RFB must equal or exceed a predetermined threshold. During each period, the experimenter calculates the RFB for each of the three groups.

If during a given period in treatment 1 of the experiment, a group's RFB equals or exceeds 13 francs ($2.60), the group's resistance is declared successful, and the Others in this group are not required to pay the DM's transfer demand. If, however, a group's RFB is less than 13 francs, the Others lose their contributions to the fund and must also pay the DM's transfer demand. In addition to three sessions of treatment 1 as described, we also conduct two sessions of treatment 2, with a resistance threshold of 29 francs ($5.80).

Before learning the group's RFB during a given period, all subjects (the DMs and Others) are asked to forecast the RFB for that period, and subjects receive $0.25 each period for recording their forecast. After the forecasts are recorded, the RFB of each group is announced to the participants. However, they are never told the amount contributed by individual members of their group. After learning whether resistance was successful or not, the subjects calculate their period earnings. The subsequent periods repeat these steps, with all subjects beginning each period with a fresh endowment of 25 francs. After completing the 10 (8) decision periods, participants complete a post-experiment questionnaire that includes demographic questions as well as questions regarding their reaction to the experiment. To motivate thoughtful responses, they receive $4 for completing the questionnaire. After completing the questionnaire, the experimenters pay the subjects privately in cash.

In a one-shot version of this game with a resistance threshold of 13 (29) francs, the efficient, subgame perfect equilibrium strategies are the following: (a) the DM makes a transfer demand of 3 (7) francs, and (b) the Others contribute nothing to the resistance fund. Using backward induction, the equilibrium strategies of a multi-period version of this game is the same as for the one-shot version. Because the two resistance thresholds – 13 and 29 francs – are not evenly divisible by the number of Others, the game does not have a unique equilibrium. For example, with a threshold of 13 francs, three subjects could contribute 3 francs, and the remaining subject would have to contribute 4 francs to resist a DM's transfer demand. Thus, there are four equilibrium strategies: $(T; C_1, C_2, C_3, C_4) = (3; 4, 3, 3, 3)$, $(3; 3, 4, 3, 3)$, $(3; 3, 3, 4, 3)$, and $(3; 3, 3, 3, 4)$, where T is the DM's transfer demand and C_i is Other i's $(= 1, \ldots, 4)$ contribution to the resistance fund. This feature of the experiment makes coordination by the Others on the efficient, subgame perfect equilibrium strategy more difficult because one and only one member of the group should step forward and make the larger contribution to the resistance fund.

Assuming that all subjects employ equilibrium strategies throughout a session, a DM's total payoff in treatment 1 (2) would be 280 (320) francs or \$56 (\$74), and the total payoff to an Other in treatment 1 (2) would be 220 (180) francs or \$44 (\$26). We proceed with a detailed discussion of our findings.

3. Summary of Findings

This section is organized as follows. We begin by briefly discussing the descriptive statistics of our sample. Next, we discuss the frequency distribution of transfer demands and the frequency distribution of successful resistance, conditional on a transfer demand. Then, we discuss the results of our econometric models of the DMs' and Others' decisions or strategy choices. Finally, we discuss the frequency distribution of correct forecasts of resistance.

Table 10.1 reports the descriptive statistics for our sample of 719 decisions by 75 subjects. The sample consists of 144 transfer demands by 15 DMs and 575 contribution decisions by 60 Others. Of the 15 DMs, 9 participated in treatment 1, making 84 transfer demands, and 6 participated in treatment 2, making 60 transfer demands. Meanwhile, 36 Others participated in treatment 1 and 24 in treatment 2, and they made 335 and 240 contribution decisions, respectively. The average transfer demand is 9.85 francs, and the average transfer demand is greater in treatment 2 than in treatment 1. The average contribution to the resistance fund is 4.02 francs. Again, the average contribution is slightly greater in treatment 2 than in treatment 1. However,

Table 10.1. *Summary statistics*

Variables	Others						Decision makers					
	All		Treatment 1		Treatment 2		All		Treatment 1		Treatment 2	
	Mean	Std dev	Mean	Std dev	Mean	Std dev	Mean	Std dev	Mean	Std dev	Mean	Std dev
Transfer demand (francs)	–	–	–	–	–	–	9.85	6.49	8.74	6.42	11.40	6.34
Contribution to resistance fund (francs)	4.02	3.91	3.39	3.05	4.89	4.73	–	–	–	–	–	–
Forecast of resistance fund balance (francs)	18.23	17.17	15.27	10.63	22.37	22.82	16.46	8.78	13.82	7.41	20.15	9.26
Forecast error (francs)	1.95	17.22	1.47	10.04	2.61	23.88	0.29	10.97	0.11	7.84	0.57	14.33
Period earnings (francs)	17.11	5.87	19.48	4.21	13.79	6.24	40.25	21.47	33.5	14.22	49.7	26.00
Percent of transfer demands resisted	46	4.9	56	4.9	33	4.7	–	–	–	–	–	–
Age	24	6.2	22	43	25	7.9	24	7.29	21	2.69	27	10.02
Age-squared	594	372	511	246	710	474	616	443	465	130	827	612
Education (Masters student = 1, Undergraduate student = 0)	0.03	0.17	0.02	0.15	0.04	0.20	–	–	–	–	–	–
Percent black	23	4.2	27	4.5	17	3.7	–	–	–	–	–	–
Percent white	48	5.0	47	4.9	50	5.0	79	4.1	88	3.3	67	4.8
Percent Hispanic	3	1.8	2.3	1.7	4	2.0	–	–	–	–	–	–
Percent Asian	21	4.0	17	3.8	25	4.3	14	3.5	12	3.3	17	3.8
Percent other races	5	2.2	5	2.3	4	2.0	7	2.6	0	0	17	3.8
Percent Christian	50	5.0	59	4.9	36	4.8	39	4.9	21	4.1	75	4.4
Percent Catholic	9	2.9	29	2.4	14	3.4	15	3.5	21	4.1	–	–
Percent with no declared religion	28	4.5	29	4.6	27	4.5	31	4.6	45	5.0	25	4.4
Percent other religions	12	3.3	54	2.3	23	4.2	16	3.7	12	3.3	50	5.1
Percent married	11	3.2	93	2.5	18	3.9	16	3.7	–	–	–	–
Percent female	54	4.9	47	4.9	63	4.9	75	4.3	69	4.7	83	3.8
Number of Observations	575		335		240		144		84		60	

the average contribution in treatment 1, when multiplied by 4, exceeds the resistance threshold of treatment 1. In contrast, the average contribution in treatment 2 when multiplied by 4, does not exceed the resistance threshold of treatment 2.

Slightly less than 46 percent of all transfer demands are resisted. Substantially more transfer demands in treatment 1 are resisted than in treatment 2, specifically 56 percent versus 33 percent, respectively. Interestingly, the average forecast error of the RFB during each period is surprisingly small, approximately 2 francs for Others and 0.29 francs for DMs. The average age of Others (DMs) is 24 (24) years old; 48 (79) percent are white; 50 (39) percent are Christian; 11 (16) percent are married; and 54 (75) percent are female. Most of the subjects are undergraduate students, with a very small number pursuing a master's degree.

Turning to average earnings, DMs earn on average 393.75 francs ($78.75), and Others earn on average 156.26 francs ($31.25). In treatment 1, the average earnings of DMs are 312.67 francs ($62.53) and 181.30 francs ($36.26) for Others. In treatment 2, average earnings are 482.84 francs ($96.57) and 136.43 francs ($27.29) for DMs and Others, respectively.

These patterns generally are as expected. Because of the power advantage of the DMs in this game, they make more on average than the Others, irrespective of the resistance threshold. As previously discussed, increasing the resistance threshold lowers the probability of resistance. Anticipating this apparently, DMs increase their average transfer demand. That combined with a lower probability of resistance results in DMs earning more on average in treatment 2 than in treatment 1; meanwhile, Others earn less in treatment 2 than in treatment 1. As a result, the average earnings differential between DMs and Others is 3.5 in treatment 2 as compared to 1.7 in treatment 1. In other words, increasing the resistance threshold by nearly 125 percent (from 13 to 29 francs) results in a 100-percent increase in the earnings differential between DMs and Others.

It is also interesting to compare the observed earnings, described earlier, with those predicted by the theory. As previously discussed, assuming subjects employ equilibrium strategies, a DM's session earnings would be 280 (320) francs or $56 ($64) in treatment 1 (2), and the comparable figures for Others are 220 (180) francs or $44 ($36) in treatment 1 (2). Comparing these figures with the observed session averages for our subjects, we find that the average session earnings of DMs are substantially greater than that predicted by the theory, and the average session earnings of Others are substantially less than the predicted earnings. However, the

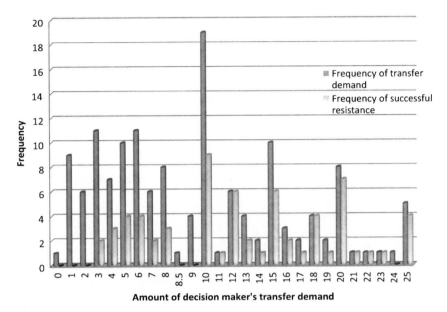

Figure 10.1. Frequency distribution of DM's transfer demand and of successful resistance (all subjects). *Note:* This figure shows the frequency distribution of transfer demands and, conditional on the DM's transfer demand, the frequency distribution of resistance for all subjects.

actual earnings differential between DMs and Others observed in our experiment for each treatment is greater than the predicted values for each treatment. According to the theory, increasing the resistance threshold should increase the earnings differential by 40 percent, but the observed increase is 100 percent.

3.1. Transfer Demands and Resistance

Figures 10.1 through 10.3 show the frequency distribution of transfer demands (in francs) and the frequency of resistance, conditional on the transfer demand, for all subjects, for treatment 1 subjects, and for treatment 2 subjects, respectively. Figure 10.1 shows that there are modes in the frequency distribution of DM's transfer demands at 10 francs, 15 francs, 20 francs, and 25 francs, suggesting perhaps that numbers evenly divisible by 5 are focal points for purposes of choosing a transfer demand. Interestingly, the distribution of transfer demands appears to be approximately uniform between 1 and 8 francs in Figure 10.1, and as we subsequently show

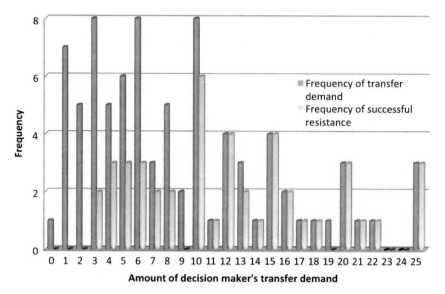

Figure 10.2. Frequency distribution of DM's transfer demand and of successful resistance (treatment 1 subjects). *Note:* This figure shows the frequency distribution of transfer demands and, conditional on the DM's transfer demand, the frequency distribution of resistance for the sample of subjects participating in treatment 1.

in Figures 10.2 and 10.3, as well. The median transfer demand for all DMs is 9 francs.

Comparing Figures 10.2 and 10.3 allows us to examine the effect of increasing the threshold on the frequency distribution of transfer demands and the ability of Others to resist such demands. Generally speaking, the frequency distributions of transfer demands in Figures 10.2 and 10.3 exhibit the same general features as those of Figure 10.1. Specifically, the distributions are approximately uniform between 1 and 8 francs, and there are modes in both figures for transfer demands of 10, 15, 20, and 25 francs, as before. The median transfer demand for treatment 1 is 8 francs ($1.80) and, for treatment 2, 10 francs ($2.00). This increase in the median transfer demand in treatment 2 relative to treatment 1 implies that DMs are responding to the increase in the threshold by increasing their average transfer demand. This suggests that they have some insight into how the parameters of the game influence the strategic choices of Others. Furthermore, as the theory suggests, very few transfer demands less than 3 (7) francs are resisted in treatment 1 (2), meaning that in such cases the RFB does not exceed the resistance threshold. In treatment 1, nearly all transfer demands greater

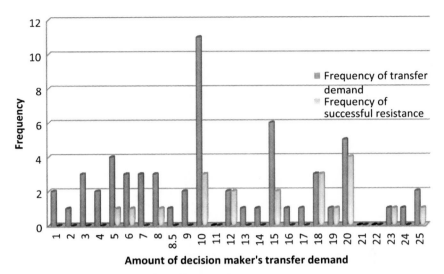

Figure 10.3. Frequency distribution of DM's transfer demand and of successful resistance (subjects in treatment 2). *Note:* This figure shows the frequency distribution of transfer demands and, conditional on the DM's transfer demand, the frequency distribution of resistance for the sample of subjects participating in treatment 2.

than 10 francs are resisted. In treatment 2, however, Others are not as successful as the treatment 1 subjects in resisting transfer demands greater than 10. This suggests that increasing the resistance threshold makes it more difficult for Others to coordinate to resist transfer demands. The increase in the difficulty of cooperating to resist transfer demands from increasing the resistance threshold also is reflected in the decrease in average period earning by Others in treatment 2 as compared to that of treatment 1. The average period earnings by Others in treatments 1 and 2 are 19.48 francs ($3.90) and 13.79 francs ($2.76), respectively.

While we can take reassurance from the fact that the theory explains some patterns in our data, it is also clear that DMs choose out-of-equilibrium strategies more often than not. This is consistent with previous findings in related literatures: out-of-equilibrium strategies are not unusual in experimental studies with repeated play. The DM may be learning about the probability of resistance by trying to separate individual preferences and group coordination issues. Furthermore, the ability to resist "outsized" transfer demands – those greater than the resistance threshold divided by the number of Others – in our data is substantially greater than that suggested by the theory, which predicts that the Others will make no contribution to the

Table 10.2. *Random effects model of the decision maker's transfer demands*

Variable	Estimated coefficient
Constant	78.00**
	(34.15)
Lagged transfer demand	0.249**
	(0.103)
DM's forecast of resistance fund balance	0.0437
	(0.079)
Lagged forecast error	0.095
	(0.058)
Resistance in previous period	− 1.166
(= 1 if resistance was successful in previous period)	(1.329)
Threshold indicator variable (= 1 if 29 francs)	− 0.621
	(1.672)
Gender (= 1 if female)	−1.514
	(1.612)
Marital status (= 1 if married)	− 2.086
	(14.06)
Age	− 4.724*
	(2.606)
Age-squared	0.0805
	(0.052)
Race (= 1 if white)	− 7.560***
	(2.340)
R^2	0.340
Number of observations	123

Clustered standard errors are reported in parentheses, clustering by thirteen DMs; two DMs are dropped because they did not report their marital status. Asterisks indicate the statistical significance of the estimated coefficient, as follows: *** indicates a p-value < 0.01; ** indicates a p-value <05; and * indicates a p-value < 0.1.

resistance fund. In other words, in the theory, everyone will try to free ride and resistance of out-sized transfer demands will always fail.

3.2. Modeling the Strategy Choices of DMs and Others

In this section, we briefly discuss the results of econometric models describing the strategy choices of DMs and Others. The estimates of these two models are reported in Tables 10.2 and 10.3, respectively.

Beginning with our model of the DMs strategy choice, we estimate a random effects model in which the dependent variable is the DMs' transfer demand (in francs). We include demographic characteristics of the DMs

Table 10.3. *Random effects OLS and 2SLS models of other contributions*

Variables	OLS	2SLS	2SLS
Constant	− 9.619	− 6.468	− 2.453
	(7.611)	(4.312)	(1.891)
Transfer demand	0.219***	− 0.102	− 0.0934
	(0.0242)	(0.147)	(0.146)
Threshold (= 1 if 29 francs)	1.075	2.548***	2.426***
	(0.734)	(0.743)	(0.774)
Correct forecast of resistance	–	0.351**	0.340*
		(0.171)	(0.177)
Age	0.615	0.413	0.0611
	(0.559)	(0.317)	(0.0553)
Age-squared	− 0.00895	− 0.00627	–
	(0.00980)	(0.00553)	
Gender (= 1 if female)	0.383	− 0.478	− 0.341
	(0.712)	(0.590)	(0.473)
Marital status (= 1 if single)	2.251	1.653	2.203**
	(1.747)	(1.047)	(0.996)
Number of years in college	− 0.521	− 0.0687	− 0.0777
	(1.808)	(1.105)	(1.107)
Black	− 1.055	0.301	–
	(1.529)	(0.929)	
White	− 0.734	− 0.325	–
	(1.433)	(0.823)	
Hispanic	− 2.372	0.115	–
	(2.624)	(1.588)	
Asian and Pacific Islander	− 1.507	0.143	–
	(1.547)	(1.083)	
Protestant	0.995	–	–
	(0.832)		
Catholic	0.877	–	–
	(1.520)		
Other religion	1.299	–	–
	(1.212)		
Number of observations	555	549	549

Clustered standard errors are reported in parentheses, clustering by the fifty-eight Others; two Others are dropped because they did not report their marital status. Asterisks indicate the statistical significance of the estimated coefficient, as follows: *** indicates a p-value < 0.01; ** indicates a p-value < 0.05; and * indicates a p-value < 0.1.

(i.e., gender, martial status, age, age-squared, and a dummy variable for white) in the model to control for unobserved differences in tastes that may influence their strategy choices. We are implicitly assuming that such tastes are correlated with certain demographic characteristics of the subject.

We estimate a random effects model to account for unobserved differences in tastes that are uncorrelated with observables, such as race, gender, age, religion, and so on. For our estimates to be consistent, the distribution of the unobservable, random taste variable must be normally distributed. We find that the estimated coefficients of age and race are negative and statistically significantly different from zero at conventional levels.[8]

We also include characteristics of the game and treatments among the regressors to control for monetary incentives embedded in the game. Specifically, we include among the regressors lagged transfer demands to account for "learning-by-doing," the DM's forecast of the RFB, the lagged forecast error, and resistance in the previous period. By including a dummy variable equal to 1.0 for treatment 2, we are able to examine the effect of changing the resistance threshold on the strategy choices of DMs, which is a focus of this regression. Somewhat surprisingly, this indicator variable is negative but statistically indistinguishable from zero at conventional levels. Among the incentive variables, only the lagged transfer demand has an estimated coefficient that is statistically significantly different from zero at conventional levels. The estimated coefficient is positive, suggesting that DMs increase their transfer demand in subsequent periods.

Turning to our results for the strategy choices of those assigned to the role of Others, we also estimate a random effects model to account for unobserved tastes that may influence strategy choices. In two specifications of this model, we estimate Two-Stage Least Squares (2SLS) to account for the potential endogeneity of the variable "correctly forecasting whether or not the RFB equals or exceeds the resistance threshold." We use the lagged value of the forecast as an instrumental variable for this potentially endogenous variable. For comparison purposes, we also report Ordinary Least Squares OLS estimates, which are reported in column 1 of Table 10.3. Finally, we estimate two specifications of the Two-Stage Least Squares (2SLS) model, one specification includes a set of race indicator variables (i.e., black, Hispanic, and Asian); the other specification does not include this set of indicator variables. These results are reported in columns 2 and 3, respectively, of Table 10.3.

Beginning with the OLS estimates, the only variable that is statistically distinguishable from zero at conventional levels is the transfer demand. The

---

[8] We report clustered standard errors, clustering on the identity of the decision maker (DMs and Others, as the case may be) to account for the fact that a set of observations apply to one individual and, thus, these observations may not be independently distributed.

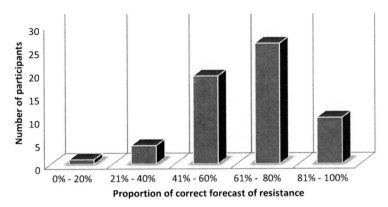

Figure 10.4. Distribution of forecast accuracy (all subjects).

estimated coefficient is equal to 0.219 (S.E. = 0.0242), and the estimate is nearly ten times its standard error. This estimate suggests that there is a positive relationship between the size of the Others' contribution to the resistance fund and the transfer demand.

Now, we turn to the 2SLS estimates reported in column 3. In contrast to our OLS specification, this model includes an indicator variable for correctly forecasting resistance. Because this variable is potentially endogenous, we estimate the model using 2SLS. The instrumental variable is the lagged forecast of the RFB. The estimated coefficient of this variable is positive and more than twice its standard error. This estimate suggests that there is a positive relationship between a correct forecast of resistance and the size of the contribution to the resistance fund. The estimated coefficient of the threshold indicator variable is positive and statistically significant at the 1 percent level, meaning that the average contribution in treatment 2 is greater than in treatment 1 as a result of the increase in the resistance threshold. Finally, the estimated coefficient of marital status (= 1 if single) is positive and statistically significant, suggesting that single subjects contribute more on average to the resistance fund than their married counterparts.

3.3. Distribution of RFB Forecast Accuracy

Now, we examine the forecasts of the RFB by the subjects in this experiment. Figures 10.4 through 10.6 show the distributions of forecast accuracy for all subjects, treatment 1 subjects, and treatment 2 subjects, respectively. The horizontal axis of these figures categorizes subjects according to the

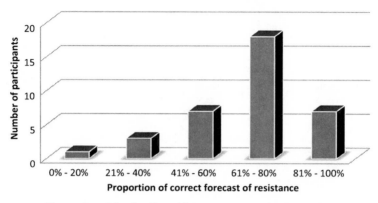

Figure 10.5. Distribution of forecast accuracy (treatment 1).

proportion of times a given subject correctly forecasts whether or not the RFB would or would not equal or exceed the threshold.

As previously noted, the forecast error of the RFB is remarkably small. This is borne out in Figure 10.4, which shows that approximately fifty-five subjects out of seventy-five are correct more than 40 percent of the time. Figures 10.5 and 10.6 show the distribution of forecast accuracy of subjects in treatments 1 and 2, respectively. The main distinguishing feature of these two distributions is that there is evidence of some deterioration in the ability of subjects to make correct forecasts under treatment 2 as compared to their ability in treatment 1. In other words, increasing the threshold appears to have adversely affected the ability of participants to correctly forecast whether or not resistance will be successful.

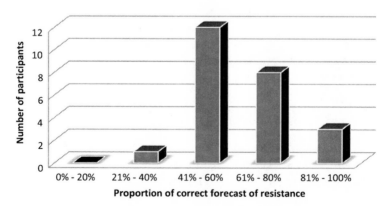

Figure 10.6. Distribution of forecast accuracy (treatment 2).

3.4. Odds and Ends

We are interested to know whether the main behavioral patterns observed in public goods games also are observed in the resistance game that is the focus of this study. Two features of multi-period public goods games are particularly noteworthy in the current context.[9] Specifically, there is considerably more giving in public goods games than predicted by the hard-nosed Nash equilibrium, and cooperation in multi-period public goods games appears to deteriorate in later rounds of a session. We also find substantial evidence of out-of-equilibrium play in our resistance game. DMs demand substantially more than predicted by the theory, and Others are more successful in resisting "outsized" transfer demands than predicted by the theory.

We also examine whether there is a decline in cooperation among Others in later periods of a session as compared to earlier periods. In the first five periods of a session, Others successfully resist transfer demands 54 percent of the time, compared to 41 percent of the time in the last five rounds of a session. For treatment 1, the corresponding figures are 64 percent and 48 percent, and for treatment 2, the figures are 37 percent and 30 percent. This observation suggests that, as in a multi-period public goods game, there is some deterioration in the ability of Others to cooperate to resist transfer demands in later periods of a session. In short, there is a decline in the ability of Others to resist coercion in later rounds of the game compared to their ability in earlier rounds. Nevertheless, the ability to resist remains rather high even in later periods of a session. The ability to cooperate in resisting transfer demands is much greater when the threshold is smaller. Curiously, the decline in the ability to cooperate between the first five periods and the last five periods of a session is steeper in treatment 1 (-26 percent) compared to treatment 2 (-18 percent).

4. Conclusion

We adapt a public goods game to investigate whether people are able to cooperate to resist coercive government actions in the face of individual incentives to do otherwise. For this purpose, we use a resistance game that is a form of threshold public goods game. The equilibrium strategy in our resistance game is for a DM to make a modest transfer demand of 3 (7) francs

---

[9] See Ledyard (1995) for a detailed review of this literature.

in treatment 1 (2) and for the Others to offer no resistance to such demands. In the case of out-of-equilibrium transfer demands, the theory suggests that Others will not attempt to resist them because of free-rider behavior. We find that the observed average earnings of DMs are substantially greater than that predicted by the efficient, subgame perfect equilibrium of our game. Furthermore, subjects' forecasts of the RFB are remarkably accurate. We also find that the probability of resistance is smaller in later periods of a session than in earlier ones. Nevertheless, the probability of resisting transfer demands is rather high relative to that predicted by the theory, even in the later periods of a session. Finally, we find that the probability of cooperating to resist coercion decreases as the obstacles to cooperation increase, as evidenced by the decline in the probability of resistance when the threshold is increased from 13 to 29 francs in treatments 1 and 2, respectively.

Regarding the topic of this volume, we find that laboratory subjects, despite the predictions of the theory, are indeed able to cooperate in resisting coercion despite the social dilemma inherent in this game. In a related study provided for this volume, Cettolin and Riedl (Chapter 11 in this volume) investigate the incidence of the free-rider problem when one member of a group is singled out to make a mandatory minimum contribution to the group fund of a public goods game. In a standard public goods game, some people appear to cooperate when they perceive others doing so and refuse to cooperate when they perceive others failing to do so. Such behavior is referred to in the literature as conditional cooperation. Cettolin and Riedl are interested to know whether conditional cooperators will make voluntary contributions to a public good when a member of the group is coerced to make a contribution to the public good. They find that coerced cooperation does not significantly affect voluntary contributions to the public good by the non-coerced members of the group. Thus, interestingly, coerced "cooperation" does not appear to mitigate the coordination problem that underlies the free-rider problem. In other words, reciprocal cooperation by conditional cooperators appears to require others in the group to take voluntary actions.

We believe that our findings make an important contribution to the public finance literature, not only from an academic perspective but also from a policy perspective. Our findings are consistent with anecdotal evidence that people find it very difficult to cooperate in resisting unpopular legislation in democratic states and even more so in the case of authoritarian and despotic regimes. In fact, our finding that increasing the resistance threshold makes it more difficult to resist coercion suggests that the more despotic the regime, the less likely it will be that people will successfully cooperate to resist it. In effect, a despotic regime increases the resistance threshold to government action allowing it to take extraordinarily coercive actions against the populous. History is replete with examples of despotic regimes, even ones engaged in the mass extermination of the population, which apparently could only be resisted, if at all, through foreign intervention to overthrow the regime. Examples of such regimes include Hitler's Germany and Pol Pot's Cambodia.

Our findings suggest future research. Our DM is a randomly assigned dictator who may impose a reallocation of initial endowments; meanwhile, Others have the option of avoiding redistribution by contributing to a resistance fund. Future research could investigate how the method used to appoint the DM, including democratic election, impacts behavior in this game. In addition, coordination mechanisms such as cheap talk or a credible pre-commitment device may have a profound impact on the ability to resist unfavorable policies.

APPENDIX

General Instructions

You have been asked to participate in a decision-making experiment. It is very important that you not talk or communicate with others throughout the experiment. The instructions that we have distributed to you are solely for your private information. If you have any questions, please ask a monitor.

During the experiment your entire earnings will be calculated in francs. At the end of the experiment the total amount of francs you have earned will be converted to dollars at the following rate:

$$5 \text{ francs} = 1 \text{ dollar}$$

At the end of the experiment your entire earnings from the experiment and the $2 bonus if you arrived on time will be paid to you immediately in cash. You will also be asked to complete a pre-experiment questionnaire before making any decisions as well as a post-experiment questionnaire, and for doing so, you will receive $4.

The experiment is divided into different periods. In all, the experiment consists of ten periods. In each period the participants are divided into groups of five. You will therefore be in a group with four other participants. Your group will consist of the same five participants throughout the experiment.

The remainder of the instructions explains exactly how the experiment is conducted. Remember that we ask that you avoid talking, signaling, or making noises to other participants at any time.

Specific Instructions

In the experiment today all members of your group will be endowed with 25 francs. One group member is referred to as the "Decision Maker or DM" and the remaining four group members as "Others." At this time no one knows who the DM is for your group (even the experimenters). It could be that you will be the DM, as we will soon describe.

At the beginning of a period the DM for your group will propose how many francs each of the Others will transfer to him/her. The proposed transfer is the same for all four group members. If you are an Other, after you are informed of the proposed transfer to the DM, you must decide whether you will voluntarily transfer the francs to the DM or resist the transfer. If you do not want to pay the transfer asked by the DM, you can pay any number of francs into a Fund for your group. Each period the experimenter will add together the contributions to the Fund made by members of your group. If in a period the Fund has 13 or more francs, the transfer to the DM is not paid. But if the Fund has less than 13 francs, you lose your contribution to the Fund and also must pay the transfer to the DM.

Here are the two alternatives:

1. The Fund has a total of 13 or more francs. None of the Others has to transfer francs to the DM, and the DM receives nothing for the period. The Others keep all francs they did not pay into the Fund. This alternative is summarized as follows, where c = an Other's contribution to the Fund:

When Fund $\geq$ 13, Other's Earnings = 25 − c and DM Earnings = 25.

Note: The contribution to the fund by each Other is their own private decision and can be the same or different from the contributions of other group members. Thus, each Other group member potentially has a different contribution (c) and different earnings.

2. The Fund has a total of less than of 13 francs. The francs paid into the Fund are lost and all Others must pay the transfer proposed by the DM. If an Other does not have sufficient funds remaining to fulfill the DM's proposal, the member transfers all remaining francs

to the DM. The DM receives the transfer proposed (or somewhat less if a group member has insufficient funds). This alternative is summarized as follows, where c = an Other's contribution to the Fund and T = transfer proposed by DM:

$$\text{When Fund} < 13, \text{Others Earnings} = 25 - T - c$$
$$\text{and DM Earnings} = 4^* T + 25.$$

In addition to the earnings decisions above, each period all group members will receive 1 franc per period to forecast the total contribution to the Fund by their group members.

The experimenter has randomly determined both group membership and which member of the group will be the DM. After the instructions are complete the experimenter will distribute decision forms to each participant here today. If your decision form is for the Decision Maker, you are the randomly selected DM for your group. Otherwise, your form will indicate you are an Other. Please do not reveal your role to other participants at any time. Also, recall that the experiment includes 10 periods.

Decisions

Please refer to the Practice Decision Forms included with these instructions. Each period will proceed as follows:

1. Each DM will record their proposed transfer (T) in column (3) from each of the Other four group members and make a forecast of the Total Fund balance in column (5) of the DM's Decision Form. All participants' folders will then be collected.
2. The experimenter will record the proposed transfer (T) in column (3) of the Others Decision Forms and return folders to all participants.
3. The Other Group Members will then record their contributions to the Fund in column (4) of their Decision Forms and also record in column (5) of their decision form the total group contribution expected this period to the Fund. Again, the experimenter will collect all folders.
4. The total Fund balance for each group will be computed and recorded in column (6) of the Others' Record Sheets and column (6) of the DM's. The experimenter will return the folders, and all participants will compute their period earnings in the final column.

After a period concludes, we move to the next period with the DM recording their proposed transfer (T) from each group member and repeat all steps above.

Do you have any questions?

Before we begin the experiment we will complete the practice exercises below, as well as a short pre-experiment questionnaire. Then, the experimenter will distribute a folder to each participant in the room. Again, if you are the randomly selected DM for your group, the Decision Form will so indicate. Otherwise, the form will indicate that you are an Other. Your role today will not be revealed to anyone in the room. Recall that group membership and the DM were randomly determined by the experimenter.

Practice Exercises

Now we will complete the practice exercises. You will complete them for an Other as well as for a DM.

1. In the first period the DM proposes a transfer of 20 francs. One Other offers resistance (c) of 4 francs. The Fund balance is 11 francs. Compute each Practice Decision Form.
2. In the second period the DM proposes a transfer of 2 francs. One Other offers resistance (c) of 10 francs. The Fund balance is 36 francs. Compute each Practice Decision Form.

We will now distribute the folders and give the DMs 5 minutes to determine their proposed transfers for period 1.

Participant Number _____

DECISION FORM
Others

(1) Period	(2) Beginning balance Francs	(3) Transfer proposed by your DM (T)	(4) Your contribution to the Fund (c)	(5) Your "Forecast" of Total Fund balance	(6) Actual Total Fund balance	(7) Earnings*
1	25					
2	25					
3	25					
4	25					
5	25					
6	25					
7	25					

8	25					
9	25					
10	25					
Total earnings in dollars [sum of column (7) divided by 5]						
Forecast earnings in dollars [1 franc for each forecast in column (5) divided by 5]						
Add $2 bonus **if** on time.						
Add $4 for completion of the pre- and post-experiment questionnaires.						

* Earnings each period are determined as follows:

When Fund ≥ 13, Your Earnings $= 25 - c$

Fund < 13,   Your Earnings $= 25 - T - c$

Participant Number _____

DECISION FORM
Decision Maker (DM)

(1) Period	(2) Beginning balance	(3) Record the proposed transfer from each of the Others (T from 0 to 25)	(4) 4*T	(5) Your "Forecast" of Total Fund balance	(6) Total Fund balance	(7) Earnings**
1	25					
2	25					
3	25					
4	25					
5	25					
6	25					
7	25					
8	25					
9	25					
10	25					
Total earnings in dollars [sum of column (7) divided by 5]						
Forecast earnings in dollars [1 franc for each forecast in column (5) divided by 5]						
Add $2 bonus **if** on time.						
Add $4 for completion of the pre- and post-experiment questionnaires.						

** Earnings each period are determined as follows:

When Fund ≥ 13, Your Earnings $= 25$

Fund < 13,   Your Earnings $= 4\text{*}T + 25$

Practice DECISION FORM: Others

(1) Period	(2) Beginning balance Francs	(3) Transfer proposed by your DM (T)	(4) Your contribution to the Fund (c)	(5) Your "Forecast" of Total Fund balance	(6) Actual Total Fund balance	(7) Earnings*
1	25					
2	25					
Total earnings in dollars [sum of column (7) divided by 5]						
Forecast earnings in dollars [1 franc for each forecast in column (5) divided by 5]						
Add $2 bonus **if** on time.						
Add $4 for completion of the pre- and post-experiment questionnaires.						

* Earnings each period are determined as follows:
When Fund $\geq$ 13,   Your Earnings = 25 – c
Fund < 13,   Your Earnings = 25 – T – c

Practice DECISION FORM: Decision Maker (DM)

(1) Period	(2) Beginning balance	(3) Record the proposed transfer from each of the Others (T from 0 to 25)	(4) 4*T	(5) Your "Forecast" of Total Fund balance	(6) Total Fund balance	(7) Earnings**
1	25					
2	25					
Total earnings in dollars [sum of column (7) divided by 5]						
Forecast earnings in dollars [1 franc for each forecast in column (5) divided by 5]						
Add $2 bonus **if** on time.						
Add $4 for completion of the pre- and post-experiment questionnaires.						

** Earnings each period are determined as follows:
When Fund $\geq$ 13,   Your Earnings = 25
Fund < 13,   Your Earnings = 4*T + 25

PRE-EXPERIMENT QUESTIONNAIRE

This questionnaire is designed to collect information to help the researchers understand decisions made throughout the experiment. Please be assured that you cannot be personally identified from your responses. You will be paid to complete the questionnaire, so please be sure to fill it out completely.

List five words that best describe who you are:

1. _____
2. _____
3. _____
4. _____
5. _____

POST-EXPERIMENT QUESTIONNAIRE

This questionnaire is designed to collect information to help the researchers understand decisions made throughout the experiment. Please be assured that you cannot be personally identified from your responses. You will be paid to complete the questionnaire, so please be sure to fill it out completely. Please double-check to ensure that you have not inadvertently skipped a question when you are finished and answer all questions as fully as possible.

1. What is your standing in your university? (check one)
   _____ undergraduate student _____ masters student _____ PhD student _____ Other
2. Based on your current standing (i.e., undergrad, masters, PhD), what is your year of study (e.g., 1st, 2nd, 3rd, 4th)? _____
3. What is your college (e.g., management, education?) _____
4. What is your major area of concentration (e.g., accounting, biology)?
   _____
5. What is your sex? (check one) male _____ female _____
6. What is your age? _____ years
7. What is your race/ethnicity? (check one)
   Black (not if Hispanic origin) _____ White (not of Hispanic origin) _____ Hispanic _____
   Asian or Pacific Islander _____ American Indian or Alaska Native _____ Other (please detail) _____
8. How would you characterize your current economic situation? (circle number)

Poor 1—2—3—4—5—6—7—8—9—10—11   Wealthy

9. How interesting did you find this experiment?
Not Very   Very
Interesting 1—2—3—4—5—6—7—8—9—10—11   Interesting

10. How would you characterize the amount of money earned in this experiment for the time required?
Nominal   Considerable
Amount 1—2—3—4—5—6—7—8—9—10—11   Amount

11. In general, how would you characterize your political attitudes?
Very   Very
Liberal 1—2—3—4—5—6—7—8—9—10—11   Conservative

12. In general, how would you characterize your religious beliefs?
Not Religious   Very
At All 1—2—3—4—5—6—7—8—9—10—11   Religious

13. How would you characterize your behavior today?
Very   Very
Selfish 1—2—3—4—5—6—7—8—9—10—11   Generous

14. How would you characterize the decisions of your group?
Very   Very
Selfish 1—2—3—4—5—6—7—8—9—10—11   Generous

15. How would you characterize people, in general?
Very   Very
Selfish 1—2—3—4—5—6—7—8—9—10—11   Generous

16. Are you married? (check one) yes _____ no _____
If not, are you in a committed relationship? (check one) yes _____ no
_____

17. How many children do you have? _____

18. What is your religious affiliation? _____

19. How important are groups for you in general?
Not at all 1—2—3—4—5—6—7—8—9—10—11   To a great extent

20. Are you feeling happy today?
Not at all 1—2—3—4—5—6—7—8—9—10—11   To a great extent

21. Please give a brief statement on what you think about groups in general and what your experiences (positive or negative) are.

22. How would you characterize your **Decision maker's** (DM's) behavior today?
Check if you were the DM: N/A _____

Very   Very
selfish 1—2—3—4—5—6—7—8—9—10—11   generous

23. How would you characterize your Other **group** members' behavior today?

Very   Very
cooperative 1—2—3—4—5—6—7—8—9—10—11   uncooperative

References

Ledyard, John (1995). "Public Goods Experiments." In Kagel, John H. and Alvin E. Roth (eds.), *Handbook of Experimental Economics*. Princeton, NJ: Princeton University Press, 111–194.

Mertins, Vanessa (2008). "Procedural Satisfaction Matters – Procedural Fairness Does Not: An Experiment Studying the Effects of Procedural Judgments on Outcome Acceptance." IAAEG Discussion Paper No. 2008/07. Institute for Labour Law and Industrial Relations in the European Community.

11

Partial Coercion, Conditional Cooperation, and Self-Commitment in Voluntary Contributions to Public Goods

Elena Cettolin and Arno Riedl

1. Introduction

In its purest form the consumption of a public good is non-rival and non-excludable leading to well-known undersupply results that are presented and discussed in all undergraduate and graduate textbooks in public economics (Rosen and Gayer 2010, Laffont 1988). The problem of insufficient contributions to public goods when organized in a decentralized and voluntary way is perhaps one of the best known examples in which individual and collective interest are standing in stark contrast. When pondering about whether to voluntarily contribute to a public good, individual material self-interest dictates to free ride on others' contributions whereas collective interest asks for high contributions of all involved. Traditionally it is assumed that in such a situation individual material self-interest prevails and that the economy indeed ends up with an inefficiently low supply of public goods. Therefore, and because a sufficient supply of public goods is perceived of utmost importance for any economy, the development of means and mechanisms to overcome undersupply has a long history in economics (e.g., Lindahl 1919/1958).

Following the pessimistic statement of Samuelson (1954) that in public goods economies no decentralized process can lead to efficient allocations of resources, the traditional theoretical economic literature developed sophisticated mechanisms proving Samuelson wrong on theoretical grounds. The proposed mechanisms indeed ensure that people contribute to public goods when it is in their interest to not contribute in the absence of the mechanism. For instance, the Groves-Ledyard mechanism (Groves and Ledyard 1977) is a decentralized mechanism in which the government sets a taxation-allocation scheme such that it is in each individual's interest to contribute the efficient amount. A similar but simpler mechanism is proposed by

Falkinger (1996). Ledyard (2010) provides a recent critical survey of these and other mechanisms discussed in the literature. All proposed mechanisms, although allowing for decentralized individual decisions, rely on the assumption that some benevolent decision maker can coerce people to contribute their share, usually by sanctioning deviations from the target contribution. Thus, these mechanisms all rely on centralized means of coercion and a paternalistic government.

Laboratory experiments testing these mechanisms show that if the centralized sanctioning is severe enough, the mechanisms indeed implement efficient outcomes (see, e.g., Chen and Plott 1996, Falkinger et al. 2000). The experimental literature on public goods also suggests that there may be other, truly decentralized, ways to ensure efficient or close to efficient provisions of public goods. The research investigating the role of decentralized costly punishment and reward (see, e.g., Fehr and Gächter 2000, Sefton, Shupp, and Walker 2007) indeed shows that especially decentralized individual punishment can have positive efficiency effects in public goods problems, at least when people interact repeatedly (Gächter, Renner, and Sefton 2008).[1] These are informative and important results, but it is unlikely that decentralized costly punishment alone is a sustainable solution for overcoming the underprovision problem to public goods in complex developed societies. For instance, recent experimental research has shown that heterogeneity among economic actors may undermine the effectiveness of this decentralized enforcement mechanism (Tan 2008, Reuben and Riedl 2009). In addition, decentralized punishment may not be feasible in many "real life" situations. For instance, citizens of a society may not have sufficient information about individual contributions to fine-tune punishment toward free riders, which has been shown to be essential for the success of punishment in increasing contributions and efficiency (see, Herrmann, Thoni, and Gächter 2008). Even if all citizens could know all others' contributions, they may still lack appropriate punishment technologies for targeted sanctioning, or the law may simply not allow citizens to privately enforce contributions (see also Kosfeld and Riedl 2007). Another potential limitation of decentralized punishment is that it may be too costly for sustaining efficient contributions to the public good (Anderson and Putterman 2006, Carpenter 2007) or not effective enough

---

[1]   In experiments where people only interact once this positive efficiency effect is either very weak (Fehr and Gächter, 2002) or not existent (e.g. Egas and Riedl, 2008). For a recent overview of the effects of decentralized punishment on contributions and efficiency see Gächter and Herrmann (2009).

(Egas and Riedl 2008, Nikiforakis and Normann 2008). Hence, it is likely that some coercion by a central planner will be unavoidable for sustaining efficient levels of public good provision.

An important behavioral regularity uncovered by experimental studies on public goods problems is that many people are conditional cooperative (Keser and van Winden 2000). Being conditional cooperative means that one is ready to contribute one's share if one believes or, better, can be sure that others also contribute their share. Some studies indeed show that beliefs about others' contribution behavior strongly influence a person's actual contributions to a public good (Fischbacher, Gächter, and Fehr 2001, Fischbacher and Gächter 2010). What these studies also show is that voluntary contributions triggered by conditional cooperation are fragile because they depend on a person's expectation about others' contributions. Such uncertainty is inherent in the simultaneous move nature of most public goods problems, and together with pessimistic expectations about others' contributions, it may easily lead to a breakdown of voluntary contributions to the public good.[2] One way of taking out this uncertainty in simultaneous move public goods problems is to coerce a subset of players to contributing a minimum amount.

In this essay we combine the idea of conditional cooperation and coercion. In particular, we investigate if partial coercion can be sufficient for guaranteeing high contribution levels to the public good. The idea is that if conditional cooperation is indeed such a strong force as suggested in the literature, then coercion of parts of the society could be used to coordinate beliefs of those not coerced. However, there could also be a downside. The knowledge that some people are forced to contribute their share may increase temptation to free ride on them. In that case, partial coercion may lead to even worse results than no coercion at all.

In brief we conduct the following public goods experiment, which is played only once. Three subjects are randomly matched into a group in which they receive fifty tokens (the experimental money unit) as endowment. They have to decide individually about their contribution to a linear public good. In a baseline treatment everybody is free to contribute whatever amount. In a low-coercion treatment one of the three subjects is randomly chosen and coerced to contribute at least thirteen out of fifty tokens, and in a high-coercion treatment one subject has to contribute at least thirty-eight tokens. In a final treatment, we explore the effectiveness of voluntary self-commitment in comparison to exogenous coercion and allow subjects to

---

[2] For a comparison of simultaneous and sequential move public goods problems see, e.g., Andreoni et al. (2003), Coats et al. (2009), and Gächter et al (2010).

self-commit to minimal contributions of either zero, thirteen, or thirty-eight tokens.

The main result of the experiment is that partial coercion has no positive effect on contributions beyond the pure coercion effect. In particular, although the non-coerced subjects rationally adjust their beliefs about the contributions of coerced subjects, they do *not* adjust their contributions. The picture is very similar in the self-commitment treatment in which we observe in addition a self-selection effect. Those who do not self-commit are also those who free ride in the public good game.

The rest of the essay is organized as follows. Next we give a brief overview of the most closely related experimental literature. Thereafter, Section 2 introduces the experimental design and reports on the procedures, Section 3 presents and discusses the results regarding contributions to the public good, the role of beliefs, and the effect of the possibility of self-commitment. Section 4 provides a brief discussion and concludes.

2. Related Literature

To the best of our knowledge, there are no experimental papers directly investigating how cooperation in public good games is affected by the presence of players who are obliged (coerced) to contribute a certain amount. However, there are a few studies on the related questions of how (perceived) obligations affect voluntary contributions to public goods.

In the theoretical law and economics literature obligations are thought to facilitate coordination and cooperation. Besides introducing incentives for compliance, obligations may make the prescribed outcome salient, or focal (McAdams 2000). The positive effects of obligations on cooperation levels are indeed supported by some experimental studies. Tyran and Feld (2006) experimentally analyze the effects of a law that makes full contribution to a public good game obligatory while mildly sanctioning free riding. The effects of such mild, non-deterrent law are compared to those of a severe law and to the absence of any legal obligation to contribute. The authors find that an obligation backed by mild incentives does not significantly increase contributions when it is exogenously imposed. However, contributions increase significantly if the mild law is approved in a referendum – the fact that the majority votes in favor of the law seems to induce self-fulfilling expectations of cooperation.

The influence of obligations on beliefs about others' behavior is supported by two studies of Galbiati and Vertova (2007, 2008). In the public good game studied by the authors in the 2008 paper, individuals face an exogenously fixed obligation of minimum contribution; individuals contributing less (more) than the minimum are subject to a probabilistic punishment (reward). The minimum level of contribution varies across treatments, while marginal incentives stay the same: the classical prediction for all treatments is that the obligation to contribute does not affect individual behavior. Instead, the authors find that obligations per se significantly affect the average level of contributions although cooperation cannot be sustained by obligations over time. In Galbiati and Vertova (2007) the authors investigate whether obligations affect cooperation by coordinating individuals' beliefs about others' contributions to a focal point. The study shows that obligations have indeed a positive effect on individuals' expectations about others' contributions, which is consistent with conditional cooperative behavior, as discussed earlier. The authors also suggest that a minimum obligatory contribution can have direct effects on preferences if it urges people to update their contribution norms. By looking at conditional contribution schedules, the authors conclude that the presence of the obligation positively influences preferences for cooperation.

Kroll, Cherry, and Shogren (2007) investigate cooperation in public good games when collective agreements on obligatory contribution levels are possible. Each participant proposes a desired contribution level and votes for a proposal in her group. In the binding vote treatment, the winning proposal is imposed on all members in a group. In the non-binding treatment, voting is cheap talk, and participants can deviate from the chosen contribution level. In the non-binding treatment with punishment participants can sanction group members who deviate from the voting outcome. The authors observe that voting always increases contributions to the public good, especially when the outcome of the vote is imposed on all members. However, contributions in the non-binding treatment only increase marginally and temporarily, suggesting that the contribution norm established with the vote does not survive if violators cannot be punished.

Finally, cooperation is enhanced also by mechanisms other than obligations that seemingly coordinate beliefs around a focal point. Croson and Marks (2001) study the impact of non-binding recommendations on contributions to a threshold public good. The authors find that when valuations for the public good are heterogeneous, recommended contributions significantly increase the likelihood of efficient provision.

3. Experimental Design and Procedures

The basic game in our experiment is a linear public goods game, also known as voluntary contribution mechanism (VCM). The game is played after all subjects have participated in another, unrelated experiment. The preceding experiment is separated from the reported public goods game by means of a filler task that lasts approximately seven minutes. Each participant takes part in only one of four experimental treatments. The treatments differ in the extent to which players are coerced to contribute to the public good. The game is played only once, in groups of three participants. We employ a procedure guaranteeing that participants who interacted in the previous experiment are never in the same group. All participants are informed about this.

At the beginning of the experiment each participant $i \in \{1, 2, 3\}$ receives detailed instructions on the computer screen. Participants are informed that everyone in the group receives an endowment of 50 tokens: 1 token being equal to 0.025 Euro. The marginal monetary benefit of keeping a token is equal to 1, whereas the marginal monetary benefit of contributing a token to the public good is given by $\alpha = 0.5$. Therefore, from a self-interested monetary perspective, the dominant strategy of each participant i is not contributing any token to the public good.

In treatment 1 (baseline), after reading the instructions, all participants in a group independently and simultaneously decide how many tokens, if any, they want to contribute to the public good. In treatment 2 (low coercion) after reading the instructions and before the contribution stage, one member per group is randomly selected. The selected group member is coerced to contribute at least 13 tokens, approximately 25 percent of the endowment, to the public good. In treatment 3 (high coercion) a group member is also randomly selected after the instruction phase and is then coerced to contribute at least 38 tokens, approximately 75 percent of the endowment, to the public good. In both treatments, the fact that a member will be obliged to contribute a minimum amount to the public good is common knowledge in the group. In treatment 4 (endogenous coercion) after reading the instructions and before the contribution stage, subjects decide if they want to voluntarily commit to contribute a certain minimum amount to the public good. The level of commitment can be low, 13 tokens, or high, 38 tokens. Commitment levels are always binding and revealed to all group members before the contribution stage.

The final earnings of a participant i from the public good are given by:

$$\pi_i = 50 - c_i + \alpha \sum_{j=1}^{3} c_j,$$

where in the low-coercion treatment $c_i \geq 13$ for one randomly selected i, in the high-coercion treatment $c_i \geq 38$ for one randomly selected i, and in the self-commitment treatment $c_i \geq 13$ or $c_i \geq 38$ for any i who chooses to commit to the respective minimum contribution.

Apart from contributions, we are interested in the effect of coercion on players' anticipation of what the other group members will contribute. This is of importance because other studies (Fischbacher et al. 2001, Fischbacher and Gächter 2010) have shown that many people condition their behavior on their beliefs about others' contributions. Specifically, if they expect others to contribute much, they contribute more than if they expect others to contribute little. Therefore, in all treatments, right before deciding how many tokens they want to contribute to the public good, participants are asked to guess how much the other group members will contribute to the public good. Rather than eliciting a point belief, we decided to elicit an interval, which also gives us as an idea about the guesser's confidence. Specifically, each participant is asked to indicate what she/he thinks will be the minimum and maximum contribution of each group member. The belief elicitation is incentivized using the interval scoring rule (Schlag and van der Weele 2009). The rule works as follows: If the true contribution of another member lies in the indicated interval, the guessing subject earns an amount that is inversely related to the length of the indicated interval. If the true contribution of a member lays outside the indicated interval, the subject earns nothing. More precisely, let c_j be the actual contribution of j, and $\underline{c}_{ij}$ and $\overline{c}_{ij}$ be the minimum and maximum, respectively, of the interval indicated by i regarding j's contribution, then the earnings of i from guessing j's contribution is determined as follows:

$$\pi_{ij} = \begin{cases} 0.12 \times (50 - (\overline{c}_{ij} - \underline{c}_{ij})), & \text{if } c_j \in [\underline{c}_{ij}, \overline{c}_{ij}] \\ 0, & \text{if } c_j \notin [\underline{c}_{ij}, \overline{c}_{ij}], \end{cases}$$

with $c_j, \underline{c}_{ij}, \overline{c}_{ij} \in [0, 50]$.

Eliciting an interval has the advantage that it gives information not only about the location of the belief distribution, but also about its dispersion. Indeed, the width of the interval determines an upper bound on the variance of the belief distribution. This makes the width of the interval a proxy for how confident the decision maker is about his/her guess. Furthermore, these implications hold for any risk-neutral or risk-adverse decision maker.

In the self-commitment treatment subjects may also form beliefs about the other group members' level of commitment to the public good. Therefore, after the commitment phase and before eliciting beliefs on the contribution levels, we ask subjects to indicate the likelihood in percentage points of the six possible commitment scenarios. In the first scenario none of the other group members commits, and in the last scenario both commit to contributions. This belief elicitation is incentivized with the quadratic scoring rule, which rewards subjects for the accuracy of their prediction according

Table 11.1. *Group-level contributions*

Treatment	Average	St. dev.	Median	No. of obs.
Baseline	15.61	11.18	16.67	24
Low coercion	18.75	8.76	20.17	24
High coercion	25.52	8.64	25.17	20
Self-commitment	16.61	9.51	16.67	24

Note: Unit of observation is group average contribution.

to the following formula:

$$\pi_i = 3 - 0.00015^*[(p_0 - r_0)^2 + (p_{13} - r_{13})^2 + (p_{26} - r_{26})^2 \\ + (p_{38} - r_{38})^2 + (p_{51} - r_{51})^2 + (p_{76} - r_{76})^2],$$

where p_n indicates participant's i likelihood estimate, expressed in percentage points, that the sum of commitments equals n. As an example, if i believes that with 50 percent chance both the other members commit to contribute 13 tokens then $p_{26} = 50$. The realized commitments are indicated by r_n. If, for instance, i's other group members commit to contribute respectively 13 and 38 tokens, then $r_{51} = 100$ and all other r_n equal zero.

The experiment ends after the contribution phase in which subjects are informed about the total amount contributed to the public good and about their earnings from the public good game and the beliefs elicitations. Thereafter they answer a short questionnaire, are paid in cash, and dismissed from the laboratory. The experiment lasted approximately 25 minutes inclusive of the instructions. In total 276 subjects participated in the experiment: 72 in each of the baseline, low-coercion, and self-commitment treatments and 60 in the high-coercion treatment.

4. Results

In the following we first report on group level contributions to the public good for all treatments. We then proceed with a discussion of contributions of non-committed group members, in which we also zoom into the role of beliefs in contribution behavior. Finally, we report the results of the self-commitment treatment in more detail.

4.1. Contributions to the Public Good

Table 11.1 reports first and second order descriptive statistics of the contributions to the public good, separate for treatments.

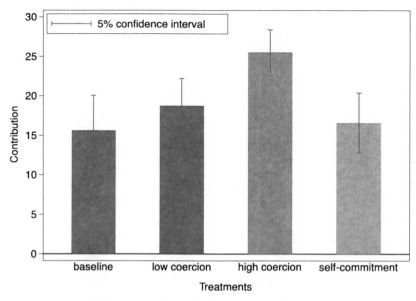

Figure 11.1. Group-level average contributions.

Result 1. *On the group level contributions are highest in the high-coercion treatment, followed by the low-coercion, the self-commitment, and the baseline treatment. The difference between high-coercion and the other treatments is statistically significant. All other differences are insignificant.*

Support for this result can be found in Figure 11.1 and Table 11.1. Average contributions to the public good vary roughly between 15 tokens (30 percent) in the baseline treatment and 25 tokens (50 percent) in the high-coercion treatment. The medians of contributions are very close to the averages. When comparing the group average contributions across all four treatments, a Kruskal-Wallis equality-of-population rank (henceforth, KW) test detects a significant difference ($\chi^2_3 = 11.831$, $p = 0.0080$, two-sided). Pair-wise comparisons between treatments with Mann-Whitney rank sum (henceforth, MW) tests reveal that contributions in the high-coercion treatment are significantly higher than in all other treatments ($p \leq 0.0328$, two-sided). All other pair-wise comparisons of group average contributions return insignificant results ($p > 0.1766$, two-sided).

We are especially interested in the contribution behavior of non-coerced (non-committed) subjects. If it holds that conditional cooperation is an important behavioral mechanism for achieving high voluntary contribution rates, then the knowledge that some subjects are coerced into (committed

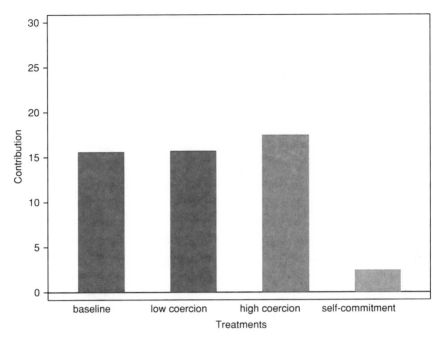

Figure 11.2. Average contributions of non-coerced (non-committed) subjects.

to) relatively high contributions should have a positive effect on the contributions of non-coerced (non-committed) subjects. Specifically, we expect that non-coerced subjects in the low-coercion treatment contribute more than subjects in the baseline treatment and, in turn, that subjects in the high-coercion treatment contribute more than subjects in the low-coercion treatment. Our next result shows that these hypotheses are not supported by the data.

Result 2. *In the low- and high-coercion treatments those subjects who are not coerced contribute the same amount in both treatments and not more than the average amount observed in the baseline treatment. In the self-commitment treatment non-committed subjects in groups with at least one self-committed subject contribute significantly less than non-coerced subjects in the other treatments.*

Figure 11.2 and Table 11.2 show data in support of the result. When comparing the group average contributions of non-coerced (non-committed) subjects across all four treatments a KW test detects a significant difference ($\chi_3^2 = 26.221$, $p = 0.0001$, two-sided). Pair-wise comparisons between

Table 11.2. *Average contributions of non-coerced (non-committed) subjects*

Treatment	Average	St. dev.	Median	No. of obs.
Baseline	15.61	11.18	16.67	24
Low coercion	15.71	11.80	12.75	24
High coercion	17.48	13.28	18.25	20
Self-commitment	2.06	4.13	0.0	18

Note: In the baseline treatment the unit of observation is the group average contribution, in the low- and high-coercion treatments, it is the average contribution of non-coerced subjects in a group, and in the self-commitment treatment it is the average contribution of not self-committed subjects in groups with at least one self-committed subject.

treatments with MW tests reveal that in the self-commitment treatment contributions of not self-committed subjects in groups with at least one committed subject are significantly lower than contributions of non-coerced subjects in either of the other three treatments ($p < 0.0001$, two-sided). All other pair-wise comparisons of average contributions return insignificant results ($p \geq 0.6540$, two-sided).[3]

This result is twofold surprising. First, the fact that knowing that others are coerced to contribute relatively high amounts to the public good does not have any positive effect on contributions of those who are not coerced seems to be in complete opposition to the conditional cooperation hypothesis. Second, the fact that not self-committed subjects contribute even less when they know that others self-commit to relatively high contributions than when there is no self-commitment possible reinforces this interpretation and also suggests that self-commitment may work as a selection device. However, the studies on conditional cooperation also point out that conditional cooperators contribute only when they expect others to contribute. Hence, it could be that our treatment manipulations failed to induce correct beliefs. Therefore, we next investigate the role of beliefs in contribution behavior.

4.2. The Role of Beliefs

Conditional cooperation can increase contributions in our coercion treatments only if non-coerced subjects adjust their beliefs about coerced subjects accordingly. The next result shows that this is the case for non-coerced

---

[3] The above result does only change marginally when also taking those groups into account where no subject self-committed in the self-commitment treatment (see Appendix 5).

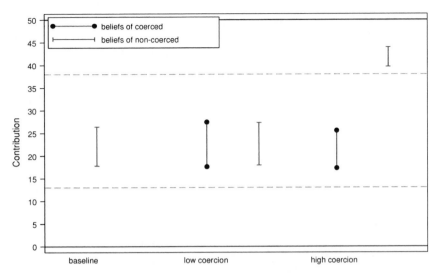

Figure 11.3. Average belief intervals of coerced (non-coerced) subjects about non-coerced (coerced) contributions.

subjects in the high-coercion treatment, but that otherwise coercion has no effect on beliefs about others' contributions.

Result 3. *Neither in the low- nor in the high-coercion treatment does coercion affect a coerced subject's beliefs about the contributions of the non-coerced subjects. The non-coerced subjects adjust their beliefs only in the high-coercion treatment.*

Figure 11.3 shows the average belief intervals regarding the contributions of the other group members in the baseline treatment as well as the average belief intervals of coerced (non-coerced) group members regarding their non-coerced (coerced) counterparts in the low- and high-coercion treatments. The figure indicates that beliefs of coerced subjects about the contributions of non-coerced subjects do not differ between the low- and high-coercion treatments and are also not different from beliefs in the baseline treatment. This visual impression is corroborated by a KW test. When testing the equality of beliefs of minimum contributions between the baseline and the two coercion treatments, the test does clearly not reject the null hypothesis ($\chi_2^2 = 1.284$, $p = 0.5263$, two-sided). The same holds for the beliefs of maximum contribution ($\chi_2^2 = 0.150$, $p = 0.9279$, two-sided) and the belief interval length ($\chi_2^2 = 1.108$, $p = 0.5745$, two-sided). Hence, coerced subjects believe that neither the non-coerced subjects will conditionally contribute nor that they will exploit the situation and free ride more strongly than in the baseline treatment. As one would expect, non-coerced subjects' beliefs about coerced subjects are affected by coercion. When testing equality of minimum, maximum, and interval length of beliefs about coerced subjects' contributions, the null hypothesis of equality of distributions is clearly rejected ($\chi_2^2 = 41.957$, $p = 0.0001$; $\chi_2^2 = 34.055$, $p = 0.0001$, $\chi_2^2 = 15.848$, $p = 0.0004$, respectively; all two-sided). Pair-wise comparisons with MW tests show that this difference is solely driven by beliefs in the high-coercion treatment in which coerced subjects had to contribute at least 38 tokens. In particular, there is no belief shift in the low-coercion treatment in comparison to the baseline treatment. When comparing the minimum, maximum, and interval length of beliefs of non-coerced subjects in the baseline and low-coercion treatment with the high-coercion treatment, MW tests reject equality of distributions for all pair-wise comparisons and all three measures ($|z| \geq 3.258$, $p \leq 0.0011$, two-sided). In contrast, when comparing beliefs in the low-coercion and the baseline treatment, the null hypothesis of equality of contributions is not rejected for any of the belief measures ($|z| \leq 0.712$, $p \geq 0.4764$, two-sided).

In the previous section we have seen that neither low nor high coercion changes the contribution behavior of non-coerced subjects. The preceding results on beliefs of coerced subjects show that they correctly anticipate this contribution behavior of their counterparts. A precondition for the existence of conditional cooperation is that contribution behavior is positively correlated with the expectations about others' contributions. Figure 11.4 shows the relation between the elicited (average) belief intervals and the (average) contributions in the baseline treatment and for both the coercion treatments, with in the latter cases separate for coerced and non-coerced subjects.

For the baseline and the low coercion treatment, the plots indicate a positive correlation between the belief intervals and the own contribution. Hence, there is evidence for conditional cooperative behavior in both treatments and in case of low coercion, for both coerced and non-coerced subjects (cf. Figures 11.4 a and b). Indeed, Spearman rank order correlations between beliefs about minimum contributions of others and own contributions are positive and statistically significant in the baseline treatment and for coerced as well as non-coerced subjects in the low coercion treatment (baseline: $\rho \geq 0.6565$, $p = 0.0005$; low coercion – coerced subjects: $\rho \geq 0.7221$, $p = 0.0001$; low coercion – non-coerced subjects: $\rho \geq 0.7188$, $p = 0.0001$; all two-sided).

In the high-coercion treatment (cf. Figure 11.3), there is a significantly positive correlation between non-coerced subjects' own contributions and

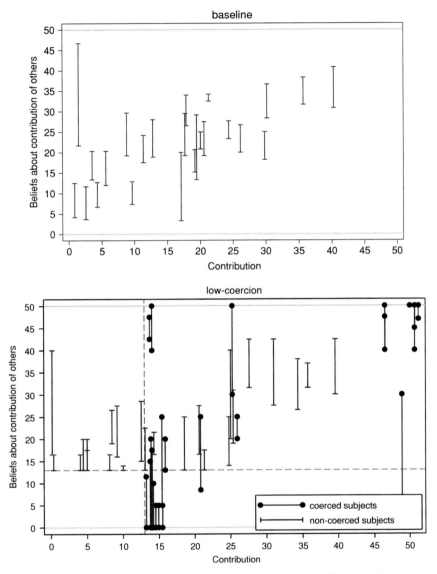

Figure 11.4. Relation between own contribution and belief (interval) about others' contribution in the baseline and the two coercion treatments. *Note:* In baseline treatment group level data, in coercion treatments type level data; small random noise added to contributions to avoid overlap in graph.

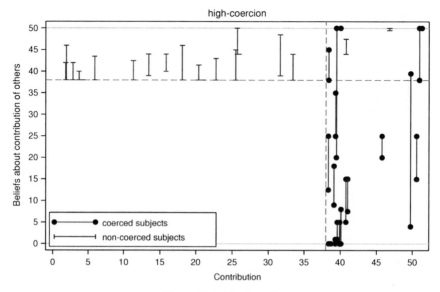

Figure 11.4 (*continued*)

their beliefs on coerced subjects' minimum contribution ($\rho = 0.5902$, $p = 0.0062$, two-sided). For coerced subjects there is also a positive but statistically insignificant correlation between their contributions and their beliefs ($\rho = 0.3079$, $p = 0.1867$, two-sided). We attribute this insignificance to the much smaller room left for coerced subjects to act according to their beliefs.[4] Indeed, Tobit regressions correlating contributions on believed minimum contributions and believed contribution interval length largely corroborate the nonparametric tests and also indicate a statistically significant positive correlation between coerced subjects' beliefs on the minimum contributions of their non-coerced counterparts and their own contributions. Table 11.3 reports these estimates. The regressions are run separately for each treatment, and within the coercion treatments, separately for coerced and non-coerced subjects.

We summarize the preceding evidence in our next result.

Result 4. *In the baseline and both coercion treatments coerced and non-coerced subjects' contributions are positively correlated with their beliefs about their counterparts' contributions.*

---

[4] The correlation statistics do not change significantly when looking at the believed maximum of the other subject type's contribution.

Table 11.3. *Tobit regressions of contributions as function of believed contribution by others*

	Baseline	Low-coercion		High-coercion	
		Coerced	Non-coerced	Coerced	Non-coerced
belief_minimum	0.893***	0.692***	1.474***	0.178*	3.242***
	(0.207)	(0.144)	(0.254)	(0.071)	(0.726)
belief_interval	−0.378	0.358	0.032	0.115	1.122
	(0.385)	(0.364)	(0.311)	(0.130)	(0.831)
const	2.619	10.454	−11.242*	38.168***	−116.181***
	(5.643)	(5.483)	(4.829)	(2.060)	(30.315)
LRχ_2^2	15.71	17.55	22.07	6.21	13.59
Prob $> \chi^2$	0.0004	0.0002	0.0000	0.0448	0.0011
No. of obs.	24	24	24	20	20

Note: *** (**) [*] indicate two-sided significance levels at 0.1 (1) [5] percent; standard errors between parentheses.

Table 11.4 reports average contributions for non-coerced subjects split according to whether their beliefs about minimum contributions of coerced subjects were less than or equal to the coercion level or strictly more than it. For the coercion treatments this returns the contributions of those who believe that the coerced subjects contribute minimally exactly the coerced level. For the baseline treatment it returns the contributions of those who

Table 11.4. *Non-coerced subjects' average contributions for beliefs less than and more than coercion levels*

	Average contributions for minimum beliefs			
	Equal or below 13[†]	Strictly above 13	Equal or below 38[†]	Strictly above 38
Baseline	5.44	19.00	15.61	–
	(6.24)	(10.43)	(11.18)	–
	[n = 6]	[n = 19]	[n = 24]	[n = 0]
Low-coercion	8.00	21.21		
	(6.86)	(11.63)		
	[n = 10]	[n = 14]		
High-coercion			12.12	27.43
			(10.83)	(12.10)
			[n = 13]	[n = 7]

Note: [†] for the low- and high-coercion treatments, these are the average contributions of non-coerced subjects who believe that the minimum of contributions of their coerced counterparts is exactly 13 and 38, respectively.

believe that their other group members (who are not coerced by definition) will contribute less than the coercion levels of the coercion treatments. The question we want to answer here is if a "forced" lift in expectations of others' contributions as a result of coercion makes those who are otherwise pessimistic contribute more. If conditional cooperation is an important motivational force in contribution behavior, even if contributions are exogenously enforced, we should find that contributions are higher in case of lifted expectations. The results reported in Table 11.4 provide some indication that this might be the case in the low-coercion treatment. Comparing contributions in that treatment with those in the baseline treatment indicates that lifted expectations increase contributions from 5.44 tokens to 8.00 tokens. However, a MW test rejects the hypothesis that this difference is statistically significant ($z = -0.707$, $p = 0.4798$, two-sided). Interestingly, in comparison to the baseline treatment, in the low-coercion treatment the belief that the minimum contribution of coerced subjects will be strictly larger than the coercion level is less frequent (79 percent in baseline vs. 58 percent in low coercion). This is different in the high-coercion treatment in which the frequency of beliefs that contributions of coerced subjects will be strictly more than the coercion level of 38 is 29 percent, whereas it is 0 percent in the baseline treatment. However, in high-coercion treatment exogenously lifted beliefs have a negative, albeit statistically insignificant, effect on contributions. Comparing contributions in that treatment with those in the baseline treatment indicates that lifted expectations decrease contributions from 15.61 tokens to 12.12 tokens ($z = 0.764$, $p = 0.4448$). This following result summarizes.

Result 5. *For low coercion exogenously lifted expectations insignificantly increase contributions but make less non-coerced people than in baseline believe that the coerced ones will contribute strictly more than the coercion level. For high coercion more non-coerced people than in baseline believe that the coerced ones will contribute strictly more than the coercion level, but exogenously lifted expectations insignificantly decrease contributions of non-coerced subjects.*

This and the preceding results in this section indicate that, on the one hand, subjects are conditionally cooperative in the sense that they contribute more the more they expect others to contribute, but that, on the other hand, coercion fails to create an upward shift in contributions of non-coerced subjects. The latter holds, despite the fact that non-coerced subjects consistently adjust their expectations regarding coerced subjects' contributions. In addition, in both coercion treatments there are counter-vailing forces at work regarding the effect of lifted expectations. Together these results explain why the contributions of non-coerced subjects in the coercion treatments do not significantly differ from subjects in the baseline treatment in which nobody is coerced by definition (cf. RESULT 2).

An open question is whether non-coerced subjects' beliefs regarding the other non-coerced subject contributions is negatively (or positively) influenced by the fact that there is one subject coerced to contribute a minimum amount. Even conditional cooperative people may refrain from contributing more in the coercion treatments when they believe that the other non-coerced subject will free ride on the coerced subject. The data show that there is neither a positively nor a negatively significant effect of coercion on these beliefs. In the baseline treatment subjects' beliefs about the other members' minimum and maximum contributions are 17.8 and 26.4 tokens, respectively. In the low- and high-coercion treatments these beliefs are 15.7 and 15.2, respectively, for the minimum contributions, and 25.7 and 26.1, respectively, for the maximum contributions. The belief interval lengths in the baseline, low-, and high-coercion treatment are 8.6, 10.0, and 10.8, respectively. None of these differences is statistically significant (KW tests: $\chi_3^2 < 2.246$, $p \geq 0.3254$, two-sided).

4.3. Self-Commitment and Contributions

In this section we focus on the results in the treatment in which subjects could freely choose to commit themselves (i.e., self-coerce) to either a low (13 tokens) or a high (38 tokens) minimum contribution level. We first report whether subjects self-commit, and if so, on which levels. Thereafter, we examine how this effects contributions behavior of non-committed subjects. (Recall, that it is public knowledge to all group members how many in the group have committed themselves and at which levels.) The first result for this treatment shows that many subjects are indeed ready to self-commit to minimum contribution levels.

Result 6. *In the self-commitment treatment a slight majority of individuals self-commits to a minimum contribution level. About one-third commit to contribute at least 13 tokens and almost 20 percent to contribute at least 38 tokens.*

Support for this result can be found in Figure 11.5. It shows that in total about 53 percent of all subjects commit to either a low (33.3 percent) or a

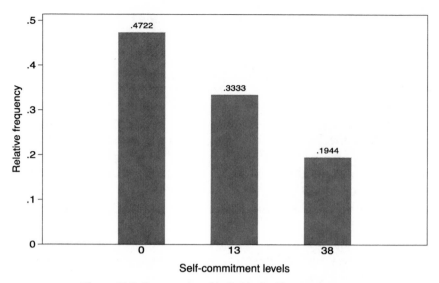

Figure 11.5. Frequencies of individual self-commitments.

high (19.4 percent) minimum contribution level. In addition, Figure 11.6 shows the frequency of all possible combinations of self-commitment levels across groups. It can be seen that all possible combinations occur at least once, except for the combinations in which two group members choose 13 and one chooses 38 and in which all three group members choose the high self-commitment level of 38 tokens. The most frequent combination (25 percent) is when each group member chooses a different self-commitment level. Perhaps not surprisingly, the self-commitment combinations involving a majority of group members choosing a high commitment level are rather scarce (8.34 percent in total). Interestingly, no self-commitment at all is also rather infrequent. It happens only in 12.5 percent of the cases that no member in a group commits.

Figure 11.6 also shows the average contributions in groups given the indicated combinations of commitment levels. Not surprisingly the average contributions increase with the strength of the commitments. Groups that do not commit at all contribute on average close to zero (4.67 tokens, $n = 3$). The one group in which two members commit to at least 38 tokens and one member commits to at least 13 tokens contribute a group average of 45 tokens, which is clearly more than their average commitment level of 29.67 tokens. Similarly, the groups in which all three members committed to at least 13 tokens contribute on average 17.17 tokens. Hence, these examples suggest that the possibility to commitment may have increased the overall contributions.

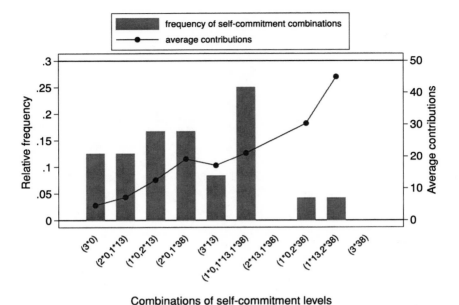

Figure 11.6. Frequencies of self-commitment combinations and associated average contributions.

However, recall from Section 3.1 (RESULTS 1 and 2) that taken overall groups' contributions in the self-commitment treatment are not higher than in the other treatments and that subjects who do not self-commit are contributing significantly less than non-coerced subjects in the other treatments. This suggests that in groups with self-commitment of some but not all members, the not self-committed members strongly free ride. Figure 11.7 shows that this is indeed the case. Figure 11.6 depicts a scatter plot of average contributions of committed and non-committed subjects on the average self-commitment level in the group. It clearly shows that not self-committed subjects contribute very little and that they do not increase their contributions with higher commitment levels of the other group member(s). The visual impression is corroborated by a correlation analysis. Spearmans rank order correlation coefficients of contributions on commitment levels is even marginally significantly negative ($\rho = -0.3953$, $p = 0.0761$, two-sided, $n = 21$) for not committed subjects. Clearly, for self-committed subjects there is a strong and significant positive correlation between contributions and commitment levels ($\rho = 0.5675$, $p = 0.0073$, two-sided, $n = 21$). Figure 11.6 shows alternatively that for each chosen commitment combination the contributions of not committed subjects are very low. In fact, their contributions are highest when no one in the group

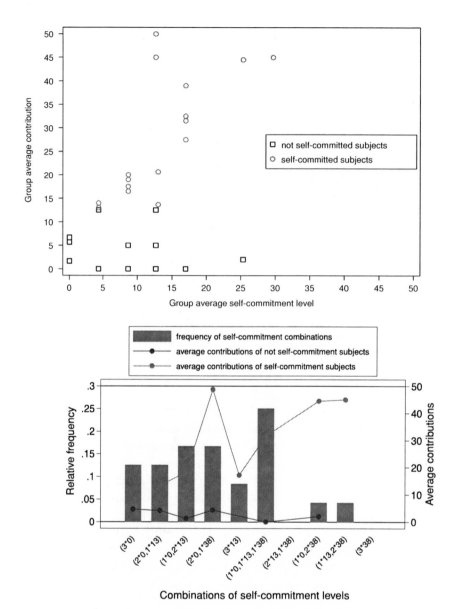

Figure 11.7. Relation between commitment levels and contributions of (not) self-committed subjects. (a) Average contributions of (not) self-committed subjects as a function of average commitment levels. (b) Self-commitment combinations and associated average contributions of (not self-committed subjects).

self-committed, but even in that case it only reaches a level of 4.67 tokens on average. Hence, basically all positive contributions are made by those who so self-commit to some minimum level. We summarize in our last result.

Result 7. *In the self-commitment treatment almost all positive contributions are made by self-committed subjects, whereas not committed subjects almost fully free ride.*

An interpretation of this rather somber result is that self-commitment works as a selection device. It is those subjects who have an inclination to conditionally or unconditionally contribute who commit to minimum levels. Those who do not commit could in principle be pessimistic conditional cooperators or free riders. The data strongly suggest that it is rather the latter type of subjects who does not self-commit, because even in groups with high commitment levels not self-committed subjects do contribute close to zero.

5. Discussion and Conclusion

In this essay we experimentally investigate whether partial coercion or self-commitment can increase voluntary contributions to a public good. The hypothesis that coercing a subset of people positively affects contributions of those not coerced is based on the well-documented empirical observation that many people are conditional cooperative (Keser and van Winden 2000 Fischbacher et al. 2001, Fischbacher and Gächter 2010). Conditional cooperators contribute more to a public good the more others contribute or the more they expect others to contribute. If, as in our experiment, some of these others are coerced to contribute a minimum amount, there is no uncertainty about these contributions, and conditional cooperators should in principle be willing to contribute, too. Our results do not support this hypothesis. Although non-coerced subjects rationally adjust their beliefs about contribution behavior of coerced subjects, they do not increase their own contributions to the public good accordingly. In consequence, the overall contribution levels in the two environments with high and low partial coercion do not differ from an environment in which all subjects are free to choose any contribution to the public good.

Notably, we observe this result although our subjects are clearly conditional cooperative minded. That is, most of our subjects behave conditionally cooperative in the sense that they contribute more the more they believe others to contribute. This, however, is only a second order effect. What partial coercion fails to create is a first order effect: it neither creates an upward shift in beliefs of coerced subjects about non-coerced contributions nor does it – thereby fulfilling these pessimistic beliefs – lead to an upward shift in contributions of non-coerced subjects. It seems that conditional cooperation only "works" when positive contributions of others to the public good are perceived as voluntary and not if they are enforced by some third party. This strongly suggests that intentions (e.g., Falk, Fehr, and Fischbacher 2008) and accountability (e.g., Konow 2000) matter. Hence, for conditional cooperators it is not enough that others contribute large positive amounts, they also must "mean" it. That is, conditional cooperators respond with higher contributions to high contributions of others if they believe that others had the intention to do so voluntarily and if they can be made responsible for these contributions.

Our finding may also be viewed as a special new case of motivation crowding-out (e.g., Frey 1997, Frey and Jegen 2001). In the motivation crowding-out literature it is shown that external intervention can undermine intrinsic motivation. For instance, Gneezy and Rustichini (2000) show that introducing a fee for parents coming late to pick up kids at a day-care center has adverse effects on pick-up time, and more recently, Holmås et al. (2010) found evidence that monetary incentives intended to decrease hospital length of stay instead increases it. These and other examples of motivation crowding-out refer to direct effects, whereas the results in our experiment point to an indirect crowding-out effect. It is the external intervention that forces *others* into a particular behavior that crowds out one's own motivation to contribute to the public good in response to the increased contributions of other people. Admittedly this interpretation is to some extent speculative, and more evidence is needed to see whether such indirect crowding-out indeed takes place.

Our results regarding the effect of partial coercion on contributions to a public good put some doubt on the idea pursued in legal theory that people obey laws, pay their taxes, or – more generally – contribute to public goods, because they know that others will be forced if necessary (Hart 1961). This severely limits the range of legal government intervention in cases in which coercion is not complete. Hence, the public enforcement and punishment of, for instance, caught tax dodgers may not have the desired effect on other potential tax dodgers. The government may achieve better results in terms of tax compliance by "manipulating" the beliefs of tax payers about other tax payers' compliance behavior. Indeed, survey evidence suggests that there exists a high correlation between perceived tax evasion and tax morale (Frey and Torgler 2007). A recent experimental study by Lefebvre et al. (2011) conducted in four different European regions shows that negative information about others' tax evasion behavior indeed has adverse effects on tax compliance. We believe that these are interesting observations that are also important for the theoretical modeling of coercion (Winer, Tridimas, and Hettich, Chapter 7 in this volume). Usually these models are silent about the fact that a large fraction of people is willing to pay their taxes as long as others do. In addition, our experiment has revealed a potentially important additional cost of coercion, namely that it may crowd out some of this intrinsic motivation. It also indicates that some of the costs of coercion as defined in Winer et al. could be avoided by using information policy instead of legal coercion to make citizens contribute to a public good. This is also of interest in the light of the study by Rider, Ackert, and Gillette (Chapter 10 in this volume) who experimentally investigate the willingness of resisting coercion. Such costly resistance actions may also be avoided when citizens voluntarily contribute because they believe that (most) others also voluntarily contribute.

In our experiment we have also tested if self-commitment – that is, self-coercion – to a minimum contribution level can overcome the free-rider problem in public good provision. Here we find that a majority of people is indeed willing to commit themselves even if they believe that others may not do so. However, overall this inclination to self-commitment does not lead to higher voluntary contributions to the public good. The main reason for this negative result is that those who do not self-commit are not contributing anything to the public good. Hence, self-commitment serves "only" as a selection device. Those who do not self-commit are those who prefer to fully free ride on the contributions of others. This result resonates with the finding in Kosfeld, Okada, and Riedl (2009) who investigate the voluntary establishment of organizations that can coerce their members to contribute fully to the public good. Importantly, in their experiment not everybody had to join an organization to establish it. If only a subgroup was organized, those outside the organization could choose any contribution level. Their main result is that most of the time organizations are formed only if all people join, thereby eliminating the possibility of free riding. However, in some circumstances only subgroups formed an organization, and in these cases those outside the organization indeed showed a tendency to free ride completely. A behavior very similar to the behavior we observe for the not self-committed subjects. However, in contrast to our experiment, Kosfeld et al. find that the voluntary establishment of coercive organizations does increase the supply of public goods. This indicates that self-commitment can increase public good provision, but only if it is embedded in an appropriate institutional environment.

Table 11.5. *Group level contributions of non-committed subjects*

Treatment	Average	St. dev.	Median	No. of obs.
Baseline	15.61	11.18	16.67	24
Low coercion	15.71	11.80	12.75	24
High coercion	17.48	13.28	18.25	20
Self-commitment	2.43	4.01	0.0	21

Note: In baseline unit of observation is group average contribution; in low and high coercion the average contribution of non-coerced subjects in a group; in self-commitment the average contribution of not self-committed subjects in groups with at least one self-commitment.

APPENDIX

Additional Results

Table 11.5 and Figure 11.8 show the group level contributions of non-coerced (low and high coercion treatments) and not self-committed subjects. A Kruskal-Wallis test indicates statistically significant differences

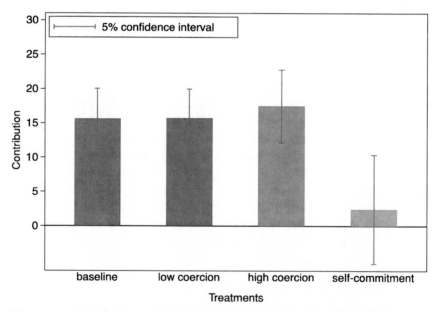

Figure 11.8. Group level average contributions of non-committed subjects. *Note:* In self-commitment treatment also those groups in which nobody committed are taken into account.

between treatments ($\chi_3^2 = 27.311$, $p = 0.0001$, two-sided), and Mann-Whitney tests show that in the self-commitment treatment contributions of not self-committed subjects are significantly lower than contributions of non-coerced subjects in the other three treatments ($p < 0.0001$, two-sided). All other pair-wise comparisons of average contributions return insignificant results ($p \geq 0.6540$, two-sided).

References

Anderson, C. M., and L. Putterman (2006). "Do Non-Strategic Sanctions Obey the Law of Demand? The Demand for Punishment in the Voluntary Contribution Mechanism." *Games and Economic Behavior* 54: 1–24.

Andreoni, J., W. Harbaugh, and L. Vesterlund (2003). "The Carrot or the Stick: Rewards, Punishments, and Cooperation." *American Economic Review* 93(3): 893–902.

Carpenter, J. P. (2007). "The Demand for Punishment." *Journal of Economic Behavior and Organization* 62(4): 522–542.

Chen, Y. and C. R Plott (1996). "The Groves-Ledyard Mechanism: An Experimental Study of Institutional Design." *Journal of Public Economics* 59: 335–364.

Coats, J. C., T. J. Gronberg, and B. Grosskopf (2009). "Simultaneous Versus Sequential Public Good Provision and the Role of Refunds – an Experimental Study." *Journal of Public Economics* 93(1–2): 326–335.

Croson, R. T. A., and M. B. Marks (2001). "The Effect of Recommended Contributions in the Voluntary Provision of Public Goods." *Economic Inquiry* 39(2): 328–249.

Egas, M., and A. Riedl (2008). "The Economics of Altruistic Punishment and the Maintenance of Cooperation." *Proceedings of the Royal Society B* 275(1637): 871–878.

Falk, A., E. Fehr, and U. Fischbacher (2008). "Testing Theories of Fairness-Intentions Matter." *Games and Economic Behavior* 62(1): 287–303.

Falkinger, J. (1996). "Efficient Private Provision of Public Goods by Rewarding Deviations from Average." *Journal of Public Economics* 62(3): 413–422.

Falkinger, J., E. Fehr, S. Gachter, and R. Winter-Ebmer (2000). "A Simple Mechanism for the Efficient Provision of Public Goods: Experimental Evidence." *American Economic Review* 90: 247–264.

Fehr, E., and S. Gächter (2000). "Cooperation and Punishment in Public Goods Experiments." *American Economic Review* 90: 980–994.

Fehr, E., and S. Gächter (2002). "Altruistic Punishment in Humans." *Nature* 415: 980–994.

Fischbacher, U., and S. Gächter (2010). "Social Preferences, Beliefs, and the Dynamics of Free Riding in Public Goods." *American Economic Review* 100(1): 541–556.

Fischbacher, U., S. Gächter, and E. Fehr (2001). "Are People Conditionally Cooperative? Evidence from a Public Goods Experiment." *Economics Letters* 71: 397–404.

Frey, B. S. (1997). "The Cost of Price Incentives: An Empirical Analysis of Motivation Crowding-Out." *American Economic Review* 87(4): 746–755.

Frey, B. S., and R. Jegen (2001) "Motivation Crowding Theory." *Journal of Economic Surveys* 15(5): 589–611.

Frey, B. S., and B. Torgler (2007). "Tax Morale and Conditional Cooperation." *Journal of Comparative Economics* 35(1): 136–159.

Gächter, S., and B. Herrmann (2009). "Reciprocity, Culture and Human Cooperation: Previous Insights and a New Cross-Cultural Experiment." *Philosophical Transactions of the Royal Society B: Biological Sciences* 364(1514): 791–806.

Gächter, S., D. Nosenzo, E. Renner, and M. Sefton (2010). "Sequential vs. Simultaneous Contributions to Public Goods: Experimental Evidence." *Journal of Public Economics* 94(7–8): 515–522.

Gächter, S., E. Renner, and M. Sefton (2008). "The Long-Run Benefits of Punishment." *Science* 322: 1510.

Galbiati, R., and P. Vertova (2007). *Behavioral Effects of Obligations.* Econpubblica Working Paper 120. Bocconi University

Galbiati, R., and P. Vertova (2008). "Obligations and Cooperative Behavior in Public Good Games." *Games and Economic Behavior* 64: 146–170.

Gneezy, U., and A. Rustichini (2000). "A Fine is a Price." *Journal of Legal Studies* XXIX(1): 1–18.

Groves, T., and J. Ledyard (1977). "Optimal Allocation of Public Goods: A Solution to the 'Free Rider' Problem." *Econometrica* 45(4): 783–809.

Hart, H. L. A. (1961). *The Concept of Law.* Oxford: Oxford University Press.

Herrmann, B., C. Thoni, and S. Gachter (2008). "Antisocial Punishment Across Societies." *Science* 319: 1362–1367.

Holmås, T. H., E. Kjerstad, H. Lurås, and O. R. Straume (2010). "Does Monetary Punishment Crowd Out Pro-Social Motivation? A Natural Experiment on Hospital Length of Stay." *Journal of Economic Behavior and Organization* 75(2): 261–267.

Keser, C., and F. van Winden (2000). "Conditional Cooperation and Voluntary Contributions to Public Goods." *Scandinavian Journal of Economics* 102: 23–39.

Konow, J. (2000). "Fair shares: Accountability and Cognitive Dissonance in Allocation Decisions." *American Economic Review* 90: 1072–1091.

Kosfeld, M., A. Okada, and A. Riedl (2009). "Institution Formation in Public Goods Games." *American Economic Review* 99(4): 1335–1355.

Kosfeld, M., and A. Riedl (2007). "Order Without Law? Experimental Evidence on Voluntary Cooperation and Sanctioning." *KritV – Kritische Vierteljahresschrift fur Gesetzgebung und Rechtswissenschaft* 90(1–2): 140–155.

Kroll, S., T. L. Cherry, and J. F. Shogren (2007). "Voting, Punishment, and Public Goods." *Economic Inquiry* 45(3): 557–570.

Laffont, J. J. (1988). *Fundamentals of Public Economics.* Cambridge, MA; London: MIT Press.

Ledyard, J. O. (2010). "Non-coercion, Efficiency and Incentive Compatibility in Public Goods Decisions." mimeo. California Institute of Technology.

Lefebvre, M., P. Pestieau, A. Riedl, and M. C. Villeval (2011). "Tax Evasion, Welfare Fraud, and 'The Broken Windows' Effect: An Experiment in Belgium, France and the Netherlands." Working Paper 3408. Munich, Germany: CESifo.

Lindahl, E. (1919/1958). "Die Gerechtigkeit der Besteuerung," translated (in part) as "Just Taxation: A Positive Solution." In R. Musgrave, and A. Peacock (eds.), *Classics in the Theory of Public Finance.* New York: Macmillan, 168–176.

McAdams, R. H. (2000). "A Focal Point Theory of Expressive Law." *Virginia Law Review* 86: 1649–1729.

Nikiforakis, N., and H. T. Normann (2008). "A Comparative Statics Analysis of Punishment in Public Goods Experiments." *Experimental Economics* 11(4): 358–369.

Reuben, E., and A. Riedl (2009). "Cooperation and Punishment in Privileged Groups." *Journal of Conflict Resolution* 53(1): 72–93.

Rosen, H. S., and T. Gayer (2010). *Public Finance*, 9th edition. New York: McGraw-Hill.

Samuelson, P. (1954). "The Theory of Public Expenditure." *Review of Economics and Statistics* 36(4): 387–389.

Schlag, K., and J. van der Weele (2009). "Efficient Interval Scoring Rules." Economics Working Papers 1176. Universitat Pompeu Fabra.

Sefton, M., R. Shupp, and J. Walker (2007). "The Effects of Rewards and Sanctions in Provision of Public Goods." *Economic Inquiry* 45(4): 671–690.

Tan, F. (2008). "Punishment in a Linear Public Good Game with Productivity Heterogeneity." *De Economist* 156(3): 269–223.

Tyran, J. R., and L. P. Feld (2006). "Achieving Compliance When Legal Sanctions Are Non-Deterrent." *Scandinavian Journal of Economics* 108:135–156.

Discussion

Coercion in the Lab!

Michael McKee

Coercion in the lab! Well, there are some things we can no longer do with lab subjects, of course, and this limits the domain of coercion treatments. Some may recall the infamous "obedience" experiments of Stanley Milgram. However, the rules changed, and for the most part we must confine coercion to monetary penalties or fairly innocuous social penalties.[1] In this setting, we have two essays in this section that experimentally examine the scope for coercion to increase economic efficiency via the provision of public goods.[2] Although both essays incorporate coercion in public good settings, they do so in quite different ways to address different issues. In my discussion I will attempt to place these essays into the broader literature on public good provision, beginning with the chapter by Elena Cettolin and Arno Reidl.

Simply having public goods provided has long been an area in which coercion was seen as necessary. Because such goods are non-excludable, the Nash dominant strategy is to free ride. The result is, of course, suboptimal levels of provision of public goods; hence, the need to *coerce* contributions to the provision of these good. This is the opening argument of Cettolin and Riedl in this section of the book. They argue that coercion to contribute is a requirement of public good provision in general. The authors then explore whether or not the coerced contributions of some will induce reciprocal contributions by others. Cettolin and Riedl characterize their setting as one of possible conditional cooperation, but they find that the non-coerced group members do *not* increase their contributions in response, and the

---

[1] Some experimentalists have been able to invoke non-monetary penalties (see Masclet et al. 2003, for example), but many institutional review boards limit such mechanisms.

[2] There is an extensive experience with the use of monetary sanctions in the lab and these have been found to motivate behavior in predictable and significant ways. I am most familiar with the work on tax compliance (coerced payments) and the use of monetary penalties here (see Alm and McKee 2006 and Alm, Jackson, and McKee 1993).

authors take this to imply that conditional cooperation will not solve the public good provision dilemma.

I would argue that because coerced contributions are not the result of cooperative behavior, we are not looking at a straightforward conditional cooperation setting of the usual kind here. Coerced cooperation apparently does resolve the uncertainty regarding others' behavior in the experiments as Cettolin and Riedl note. However, the contributions observed are not, I suspect, just the result of cooperative behavior. It is possible that the requirement that one person is forced to contribute and the others are free to contribute or not may lead to responses that depend on subjective assessments of fairness and/or inequality aversion (Engleman and Strobel 2004). Finding that coercing a contribution from a subset does not lead to subsequent voluntary contributions suggests to me that the subjects in this setting do not regard the inequality as unacceptable.

Following on with this line of thinking, one can also say that the experiments conducted here open up the possibility of investigating the effects of using income distribution to select the individuals required to contribute. In a real-world tax setting, if we were permitted, such an investigation might amount to choosing a subset of the group to be subjected to tax withholding according to income or other characteristics, whereas others are allowed to self-report tax liabilities.

The fact that the results reported here indicate that coercing contributions is not an effective inducement to cooperation, when coupled with the fact that coercion is costly, reinforces the view that we must be careful to apply coercion in a manner that induces greater cooperation. Indeed, a typical result in experimental work in which direct coercion via punishment requires the use of resources is that the efficiency gains from greater cooperation are (more than) exhausted by the coercion activity (Fehr and Gachter 2000). Such an outcome is disappointing to those who would design mechanisms to coerce contribution to the public good. Ideally, the *threat* of coercion, which consumes few resources, will be sufficient to dissuade cheating among those not having the coercion imposed, resulting in a net increase in social welfare. Cettolin and Riedl are clearly aware of these issues as they note in the final sentence of their concluding section.[3]

---

[3] An individual may wish for coercion. According to the Talmudic dictum one may be coerced until he says "I am willing." Thus, "It is only that his evil inclination has overpowered him. So if he is beaten so that his evil inclination is weakened, and he says: 'I am willing,' he has willingly complied ... he is not considered 'coerced' – on the contrary, it is his evil character which has forced him, against his true will, in the first place."

Despite the limitations on the form of experiments that we can conduct, coercion in the lab can still take many forms. Lucy Ackert, Ann Gillette, and Mark Rider (AGR) present the results of another novel experiment in which the public good is protection of private property rights – that is, the prevention of expropriation by the government. Expropriation reduces the size of the economy by reducing the incentive to invest in productive (public good) assets. Because the mechanism to prevent expropriation in the AGR experiments is subject to scale effects, public good production here requires a minimum level of contributions or a provision point, and in these experiments the provision point is implemented without a money-back guarantee. The AGR team finds relatively high levels of cooperation in this setting, a finding that is supported by results reported in Croson and Marks (2000).

The "government" in AGR is implemented as a decision maker (DM) who can set the expropriation or amounts taken from the other members of the economy (Others). The Others then choose how much to contribute to the prevention fund. If the threshold is met, there is no expropriation. In any case, the contributions are not returned. Because the DM can set the expropriation level and there is a cost of preventing the expropriation, an equilibrium in this sequential game has the DM set the expropriation level less than the threshold for prevention and the Others contributing nothing to prevention. In this case, the usual prediction is that the experimental results would show no contribution to the prevention of expropriation as none is needed. The actual results, however, show a much higher level of DM expropriation and a higher than predicted level of resistance.[4] This is an interesting setting in that it reverses the usual frame for public good experiments, as the public good is the prevention of a bad. However, the

---

[4] There are a few experimental details that I find puzzling. The fixed payments for the forecasts and completion of the questionnaires likely have no effect because there is no marginal payment for correct forecasts or truthful responses. Although the AGR design eliminates a potential confound because of inequality aversion, it still requires the DM to take the action of demanding money. Evidence from dictator games (Cherry, Frykblom, and Shogren 2002) suggests that earned dictator rights produce behavior more consistent with the theoretical predictions. As an aside, I would suggest running the same experiment with the DM's decision exogenous to eliminate the interaction effect and allow focus on the behavior of those contributing to resist coercion. The DM could have a binary decision – expropriate or not – and the Others choose a level of contribution to the prevention fund after this is announced. Further, the interesting setting is the one in which the DM sets the expropriation level more than that necessary to induce the Others to resist. Thus a setting in which the DM has a strong incentive to expropriate provides the necessary tension for this story to be interesting.

results are consistent with those from experiments investigating the direct provision of a (public) good.

A general question raised by the experimental work of Cettolin and Riedl and by that of AGR is whether coercion can establish a social norm leading to cooperative outcomes in public goods settings, an issue raised early on in this volume by John Wallis (see Chapter 2) as well as by the editors in their Introduction. In recognizing the value of cooperation and the individual incentive to cheat on such cooperation, "we" establish institutions to coerce behavior because sanctions imposed on cheaters give us confidence that the overall behavior will be cooperative.

Social norms may be established in a variety of ways. In an earlier, and simpler, research program Alm, Jackson, and McKee (1993) investigated the effect of the "legitimacy" of the spending financed through the taxes on the level of voluntary tax compliance. They report that, holding enforcement effort constant, compliance increases when the expenditure financed by the tax is widely supported *and* the decision mechanism is viewed as representing the wishes of the taxpayers. Extrapolating from this work, it is reasonable to think that a setting in which individuals vote on a coercion rule to impose in the event of cheating may experience greater success if the rule is seen to enjoy widespread support, although this issue remains to be studied directly.

The general question of what the optimal level of coercion is also arises. Although the Wicksellian ideal of unanimity is not possible, it is unlikely that we require universal support for the existence or application of coercion to lead to acceptable levels of public good provision. One might appeal here to a calculus of balancing the costs of achieving unanimity with the costs of not achieving the efficient level of provision, following Buchanan and Tullock (1962).

It must be noted that in some settings, coercion by an authority does appear to work. Tax compliance in most countries is much higher than would be supported by the expected penalties from an audit. Because taxation is an enforced contribution to a public good, it is informative to explore the effects of coercion in this setting. Slemrod, Blumenthal, and Christian (2001), for example, report results from a field experiment in which individuals were simply informed that their tax return for the current year had been pre-selected for closer scrutiny. Taxpayers receiving this letter generally reported higher taxable incomes than in the previous year. Such induced effects – these individuals were not actually audited – are also supported in lab experiments (Alm and McKee 2006). One may also note that in both these field and the lab settings, coercion costs were less than the increase in revenues.

Implementation games stemming from the mechanism design literature coerce by imposing costs for failure to contribute to the public good and by solving the *ex post/ex ante* dilemma inherent in the free-riding problem. It has long been known that the production function (for the public good) affects whether voluntary contributions are sufficient to have the good provided. The usual mode in the literature emphasizing free riding has assumed an additive production function (or linear public good) because each member of the group perceives her contribution as inframarginal. However, Hirshleifer (1983) compared outcomes of this additive (linear) production function with alternate production functions. In his "weak link" setting the aggregate public good is determined by the smallest individual contribution. In his "best shot" setting the aggregate public good is determined by the maximum individual contribution. The weak link is, of course, far more conducive to having a public good provided through voluntary contributions as has been shown in lab experiments (Harrison and Hirshleifer 1989). Other production functions can also lead to efficient private (voluntary) provision. Bagnoli and Lipman (1989) extended the "minimum contributing set" (MCS) setting of van de Kragt, Orbell, and Dawes, (1983) to one in which member contributions could be varied from zero to the individual endowment. This transforms the MCS to a provision point (PP) production function for the public good. If the aggregate contributions are not equal to or greater than the PP, the good cannot be provided. In this setting, the undominated perfect equilibrium (with risk-neutral players) is the efficient level of contributions: the PP. Later Bagnoli and McKee (1991) experimentally investigated the performance of PP settings in which a money-back guarantee was implemented to address risk aversion. The PP setting can be applied in multiple unit settings, as AGR demonstrate, but the results have been more mixed. Croson and Marks (2000) provide a meta-analysis as well as some new experimental results in the step level setting. What is key to all such settings is the conditional provision rule – the public good is supplied only when the money has been collected.

The situation becomes even more complicated when we introduce multiple public goods typically financed from general revenues rather than earmarked taxes. Although the government can induce trust that all will "contribute" to revenue via the use of some sort of compliance enforcement effort, the larger question that arises in this more realistic setting is whether the public will trust that the government will provide the goods promised. Studying this in the lab requires that we investigate more complicated settings in which the collections are enforced reliably but in which there is the possibility that the preferences of the public good provider (the government) will lead to spending that is not congruent with the preferences of citizens. Such situations are likely numerous in real life; as one example, I note that in U.S. states with lotteries, it is often the case that revenues are diverted from their intended or stated purposes (largely education) when the lotteries were enacted.

It is easier to link tax compliance to the uses of the public funds when the allocation of those funds is easily monitored and, thus, government behavior is credible, as Alm et al. (1993) have demonstrated. A useful line of future experimental inquiry would be to decouple the link between compliance, or coercion, and the use of public funds and to study the willingness to be coerced and its effectiveness in the absence of the direct link between revenues and expenditures. In other words, more coercion in the lab is warranted.

References

Alm, J., and M. McKee (2006). "Audit Certainty and Taxpayer Compliance." *National Tax Journal* LIX: 801–816.

Alm, J., B. R. Jackson, and M. McKee (1993). "Fiscal Exchange, Collective Decision Institutions, and Tax Compliance." *Journal of Economic Behavior and Organization* 22(3): 285–303.

Bagnoli, M., and B. Lipman (1989). "Provision of Public Goods: Fully Implementing the Core through Private Provision." *Review of Economic Studies* 56: 581–603.

Bagnoli, M., and M. McKee (1991). "Voluntary Contribution Games: Efficient Private Provision of Public Goods." *Economic Inquiry* 29: 351–366.

Buchanan, J., and G. Tullock (1962). *The Calculus of Consent.* Ann Arbor, MI: University of Michigan Press.

Cherry, T., P. Frykblom, and J. Shogren (2002). "Hardnose the Dictator." *American Economic Review* 92: 1218–1221.

Croson, R. T. A., and M. B. Marks (2000). "Step Returns in Threshold Public Goods: A Meta- and Experimental Analysis." *Experimental Economics* 2: 239–259.

Engleman, D., and M Strobel (2004). "Inequality Aversion, Efficiency, and Maximin Preferences in a Simple Experiment." *American Economic Review* 94: 857–869.

Fehr, E., and S. Gachter (2000). "Cooperation and Punishment in Public Goods Experiments." *American Economic Review* 90: 980–994.

Harrison, G. W., and J. Hirshleifer (1989). "An Experimental Evaluation of Weakest Link/Best Shot Models of Public Goods." *Journal of Political Economy* 97: 201–225.

Hirshleifer, J. (1983). "From Weakest-Link to Best-Shot: The Voluntary Provision of Public Goods." *Public Choice* 41: 371–386.

Masclet, D., C. Noussair, S. Tucker, and M. C. Villeval (2003). "Monetary and Nonmonetary Punishment in the Voluntary Contributions Mechanism." *American Economic Review* 93: 366–380.

Slemrod, J., M. Blumenthal, and C. Christian (2001). "Taxpayer Response to an Increased Probability of Audit: Evidence from a Controlled Experiment in Minnesota." *Journal of Public Economics* 79: 455–483.

Van de Kragt, Alphonse, John Orbell, and Robin Dawes (1983). "The Minimal Contributing Set as a Solution to Public Goods Problems." *American Political Science Review* 77: 112–122.

Name Index

335

Subject Index